# MODERNISM, EMPIRE, WORLD LITERATURE

After World War I, American, Irish and then Caribbean writers boldly remade the world literary system long dominated by Paris and London. Responding to literary renaissances and social upheavals in their own countries and to the decline of war-devastated Europe, émigré and domestic-based writers produced dazzling new works that challenged London's or Paris's authority to fix and determine literary value. In so doing, they propounded new conceptions of aesthetic accomplishment that were later codified as 'modernism'. However, after World War II, an assertive American literary establishment repurposed literary modernism to boost the cultural prestige of the United States in the Cold War and to contest Soviet conceptions of 'world literature'. Here, in accomplished readings of major works and essays by Henry James, Ezra Pound, W. B. Yeats, T. S. Eliot, James Joyce, F. Scott Fitzgerald, Eugene O'Neill and Derek Walcott, Joe Cleary situates Anglophone modernism in terms of the rise and fall of European and American empires, changing world literary systems, and disputed histories of 'world literature'.

JOE CLEARY is Professor of English at Yale University. His earlier books include *Literature, Partition and the Nation-State: Culture and Conflict in Ireland, Israel and Palestine* (2001) and *Outrageous Fortune: Capital and Culture in Modern Ireland* (2007). He is also the editor of *The Cambridge Companion to Irish Modernism* (2014) and co-editor of *The Cambridge Companion to Modern Irish Culture* (2005).

# MODERNISM, EMPIRE, WORLD LITERATURE

JOE CLEARY

*Yale University*

CAMBRIDGE
UNIVERSITY PRESS

# CAMBRIDGE
## UNIVERSITY PRESS

University Printing House, Cambridge CB2 8BS, United Kingdom

One Liberty Plaza, 20th Floor, New York, NY 10006, USA

477 Williamstown Road, Port Melbourne, VIC 3207, Australia

314–321, 3rd Floor, Plot 3, Splendor Forum, Jasola District Centre, New Delhi – 110025, India

103 Penang Road, #05-06/07, Visioncrest Commercial, Singapore 238467

Cambridge University Press is part of the University of Cambridge.

It furthers the University's mission by disseminating knowledge in the pursuit of
education, learning, and research at the highest international levels of excellence.

www.cambridge.org
Information on this title: www.cambridge.org/9781108492355
DOI: 10.1017/9781108698146

First published 2021

Printed in the United Kingdom by TJ Books Limited, Padstow Cornwall

*A catalogue record for this publication is available from the British Library.*

*Library of Congress Cataloging-in-Publication Data*
NAMES: Cleary, Joe (Joseph N.), author.
TITLE: Modernism, empire, world literature / Joe Cleary.
DESCRIPTION: Cambridge, United Kingdom : Cambridge University Press, 2021. |
Includes bibliographical references and index.
IDENTIFIERS: LCCN 2020054408 (print) | LCCN 2020054409 (ebook) | ISBN 9781108492355
(hardback) | ISBN 9781108729277 (paperback) | ISBN 9781108698146 (epub)
SUBJECTS: LCSH: Literature, Modern–20th century–History and criticism. | American
literature–20th century–History and criticism. | English literature–20th century–History
and criticism. | English literature–Irish authors–History and criticism. |
Modernism (Literature)–United States. | Modernism (Literature)–Ireland.
CLASSIFICATION: LCC PN771 .C46 2021 (print) | LCC PN771 (ebook) | DDC 809/.9112–DC23
LC record available at https://lccn.loc.gov/2020054408
LC ebook record available at https://lccn.loc.gov/2020054409

ISBN 978-1-108-49235-5 Hardback

*For Conor*

# Contents

vii

# *Acknowledgements*

Books are written against the odds and take a terrific toll in time. This one was written in Ireland and the United States and has survived life's vicissitudes thanks to many people's support.

Ray Ryan, Senior Commissioning Editor at Cambridge University Press, gave the project matchless support from start to finish. Edgar Mendez, Senior Editorial Assistant at the press, offered kindly assistance. Special thanks also to the copyeditor, Beth Morel, and to Sharon McCann at Cambridge University Press. Three initially anonymous Cambridge readers of two early chapters returned thoughtfully encouraging responses. One of them, Jed Esty, has become a valued friend and colleague in transatlantic modernist studies. Ato Quayson and Eric Falci each offered telling responses to later sections of the work. Seamus Deane, Emer Nolan and Luke Gibbons commented on and significantly improved some draft chapters.

My understanding of modernism, empire and world literature owes too much to too many people to acknowledge here. Some will find their works listed in chapter endnotes. For present purposes, I must mention especially Steph Newell, Caz Phillips, Michael Denning, David Quint, Lanny Hammer, Katie Trumpener, Ardis Butterfield, Dudley Andrew, Katerina Clark, Günter Leypoldt, Marc Robinson, Michael Warner, Joe North, Jill Campbell, John Peters and Jill Richards, all of whom in conversations at Yale deepen my sense of literature. Longtime Irish colleagues, including David Lloyd, Barry McCrea, Stephen Rea, Sinéad Kennedy, Michael Cronin, Catherine Morris, Liam Lanigan, Mark Quigley, Tony Crowley, Ronán McDonald, Lionel Pilkington, Heather Laird, Kevin Honan, Bridget English, Barra Ó Seaghdha, Ronan Sheehan and Kevin Whelan, have shared passions for Irish politics and modernist letters. Friends in the Red Stripe Collective (Maynooth University) and the Left Literary Studies group (Yale University) have afforded solidarity and intellectual stimulation. So have people associated with *boundary 2*, especially Paul Bové, Meg

Havran, Bruce Robbins and Aamir Mufti. The students who took my modernist seminars at Yale were a formidable crew, among whom special mention must go to Jordan Brower, Julia Chan, Margaret Deli, Seo Hee Im, Edward King, Lukas Moe and Chris McGowan. Julia Chan offered invaluable assistance with the final copyediting process. Whenever the heart sang or sank, I found resource in the company of David and Jane Kastan and Eddie Higgins & Co. in Trinity Bar in New Haven. Margaret Spillane and Bruce Shapiro have made New Haven brighter and more convivial in dark times. Colleen Lye and David Pickell have remained steadfast friends across time and continents. So too have Dermot Dix and Chandana Mathur.

Erica Sayers, Jane Bordiere, Jamie Morris, Sarah Harford and Sue Penney are the pillars on which the Yale English department rests and have been pillars to me too. The Yale librarians are unsurpassable. Wonderful lectures offered at the Notre Dame Irish Seminar in Dublin by Edward Said, Perry Anderson, Giovanni Arrighi, Jacqueline Rose, James Chandler, Paul Bové, Jed Esty, Seamus Deane, Emer Nolan, David Lloyd, Luke Gibbons and many others leave traces here somewhere.

First and last, I thank my mother, brothers and sisters for their ongoing support and dedicate the book to my son, Conor, the nonpareil. Up the Reds!

# 'A Language That Was English': Peripheral Modernisms and the Remaking of the Republic of Letters in the Age of Empire

[British literature] was kept alive during the last century by a series of exotic injections [...] There was a faint waft of early French influence. Morris translated sagas, the Irish took over the business for a few years; Henry James led, or rather preceded, the novelists, and then the Britons resigned *en bloc*; the language is now in the keeping of the Irish (Yeats and Joyce); apart from Yeats, since the death of Hardy, poetry is being written by Americans. All the developments in English verse since 1910 are due almost wholly to Americans. In fact, there is no longer any reason to call it English verse, and there is no present reason to think of England at all.

We speak a language that was English.

Ezra Pound, 'How to Read', *New York Herald Tribune*, 1929.[1]

So one effect of the twentieth century's International Modernism was that 'English' ceased to belong in its totality to a people resident on one storied island where they shared usages, intonations, hence memory, a history. Until recently it was they who had owned it all; if you were not one of them and chose to write in English, you either courted assimilation, like Washington Irving, or remained a barbarian, like Herman Melville. Such American or Irish literature as mattered was English Literature that by some accident had been written somewhere else. But now England's literature became a special case, the literature of one province among several. It is all like the separation of the French and Spanish literatures from Latin, which in turn mutated in its homeland into Italian.

Hugh Kenner, 'The Three Provinces', in *A Colder Eye: The Modern Irish Writers*, 1983.[2]

# I

This book is about modernism and the remaking of the modern world literary system in the period between approximately 1890 and the 1950s. More specifically, it is a study of the rise of Irish and American literary modernisms in the decades immediately before and after World War I, and of the various ways in which these modernisms contributed to the eventual transformation of the London-centred English literary world in the same period that English went on to displace French as a 'global language'. The final chapter on Derek Walcott's *Omeros* extends the study into the late twentieth century, examining a major poem from the Caribbean that wrestles with a literary system no longer centred in Europe but now in the United States. The observations of Ezra Pound and Hugh Kenner that serve as epigraphs to this chapter anticipate the history that this book investigates. With Pound and Kenner, I share the view that the ambitions that inspired early twentieth-century English-language high modernism came in the main from a revolt in the peripheries of the Anglophone literary world against long-established English metropolitan literary dominance. In its early stages at least, that revolt came primarily from Ireland and the United States; later, and in some similar, some different ways, literary and political movements in the Caribbean and other parts of the Anglophone world triggered further significant changes to the wider Anglophone literary system.

In the nineteenth century and up to World War I and beyond, London dominated the world of English-language letters. English writers and critics and English publishing houses and journals set the terms for what mattered in 'English literature' not just in Great Britain but across the English-speaking world, then largely a colonial world. In the era when what we now know as 'high modernism' flourished, the more or less absolute dominance of London was broken. Irish writers like Oscar Wilde and George Bernard Shaw, William Butler Yeats and James Joyce, and American writers including Henry James, T. S. Eliot, Ezra Pound, Gertrude Stein, F. Scott Fitzgerald and Eugene O'Neill were too significant to be relegated to the margins of 'English literature'. The kinds of works they produced were too different to those of the great English Romantic and Victorian poets and dramatists and too foreign to the works of the great English realist novelists neatly to accommodate some expanded 'great tradition' of English literature. Besides, the Americans in this era were developing their own elite universities and producing critics more cosmopolitan-minded and receptive to new currents in European literature than most of their English contemporaries. These critics were no longer content to take their literary tastes or leads only from London. From the Gilded Age onwards, Americans were building museums and galleries, great concert halls and orchestras, and great public and private libraries in a bid to match or outdo Europe culturally. The United States' immense wealth and increasing global power in this period allowed it to acquire old and new art collections from all over the world, and especially from Europe, and it also attracted European sculptors, composers, directors and architects to its shores. Long a cultural colony of Great Britain, the United States was ceasing to be so and becoming a 'world leader' in the arts in its own right. After World War II and during the Cold War, the American state made even greater efforts to assert an American presence in the arts and literature in Europe and beyond.

The Irish case was clearly different. The Irish Free State came into existence in 1922. After a civil war, that state was consolidated in the same decade that *Ulysses* was published, that Yeats published his first version of *A Vision, The Tower* and *The Winding Stair*, and that Sean O'Casey's 'Dublin Trilogy' (*The Shadow of a Gunman, Juno and the Paycock, The Plough and the Stars*) was produced in Dublin. Yeats and Shaw won their respective Nobel Prizes in Literature in that decade, Yeats in 1923, Shaw in 1925. Dublin would never possess the great clusters of libraries, museums, art houses or concert halls that afforded New York such tremendous lustre as it rose to become a great world city and centre for the arts. The Irish universities or literary circles did not produce critics of a stature to match T. S. Eliot, Ezra Pound, Edmund Wilson, R. P. Blackmur, Cleanth Brooks, Lionel Trilling, Richard Ellmann, Clement Greenberg and so many others who would make such significant contributions to English-language literary or art criticism almost everywhere. However, whereas the Americans took over from the British in running a world empire, the Irish broke with an empire and had the audacity to establish their own state and to cultivate a literature of some distinction in its own right. The significance of this achievement was not lost on contemporaries. In Harlem and the Caribbean, in India and China, in Korea and Nigeria, in Russia and Australia, the Irish example was noted with interest. It wasn't just the Swedish Academy or American academic critics who took heed of the examples of J. M. Synge and Augusta Gregory, Joyce and Yeats, O'Casey and, later, Beckett. Elsewhere, writers like Lu Xun, Alain Locke, Claude McKay, Chinua Achebe, Ngũgĩ wa Thiong'o and Derek Walcott were also attending to Irish examples. Their national situations and literary circumstances were naturally different to Ireland's, but the Irish case established that long-term colonial domination by British or other European powers did not have to mean enduring literary subsidiarity. In short, the combined efforts of the Irish and American literary writers and intellectuals in this period diminished nineteenth-century deference to London, showed that new cultural projects could be attempted in new ways, and made the

English literary capital just one node (though still an important one) in a more complex circuit of Anglophone literary transmission.

Nevertheless, although the narrative about the overthrow of English literary dominance that this book unfolds over its six chapters intersects with those of Pound and Kenner cited above, my account is more dialectical and historical materialist than theirs. The emergence of Irish and American and other later Anglophone literary modernisms has helped to provincialize English literature and permanently transform the Anglophone literary world. Yet, although these modernisms emerged initially from two long-standing cultural colonies of England, they developed in quite different national contexts and socio-literary situations. Early twentieth-century Ireland was engaged in a national liberation struggle to extricate itself from the British Empire, and the modernism that it produced in this moment emerged from a small, economically underdeveloped, largely agrarian colony, geographically proximate to London. American modernism was the product of a more distant former colony that had won its national independence much earlier, in the American Revolution, and the United States had by the early twentieth century become a continental-sized and industrially advanced nation-state already poised to take over from Great Britain as the world's leading political and economic superpower. The story of how these two modernisms of such different provenance intersected with each other at this momentous juncture in modern imperial history is a fascinating one, but one to which many if not most histories of modernism seem even now strangely oblivious or indifferent. To make sense of these interknitted histories, critics need to do more than to pair Irish and American writers comparatively or to close-read some of their works. The longer-term intellectual, cultural and material histories that underpinned the works of Henry James, James Joyce, Ezra Pound, W. B. Yeats, T. S. Eliot or Derek Walcott also need to be part of any examination of the nature and consequence of their combined creations. The ways in which the literary system of the day conditioned these writers and their works, and, dialectically, the ways in which their works reflect and respond to the constraints of that system, need to be part of the analysis.

My concept of a world literary system owes much to Pascale Casanova's *The World Republic of Letters*, one of the more controversial works of literary scholarship in recent times.[3] For Casanova, as for world literary systems analysis more generally, the term 'world' refers not to something that necessarily enjoys planetary reach or compass, but rather 'to the quality of worldedness, the self-constituting and inner-directed force, of a given world system'.[4] Thus conceived, a world system is a largely self-contained 'whole' or demarcated field with its own procedures of transmission and regulation. Hence, a world literary system is more than an aggregate of its component national or regional literatures: a 'world literary system' constitutes a unified if unequal structure in which the component national or regional literatures are competitively organized and stratified by the manner in which they are integrated into the larger whole.[5]

Some literal-minded critics will ask if a 'world literary system' is anything more than a phrase. Do such 'systems' even exist? It is true that 'systems' of this kind cannot be documented in the same way that the workings of a federation of universities, the archives and anthologies that constitute a national literature, or the transactions of a national academy might be. Though the two are not the same thing, nor one merely superstructure to the other, a world literary system has, like the capitalist world system, to be deduced from its laws of operation, the kinds of transactions it allows, what it enables and rewards. One has to work backwards from the observed effects or consequences of the system to begin to grasp how it might work. In seems evident enough that by the nineteenth century Britain and France were the world's two leading imperial as well as literary powers. For much of the modern period, France and French culture dominated the European continent. In an essay on the French novel written in 1949, the great German critic E. R. Curtius could attest without qualification to the long-standing dominance of French culture:

> Nations, like individuals, are distinguished by their gifts. As early as the twelfth century France supplied all of Europe with verse romances and narrative matter. In the nineteenth century, which for France begins in 1789, it outdoes all other nations in three fields: painting, the novel, and revolution. From David (1748–1825) to Cézanne (1839–1906) French painting dominates, as did Italian during the Renaissance, Spanish during the Baroque. It is not as though a talent of genius came to the fore from time to time; no, an abundance of first-rate masters is found together in a small area; they relieve each other, form schools, invent formulas, set the pace for all of Europe. Whoever wishes to learn how to paint must do so in France.[6]

What Curtius says of the French in nineteenth-century Europe applies in different respects to English writers and critics in the same era throughout the British colonies and dominions. The nineteenth-century English produced not just two or three great poets or novelists, but a steady succession of such talents. England's leading universities, distinguished literary reviews, and that nation's most famous writers, intellectuals and literary critics were admired not just in England but across the English-speaking empire. English publishing houses circulated English-language texts – bibles, dictionaries, grammars, readers, encyclopaedias, treasuries of hymns and verse – across the world. New school systems and academies in the colonies encouraged reverence for things English. Writers like Wordsworth and Shelley, Austen and Scott, Dickens and George Eliot, Tennyson and Browning, Carlyle and Mill, Arnold and Ruskin set the pace all over the English-speaking world as Curtius says the French painters, novelists and revolutionaries did all over Europe. Everywhere, from Ireland to the United States, Australia to South Africa, Canada to Nigeria, the educated classes interested in culture were largely Anglophile and looked for direction to what was happening in England. These elites, their luminaries often schooled in English universities or frequenting London's literary circles, often knew English literature far better than that of their own regions. In those cases where they did not actively discourage local literatures, they nevertheless held up English standards to their local writers as those to emulate. Writers and scholars from the colonies often moved to England to make their careers, or pined for contracts with English publishers, or for good reviews from the leading British reviews of the day. Just as other European cultures for a long time rotated like so many satellites around a sun that was Paris, so too the English-speaking cultures beyond England were drawn to smoggy London as to a candle.

A world literary system, however, is composed of more than just a capital and its subsidiaries. It depends on that capital's lasting capacity to produce a continuous relay of writers or painters, schools and coteries that 'invent formulas' in the manner Curtius describes. It requires that capital to be able to continue to give intellectual leadership, to set canons of taste and to secure reputations that will endure not just for a passing moment but a century or longer. The capital must be able to disseminate its influence beyond the nation-state by exerting a soft cultural sway over other far-scattered sub-capitals that work with the centre in a series of feedback loops. This circuitry of exchange operates most effectively if the sub-capitals are themselves lively hubs of creativity but still have reasons to defer to the authority of the centre because they cannot match it for material and intellectual resources and for some ineffable sense of greatness. A world literary system, then, becomes visible in what it produces and regulates. Its effects may be seen in the types of literary productions the system creates and canonizes and in the kinds of pilgrimages from periphery to centre it encourages and rewards over some *longue durée*. The system is manifest in the kinds of stimuli, deferences and challenges – whether from older faded centres, other rival centres outside its bounds or its own sub-capitals – the centre can cultivate and manage to its advantage over a long period. Only when the centre cannot hold do things dramatically change; then, a new centre restructures an alternative system after its own interests.

Systems have histories. As Casanova tells it, the history of the modern world literary system is to a considerable extent the story of how Paris established itself as the world's leading literary capital by becoming from the early modern period onwards the city with the greatest literary prestige on earth. In her view, a formative episode was the establishment of the French Pléiade and the publication in 1549 of Joachim du Bellay's *La deffence et illustration de la langue françoyse*, a programme for the enrichment of the French language and manifesto for a new literature able to compete with the pan-European intellectual hegemony of Latin. By culturally asserting themselves against Latin, Casanova avers, the French established an early process of national literary differentiation – something that then became a basic organisational reflex of the modern world literary system, a recurrent, competitive, centrifugal impulsion that continues to this day. By the Age of Versailles, Casanova contends, Paris had already become a leading centre for the arts, fashion, civility, *belles lettres* and fine living, and the French language had established itself as the *lingua franca* of the aristocracies and intelligentsias all across Europe, and would remain so for several centuries to come. After 1789, Paris multiplied this already impressive *ancien régime* cultural capital by also becoming the city that symbolized the Revolution and Enlightenment modernity. Until World War II at least, the city's heady mixture of old-world cultural sophistication and vanguard political radicalism attracted a steady influx of political and artistic immigrants from abroad, and many nationalist movements and national literatures from across the world first found their tongues, so to speak, in French exile.[7]

Once France had consolidated its position at the centre of the European literary system, that system's next major overhaul and expansion, Casanova argues, was brought about by English and German pushbacks against French supremacy. By the end of the eighteenth century, through the efforts of men of letters, grammarians and lexicographers, the main outlines of modern English were fixed, though significantly without a centralizing legislative institution on the model of the Académie Française. If the French claimed to exemplify literary 'sophistication', 'worldliness' and 'rational universality', the English responded by laying claim to a literature that was firmly rooted in the 'local' and 'national' and not, as its French rival pretended to be, abstractly 'universal'.[8] Such distinctions are the common stock-in-trade of national stereotype, but were nonetheless constitutively important to the deeper value systems that conditioned French and English literatures in the nineteenth century. In this period, the English challenge to French hegemony was abetted by its German counterpart. Goethe may be deemed the father-founder of modern German letters, but the decisive figure here, for Casanova, was Herder, whose theories 'brought about the first enlargement of literary space to include the European continent as a whole' (75). Herder's work not only formulated a rationale for German cultural emancipation from French hegemony, but 'also provided the theoretical basis for the attempt made in politically dominated territories, both in Europe and elsewhere, to invent their own solutions to the problem of cultural dependence' (75). Where French literary nationalism was unashamedly elitist, classicist or neoclassicist and universalist in self-conception, Herder proposed that an authentic national literature could only emerge via a long evolutionary process and that literary 'genius' and artistic fertility were best nurtured by a rootedness in national-popular vernacular traditions. This articulated the national and the popular in ways that, as Casanova puts it, 'shattered all the hierarchies, all the assumptions that until then had unchallengeably constituted literary "nobility" – and this for a very long time' (77). By asserting the dignity of all cultures and locating the sources of literary fertility or genius in the vernacular cultural life of the people as a whole, Herder's work re-wrote the rules of international literary consecration and prestige, and legitimated new mechanisms for the accumulation of international literary capital. For Herder, exemplary forms of national-popular literature included popular song, Ossian and Shakespeare.[9]

Viewed thus, a world literary system comes into being by means of international struggles for cultural distinction. Once the basic laws of mimetic rivalry between countries have been set in place, the system can then extend outwards and develop. As England and Germany in their revolt against French letters had established themselves as major cultural centres in their own right, so too in turn their respective intellectual provinces also began to contest English and German artistic domination. Thus, the English struggle against French supremacy in the late eighteenth and early nineteenth centuries was accompanied, more or less concurrently, by Irish and American attempts to bolster their resistances to English cultural domination. In the same period, the Scandinavians and Russians attempted to find ways to counter French and German intellectual dominance. In this intellectually and aesthetically combative system, national literatures drew a large part of their self-definition from direct rivalries, long embedded, with other national spaces: German *vs* French, Scottish *vs* English, Irish *vs* English, Czech *vs* German, American *vs* English, Russian *vs* German and so forth.[10]

It is clear from this bald summary account that for Casanova the modern world literary system originated in Europe and found its centre of gravity in Paris when French became the adoptive culture for the upper classes and the higher intellectual strata all across that continent from Madrid to Moscow. That world system was then expanded outwards by way of a series of semi-peripheral nationalist 'revolts' conducted initially in the countries directly bordering on France, then in the more semi-peripheral countries culturally subordinate to England and Germany. In the twentieth century, Casanova's account implies, these literary revolts continued to erupt in the outermost peripheries of the Paris-centred world system, this time in the vast colonial territories beyond Europe that had been subjected, however unevenly, by way of European imperialism to European linguistic, intellectual and literary domination. The most radical literary experiments in the twentieth-century postcolonial peripheries, those of the Latin American Boom being an exemplary instance for Casanova, are thus taken to be fundamentally continuous in tendency with the earlier revolutions of the French against the universalism of Latin, of the English and Germans against French cultural hegemony, and of the Irish or Norwegian cultural struggles against English or German supremacy.[11] As new European centres vie with old ones, and as new national literatures across Europe and other continents struggle with more prestigious neighbouring literatures for recognition, the mimetic logic of the world system remains the same and the reach of that system is increased, not diminished, by such relentless competition.

Immensely suggestive though it is for the study of the formation of national literatures generally and for the analysis of modernism more particularly, *The World Republic of Letters* suffers in my view from a number of conceptual restrictions that I hope to avoid in this study.[12] To begin with, for instance, Casanova's work stresses the significance of literary peripheries to modern literary innovation and linguistic experiment and thus to the continuous renovation of world literature. Whereas writers and intellectuals situated in core metropolitan zones like France and England tend generally by virtue of their exalted position, she argues, to take the literary norms and privileges enforced by that system for granted, their counterparts in the peripheries are by necessity much more anxiously or cannily conscious of the hierarchical nature of the world of letters. Thanks to their lower place in that system's hierarchy, they have every reason to be more sensitively attuned to the unspoken rules of the game, to its mechanisms of consecration and to the prevailing conceptions of literary backwardness or modernity that it sustains. Because they know their own national literatures are deemed to be unsophisticated, many writers from the peripheries have always elected to adapt their literary production as best they can to metropolitan norms. For this reason, many have migrated to the core capitals of the world system in search of standards or literary recognition and rewards not available in their own more destitute nations. However, not everyone is equally content to adapt ambitions to the rule of the centre. Other writers from the peripheries have been provoked by similar circumstances to challenge the normative values enforced by the core literary powers and have struggled mightily to add to the value of their own national literatures. In Casanova's view, these peripheral areas tend to be sites of restive (and mimetically resentful) literary activity in which both emulation of and rebellious challenges to metropolitan norms are recurrent systemically determined reflexes and stimuli to literary production. An anxious sense of literary backwardness, and a consequent desire on the part of writers either to assimilate the styles and values of the centre or else to challenge and repudiate that centre in some way, are, in Casanova's work, defining features of a literary periphery. Even so, these anxieties are what make the peripheries sites of intensely lively activity despite their relative lack of prestige, and that occasionally even make them the sites where revolutionary upheavals that will alter the existing system begin.

Nevertheless, despite her sense that French cultural dominance in Europe has a history and her welcome stress on the restive or rebellious creativity of the peripheries, there is something troublingly static in Casanova's overall conception. For one thing, the centre of her system, Paris, appears to be extraordinarily fixed and stable. It dominates from the seventeenth century to the 1960s, when its dominance, Casanova allows, though even then she hesitates, may have finally begun to wane. For Casanova, revolts in marginal zones against metropolitan capitals are literary events of consequence; these revolts bring new national literatures, new literary movements and great works of literature into being. Yet because for her everything that happens in the system's margins has to be recognized, processed and canonized first in the centre, the ultimate effect of all this peripheral literary revolt is that the world literary system is spatially expanded but continues nonetheless to be centripetally dominated by Paris and, to a lesser extent, London. Thus, more than two centuries of peripheral 'revolutions', initially articulated in Scandinavia and Russia, Ireland and the United States, and followed by the subsequent revolutions of the modern postcolonial literatures of South America, Asia and Africa, have not, in her account at least, proved sufficient to change in any really substantive way either the basic institutional structures of the world literary system or the dominance of the core regions of the system, namely France, England and Germany. In her account, the more the system changes, the more fundamentally it stays the same. Mimetic logic remains its motor, Paris its regulative centre.

In some fundamental respects, Casanova's position seems perfectly plausible and even confirmed by contemporary common-sense experience: French, English and German remain, after all, the core literatures of comparative literature programmes throughout Europe and the Americas. Much of the early twentieth-first-century controversy in the Euro-American academy about the tenability of the concept of 'world literature' continues to focus on the privilege accorded to these Western European literatures.[13] Even so, Casanova's conception of a world literary system, continually agitated from its edges yet always remaining fixed at the centre, suggests that there is something agglomerative in her overall conception of literary revolt: once the core of the system is established, with Paris as its supreme capital and with France, England and Germany at its axial centre, the changes that occur thereafter seem fundamentally additive rather than qualitative in character. Thus, in the nineteenth and twentieth centuries new national literatures emerge and try to secure for themselves what recognition they can, but the effect is merely to expand the reach of the overall system globally without ever forcing major reconfigurations of the basic order of things.

*Modernism, Empire, World Literature* will argue that the modernist period that extended from roughly 1890 to the Cold War represents a moment when that Western European literary system, as it had hitherto been regulated by France and England, was in fact decisively restructured. In this period, it will suggest, Europe experienced an extraordinary and overlapping, though not by any means concordant, series of literary 'revolutions' both in its metropolitan core countries and in its peripheries, the combined effect of which was to transform the world literary system more convulsively and with more lasting effect than Casanova's account allows. The modern world system as a whole, of course, changed enormously between 1890 and 1945. Casanova is right to stress that the world literary system has its own structural coherence and enjoys at least a relative autonomy from political and economic determinants, but it was not in the end immune to the wider international turbulence of the politico-economic conjuncture of these decades. Rather, I will argue, it was subjected to its own field-specific seismic changes.

The convergence of Irish and American literary modernisms in the interregnum between the two world wars constituted only one episode in the titanic political, economic and cultural convulsions that ran from the *belle époque* to the Cold War. However, that episode was not without significance or consequence. Something more than disturbances on the fringes of the system that created a stir to be savoured and assimilated in Paris and London took place. 'We speak a language that was English', Pound writes in 'How to Read' in 1929. The English language, he implies, may still appear to be English but it is now undergoing a transformation of such magnitude that it is no longer the metropolitan English it once was or no longer perhaps coupled to the country England. In Pound's view, these changes in English language and literature are indicative of some new order of things still emerging into view. In George Bernard Shaw's futuristic satire *The Apple Cart*, staged the same year, first in Warsaw in June and later that August in London, the American diplomat Vanhattan proposes to the King and Queen of England an 'amalgamation of the British Commonwealth with the United States'.[14] 'The United States, ma'am', Vanhatten observes, 'have absorbed all the great traditions, and blended them with their own glorious tradition of Freedom into something that is unique and universal' (97). For the English King, Magnus, America's proposal to tear up its Declaration of Independence and to rejoin the British Empire is not at all the English victory it seems, but an elaborate ploy to incorporate Britain as a regional province of a new American Empire. Further, this conspiracy, he learns, has been instigated not by the American president, but by a Sinn Féin president of the new Irish Free State:

> MAGNUS. [*pulling himself together with a visible effort*] May I ask, Mr Vanhattan, with whom did this – this – this master-stroke of American policy originate? Frankly, I have been accustomed to regard your President as a statesman whose mouth was the most efficient part of his head. He cannot have thought of this himself. Who suggested it to him?
>
> VANHATTAN. I must accept your criticism of Mr Bossfield with all doo reserve, but I may mention that we Americans will probably connect the good news with the recent visit to our shores of the President of the Irish Free State. I cannot pronounce his name in its official Gaelic form; and there is only one typist in our bureau who can spell it; but he is known to his friends as Mick O'Rafferty.

MAGNUS.   The rascal! Jemima: we shall have to live in Dublin. This
is the end of England.

VANHATTAN.   In a sense that may be so. But England will not
perish. She will merge – merge, sir – into a bigger and brighter
concern. Perhaps I should have mentioned that one of our
conditions will be that you shall be Emperor. King may be
good enough for this little island; but if we come in we shall
require something grander.

(94–95)

For both the obstreperous American poet and the satirical Irish playwright,
the old political and literary Anglophone world, long dominated by
London, was already fast disappearing by the end of the 1920s. And as
global power shifted across the Atlantic to England's former province in
America, Anglophone literary relations and even the English language were
simultaneously undergoing their own sea changes. For both Pound and
Shaw, London no longer commanded things in Ireland or the United
States; rather, it was being sucked into a new world larger than itself and
beyond its capacity to manage. Some disturbing combination of
Americans, Irish Americans and Irish, Shaw insinuates, is now tumbling
the old applecart. The colonial upstarts are taking their revenge, the
English aghast at the prospect but helpless to change it. Irish and
American modernisms, this volume will contend, were one of the means
by which a significant re-ordering of older literary relations was conducted.

Still, if Pound's boast that English language and English literature were
now 'in the keeping' of the Irish and the Americans carried weight, Shaw's
conception of a new American pre-eminence was also valid. The Irish and
American modernist revolt against the cultural supremacy of London
represented a revolt in the peripheries against the centre and an emancipation from one long-standing kind of English literary dominance. The
literary issue of that revolt would eventually be assimilated, however, by an
ascendant United States determined to 'absorb all the great traditions' and
to 'blend them' into something 'that is unique and universal', this the
better to reflect its own cultural dominance and its claim to be the
guardian 'of their own glorious tradition of Freedom'.

In sum, what initially began as a revolt by two minor Anglophone
peripheral literatures against one kind of English metropolitan dominance
may well have been converted – though not without resistance and
inassimilable remainder – into a new form of cultural capital stockpiled
by a new metropolitan power, the United States, as a means to assert
itself as a new world literary centre. Or, to put matters another way, when

Pound, Eliot, Stein, Wilde, Shaw, Joyce and others left their home countries for London or Paris before World War I they did so as lowly 'provincials' from what were still regarded at the time as Irish and American literary backwaters. Several decades later, when their works and those of their most distinguished fellow-national émigrés or stay-at-home experimental writers had been collocated and converted into the 'classics' of what we now call modernism, the relative status of English, Irish and American national literatures had changed enormously, and in a remarkably short time. In the same period, the relative status of the United States and Western Europe, and of New York and London as global cultural capitals, had shifted too. Modernism, Franco Moretti has claimed in a flamboyant formulation, represented Europe's 'last *literary season*'. In and around World War I, Moretti proposes, Europe witnessed the creation of 'an extraordinary concentration of literary masterpieces'. Nevertheless, what is remarkable about this abundant literary harvest, he adds, is that it constituted 'the last *literary season* of Western culture. Within a few years European literature gave its utmost and seemed on the verge of opening new and boundless horizons: instead, it died. A few isolated icebergs, and many imitators: but nothing comparable to the past'.[15]

Whether or not this is the case (it may be too soon to tell as Mao Tse-Tung was reported to say when asked whether the French Revolution had succeeded), there can be little doubt that the ingathering and cultivation of modernism in the galleries, museums, concert halls, literary magazines and presses in the United States in the period between 1914 and 1940, and the canonization of literary modernism in that country's leading universities during the Cold War especially, represented America's first 'literary season' as a new global cultural as well as economico-military power.[16] In Casanova's account of the emergence of the world literary system, the Germans and the English were able to contest French cultural dominance in Europe in the early nineteenth century only by pooling each other's resources and devising new Herderian literary value systems and modes of consecration to establish literary worth on terms different to those favoured by the French. Teutonist and Anglo-Saxonist racial theory that stressed the common origins of English and Germanic peoples, and their differences to Slavic and Celtic races, helped to facilitate such cross-cultural exchange. The German recruitment of Shakespeare as a great Teutonic author; the construction of Goethe as a modern Shakespeare; and the English assimilation of German aesthetic idealism by way of the Romantic poets, Coleridge, Carlyle and Arnold, all contributed to this larger process of contesting French hegemony. A century later, the informal league of

Irish and American modernists – Pound's collaboration with Yeats, Eliot's rivalry with Yeats, Eliot's enthusiasm for Joyce, the extraordinary receptivity of American critics to Joyce and Yeats, the influence of Shaw and O'Casey on Eugene O'Neill, Joyce's importance for Faulkner or Claude McKay – represents a collaborative recruitment of then semi-peripheral Anglophone national resources to similar ends. In and around World War I, the Americans and Irish found London ripe or rotten enough, so to speak, for the taking, just as the German and English were able to dispute French cultural supremacy, especially after Waterloo.

Like their antecedents, the Irish and Americans still needed each other to challenge so formidable an establishment as London's remained up to 1914 and they also needed new rules of consecration to legitimate the new kind of literature they were keen to distinguish from the older English (and Irish and American) sort. 'Modernism' is the name we now assign to that new aesthetic code through which the transformation in English letters that shifted Anglophone literary supremacy from London to New York was effected. Whatever else it meant, 'modernism' signalled a challenge to earlier aesthetic isms all strongly associated with eighteenth- and nineteenth-century Europe – Romanticism, realism, naturalism, symbolism, Victorianism – and a cross-Atlantic reorganization of the then-prevailing literary system and relations of letters that London and Paris, whether they wanted to or not, had to swallow. A new and in many ways exasperatingly elastic or hazy term had arrived to describe new kinds of literary and artistic activity; though some of that activity took place in Paris or London, what was 'modern' or 'modernist' in the arts now seemed to span regions and continents no longer under France's or Britain's cultural control.

## II

In his remarkable *The Long Twentieth Century: Money, Power and the Origins of Our Times*, Giovanni Arrighi situates the period that ran from the *belle époque* to the end of World War II in terms of the *longue durée* of modern industrial and finance capital, imperial expansion, and the institutions of state and international governance.[17] For Arrighi, the twinned development of modern capitalism and imperialism has evolved in terms of four systemic cycles of capitalist accumulation, each encompassing what he terms a 'long century'. The globalizing thrust of the modern capitalist world system was inaugurated, he contends, with a Genoese-financed Iberian cycle of imperial expansion and capital accumulation extending from the fifteenth to the seventeenth century. This Genoese-Spanish cycle was followed by a Dutch cycle, stretching from the late sixteenth to the late eighteenth century, and then by a British cycle, which ran from the mid-eighteenth to the early twentieth century. After World War I, British hegemony was seriously weakened, and the United States led a new cycle of accumulation and world domination lasting from the late nineteenth century into the contemporary moment.[18] For Arrighi, each of these 'long centuries' is defined by a distinctive operational clustering of fiscal institutions and inter-state structures that provide the conditions for a long initial phase of relatively stable capitalist commodity production in the core regions of the world economy. But these periods of stability create surpluses of capital in these core regions that sooner or later give rise to 'autumnal' moments of financial expansion that represent both the zenith and the beginning of the end of that particular regime of accumulation. In other words, each distinct cycle traverses in its course the successive component elements of Marx's general formula for capitalism, MCM', where M stands for money capital, C for commodity capital, and M' for a financial capital that breaks free of commodity capital and in which accumulation proceeds primarily through intensified series of transnational financial transactions. 'In phases of material expansion', Arrighi contends, 'money capital "sets in motion" an increasing mass of commodities (including commoditized labor-power and gifts of nature); and in phases of financial expansion an increasing mass of money capital "sets itself free" from its commodity form, and accumulation proceeds through financial deals (as in Marx's abridged formula MM'). Together, the two epochs or phases constitute a full *systemic cycle of accumulation* (MCM')' (6, italics in original).

In Arrighi's view, the 'autumnal' moments when finance capital dominates in this manner are by definition inter-cyclical: they mark turbulent transitional conjunctures during which one regime of capitalist accumulation reaches its climax in flurries of financial speculation and when control passes from an old metropolitan centre to a newly emergent centre that now possesses a stronger capacity to re-establish a more stable cycle of capitalist accumulation. The period from the end of the sixteenth to the beginning of the seventeenth century; the mid- and final decades of the eighteenth century; the decades spanning the interval between the *belle époque* and World War I; and the closing decades of the twentieth century constitute for Arrighi the successive 'autumnal' moments of the various 'long centuries' he describes. These key crises, he argues, took place as capital migrated from a declining centre to a newly emergent one: first, from the Genoese-centred financial headquarters of the Spanish empire to Holland following the Treaty of Westphalia; second, from Holland to the London Exchange as the Dutch banking and colonial trading monopolies were overtaken in the course of the eighteenth century by British chartered companies; and, third, in the early twentieth century when British and French debts incurred in World War I, together with the growing might of the American economy, transferred financial dominance of the modern world system from the City of London to New York's Wall Street.[19]

As in previous historical moments, this latest transfer of the hegemony of the capitalist world system from an old centre to a new rival centre was marked by social and political upheavals of the most extraordinary kinds. The *belle époque* of the Edwardian era, Arrighi contends, marked the high point of British free-trade imperialism and a moment in which the wealth of the propertied classes of Britain and the Western world more generally had attained unprecedented heights. That wealth notwithstanding, the deeper crises of the British-regulated world system were not to be resolved by those dominant classes, and within a generation the consequences would, in Arrighi's words, 'bring the entire edifice of nineteenth-century civilization crashing down' (269). One of the most obvious manifestations of the deeper crisis of the era was a dramatic rise in inter-imperial tensions within the larger system as newly emergent leading industrial states, including Germany, the United States, Italy and Japan, vied for position with the older core powers, Britain and France. The *pax Britannica* enforced by long-standing British dominance of the international system had created the conditions for a period of relative economic stability in Europe marked by dramatic increases in domestic and transnational production and trade. However, that period of sustained growth was followed by a cyclically determined period of market saturation, rising prices and falling profit rates, which triggered a switch from commodity to finance capital and set in motion a hectic chase for cheaper raw materials for European manufacturing and more profitable sites of overseas investment for finance capital both in North America and in the territories of the European empires. Some manifestations of this process included the infamous 'Scramble for Africa', a huge migration of Western European capital and labour to the United States in the period leading up to 1914, and a rapid militarization of the most advanced capitalist states, and of Britain and Germany in particular.

Under these pressures, the framework of international political and trading agreements established during the *pax Britannica* gradually came asunder: the upshot was that the major European imperial powers were catapulted into a devastating continent-wide collision with each other in World War I. That war in turn paved the way in the east to the Bolshevik Revolution of 1917 and the establishment of the Soviet Union, and, in the west, to the inexorable rise of the United States. That state not only escaped most of the human and infrastructural devastation of the fighting in Europe but was also able to take advantage of British and French post-war indebtedness to buy back at bargain prices many of the massive foreign investments that had stimulated the development of America's domestic economy before the war. In the period before 1914, capital had flowed from Europe into the burgeoning United States; after the war, the United States was able to become a creditor-nation and to invest its surplus capital in the rebuilding of Europe.[20]

As is widely accepted, the post–World War I settlements resolved few of the more fundamental problems that troubled the wider system before 1914; indeed, in some ways the settlement arrangements further aggravated older underlying pressures. The emergence of the Soviet Union as a non-capitalist state constituted a major threat of a brand-new kind to the capitalist world system. This in turn provoked a backlash that can be understood, Arrighi argues, in three different categories: a conservative counter-movement pressed by Britain and France designed to re-establish the terms of the international system that had prevailed before World War I; a reactionary backlash led by Germany, Japan and Italy that proposed to remake the world system in fascist terms; and a reformist counter-movement led by the United States as it manoeuvred to take charge of the world system from an increasingly fractious European core.[21] Some of the more obvious landmarks of this period of interstitial crisis included the Great Depression, the rise of economic protectionism and national autarchy; the collapse of the League of Nations in favour of rapidly re-militarizing autarchic empires; and the Soviet Five Year Plans and the American 'New Deal'. By 1940, the great powers of the inter-state system were plunged into yet another military conflagration, and when it ended the new world order was dominated by two continental-sized states, the United States and the USSR. Of these two, the United States was the more economically dynamic and to it had accrued most of the gains of the final breakdown of the old British-dominated system.[22]

Like Venice in the fifteenth century, the United Provinces in the seventeenth century, and Great Britain in the eighteenth century, the United States had grown enormously wealthy and powerful in the course of an extended period of world systemic chaos. Consequently, it now had to shoulder the responsibility to restore and govern the capitalist world system it had rescued from the revolutionary, reactionary and conservative forces that had threatened it since 1917. However, two world wars had also weakened the old European empires in Asia and Africa, and their non-European subjects were now pressing for national independence. Thus, as the capitalist world system's centre was transferred across the Atlantic from Great Britain to the United States between 1890 and 1945, so too the axes of anti-systemic challenge were reconstituted along new East–West and North–South lines.

The period of world-systemic chaos and transformation that Arrighi describes coincided with the effervescence of the very heterogeneous array of experiments and innovations in the arts that are now commonly described as 'modernism'. To say that modernism emerged from the crashing down of what Arrighi calls 'the entire edifice of nineteenth-century civilization' is a commonplace; the altogether more difficult challenge is to conceptualize the dialectical connections between the wider changes underway within the world capitalist system and the world literary system of this period. In very broad, necessarily schematic strokes, though, a few crucial vectors of development may be sketched.

One of the key features of the modernist moment was the emergence within Europe of several waves of avant-garde movements of very different aesthetic stripe and political tendency: the Impressionists, Symbolists, Futurists, Dadaists, Cubists, Imagists, Vorticists, Constructivists, Expressionists and Surrealists are only some of the most notable of these formations. Historians of the European avant-gardes trace their origins to the defeat of the Paris Commune and to the emergence of dissident bohemian enclaves within the larger European cities. These avant-gardes were for the most part concentrated in the major cultural capitals of the European-centred world literary system and they seem to have proved especially important in those societies where the higher arts were regulated by national academies that had been created in the days of the absolutist state and the *ancien régime*. These academies usually reflected, therefore, the impress of the aristocracy and the haute bourgeoisie that were their patrons. Emerging in Paris, Vienna, Berlin, Prague, Moscow and St. Petersburg and other capital cities, the avant-gardes challenged nineteenth-century conceptions of what constituted literature and the higher arts, and to this end they chiefly targeted the *art institutions* that regulated the mechanisms of artistic production and distribution and that monitored traditional canons of taste. Avant-gardes of this militant kind seem to have played a much less decisive role in England or the United States or indeed in the Anglophone world more generally than in continental Europe. This may be because the Anglophone countries never had the tightly centralized states of the great absolutist monarchies (in France, Spain, Austro-Hungary, Prussia and Russia, for example). They had also been more fully capitalist than their European counterparts for longer and had prided themselves on the fact that their academies, perhaps fewer in number than those in continental Europe, cultivated more variety and more 'natural' empirically based art than the theory-based academicism of the European systems.[23] Whatever their specific aesthetic or political commitments, the avant-gardes in any event sought to challenge what they regarded as outmoded conceptions of art and to advance the self-critique of art as a bourgeois institution without, however, capitulating to the idea of art as merely another market-driven commodity.[24]

A second major development that challenged the Old World literary system in this period was the establishment of the Soviet Union and its attempt to generate a non-capitalist literary world with Moscow as its capital. Like so many other European literatures, modern Russian literature had developed by way of a competitive dialogic rivalry with French and German literatures in particular.[25] In the period leading up to and following the Bolshevik Revolution, Russia had also produced its own wave of modernist artistic experiments as the old tsarist institutions of literature and art were challenged by artists associated initially with the liberalizing middle classes, later with the revolutionary forces. However, as the new Soviet state consolidated in the 1920s and 1930s, its communist intellectual elites began to develop a specifically Soviet vision of 'world literature' and tried to establish Moscow as a rival world literary capital to Paris. Pointing to phenomena such as imperialist, class and racial exploitation, the Great Depression, and the rise of Nazism, this emergent Soviet intelligentsia conceived of the capitalist West as 'a combination of Dostoevsky's "Europe as graveyard" and Spengler's "Decline of the West"'.[26] From the Soviet perspective, there were really two antithetical worlds vying for survival in the contemporary moment: a doomed capitalist West displaying the social and cultural morbidity of advanced civilizational decline and a rising communist world in the East opening up a bold new stage of history, civilization and artistic production. Thus, the Soviets fashioned a historical grand narrative in which the French Revolution and the Paris Commune found their logical culmination in the Russian Revolution and a corresponding literary grand narrative in which a once-revolutionary and democratizing European bourgeois literature had lost its way and entered a stage of decadence and formalist senescence in the later nineteenth century. In this view, Western

European modernism represented the final decadence of European Enlightenment intellectual and literary culture, and the emerging proletarian and socialist realist literatures cultivated in the new communist world pointed the way to the future.[27] Under the influence of the Popular Front and the anti-fascist internationalism of the mid-1930s in particular, the Soviet cultural intelligentsia made a determined attempt to fashion its own version of 'world literature' – the term found sanction in the writings of Goethe and in Marx and Engels of *The Communist Manifesto* – and to formulate a canon that sequenced the most progressive 'world writers' of the European literary world with those of the contemporary Soviet Union.

Although Moscow conceived of itself as an intermediary between European and Asian civilizations, its conception of 'world literature' was in practice heavily European and in literary terms it placed an emphatic stress on 'realism'. Hence, the activities of the European avant-gardes were regarded as jejune and infantile in the face of the pressing world crisis, and the formally experimental writings of the high modernists were construed as evidence of the morbid aestheticist decadence of the Western European intelligentsia. Even if Moscow never managed to outshine Paris as a world literary capital, the conception of the Soviet Union as a new kind of world civilization that was pioneering a new kind of literature and art represented a major rupture within the established world literary system centred on Paris.[28] In the turbulent period between the world wars, and especially in the throes of the apparent capitalist meltdown of the Great Depression, many writers across the globe looked not just to Paris and Western Europe but also to Moscow and the new Soviet Union as arbiters of literary modernity and progress.

If Moscow represented one kind of challenge to Parisian cultural preeminence in the period after World War I, there were also other rivals nearer to hand. Following the unification of Germany, Berlin experienced several decades of accelerated growth, its population climbing from less than a million in 1871 to over two million by 1905. Berlin, the seat of the German Imperial Parliament, was determined not only to surpass Munich as Germany's primary cultural capital but also to rival Paris in architectural magnificence and artistic lustre. Conscious of its Scandinavian and Low Countries ethnic hinterlands to the north and the east, the city saw itself not merely as a German state capital but also as a metropolitan centre for a wider 'Nordic tradition' extending across Northern Europe. A centre for the theatrical and visual arts in particular in the late nineteenth century, Berlin was the city in which many of Ibsen's greatest plays were produced, as were those of the German naturalist, Gerhardt Hauptmann; the two were conceived by many German critics of the period as the Marlowe and Shakespeare of a new 'German' drama. Northern European writers, musicians and painters (among them Ola Hansson, Gunnar Heiberg, Edvard Munch and Jean Sibelius) also gravitated towards Berlin as did artistic émigrés to the east. The Swedish playwright August Strindberg lived for a time in the city in 1892–93 and Otto Brahm's Freie Bühne theatre premiered some of his groundbreaking works in Berlin, including *The Father* and *Miss Julie*. Following Germany's defeat in World War I, the Weimer Republic had opened up the German university system to Jewish students and liberalized culture generally. This created the conditions for a major new wave of modernist experimentation in all of the major arts, some of the more notable examples of which include the Bauhaus movement, the new Objective Style, German Expressionism and the Berlin cabaret scene of the 1920s and 1930s.[29]

Further to the south and east, Vienna, the capital of the Austro-Hungarian Empire, was another polyglot emigrant metropolis that also served as a crucible of early modernism. Counting Prague and Budapest as its cultural satellites, Vienna was also a magnet for aspiring Jewish artists and intellectuals from across the eastern regions of the Habsburg Empire. The birthplace of psychoanalysis, home to the Viennese School of composers and the Vienna Secessionist movement, the city produced a powerful body of modernist experiment both in the *fin-de-siécle* era leading up to the collapse of the empire in 1914, and again in the 1920s and early 1930s as the crisis of the Austrian Republic intensified. However, with Hitler's ascension to power in Germany in 1933, and the Anschluss of 1939, modernism was suppressed in official German culture as an unhealthy symptom of 'decadence'. Thereafter, many of those most associated with modernism, as well as Jews, socialists and anti-fascists of all sorts, had to flee Germany into exile, many taking refuge initially in Paris or London, but later emigrating further westwards to the United States.[30]

If Paris, then, survived the turbulent period between the *belle époque* and World War II as continental Europe's leading literary capital, it did so not simply because its position was always unassailable but thanks to a considerable degree of historical contingency or good luck. Paris was never as stable as London – the Prussians had paraded through the city in 1871 to mark the German victory in the Franco-Prussian War; the workers' uprising of the Paris Commune followed quickly afterwards; the city almost fell again to the invading Germans in 1914; and it was occupied by the Nazis in World War II. These upheavals throughout this period were possibly a stimulus to Parisian nineteenth-century literary and modernist vitality. Similar affinities between social and political rupture and the momentum of modernist experiment may be sensed in Vienna, Berlin and Moscow. Parisian modernism was often denounced by domestic nationalists as the work of foreigners animated by 'anti-French' sensibilities and tastes. The Cubists, for example, were frequently described as *métèques* ('damned foreigners') and the prominence of other leading émigrés such as the Russian Sergei Diaghilev, the Spaniard Pablo Picasso or the Irishman James Joyce in Parisian modernist experiment led some French cultural nationalists to interpret modernism as a 'barbarian' assault on the canons of French classicism.[31] However, because it had prided itself for centuries on being not just a French national capital but also a great world city of culture and the arts, and because it had neither suddenly lost its empire as Vienna had when the Habsburg regime collapsed during World War I, nor was associated with a domestic suppression of modernism as Berlin and Moscow each were under their Nazi and Soviet Communist regimes of the 1930s, Paris's international cultural prestige remained comparatively higher after 1945 than that of any other continental competitor capital in Europe. By the beginning of the Cold War in 1947, the Soviet Union had largely ceded modernism to the West, Berlin was divided into Eastern and Western zones in a partitioned and devastated Germany and Vienna had shrivelled almost thirty years earlier to the capital city of Austria and of European angst.

The Scandinavian and German countries probably had better claims than the French to the initial developments in modernist drama, as did the Austrians and Russians to the inauguration of modernist art music and ballet. The Germans and the Americans did more than their French counterparts to pioneer modernist architecture and the cinema industry. While there were indeed prominent metropolitan French waves of modernist experimentation across a wide spectrum of the more small-scale 'artisanal' art forms, Paris's claim to be the capital of twentieth-century modernism owed a great deal to its magnetic capacity to serve as sanctuary city for expatriate modernists from other countries in the interwar decades of the 1920s and 1930s. It was also home to a resurgence of 'late modernism' in the aftermath of France's liberation from Nazi occupation in 1945. Nevertheless, after 1945 the world was no longer as it was before, and new claimants to the title of world literary capital had emerged to the East in Moscow and the West in New York.

Paris's international prestige, accumulated and consolidated over so many centuries, did not immediately fade, of course. However, its most internationally distinguished post-war intellectual luminary, Jean-Paul Sartre, was under no illusion that its former grandeur and that of its writers would not be restored to old glory. In 'The Situation of the Writer in 1947', a magnificent essay first published in *Les Temps modernes*, he offered a clear-eyed appraisal of the congeries of challenges now confronting progressive French writers.[32] The essay acknowledged that in some ways contemporary French writers had enjoyed more 'luck' than many of their European counterparts. The achievements of the great French Enlightenment writers who prepared the way for the Revolution were such that later generations of French writers, including his own, were always more feared, and hence revered, by French society than their counterparts elsewhere. 'Our confrères in London, who do not have these glorious memories', Sartre remarked, 'do not frighten anyone; they are considered quite harmless', while in Italy 'where the bourgeoisie, without ever having counted for much, has been ruined by fascism and defeat, the condition of the writer, needy, badly paid, lodged in dilapidated palaces too vast and grandiose to be heated or even furnished, at grips with a princely language too pompous to be supple, is far removed from ours' (142). However, if the French writers still enjoyed conditions of relative privilege, their cultural capital, Sartre allowed, was fast declining, and the old supports of great traditions and a once-sturdy bourgeois class were no longer to be counted on. Modernism, in Sartre's view, had been a war waged by bourgeois writers on the bourgeoisie:

> But 1945 does not resemble 1918. It was fine to invoke the flood upon a victorious and smug France which thought that it would dominate Europe. The flood has come. What remains to be destroyed? The great metaphysical destruction of the other post-war period was carried on joyously, in a spirit of unleashed explosion. Today, there is the threat of war, famine, and dictatorship. We are again super-charged. 1918 was holiday-time. A bonfire might be built of twenty centuries of culture and accumulations. Today the fire would go out by itself or would refuse to catch. It will be a long time before the holiday season comes round again.
>
> (189)

For Sartre, '[t]he fate of the bourgeoisie', one to which the fate of French writing was antagonistically affiliated, 'was tied up with European supremacy and colonialism' (200). But as France now lost its colonies and control over Europe, the French bourgeoisie also lost its power, and the writer had now to seek new publics, even though the arrival of new media – radio, television, the cinema – complicated the very idea of a public for those committed to literary writing. The working classes might now be the most progressive class to which to turn to find that new public, but access to that class was controlled by the Communist Parties, which gave their allegiance to Moscow and distrusted writers and criticism. Across the Atlantic, the United States, a country whose disaggregated writers had always had to manage without the kinds of supports enjoyed by their European counterparts, offered no reassurance either. Today, Sartre concluded, '[t]wo world powers, neither of which is bourgeois and neither of which is European, are disputing the possession of the universe. The triumph of one means the advent of state control and international bureaucracy; of the other, the coming of abstract capitalism' (200). Paris might have been saved the sorrier fates of Vienna, Rome or Berlin, then, but it was fatuous, in Sartre's view, not to see how drastically things had changed, how little either the European bourgeoisie or working class still governed their own fates, how much 'history is written elsewhere' (211).

### III

Nineteenth-century London was always a larger and more fully modernized city than Paris. By the second half of the century, England had completed its industrial revolution and was an overwhelmingly urbanized country, whereas France remained a much more mixed society with many regions that were still largely agrarian and not nearly as fully industrialized as their English counterparts. If, as many cultural historians now argue, modernism flourished most hectically, not in the most wholly modernized societies but rather in those marked by a combined and uneven development that brings modern and non-modern cultural milieux into violent and mutually estranging contact with each other, then, as Evan Horowitz has remarked, '[t]he problem with London was that it was too advanced, no longer allowing for the kinds of mixed phenomena that so defined the landscape of nineteenth-century Paris'.[33] In France, the middle classes had had to wrest political power from the *ancién regime* in a violent revolution in 1789, and then to confirm their control of an advanced and strongly centralized state against proletarian (not to mention German) challenges in 1830, 1848 and 1870–71. By contrast, in England, the absolutist state had never been so long or sturdily developed and the English middle classes had come to power earlier and by a more gradualist process; they had also achieved a more stable class compromise with the aristocracy and a more secure dominance over a more deferential proletariat. To cite Horowitz again, 'The reason that London lacked a culture of bohemia was not because it trailed France, but precisely because it had managed, over time, to accommodate and institutionalize both the new forces of industrial capitalism and the new powers of the middle class' (115). Whereas late nineteenth-century Paris, in short, was a city in which its *flâneurs* could still function, in Walter Benjamin's words, as '[t]he errant negotiators between the old and new',[34] London was a more consummately modernized metropolis, and for many, as Horowtiz puts it, it was already 'a nightmare of fulfilled modernity' (116). If Parisian modernism, then, was a partly French, partly émigré and partly avant-garde, partly high mandarin affair, in London the émigré element was much more strongly pronounced, the radical avant-garde element much less so.[35]

Politically, London was much less badly battered than was Paris – with its revolutions, its massive imperial rebuilding project under Louis Napoleon, invaded in 1870 and 1940, almost so in World War I – during the moment of world systemic crisis between the *belle époque* and 1945. Because it had always been Paris's strongest rival as cultural capital in the nineteenth century, the British capital ought in theory to have taken over from Paris as Europe's leading cultural capital after 1945. The moment for it to do so seemed ripe. London had not been occupied by Nazi Germany as Paris was; it had not been divided like Berlin; it had not retreated behind an Iron Curtain like Moscow. Nevertheless, precisely because Great Britain had been the world's pre-eminent imperial and financial power as this systemic crisis began, but had by 1945 ceded its leading place to the United States, London may ultimately have suffered a more immediate and greater loss of cultural prestige than did Paris in this period. Post-1945 Paris, as Sartre noted, was trapped in subsidiarity between the United States and the Soviet Union, but London had become a sub-capital of its former Atlantic colony. In that sense, it was no longer even in control of its own former Anglophone linguistic or literary jurisdiction.

At the outset of the *belle époque* London was the undisputed cultural capital of the English-speaking world. Dublin, although economically second to Belfast, was the cultural capital of Ireland. It might style itself the 'second city' of the empire, but for most of the nineteenth century it was a bypassed capital in an imperial Union. After the Scottish Treaty of Union in 1706 and the Irish Act of Union in 1801, respectively, Scotland and Ireland had both ceded their local parliaments to 'the mother of parliaments' in Westminster, and throughout the nineteenth century writers and intellectuals (as well as politicians) from both countries had flocked to London to assimilate into English culture. The calamity of the Great Famine running from 1845 into the early 1850s led to the immediate deaths of a million people and to the emigration of a million others, mainly to Great Britain and the United States. It had also precipitated a major transformation in Irish cultural and property systems that fuelled ongoing emigration overseas: more than four million Irish people emigrated permanently between the Great Famine and World War I – most to the United States but many also to Britain and to the white settlement colonies in Australia, Canada, New Zealand and South Africa.[36] One of emigration's consequences was that Ireland and Dublin suffered an ongoing sense of economic retardation relative to an England that had become the workshop of the modern world. Yet the Irish capital became, as part of the slow-burn politico-cultural reaction to the Famine and to Britain's contrasting world domination, a centre of nationalist agitation and increasingly conscious of itself as the capital not just of a subject nation but also of a far-flung diaspora of 'the Gael overseas'. Standish O'Grady was born in 1846, George Moore and Augusta Gregory in 1852, Oscar Wilde in 1854, George Bernard Shaw in 1856, Douglas Hyde in 1860, William Butler Yeats in 1865. All came of age in an Ireland recovering from the aftershocks of a great calamity, but by the late nineteenth century some were already achieving fame or notoriety in London, others leading soon-to-be-notable Irish- and English-language literary revivals in Ireland.

The American Civil War of 1861–65 was a watershed in US history, as convulsively transformative of the established structures of that society as the Great Famine had been in Ireland, but the economic consequences were very different because the Civil War and Reconstruction stimulated an accelerated period of American industrialization, especially in the North. By the outset of the twentieth century two leading American cities, New York and Chicago, rivalled or surpassed London in size. Despite the United States' enormous advances in industrial and economic power in the later nineteenth century, no American city in 1900 could rival London's long-accumulated literary prestige and none claimed to do so. Rather, American literary critics in this era bemoaned the lack of an American cultural capital, and American cultural nationalists in the early twentieth century repeatedly fretted, as they had done throughout the nineteenth century, over American literary backwardness and over expatriatism in London and Paris, one of the many consequences of that felt backwardness. In an essay on 'American Literary Centres' published in *Literature and Life* in 1902, William Dean Howells, for example, commented that the United States had 'no more a single literary centre than Italy or than Germany has (or had before their unification)'.[37] The United States, Howells continued, had possessed a succession of small literary capitals in eighteenth- and nineteenth-century Philadelphia, New York and Boston, but before the Civil War, he surmised, 'we had really no use for an American literary centre' because '[u]p to that time we had a Colonial literature'; it was only in the aftermath of that great conflict that 'we really began to have an American literature' (175). In the contemporary moment, Howells noted, literary publishing was gravitating away from Boston to New York, but though the latter city was now 'a vast mart, and literature is one of the things marketed there', New York, he opined, 'does not care nearly so much for books as for horses or for stocks' (179). Nineteenth-century Boston, he ventured, had once been an authentic small literary capital like Weimar or Edinburgh; modern New York had grown to be a huge urban megalopolis like London, but was still a crude commercial centre that lacked literary sophistication and thus could not be considered an authentic cultural as well as financial capital in the English or European manner.

In 1918 we can still find a senior American critic like Van Wyck Brooks lamenting in *Letters and Leadership* the fact that despite the United States' new importance in world affairs consequent to World War I, it still has little to offer that world by way of a coherent culture. 'But what', Brooks asks his readers, 'have we to put beside those finer elements in European life that the war has not been able to destroy and that are even now giving birth to whatever the future seems to hold of promise for the human spirit?'[38] 'A great deal', Brooks answers himself, 'but little indeed in presentable form', something that 'enables our unkinder critics to assert, with a certain air of plausibility, that we really have nothing at all' (xii). Citing Thomas MacDonagh's *Literature in Ireland*, a critical work by the young Irish poet and critic executed by the British for his role in the Easter 1916 Rising, Brooks noted the discrepancy between societies like Ireland and America that have to juggle 'a full-grown [English and European] criticism side by side with what [MacDonagh] calls a baby literature' (90). 'For Ireland and America really are alike', Brook surmises, 'in that they inherit a dominant academic tradition colonial in essence, having its home in centers of civilization remote from the springs of national life which has only of late come into its own consciousness' (91). One of the several things that had retarded the emergence of an ambitious American national literary consciousness, Brooks concluded, citing Goethe in 1795, was the lack of 'any central point of social culture, where authors might associate with one another and develop themselves by following, each in his own special branch, one aim, one common purpose' (120). For Brooks after the war, as for Howells before, the United States lacked the cultural coherence and integration that such a centre might confer and still needed to create a national literature and a critical culture that could match that of Europe and express some sense of higher vision than American industry and military might could offer the world.

By the end of World War II much had changed in the wider Anglophone political and literary worlds. Irish republican nationalists, disappointed by the British deferral of Irish Home Rule at the outset of World War I, staged the Easter Rising in Dublin in 1916 and waged a war of independence in the aftermath of the Great War that issued in the establishment of the Irish Free State, which included most of Ireland except the six north-eastern counties that became Northern Ireland in 1921. The Irish Literary Revival, or Literary Renaissance to use another contemporary term, had been underway since the 1890s, its early activities dispersed across Belfast and London's expatriate Irish community as well as Dublin. The separatist political revolt and the intensified national climate after 1916 galvanized Irish literary activity and brought the Revival to even greater international attention. When the Irish Free State was established, Dublin had acquired the reputation not only of a rebellious new political capital that had taken on the might of the British Empire but also – thanks to the Gaelic League, the Abbey Theatre, Wilde, Shaw, Synge, Yeats and Joyce (the latter working initially in Trieste but in Paris from the 1920s onwards) – the reputation of a new centre of literary experiment.[39] In the same period, New York had become the largest city in a United States that the census of 1920 had declared for the first time to be an urban continent or nation.[40] By the 1920s, publishing and printing represented New York's second largest industry, second only to the making of women's garments.[41] The destination for hundreds of thousands of former African Americans migrating from South to North in the Great War era, and host to smaller immigrant Black communities from the West Indies, post-war New York also became home to the Harlem Renaissance. For some, the music and literature of that Renaissance represented the discovery of America's own authentic primitivist 'folk culture'; for others, the development of new urban vernacular modernisms such as jazz and swing.[42] In the same decades, Greenwich Village emerged as a vibrant polyglot bohemian quarter of intellectuals and artists – the milieu was more socially and ethnically mixed, culturally brasher and less traditionalist than London's Bloomsbury.[43] Though American writers such as Djuna Barnes, John Dos Passos, F. Scott Fitzgerald, Ernest Hemingway, Claude McKay and many others continued to migrate to Paris in the decade after World War I, émigré activity tapered off dramatically after the stock market crash of 1929 as the ensuing economic depression forced many expatriates to return home. Soon afterwards, World War II and the German occupation of Paris virtually ended the American presence.[44]

Meanwhile, the American expatriates Pound and Eliot had become commanding presences or impresarios in literary London, Eliot especially becoming perhaps the most powerful arbiter of cultural taste in the English-speaking world after the publication of *The Waste Land* in 1922.[45] When he assumed editorship of *The Criterion* in October 1922 and became poetry editor with Faber and Gwyer in 1925, Eliot consolidated his position as the leading mandarin of English letters and in so doing becoming the first American ever to assume such exceptional authority in the British capital. There was no equivalent takeover by an émigré critic in Paris. There, Sartre, though conscious of Paris's decline, remained the controlling presence in the French capital.

Eliot's commanding position in London as 'the Pope of Russell Square' was a sign of changing times in Anglo-American literary relations. However, whereas Eliot, despite his adamant social conservatism, remained receptive to various currents of European literary modernism, the British literary establishment more generally was typically indifferent or more hostile. Whether it was because modern British literature had been constitutively formed in reaction against the French Revolution, and was thus inherently attached to concepts of traditionalism, organicism and homely rootedness, or because the accumulated prestige of English letters and English realism was such that the English literati felt that they had less to gain and more to lose from modernist experiment than their American or Irish counterparts is difficult to tell.[46] Whatever the explanation, the concurrent rise to eminence of two successive generations of Irish and American literary expatriates in London and Paris – a first pre-war generation that included Henry James, James McNeill Whistler, George Moore, Oscar Wilde, George Bernard Shaw and W. B. Yeats; a second generation whose careers got underway after the war and that comprised Gertrude Stein, Ezra Pound, T. S. Eliot, Hilda Doolittle, James Joyce, Sean O'Casey and Samuel Beckett and that, thanks to Pound, co-opted Yeats to itself – did much to confirm a wider perception that the domestic wellsprings of British literary energies were running dry and that the really pacesetting forces in modern English-language literature were now to be found elsewhere. This was the gist of Pound's 1929 'How to Read' essay, first published in the *New York Herald Tribune*, when he declared the English language now 'in the keeping' of the Irish and the Americans and that there was 'no longer any reason to call [the poetry produced by these writers] English verse; and there is no reason to think of England at all' (34). Though never as brashly Yankee as Pound, and always committed to the idea that national literatures were secondary to a superior international literature that, whatever its origin, would always remain 'English', Eliot nevertheless had sounded a similar note when he had declared in 1922, the *annus mirabilis* of high modernism, that:

> the advance of 'American literature' has been accelerated by the complete collapse of literary effort in England. One may even say that the present situation here has now become a scandal impossible to conceal from foreign nations; that literature is chiefly in the hands of persons who may be interested in almost anything else; that literature presents the appearance of a garden unmulched, untrimmed, unweeded, and choked by vegetation sprung only from the chance germination of the seed of last year's plants.[47]

Deploying the language of *Hamlet*'s 'unweeded garden' to reprimand Shakespeare's modern literary heirs for having allowed the garden of English letters to grow so rank, Eliot's pronouncement of a 'complete collapse of literary effort in England' is damning. Contemporary English letters, he says in effect, are an effete late bloom that depends largely on 'the chance germination of the seed' of earlier English generations; the scale of the present decline, he asserts, has become in his time a national 'scandal' that can no longer be concealed from 'from foreign nations'.

Confronted with the Irish Renaissance centred in Dublin on one flank and by the emergence of New York as a brashly dynamic centre of both modernist and mass culture on the other, it is no great surprise perhaps that the English literary establishment in the main adopted what might be called a siege mentality towards modernism. A suspicion of things French and Continental had long been a staple of the national culture of the 'sceptred isle'; likewise, a settled sense of British cultural superiority with regard to backward, violent and impoverished Ireland and wealthy but backwoods and unvarnished America. Given modernism's associations with these multiple kinds of foreignness and the more general climate of national anxiety that issued from the perception of a slow but inevitable corrosion of British hegemony in the wake of World War I, the British establishment's suspicion of modernism was probably overdetermined by the conjuncture. In any event, Geoffrey Elton expressed a wider English anti-modernist sentiment when he remarked in 1941 that:

> The most admired writing of the twenty years' Armistice is almost impossible to read now. It dates more glaringly than the Victorians themselves. Not much of it was written by the English. It was deracinated stuff, the work of Americans living in London, or Irishmen who had settled in Paris. [...] In every capital, international publishing houses and international galleries controlled, as often as not, by men who were at home in all countries and in none, could print or hang it for the admiration of the

same drearily heterogeneous public. It was in revolt against all tradition, for it was in revolt against the ordinary man, who is compounded of tradition. [. . .] And, for the same reason, it proceeded too much from the head, too little from the heart. For it was in the qualities of the heart that, when the tempest last descended upon us, the common man had excelled the intellectuals, and had earned their resentment. And so, like all those political blueprints of Utopia which ignored humanity, treating men and women as abstract units in a vast mathematical problem, the new art inevitably over-valued theory.[48]

The denunciation of modernism as a kind of American and Irish preposterousness, composted of a rootless exilic cosmopolitanism – the deracinated stuff of 'men who were at home in all countries and in none' – and as an abstract utopianism hostile to all tradition, an aridly cerebral literature contemptuous of 'the ordinary man', would find recurrent echo in English letters. The terms of this dismissal, repeated from George Orwell to John Carey, were not the same as those of the Soviet Union where modernism was deemed a symptom of Western 'bourgeois decadence', but they weren't entirely different either. Even the more modernist English-based writers seemed to consider modernism's more extravagant experiments too much; one thinks of Virginia Woolf's or D. H. Lawrence's scepticism of Joyce, or of the later Eliot's turn to Anglicanism and English tradition in *The Four Quartets*. Hence the aptness of Jed Esty's memorable phrase that the works of the domestic English modernists between 1914 and 1945 'reveal the inner logic and stylistic contours of a major literature caught in the act of becoming minor'.[49]

The English literary establishment's hesitations about modernism no doubt abetted an emerging American literary establishment's enthusiasm to appropriate it. As mentioned earlier, American literary expatriates in Europe had long been a source of anxiety for American cultural nationalists because expatriatism was usually taken to confirm American cultural backwardness. But as early as 1902 William Dean Howells, with Henry James patently in mind, had demurred from this assessment and had suggested that Americans were the true cosmopolites and that country's overseas artists 'may be the vanguard of the great army of adventurers destined to overrun the earth from these [American] shores, and exploit all foreign countries to our advantage'.[50] Lacking an advanced and sophisticated literary culture of their own, Americans, Howells proposed, were disposed to regard all of Europe's literary patrimonies as theirs to select from at will, and thus they could, as Henry James had put it, 'pick and choose and assimilate and . . . claim our property wherever we find it'.[51] Once it felt itself begin to emerge as a major world power after World War

I, the United States had multiple incentives to appropriate modernism. First, whereas from a British perspective modernism was associated with an assault on the prestige of nineteenth-century British realism (an assault usually taken to have been initiated by a grim French naturalism and then pressed to extremes by Irish and American high modernist experiments), in the United States modernism was associated with America's politico-economic and literary coming-of-age internationally and with its assumption of the 'burden' of world power. Second, for many American intellectuals of diverse political leanings, American provincialism, anti-intellectualism and Protestant philistinism remained troubling debilities of the national culture, all the more so now that the United States was emerging onto the world stage. For some of these, the appropriation of modernism served to redress inherited national liabilities and a means to nurture the more cosmopolitan cultural disposition that all great powers ought to possess. Later, when Hitler's Germany suppressed modernism as decadent and when the Soviet Writers' Congress of 1935 declared socialist realism the official literary mode of the Communist world and effectively suppressed Russian modernism, the United States had an even stronger incentive to embrace modernism because by doing so it could now offer itself to the world as the guardian of an imperilled Western artistic heritage and as a protector of artistic freedom and innovation. As European intellectual emigrants fled from Nazi Germany and the Soviet Union or from war-torn Europe generally and found shelter in the American university system from the 1930s onwards, they lent further impetus to this by bringing their own interpretative élan to the American appropriation.[52] More reactionary motives were also undoubtedly part of the process: the appropriation of modernism allowed the United States to shore up a sense of itself as an essentially 'European civilization' even as it also claimed to be a 'world state' composed of emigrants from all over the globe. In the Cold War era, New Critical conceptions of modernism served as a counter to more populist or more directly political modes of art.[53]

In 1926, Lewis Mumford commented acerbically in *The Golden Day* on the ways in which wealthy Americans in the Gilded Age had spent fortunes in Europe 'hunting for pictures, statues, tapestries, cloths, pieces of furniture, for the epidermis and entrails of palaces and cottages and churches'. 'The essential character of all these culture-seekers', Mumford mused:

> was that their heart lay in one age, and their life in another. They were empty of the creative impulse themselves, and unwilling to nurture this impulse in the products of their own time. At best, they were connoisseurs, who could appreciate a good thing, if it were not too near; at worst, they

were ragpickers and scavengers in the middens of earlier cultures. They
wanted an outlet for their money: collection furnished it. They wanted
beauty: they could appreciate it in the past, or in what was remote in space,
the Orient or the Near East. They wanted, finally, to cover up the bleakness
of their American heritage; and they did that [. . .] by looting from Europe
the finished objects which they lacked.[54]

The American reception of modernism shared something at least with this
earlier acquisitive instinct, though in the case of modernism the phenomenon represented not only what Mumford called 'the pillage of the past'
but a staking of a claim on the present and the future too because
modernism generally managed to combine a sense of deep tradition or
even 'classicism' with connotations of vanguardist raids into the future.

The American appropriation of modernism, then, was a complex affair.
Its origins lay both in the breakdown of the old Western European–centred
world system between 1890 and 1945 and in the new American ascendancy
and assertiveness in this period as well as in the felt need of the part of the
(overwhelmingly white) American intellectual élites to repair the deficiencies
of American provincialism and cultural crudity. By the 1930s, that process
was certainly well underway. 'We are the most powerful nation', wrote
F. Scott Fitzgerald in a 1931 essay 'Echoes of the Jazz Age'; 'Who', he
asked, 'could tell us anymore what was fashionable and what was fun?'[55] In
the same year, Fitzgerald's friend, the New York–based Edmund Wilson
published *Axel's Castle: A Study of the Imaginative Literature of 1870–1930*, a
work that popularized the conception of literary modernity for a generation.
Wilson opened his work with a chapter on French Symbolism, but *Axel's
Castle's* narrative spine featured two French (Paul Valéry and Marcel
Proust), two expatriate American (T. S. Eliot and Gertrude Stein) and two
Irish (W. B. Yeats and James Joyce) writers. The closing chapter, 'Axel
and Rimbaud', offered a more general survey, but even there English
writers – including Virginia Woolf, D. H. Lawrence and (the Canadian-
born) Wyndham Lewis, who now loom large in histories of English modernism – received cursory mention.[56] Wilson was by no means uncritical of
the writers he championed. 'The disillusion and resignationism of contemporary European literature', he wrote to Max Perkins in 1928, outlining
plans for the book, 'is principally the result of the exhaustion which has
followed the war'. Americans, taking, as they had always done, their artistic
standards and techniques 'with the most recent consignments of artistic
goods from Europe', therefore have absorbed from this recent literature 'a
sea of attitudes and ideas (I mean the literary people have), which have
absolutely nothing to do with the present realities of American life and

which are largely inappropriate for us'. Nevertheless, the modernists needed to be assimilated by America and just as Joyce, Yeats, Proust, Eliot and the rest were a reaction to the earlier generation of writers like Shaw, Ibsen or Anatole France, Wilson was confident that American writers would react against this literature of exhaustion and introspection. '[I]n another generation or two, we may be leading the world intellectually. I feel that Europe is coming now to look to us for leaders while we are still respectfully accepting whatever they send us. I don't expect to wave Old Glory quite as openly as this, but I want to make the point at the end'.[57]

Only a few decades earlier, American cultural commentators had viewed the expatriation of American talent as a sure sign of American literary weakness, but as American power increased so too did a note of American confidence. As Alex Zwerdling has noted, '[f]or all their feeling of displacement at home, James, Eliot and Pound (and before them Henry Adams) [had] reflected America's ascendancy and Britain's decline. Their interpretative authority is striking: Adams's *de haut en bas* tone, James's assured use of national stereotypes, the magisterial dogmatism of Eliot's literary essays, Pound's ABC's for the benighted. Manifest destiny could claim high culture as well as territory and could cross the Atlantic'.[58] Wilson's *Axel's Castle* was the literary critical Golden Hind that helped to secure that modernist crossing, and by the 1930s and 1940s there were many able Americans to help with interpreting the treasures appropriated.

When Europe fell a second time into continental conflagration, John Peale Bishop opened an address at Kenyon College in 1941 by remarking: 'I shall begin with the simple conviction that the future of the arts is in America'.[59] Bishop's lecture went on to cite Paul Valéry on the fragility of civilizations:

> We have heard tell [...] of whole worlds that have disappeared, of empires that have foundered with all their men and all their engines; gone straight down to the inexplorable bottom of the centuries, with their gods and their laws, their academies and their sciences, both pure and applied, with their grammars, their dictionaries, their classics, their romantics and their symbolists, their critics and the critics of their critics. ... And we see now that the abyss of history is big enough for everybody. We feel that a civilization has the same fragility as a life. The circumstances which would send the works of Baudelaire and of Keats to join the works of Menander are not in the least inconceivable: they are in the daily papers.
>
> (167)

'In the Europe between 1919', Bishop surmised, when Valéry's forebodings about the sudden collapse of empires and civilizations 'were first printed, and 1939, which saw the beginning of another war, it was impossible to escape the conviction that centuries were hastening to their end. The whole order which had come into existence with the Renaissance was falling apart, and not merely the economic order that had sustained it' (167). 'For twenty years ago', Bishop continued,

> it was in Europe that the centers of our civilization were to be found. The feeling of inferiority which then so often afflicted the American as artist, in so far as it was a consequence merely of his being an American, is to be attributed to his knowing that he was remote from them. For it is in these centers that, in each art, the tradition can best be acquired and with it an intenser consciousness of one's own time. The contacts of a capital can mean many things to a young man, but none more important than this. Twenty years ago there were many capitals in the world, but in only one was it possible to know the extreme moment of time. And that was Paris.

Bishop added, 'Paris is now silent and, as it were, in exile. The actual center of Western culture is no longer in Europe. It is here' (172).

The world, including the literary world, had changed. Paris, capital of Europe and the nineteenth century, had not quite sunk to 'the inexplorable bottom of the centuries' and the 'works of Baudelaire and of Keats' had not quite been consigned to the antiquity of 'the works of Menander'. Nevertheless, Bishop's 'conviction that the future of the arts is in America' was well founded because in the post–World War II era a shattered Europe and its arts would find themselves safeguarded in American custody. The Sartre of 'The Situation of the Writer in 1947' would not have disagreed with Bishop. Sartre's conviction that the post-1918 modernist generation could still afford to assault bourgeois tradition and kindle a gorgeously joyous bonfire 'of twenty centuries of culture and accumulations' whereas his own more straitened generation could assume no such luxury registered the loss of cultural prestige accelerated by the many havocs that devastated Europe between 1918 and 1945. The American writer might well take some quiet satisfaction in the fact that America's hour had come round at last; Bishop's address is charged with a weighty sense of new worldly responsibility. His French contemporary could see the costs that would inevitably accrue when a continental-sized country so synonymous with global capitalism could now regard itself as the saviour of Europe and of culture.

## IV

My approach to Casanova's *The World Republic of Letters* differs to that of many of her severer critics. The more common critiques levelled at

Casanova's work are that it is too Francophile and too Eurocentric, that it does not allow sufficiently for cooperation and exchange as opposed to rivalry and competition between world literary capitals, or else that it privileges untenable conceptions of literary autonomy. Some of these criticisms seem to me to carry more force than others, yet despite the many charges levelled at *The World Republic of Letters* since its publication in 1999, no grander or more sophisticated account has yet appeared. *Modernism, Empire, World Literature* proposes no alternative model on the scale of her study either; rather, it attempts to historicize what it takes to be a particularly crucial moment of rupture within that system, the outlines of which I have just documented.

Casanova's volume attempts to identify the structures and relations of power that shape the ways in which national literatures and individual writers dispose themselves towards a French-dominated world literary system. As such, *The World Republic of Letters* establishes the basis for a richer cultural historical materialism than we have at present: one in which any assessment of the politics or consequences of literary works has to take into account not just of how works respond to the extra-literary 'real' world – in short, how they formally and substantively relate to society at the level of content or symbolic form – but also how they find their place in, conform to or modify the literary system that inscribes them. Despite these strengths, Casanova's model of the world literary system is too schematic and static, a limit common to most forms of structural analysis and world systems theory generally. Nevertheless, instead of taking issue with this or that weakness in Casanova's work, the aim here is to try to historicize at least one particular conjuncture in that world literary system, the dynamics of which, a century later, we literary critics and historians still only partially understand.

I have already signalled some of the more salient changes in the period under review, but a brief summary here may help to clarify matters before proceeding. The changes in question include:

(a)  The opening up of a new Soviet world literary system centred on Moscow: As noted earlier, this event instituted its own different concepts and histories of 'world literature' and its own particular systems of literary evaluation and award. For much of the twentieth century, while the communist world still reproduced itself, this meant that writers were aware of at least two quite different literary systems with distinctive values and could not fail to notice that the status conferred on different writers in each system might vary significantly. After 1918, certainly after 1945, the literary world was no longer so wholly Paris-centred as Casanova assumes. France's consecrating power remained formidable, but now writers on the radical left, whether in India, the United States, China, South America or elsewhere, could look not just to London or Paris but also to the Soviet Union for validation. London and Paris were therefore now situated in a more radically segregated literary force field than that which had existed up to 1918. The literary world was no longer a tale of two cities, but of many. Twentieth-century debates transacted in so many regions of the globe about the histories and uses of 'modernism' and 'realism', about literary autonomy and commitment, or about the 'death of the novel' generally indicate how schismatic conceptions of literature and literary matters had become in this more divided world.[60]

(b)  The challenge to the prestigious nineteenth-century institutions of art and literature issued by the metropolitan avant-gardes constituted a second rupture with the earlier literary order of things. Though they are not the topic of this study, the avant-gardes clearly instigated a consistent radical questioning of 'art' and the purpose of art and posed the question of what constituted tenable institutions of art in this era. For some, the history of the European avant-gardes is a narrative of decline in which early radical critiques of the distance between 'art' and 'life' run into the deadends of multicultural relativism, advertising industry commodification, postmodern vapidity or Eurocentric coterie narcissism. For others, it is a history of vitality that presumes the avant-gardes' continuing ability to open up post-bourgeois lifeforms and artforms. Whatever the case, the modernist avant-gardes precipitated a radical interrogation of the meaning and function of art in modern times that no amount of returns to 'tradition' have since dispelled. 'Modernism' in all its forms had shaken up the canonical certainties of nineteenth-century bourgeois forms of 'art' and 'literature' at the cost of constitutively unsettling those terms.

(c)  The de-centering of the Anglophone world long dominated by London brought about by Dublin's emergence as a much stronger regional literary capital in its immediate vicinity and, more significantly, New York's consolidation as the financial and cultural hub of a new 'world state' constituted a new order within the larger bifurcated world system described above. The nineteenth century offered no precedent for this, no moment when, for example, Boston or

Edinburgh challenged London's supremacy as a literary capital as dramatically as these parallel Irish and American developments did. The consequences of these early twentieth-century developments for London and for Paris seem complex and probably cannot be grasped in terms of some dramatic curve of 'decline' or 'ascent'. In the short run, London seems to have lost some of its earlier cultural prestige as the United States especially acquired more cultural and artistic capital. However, in the longer run the cultural dynamism of London's former literary colonies in Ireland, the United States, and then the Caribbean, and then across the British Commonwealth, may have afforded an enormous boost to a more supranational or denationalized 'global English'. The dissemination of English across so many regions controlled by the British Empire and then across regions dependent on American capital after World War II contributed to its dethroning of French as the *lingua franca* of the world of culture and the arts. This in turn contributed to some eventual downsizing of Paris's global significance as cultural arbiter. The shifting of the capital of the Anglophone literary world across the Atlantic from London to New York represented more than just a relocation from one major city to another. A nation-state can possibly shift its capital from one city to a second without major impact, but the fact that such moves are so infrequent tells its own tale: relocations disturb the status quo, unsettle a sense of history, provoke resistances. When New York and Moscow decentred and reconstituted the old literary system organized by Paris and London, they also reorganized the ways in which literature was produced, evaluated and consecrated, and the very idea of what constituted 'literature' was more disputed than ever. What we call 'modernism' was a complex reaction against and accommodation to the new American and Soviet order of things as well as a reaction against the older Paris–London dispensation.

In an era of exceptional politico-economic volatility, these factors all contributed to a more radical shake-up and restructuring of the capitalist world literary system between 1890 and the 1950s than Casanova's *The World Republic of Letters* suggests. At the start of this period, in short, the cultural prestige of Paris and London was supreme and inviolate; at the end of it, both cities retained enormous cultural prestige. By 1945, though, they were now positioned in a more multipolar literary system in which the communist literary world, the new cultural power represented by the United States, and centrifugal postcolonial forces wider and stronger than those represented by literary Dublin or literary Harlem in the earlier twentieth century were beginning to make themselves felt. As such, the history of modernism cannot be grasped without recognition of the tremendous spell that London and Paris cast on writers in these decades. Nevertheless, the history of modernism is equally the history of how the nineteenth-century world literary system dominated by these capitals came asunder and had to be salvaged and reorganized in new ways.

If modernism does not exactly constitute, to repeat Franco Moretti's term, Europe's 'last *literary season*' – a literary 'autumn' to match Giovanni Arrighi's 'autumn' of the British-dominated cycle of capitalist accumulation – it does nevertheless seem to have sounded the final knell of the aristocratic- and *haute bourgeois*–conditioned European world literary system that had emerged with the rise of European capitalism and the expansion of the Western and Eastern European empires from the early modern period onwards. To this extent, the history of modernism may be read both as one of the terminal chapters in the European-dominated capitalist world literary system and as a formative chapter in the rise of a new American-dominated late capitalist literary system that until 1989 co-existed alongside a Soviet communist system with its own jurisdictional space.

The chapters that follow will develop the conception of Anglophone modernism sketched here. In Chapter 2 I will show how perceptions of Irish and American national cultures articulated by leading nineteenth-century metropolitan British and French intellectuals, namely Alexis de Tocqueville and Matthew Arnold, continued to shape early twentieth-century Irish and American modernisms even as these modernisms also helped to emancipate Ireland and the United States from their long-standing subordination to Great Britain. Writing on America in the long shadow of the French Revolution, Tocqueville had proclaimed that democratic societies can never be expected to produce cultures with the élan to match their aristocratic counterparts; Arnold's later writings on America essentially confirmed this supposed truth. Writing on Ireland in the same period, however, Arnold argued that while Celtic cultures lacked the economic and political capabilities that had made Britain and the United States powerful and prosperous, they nonetheless possessed spiritual and imaginative attributes that could correct the philistine tendencies of advanced capitalist modernity. As Chapter 2 will suggest, even as late nineteenth- and early twentieth-century Irish and American cultural nationalisms sought to extricate themselves from English dominance, they never managed to fully disentangle themselves from these authoritative nineteenth-century discourses, nor for that matter did Irish and American modernisms manage to do so either – this despite their antipathy to any forms of narrow cultural nationalism. In the American case, the anxiety that wealth and democracy might issue only in a boorish commercial national culture was one of the things that contributed to the anti-democratic and authoritarian-accented cosmopolitanism of Pound's and Eliot's modernisms. In the Irish case, Yeats struggled to articulate a vision of a new Irish culture that would be heroically and intransigently anti-modern, thus fulfilling Arnold's conception of Celtic culture and literature in one respect, though not in the meliorist and unionist terms Arnold had proposed. In one fundamental respect, Irish and American modernisms, I will contend, were powerful decolonizing forces that liberated their respective nations from their nineteenth-century cultural deference to Great Britain; in another respect, they also represented and repudiated to varying degrees Irish and American republican traditions and perpetuated conservative colonial nineteenth-century anti-democratic ideologies.

Chapter 3 examines Henry James's *The Golden Bowl* (1904) and T. S. Eliot's *The Waste Land* (1922) as complex reflections on Great Britain's declining role as the imperial guarantor of the early twentieth-century world system and European stability and on the rise of the United States as a great industrial power. Famously Anglophilic émigrés, James and Eliot appear in many respects to conform to Casanova's conception of the 'assimilated writer', who moves from a literary periphery to a metropolitan centre and dutifully conforms to metropolitan styles and value systems to attain recognition there.[61] There is certainly some considerable 'assimilationist' element to James's and Eliot's careers in London; both careers stand in marked contrast to that of Ezra Pound. Pound's more rambunctious temperament and congenital commitment to challenging literary establishments made for a shorter and more turbulent sojourn in London and led to his eventual flight first to Paris and then to Italy where he would spend most of his later life. Nevertheless, Chapter 3 will argue that James and Eliot were never in any simple sense 'assimilated writers'. Apart from the obvious fact that both were formally innovative artists, the fact too that the first of these émigrés eventually won recognition as the most ambitious and accomplished 'English' novelist of his era while the second would become not only one of the two most feted English-language poets of his lifetime (the other being the Irishman Yeats) but also England's most authoritative critical voice between the wars and one of its most influential editors for most of his lifetime is enough to signal how much things were changing in literary London. The London-centred authority of English critics and English letters, unshakeable in the age of Arnold, Pater, Ruskin and Morris, was now being contested by interlopers like Pound, Yeats and Eliot from the 'white' colonial peripheries. In the period before World War I and in the interregnum between the two world wars, the United States had not yet entirely eclipsed Great Britain as the world's major superpower or displaced it as the leading centre of Anglophone literature, but in the careers of James and Eliot we already find registrations of the sea change underway.

*The Golden Bowl*, one of the most baffling works of James's late period, deals directly with the American 'invasion of England' and the transfer of European artistic capital to the United States in the form of Adam Verver's establishment of a great art museum in American City. That novel, Chapter 3 contends, offers a complex evaluation of the meaning of transcontinental cultural transfer and an anxious reflection on the combination of cultural tact and sophistication and steely will to power and control needed to become a great world power. Written in the wake of World War I, *The Waste Land*, as I read it, is essentially an affiliate work to that which Eliot would undertake as editor of the London-based European-minded journal, *The Criterion*, established in 1922 and running until Europe's second great collapse in 1939. At the level of content, *The Waste Land* is obviously all about collapse, decay, decadence and disintegration. However, to be properly read, the poem enforces on its serious readers an immense labour of immersion in 'world culture' and a difficult re-membering of the great European traditions whose breakdown it elegizes. Thus, despite Eliot's commitments to the reconstruction of Europe and his reservations about the capacity of the United States to function as a great world power, his career and *The Waste Land* particularly serve as intriguing harbingers to the American takeover of Europe after World War II and to the United States' commitment to the promulgation of the classics of 'Western Civilization' and 'Great Books' courses from the late 1940s and 1950s onwards. In *The Waste Land*, one might say, Eliot puts the Humpty Dumpty of 'Western Literature' back on the wall, cracks and all, after the fall of World War I. After World War II, Eliot's abandoned homeland would follow its now-famous émigré son's lead and undertake some similar rescue mission of Europe and 'Western Literature' via the

Marshall Plan and its elite universities' ambitious programmes for 'Comparative Literature' and 'Western Civilization'.

Unlike Eliot and Yeats, Joyce made his literary career in cities outside the Anglophone literary zones altogether, initially as a struggling provincial in Trieste, later as one of the feted international celebrities of Parisian literary modernism. Joyce has been widely hailed as one of the great cosmopolitans of the modernist era: as an artist whose work repudiates all nationalisms, especially Irish nationalism. This canonical version of Joyce has been challenged in recent times by Irish and postcolonial readings that have pointed to Joyce's abiding imaginative commitment to Dublin and to a sense of Irish national grievance that motivated him to subvert the dominant literary forms and idioms of the English literary world. Chapter 4 proposes that in the 'Scylla and Charybdis' episode of *Ulysses* Joyce offers an ostensibly playful but in fact analytically acute reflection on the dynamics of writerly rivalries and national literary mimesis, the ways in which national literatures emulate each other and compete for distinction. In this episode of *Ulysses*, Joyce reflects critically on the historical-cum-literary processes by which writers like Shakespeare, or Joyce himself, become 'world writers'.

In that chapter a young Stephen Dedalus, recently returned from Paris to attend his dying mother, takes on the overwhelmingly Irish Protestant literary establishment of his own still-colonial city to produce a heretical interpretation of *Hamlet*, a text viewed by many as the masterwork of the greatest 'world writer' of the modern era. Harold Bloom reads this episode as evidence of Joyce's inability to overcome the anxieties of Shakespearian influence and English literary domination. René Girard reads it as Joyce's dissection of the traps of mimetic envy and his repudiation of the deadly cycles of vengeful overcoming envy instigates. More recently, postcolonial critics propose that the 'Scylla' chapter represents Joyce's triumphant 'Calibanesque revenge' on English literature and as a defiant declaration of Irish national literary emancipation.[62]

Steering between these impressive readings, Chapter 4 argues that even as this episode registers Joyce's cocky sense of imminent triumph over both his erstwhile English literary masters and contemporary Dublin doubters, he also acknowledges the losses incurred en route to literary mastery and consecration. Stephen, a portrait of the young but greatly frustrated artist who has still to make his mark, is taunted by John Eglinton in 'Scylla and Charybdis' that the Irish 'national epic' has yet to be written. To Eglinton's chagrin, Stephen goes on to show that Shakespeare's greatness is not simply an effect of the bard's 'genius' – a pathologically vengeful genius in Stephen's telling – but something inseparable also from the rise of England to world imperial greatness and to the genius of German writers and critics who burnished Shakespeare's reputation. Stephen may not have written the epic of his youthful boasting, but in *Ulysses* the laugh is still on Dublin and its critics because Joyce has indeed written an epic work and, furthermore, has sealed his critics forever within his creation as Stephen's colonial-minded tormentors.

That said, this is no simple 'revenge'. If Shakespeare as 'world writer' belongs to a literary system shaped by European imperial great power rivalries and national competitions, then neither can 'Joyce' nor *Ulysses* hope to escape some such fate. 'World literature' emerged from competitive processes of national mimesis that have a nightmarish side, and no author can hope to be consecrated into that system without becoming party to its system-reproducing national conflicts. Winning and losing both exact costs. To be a fighting contender for permanent fame in that world literary system, it is necessary to expose one's rival national culture's pretensions, but this can be accomplished only by absorbing, imitating and outdoing that rival. This consolidates the system that had made one minor to begin with and does so in a process in which overcoming and becoming one's rival may be hard to distinguish. Stephen's triumph or defeat at the hands of his interlocutors and Joyce's unquestionable triumph with *Ulysses* are 'revenges' that challenge the idea that 'classics' or 'great books' can be elevated into some uncontaminated realm above either mundane personal rivalries or cycles of nationalized wars that cause immense bloodshed. *Ulysses* may be a great work of 'world literature' but it remains immersed in what Stephen calls the 'nightmare' of history.[63]

Chapter 5 takes the narrative across the Atlantic to the United States in the era of its ascendancy to read F. Scott Fitzgerald's *The Great Gatsby* (1925) and Eugene O'Neill's *Long Day's Journey into Night* (1956). Much has been written in recent decades about the decolonizing and anti-imperial impetus of Irish literary modernism, but very little on the character of Irish-American modernism.[64] Nevertheless, if the Irish Literary Revival and Irish modernism both brought Irish writers into complex confrontations with the metropolitan and imperial authority of English literature, their 'cousins' in the United States were involved in struggles that were parallel in some respects at least and in other ways probably even more vexed. Long taxed in nineteenth-century WASP America with all of the usual deficiencies that supposedly attended things Celtic and Catholic,

Irish Americans in the early twentieth century were, along with other non-Anglo-Saxon ethnicities, struggling to find a place for themselves in the new and more internationally assertive United States that emerged from the Gilded Age and flowered after the Great War. As part of that struggle, the Irish laid claim to racial 'whiteness' the better to shed their long-standing *lumpenproletarian* associations and to rid themselves of historical associations with 'blackness'.[65] Nevertheless, the Irish had also tended historically to identify themselves with the American republican and democratic ethos because these were considered the antithesis of an aristocratic and despotic Englishness deemed responsible for the woes of the 'old country' that had triggered the Irish exodus to the United States.

Though different in form and style, *The Great Gatsby* and *Long Day's Journey* both belong to that moment in American history when the United States' assumption of global power generated a new confidence and epic ambition in American letters checked with the aforementioned nervous sense that America might never be able to complement its enormous military strength and economic wealth with some equivalent degree of cultural sophistication. The early expressions of this anxiety in Tocqueville's *Democracy in America* will be teased out in Chapter 2, and I have already noted in passing versions of this concern in the works of critics like William Dean Howells, Van Wyck Brooks and Lewis Mumford; similar misgivings impress the works of James and Eliot examined in Chapter 3. Viewed in this wider international context, *The Great Gatsby* must be read not just as an insularly domestic national novel about the American Dream, but as a contradictory response to an emerging American ascendancy on the world stage. The novel's famous parvenu, Jay Gatsby, and his attempt to become part of the American WASP elite by marrying Daisy Fay, are clearly crucial to Fitzgerald's concerns. However, both the upstart Gatsby or his female corollary, Myrtle Wilson, and the old-moneyed Buchanans sport their putative sophistication through things borrowed from Europe: we see this in the novel's Normandy-style houses, Italian gardens, cheap replica images of the Gardens of Versailles, English suits or equestrian sports, especially Tom Buchanan's polo horses, and in Gatsby's 'Oggsford man' affectations. *The Great Gatsby*, in this reading, swings ambivalently between an epic or mock-epic-cum-pocket-epic celebration of American democracy for its openness and cultural and class mixing and a wistful repudiation of that democracy's cultural garishness and tendency towards self-destruction. At ease with neither American mass culture nor an emerging modernist high culture to which it nevertheless aspires to belong, *The Great Gatsby* reflects at the level of form the many tensions inherent to the United States' ambitions to achieve international cultural distinction through a modernism that was generally all at odds with American capitalism and the materialist optimism of the American Dream.

In O'Neill's *Long Day's Journey into Night* we discover a darker version of a similar tale. Caught between James Tyrone's commitment to the putatively high art of Shakespeare, a vocation repudiated to make his family's fortunes by acting in the commercial Broadway hit *The Count of Monte Cristo*, and his sons' preference for what seem to James the nihilistic works of Nietzsche and the Decadents, *Long Day's Journey* also narrates a tale of an impoverished parvenu who, like Gatsby, rises from nothing to secure enormous success only to see everything disintegrate about him. O'Neill's play would soon find its place in the canon of great American literature and become a triumphal landmark in American modernist theatre, but O'Neill's uncompromising sense of the disastrous directions of American society and his scarcely less intense misgivings about modernism are everywhere evident. *Long Day's Journey* represents, therefore, both a moment when American modernist theatre comes of age and acquires world stature and one in which the supposedly affirmative literature represented by 'Shakespeare' and the negative works represented by Baudelaire, Swinburne, Dowson, Wilde and others cancel each other out in the Tyrone family's death-dealing riots of despair. American literary modernism and the United States' ascent to global power may be joined to each other at the hip, but nevertheless American modernism even in its most ambitious modes could never supply the United States with the grand epic work that so many sought to secure for the country in this early Cold War period. Americanism and modernism came together to secure American international cultural distinction in the era after World War I, but their respective systems of value remained fundamentally at odds, the romance as disastrous as that of Gatsby and Daisy or of James and Mary Tyrone.

The last chapter leaps forward in time from the early Cold War era to read Derek Walcott's *Omeros* (1990) as a feat of epic creation that appeared just as the Cold War ended and that self-consciously emulates the high modernist epic accomplishments of Joyce and Yeats, Eliot and Pound, and desires thereby to insert the Caribbean into 'world literature'. Classical in its references to Homeric and Dantean epic, *Omeros* knows itself also to belong to a late twentieth-century era when the United States is now the cultural capital of the Anglophone world, and when New York, the city in which *Omeros* was published by Farrar, Straus and Giroux in 1990, has replaced London as its cultural capital. In this new world, the fate of the Anglophone writer is now more firmly attached than ever before to American consecrating authority in what Mark McGurl has called '[t]he Program Era'.[66] As I read it, Walcott's great work imaginatively shuttles between the continents of Africa, Europe and North America in a bravura bid to totalize the historical and literary systems to which the poem itself belongs. However, despite its will to formal coherence and Caribbean cultural syncretism, *Omeros* is a vexed epic haunted by a sense of self-estrangement and inner division. Even if it thrills to a sense of high literary accomplishment and announces itself as an act of Caribbean literary self-assertion, the Caribbean world the poem summons into being assimilates its European colonial masters and cultures only to find itself become an American-dominated tourist pleasure periphery. And like Joyce, Eliot and Pound before him, to achieve his high ambitions, Walcott must live out his career as an émigré in an imperial culture not his own. The world literary system and its aesthetic ideologies have changed considerably from the era of high modernists, but for the peripheral writer some problems not only persist but do so in even more acute ways than they had done in the interval between the autumn of European literary decline and the summer of American global domination.

As these short summaries indicate, change in the world literary system, as conceived in *Modernism, Empire, World Literature*, comes about by different agencies and on several different levels. On one level, it took nothing less than two massively destructive world wars and their manifold reverberations to reconfigure the world literary system marked by the relative declines of London and Paris and the increasing importance of the United States. At this level, the key events in the restructuring of the literary system are extra-literary. However, on other levels change also occurs within the literary system itself when peripheral cultures and their emissaries have the audacity and ambition to dispute a declining centre's consecrating authority. Furthermore, the most ambitious literary texts do not simply seek to find a sanctioned place within stable or destabilized literary systems; the works I examine have a capacity also to draw the structures and dynamics of the system into their own forms, to make them an object of their aesthetic reflection. In this sense, works that become canonical texts reflect the wider literary system and subsume its dynamics into their own intrinsic form and substance. These different kinds of change – extra-literary, periphery driven, textual or metatextual – work at different speeds and serve different purposes; they may not always work in tandem with each other. Ultimately, it is thanks to intersecting, multilevel agencies of these kinds that world literary systems do eventually change. We do well to study such changes if only because new transformations may soon be upon us.

CHAPTER 2

# 'It Uccedes Lundun': Logics of Literary Decline and 'Renaissance' from Tocqueville and Arnold to Yeats and Pound

America, with no past to speak of, a mere 'parvenue' among nations, is creating a national literature which in its most characteristic products differs almost as much from English literature as does the literature of France. Walt Whitman, Thoreau, Bret Harte, and Cable, to name no more, are very American, and yet America was once an English colony. It should be more easy for us, who have in us that wild Celtic blood, the most un-English of all things under heaven, to make such a literature. If we fail it shall not be because we lack the materials, but because we lack the power to use them. But we are not failing.

    W. B. Yeats, letter to the Editor, *United Ireland*, December 17, 1892.[1]

Nevertheless, America is the only place where contemporary architecture may be held to be of any great interest. That art at least is alive.

    And New York is the most beautiful city in the world?

    It is not far from it. No urban nights are like the nights there. I have looked down across the city from high windows. It is then that the great buildings lose reality and take on their magical powers. They are immaterial; that is to say one sees but the lighted windows.

    Squares after squares of flame, set and cut into the aether. Here is our poetry, for we have pulled down the stars to do our will.

As for the harbour, and the city from the harbour. A huge Irishman stood beside me the last time I went back there and he tried vainly to express himself by repeating: –

    'It uccedes Lundun.'

    'It uccedes Lundun.'

    I have seen Cadiz from the water. The thin, white lotus beyond the dazzle of blue. I know somewhat of cities. The Irishman thought of size alone. I thought of the beauty, and beside it Venice seems like a tawdry-scene in a playhouse. New York is out of doors.

    Ezra Pound, *Patria Mia*, manuscript posted to Chicago, 1913.[2]

# I

That the impetus for the re-making of the early twentieth-century Anglophone literary world system should have stemmed initially from Irish and American writers but that the modernist literature that these writers created should itself have so often proved so illiberal in temper is, on the face of things at least, something of a conundrum. After all, Ireland and the United States both had strong Enlightenment liberal and republican traditions dating back to the eighteenth century and both countries were in fact distinguished from Britain's other 'white colonies' by virtue of having been the sites of major republican rebellions against the imperial metropole. The American Revolutionary War (or War of Independence) of 1775–1783 issued in the independence of the American colonies from Great Britain and in the establishment of what most nineteenth-century observers regarded as an ambitious and unprecedented experiment in modern republican democracy. Taking inspiration from this American achievement, one in which Irish Protestant (or 'Scots Irish') settlers had played a prominent role, and from the more recent example of the French Revolution, the United Irishmen had led an insurrection in the late 1790s against British rule in Ireland to establish an Irish republic.

Unlike its American predecessor, the United Irish rebellion suffered a crushing defeat. One of the consequences of that defeat was the abolition of the semi-devolved Irish Protestant Ascendancy Parliament in Dublin and the assimilation of Ireland, by way of the 1800 Act of Union, into the United Kingdom of Great Britain and Ireland, with legislative authority over the smaller island transferred by that act entirely to London. Though there was, therefore, to be no nineteenth-century Irish republic of a French or American kind, the dream of such a republic did not disappear. Consecrated in the blood and bravery of the defeated 1798 insurrectionists, the republican idea remained a potent force in nineteenth-century historical memory, most obviously in the form of the Irish Republican Brotherhood or Fenian movement that emerged in Irish emigrant communities in North America in the period after the Great Famine and the American Civil War and that was then extended internationally to Ireland and to the emigrant Irish of the United Kingdom. Charged by the memories of 1798 and a sense of injustice compounded by the mid-century catastrophe of the Famine, Fenianism represented a militant republicanism that was deeply hostile to British governance in Ireland and strongly anti-imperialist in temper. The movement made itself felt in the Victorian period by means of dynamite campaigns conducted in

London and Manchester and by way of a rather quixotic raid by Fenian activists on British Canada in the immediate aftermath of the American Civil War.[3]

Viewed against this historical backdrop, Ireland and the United States might seem unlikely sites for the production of aristocratic-minded or authoritarian high modernisms. Republican and democratic ideals were important components of the political cultures of both societies, and for many intellectuals in the nineteenth century both countries might even be said to have represented the antithesis of the values associated with the idea of aristocracy. Ireland, for instance, was widely regarded as a backward, impoverished and chronically unstable peasant society, a country that had lost its Gaelic nobility and which, thanks to successive waves of colonization, possessed none of the unbroken continuity of tradition that defined European aristocratic societies. The United States, on the other hand, famously had no feudal or medieval past and was thus perceived to lack the time-hallowed social or cultural institutions associated with a hereditary aristocracy. How could two societies of this kind create literatures that would be aesthetically vanguardist and yet simultaneously lay claim to precisely those qualities of deep tradition, classicism, cosmopolitanism and intellectual elitism commonly associated with aristocratic culture? Or, conversely, why didn't Irish and American modernisms take a more patently republican and democratic complexion rather than the 'mandarin' or 'aristocratic', and in many cases reactionary, authoritarian and, in extreme instances, even fascist cast they eventually adopted?

The apparent paradoxes involved here might seem to dissolve readily enough. Both Ireland and the United States, it might be argued, had republican and democratic traditions, but high modernism in both countries was initially the creation of privileged Protestant cultural elites who had come to regard mass democracy as a threat to their survival and cultural integrity. Thus, one might suggest, the modernisms fashioned by these imperilled elites gave full vent to an attendant sense of civilizational wreckage and anti-populist rage. When the United States emerged as a modern industrial powerhouse in the decades after the Civil War, it attracted to its shores an influx of immigrants from Southern and Eastern Europe and from China; this further increased the ethno-cultural heterogeneity of a society that had already accommodated large emigrant communities from regions such as Ireland, Germany and Scandinavia. In the same postbellum period, the country was simultaneously beginning to witness a large-scale migration of African American labour from the rural plantations of the South to the burgeoning industrial cities of the North.

For the patrician white Anglo-Saxon elites of the eastern United States, therefore, the post–Civil War period was experienced not simply as a time of fantastically growing American power and prosperity but also as an era that threatened to capsize their class and cultural authority.

In the Irish case, the Protestant intellectual and cultural elite, though mostly professional bourgeois in composition, was closely affiliated politically with the landed Protestant Ascendancy class. Both classes viewed the rise of a Catholic middle class and its demands for democratic representation in the form of Irish Home Rule as a threat not only to the security of the existing Protestant establishment in Ireland but also as something fatal to the continuance of the Union with Britain and to the long-term stability of the British Empire. This Protestant cultural elite was internally fractured between a majority that was Unionist and imperialist in allegiance and a minority that had espoused Irish political or cultural nationalism, largely to allow Protestants to continue to provide intellectual and cultural leadership in a devolved Ireland. Whatever its political allegiances, loyalist or nationalist, this Protestant elite was always deeply conscious of its own colonial history in Ireland and was increasingly fearful as the nineteenth century progressed that any devolved and democratic Ireland would inevitably be defined in Gaelic and Catholic terms, thus reducing Protestants of all classes to a powerless 'alien' minority. On both sides of the Atlantic, therefore, once-dominant Protestant elites might be said to have viewed the advance of democracy as a threat to establishment cultures and thus to have fashioned reactionary visions of modernity and authoritarian modernisms that embraced 'aristocratic' conceptions of literature as an antidote to the conceived disorder and vulgarity of modern democracy. When British and Western European liberalism more generally suffered an extended crisis after World War I and during the Great Depression, this reaction against democracy hardened. Thus, what in some cases had started out as relatively conventional and mainstream late nineteenth-century classical liberal anxieties about democracy evolved in the 1920s and 1930s into more toxic forms of Tory authoritarianism or outright fascism.[4]

There is much to recommend this conception of things at a general level at least. An American literary lineage that extends from Henry Adams and Henry James and the 'genteel tradition' of American letters to Ezra Pound, T. S. Eliot and Hilda Doolittle; an Irish lineage that would include Standish O'Grady, W. B. Yeats, Lady Augusta Gregory and J. M. Synge: each list offers at least some support for an elitist or quasi-aristocratic genealogy of this kind. But it would then have to be allowed that the cultural and political attachments of the figures listed here are more various and complex than any singular narrative can accommodate. Furthermore, these writers do not in any event represent the whole spectrum of Irish and American modernisms because this leaves out those authors that emerged from the less traditionally privileged classes in both societies. The Harlem Renaissance modernists are the immediately obvious case in point here, but one might also want to include American figures such as Eugene O'Neill, F. Scott Fitzgerald, William Carlos Williams, Gertrude Stein, John Dos Passos and several others whose relationships to the Anglo-Saxon patrician culture of the United States were, for whatever reasons of class, religion, ethnicity or sexual orientation, a good deal more vexed than were those of the members of the 'genteel tradition'. Similarly, in the case of Ireland, middle-class Catholic modernists such as James Joyce, Thomas MacGreevy, Denis Devlin, Flann O'Brien or Máirtín Ó Cadhain all managed to steer clear of the authoritarian and eugenicist extremes of the later Yeats especially. Moreover, there were also many Protestant modernists or proto-modernists such as George Bernard Shaw, Oscar Wilde or Seán O'Casey, who espoused various forms of socialism and who will not fit the argument outlined above. And one can also point to a later generation of Protestant modernists, including Elizabeth Bowen, Louis MacNeice or Samuel Beckett (as well as the painters Jack B. Yeats and Francis Bacon), who appear to have had little enough truck with the kinds of value systems espoused by O'Grady or Yeats.

Nevertheless, even if it is important not to overly homogenize Irish and American modernisms, it would still be quite difficult to distinguish cleanly between, say, an 'aristocratic' or 'mandarin' high modernism at one end of the political spectrum and something like a 'republican-democratic' version at the other. Whatever the class attachments or political allegiances of the various authors involved, formal experimentalism, linguistic and stylistic complexity, sometimes of an extreme nature, enormous intellectual ambition and a highly self-conscious sense of international literary tradition were, early and late, defining characteristics of twentieth-century American and Irish literary modernisms. It is a common commitment to these qualities in Joyce, Beckett or Ó Cadhain or in Stein, Wallace Stevens or William Faulkner that (their diversity allowed) make them seem nearly as 'aristocratic' or at least as loftily elitist, aesthetically speaking, as Yeats or Pound who adopted more self-consciously patrician or aggressively anti-democratic stances. We may usefully discriminate between various forms of right- and left-wing authoritarian or democratic modernisms, but one of the defining features of modernism as it emerged in the early twentieth century was its shared repudiation of the dominant nineteenth-century 'mentalités'. Perry Anderson's claim in 'Modernity and Revolution' that modernism in nearly all its mutations, and however nuanced or brutal in its different ultimate allegiances, saw the bourgeois-liberal-capitalist complex as its enemy seems well founded.[5] It was these kinds of literary 'mandarinism' or 'aristocratism', moreover, that went hand in hand with a marked defiance of Victorian styles, conventions and publics that initially perplexed or outraged the London literary establishment. It was always clear that the new high modernist texts aspired to standards of erudition, elevated ambition and formal accomplishment that seemed deliberately designed to make the standards espoused by London's leading critics and journals appear in comparison complacently provincial and intellectually dull. In this pale light, Irish and American high modernisms were almost wilfully exotic distortions of a stable world. So, while some modernist literature did indeed conceal or reveal the reactionary worldview of a declining Protestant class that felt its social order imperilled by modern democracy, these were surface tremors arising from deeper disturbances. The syntax of the arts, already remoulded in French poetry between Baudelaire and Mallarmé, but still an esoteric concern, underwent a rapid, more public and scandalized transformation in the new century, most notoriously with Cubism, between 1907 and 1914. But just as the annual exhibitions of the Academy had become in Paris the target of derision and subversion in painting, so too did the institution of 'Literature' become a target for the writers of the Irish and American peripheries. The new literary modernisms from Ireland and America exhibited a high determination to outshine London and its exponents strove to create a literature of such extravagant sophistication and ambition as to defy the English capital's capacity to grasp it.

In the letter to the *United Irishman* that heads this chapter, Yeats points to the example of an emerging American literary nationalism that is generating a new literature in English that is, he asserts, almost as distinct as French literature is from English. He makes this argument for the distinctiveness of Anglo-American literature to fend off the charge of Gaelic League Irish-language nationalists that the literature of the Irish nation ought properly to be in Irish rather than in English. In doing so, Yeats adroitly appeals to the literatures of the two republics, the United States and France, to which the United Irishmen, the founders of Irish republicanism, had historically looked for inspiration. What unites Irishmen of all kinds, Yeats infers, is not language but rather 'their wild Celtic blood', the putatively 'most un-English' of Irish qualities. Simultaneous appeals to republican America and France as literary role models and to a specifically non-modern, primitivist-aristocratic and essentialist 'wild Celticism' are being blended here to produce the genome of an Irish literary identity in English that will stand in a unique, interstitial relationship with those of England or America. And when Pound, in the passage taken from *Patria Mia* (also cited above), extols New York as perhaps the loveliest of modern cities, he conscripts to his side an outsized Irishman speaking a crude English, happy to surmise that a great American city now 'uccedes Lundun'. ('Uccedes' is both 'exceeds' and 'succeeds'.) We can hear in that demotic Teague accent the note of an Irish American Fenian *ressentiment* against England, a *ressentiment* partly shared or co-opted by a Pound persona careful also to refine the Irishman's perception by suggesting that what matters is not just that New York should vulgarly 'uccede' London in size, but that it should become more aesthetically pleasing as well. His plebeian Irishman may be satisfied that New York should outstrip London in scale only, but Pound insists that bigger is not necessarily better; only if New York is also willing to become lovelier than the cities of the Old World can the United States lay claim to be the truly greater civilization. In these passages, republican and aristocratic aspirations to match or outdo England bleed into each other in rhetorically complicated ways, but in both Yeats's and Pound's cases it is a sense of literary rivalry, and a determination to 'uccede' London, that lends edge to national literary ambition.

This chapter will argue that at least in the early stages of their formation, the 'aristocratic' registers of Irish and American modernisms do not so much echo the rhetorics of pre- and post-1918 European right-wing reaction (from Boulangisme to Action Française, Freikorps to Nazism) as those of nineteenth-century classical English and French intellectual liberalism. Nineteenth-century Ireland and the United States were literary peripheries in the obvious sense that each had inherited its language and its dominant Anglophone literary models and standards from England and because London in this period was the undisputed capital of the English-speaking literary market and world system. But to be a literary periphery also meant something more than this: it meant that nineteenth-century England and France and Germany (home to cultural sages, philosophers and philologists) had the capacity to establish the critical discursive terms by which 'Ireland' and 'America' acquired meaning in the modern world in the first instance. Culturally speaking, in other words, the systems of thought and meaning by which Irish and American intellectuals made sense of their own societies and situations had largely been moulded in the metropolitan cultures of Western Europe; therefore, the articulation of modern Irish and American nationalisms, political and cultural, was conducted for the most part within these systems' discursive terms of reference.

Where literature specifically was at issue, two European writers in particular, the French Catholic liberal, Alexis de Tocqueville in the case of the United States, and, in the case of Ireland, the English Protestant liberal, Matthew Arnold, exerted huge intellectual authority. Between them, they had provided some of the constitutive terms by which Irish and American literary nationalists were to make sense of their own histories and literatures. In the two volumes of *De la démocratie en Amérique* (published in 1835 and 1840; the first American editions in 1838 and 1841) Tocqueville had allowed for the many virtues of American democracy as a political and economic system. But he had also implied that democracies are by definition so socially flattened and restlessly innovative as to be unlikely ever to produce literatures as intellectually high-brow or formally refined as the literatures of Europe's *ancien régime*. As the United States became an increasingly prosperous and powerful world state in the late nineteenth century, Tocqueville's arguments became more influential; it was becoming clear that America, as Tocqueville had predicted, would soon take its place alongside the great European powers on the world stage. Yet to many – not least to American men and women of letters – it seemed also to be true that the United States was still a long way from achieving the cultural distinction of the European nations. More worrying, was there a fundamental mismatch between cultural achievement and the political democratic and capitalist economic forms that had evolved in America?

If America faced an insurmountable cultural deficit, so too, for a different set of reasons, did Ireland. Matthew Arnold, taking cues from Ernest Renan and German philology, and writing against the backdrop of militant Fenian republican separatism, had in his *The Study of Celtic Literature* constructed Ireland as a wayward 'Celtic culture', a society that would necessarily remain dependent on Anglo-Saxon England to provide it with the good governance and material prosperity it needed because the Celts themselves had so little capacity for such matters. The Celts, for their part, Arnold hoped, would in return bring to English culture compensatory qualities of lyrical imagination and spiritual 'titanism', traits that the unlovely prosaic and materialistic culture of modern industrial England, in his view, so conspicuously lacked.[6] For Arnold, the Celts might be capable of cultural contributions worthy of note, but they would be obliged in their own interest to do so not by forming their own autonomous nation-state or distinctive national literature, but by remaining within the Union and Empire.

In the hands of Tocqueville and Arnold, Ireland and the United States were, as mentioned earlier, produced as virtual cultural opposites. The United States was viewed as an emerging industrial colossus and a youthfully emerging nation that was conducting a great unprecedented experiment in modern democracy, but that might nonetheless be destined to generate a callow culture that would always remain grossly materialistic and undistinguished, at least by comparison with the great aristocratic civilizations of Europe. Ireland, in contrast, was considered a quintessentially ancient, non-materialistic, aristocratic-and-peasant civilization out of step with a worldly middle-class modernity to which it would nonetheless be obliged, under English governance, to submit. Put bluntly, the Americans seemed likely to become a massive political and economic superpower, but to remain culturally crass and philistine; the Irish might be or become culturally interesting, but were too economically weak and politically volatile for their literature to serve as anything more than a tributary to English culture. The one society was too capitalist and materialistic to be truly 'cultural'; the other too delicately 'cultural' to be capable of economic or political self-management. Even as American and Irish cultural nationalisms gathered momentum in the late nineteenth century, the deposited terms of these authoritative discourses continued to exert their shaping force on the imaginations of both metropolitan and peripheral intellectuals alike.

However, by the beginning of the twentieth century neither Ireland nor the United States was as subservient to English cultural authority as they had been a century earlier. To the contrary, cultural nationalists in both countries had by then come to believe that they were at last undergoing a 'renaissance' (itself a highly charged European and English term) that was finally allowing them to compete with English literary glory. But even in the works of the great impresarios of these new literary movements – Yeats in the case of the Irish literary revival, Pound as the most intrepid champion of a modernist American literature – classical 'Victorian' liberal anxieties about the compatibility of modern democracy and high cultural achievement, themes sounded so influentially in the works of Tocqueville and Arnold, continued to exert enormous pressure. Indeed, as the old European imperial world order tottered in the lead-up to World War I, and as European liberalism buckled in its aftermath, these anxieties about the compatibility of democracy and high cultural achievement became amplified not just at a louder volume but also at a higher pitch. Irish and

American high modernisms were articulated in countries with strong republican histories and traditions, then, yet they nonetheless took on what look like highly 'aristocratic' and sometimes starkly illiberal and antidemocratic complexions. These rhetorics actually had their origins in European classical liberalism's own long-standing misgivings about the nature of European democracy and modernity. It only adds to the force of this paradox that, in the hands of Yeats and Pound, these misgivings would be reworked to serve as a stimulus for a modern literature perhaps even more 'aristocratic' and ambitious than many of those produced by metropolitan Europe in the modern era.

It was by such circuitous routes that the Irish and American literary peripheries revolted against the nineteenth-century capitals of the world literary system. In their remaking of that system, so long commanded by London and Paris, they replicated and aggravated the contradictions between authoritarian and democratic values of nineteenth-century England and France. The grandee modernisms of the Irish and American peripheries are in this sense a belated outgrowth of nineteenth-century classical liberalism's internal quarrels with itself, of antinomies that accumulated and then eventually intensified beyond control. These antinomies produced in time in literary modernism a strange harvest of memorable, even apocalyptic, works in alliance with a febrile politics. Throughout the twentieth century, the end of history has been predicted at regular intervals. The Last Days has by now become such a popular trope in literature, political theory and film, not to mention in evangelical religions, that they have always appeared to be imminent. This threat of extinction is curiously interlinked with earlier ideas of 'decline' and 'renaissance' that this chapter will track via Tocqueville and Arnold into some of the pre–World War I writings of Yeats and Pound as they contemplated the possibilities of national rebirths in their respective countries.

## II

Convinced that the American experiment in democracy was indicative of a wider irreversible historical development, and that the inevitable transition from aristocratic to modern democratic systems required close study if disasters of a French Revolution kind were to be averted, Tocqueville's *Democracy in America* essentially divided modern social structures into two types, the aristocratic and the democratic. Thus, the first volume of his study attempts to identify the essential differences between the characteristic legislative, executive and political systems of these two fundamental societal models; the second to diagnose the general manners, intellectual dispositions and national characters that democracies can be expected to produce. For Tocqueville, the essential difference between the two societal types is that democracies are characterized by much greater professional mobility and class malleability and hence by greater social mixing and more rapid social change than are the more socially segregated and fixed aristocratic structures. This divergence, he argues, moulds national temperaments and philosophical dispositions of a substantively different order. In aristocratic societies, he posits, the intellectual elites are naturally disposed to assumptions about the essentially static nature of society and about fundamental distinctions between various social classes or castes, an outlook that tends to favour contemplative philosophical systems and to be allergic to the advance of generalized philosophies about humankind. Modern democracies, in contrast, are disposed to more generalized philosophies about humanity and history and to demand of science and philosophy immediately useful applications and greater capacities for adaptation. In philosophical terms, Americans, in Tocqueville's view, were consequently neither so determinedly empiricist and resistant to general ideas as their more aristocratically inclined English philosophical forefathers; nor were they yet so given to abstract universalism as the eighteenth-century French *philosophes* as to manifest, like them, 'as blind a faith in the absolute truth of any theory'.[7] The French had had, unlike their English counterparts, no practical experience of anything other than the absolutist state and thus could challenge the *ancien régime* only with abstract and highly idealistic conceptions of democracy. Less aristocratic in their national temper than their English forefathers, but more practically familiar with the everyday demands of democracy than the French, Americans, in Tocqueville's view, had developed a proclivity for generalized systems and theories that were elastic enough to allow for change but that also risked conceptual superficiality.

Many Europeans, Tocqueville surmised, were disposed to believe that the socially levelling character of democracies would lead inevitably to an eventual diminution of intellectual achievement in both the sciences and the arts. There was, he contended, no basis to assume anything of the kind: the number of people actively interested in the sciences and arts would actually greatly expand in democracies and that wider level of interest would, moreover, extend to classes that would in aristocratic systems never have had either the time or the skills for such pursuits. Democracies would not, then, prove indifferent to the higher forms of learning; rather, they would develop learning in different directions than aristocratic societies had done, and both types of societies would display their own typical virtues and weaknesses in the kinds of learning they cultivated. 'Therefore, it is not true to say that men of democratic times are normally indifferent towards science, literature, and the arts; simply we have to acknowledge that they cultivate them after their own fashion and bring to them their own peculiar qualities and deficiencies' (529).

In the case of the sciences, the fundamental danger that democracies posed was that the stress on social utility and commercial return would mean that an interest in the practical application of scientific learning would eventually so outstrip interest in general theoretical principles as to lead to a stagnation in that area, something that would ultimately prove detrimental to science as a whole. 'In America', Tocqueville opined, 'the purely practical aspect of science is studied admirably and careful attention is devoted to that theoretical area which is closely related to its application'. Nevertheless, 'hardly anyone in the United States devotes himself to the essentially theoretical and abstract aspects of human knowledge' and the inevitably agitated nature of a society in which everyone was devoted to the acquisition of power or wealth was such as to raise the question of 'where could we find the tranquillity needed for deep intellectual investigations?' (530–531). In the cultural field, Tocqueville argued, the natural aversion to change characteristic of aristocratic nations and the corporatist or segmented nature of their professional structures was conducive to specialization and refinement, since all craftsmen must satisfy groups with a highly developed, often guild-regulated or corporatist sense of their own particular métier. Moreover, since those in the field of the fine arts in aristocratic societies cater almost exclusively to upper-class niche-consumers composed of wealthy, well-educated connoisseurs, refinement in the fine arts especially might be expected to be of a very high level. The dynamics of democratic societies, in contrast, required that the professions are much less commonly hereditary in character, and since society generally was also more fluid it was inevitable that both artists and the audiences to which they catered would become more heterogeneous in social and educational terms. In such circumstances, Tocqueville believed, artists would be obliged to be more commercially conscious of the socially and educationally heterogeneous audiences to which they catered. Compelled to sell his works for lower prices to a greater number of consumers, the artisan in democracies generally tends to 'find methods which enable him to work not only more effectively but also more quickly and at lower cost. If he cannot manage that, he reduces the intrinsic qualities of the objects he is making without making it entirely unsuited to its intended use'

(539). The upshot is a state of accomplished mediocrity: 'When only the rich had watches, they were almost all of excellent quality; now, mostly mediocre specimens are produced but everyone possesses one. Thus, democracy not only directs the human mind to the useful arts but also persuades craftsmen to produce many second-rate goods and consumers to put up with them' (539).

In the literary field specifically, Tocqueville asserts that aristocratic social structures encourage sophistication of expression and a rigorous embellishment of tone because the audience is primarily a restricted one with a finely developed sense of literary tradition. On the positive side, this tended to produce a literary milieu distinguished by its sensitivity to matters of style and formal accomplishment; on the negative side, to promote a fussy academicist obsession with rules for rules' sake and a degree of professional self-enclosure that issues in 'a sort of aristocratic jargon which is scarcely less removed from fine language than popular dialect' (546). On the whole, Tocqueville asserted, the literatures of democratic societies tend to be of a lower standard than those of their aristocratic counterparts because:

> Considered in its entirety, literature of democratic times could not possibly present, as it does in aristocratic times, a picture of order, regularity, science, and art; its formal qualities will normally be disregarded and sometimes despised. Style will often appear quirky, incorrect, inflated, and flabby, and almost always extreme and violent. Authors will aim more at speed of execution than perfection of detail. Writing on a small scale will occur more often than weightier books, wit more often than scholarship, imagination more often than profundity.
>
> An untutored and almost barbaric power will govern thought, accompanied by great variety and an unusual richness of writing. Writers will strive to startle rather than please and to rouse passions rather than charm the reader's taste.
>
> (548)

These, Tocqueville conceded, were ideal types or extremes of social form and the actual character of specific societies would naturally prove more mixed. Even in the more debilitating circumstances of democratic societies, a small number of writers could always be expected to react against the prevailing literary trends and standards of taste, and those who so reacted would find small but appreciative readerships of a more select and sophisticated taste. But even then, he surmised, 'those very few people who have escaped common practice in general will always relapse when it comes to details' (548–549) because even a sophisticated elite could not be expected entirely to transcend its larger ambient circumstances. However violently small intellectual elites might repudiate democratic mass culture and literary market value, they would inevitably assimilate something of the wider world they disdained.

No society, Tocqueville observed, proceeds from aristocratic to democratic extremes in one leap; rather, the transitions from one social type to the next can normally be expected to be gradual and the cultural manifestations of that change subtle and cumulative. But, generally speaking, the literatures of democracies would be markedly more heterogeneous in quality and less brilliant than those of their aristocratic counterparts. The old aristocratic literatures were not universally good, the new democratic literatures would not be universally bad; on the whole, however, the old aristocratic literatures would remain the finer of the two. The only exceptions to this general rule would arise when a cultivated society had reached a tipping point where its old aristocratic literary spirit and its new democratic literary spirit were of broadly equal strengths and came into contention with each other, both vying 'to establish their joint sway over the human mind' (549). Eighteenth-century French literature was, Tocqueville offered, one example of such 'brief but brilliant periods, when creativity avoids ebullience and liveliness avoids confusion' (549). But because the United States, unlike France, had never had an established aristocratic culture to begin with, Tocqueville's work did not seem to provide any basis to assume that America would experience a similar moment of contentious but fructifying equilibrium between aristocratic and democratic tendencies or allow for the 'brief but brilliant' moment of literary efflorescence that such tipping-points might yield.

Moving from democracies as a type to America particularly, Tocqueville commented, as many before him had done, that 'strictly speaking, the inhabitants of the United States have not yet gained a literature' (544). Nevertheless, he allowed, a great number of Americans were interested in literary matters, but for the present at least American dependence on European culture generally and on English writing, scholarship and taste-making more particularly remained almost complete. Almost all the great works read by the American public were classic English works republished in the United States and thus '[t]he literary genius of Great Britain still darts its beams into the depths of the New World forests' (544). But even more than this, among those given to literary and intellectual matters, 'the majority are English in origin and above all in style' (544). Cultivation of things English meant that American writers 'transplant into the heart of a democracy ideas and literary uses which are current in the aristocratic nation they take as their model' (544). The upshot, Tocqueville concluded, was that so-called American authors 'paint with colors borrowed from foreign customs and are rarely popular in the country of their birth because they almost never represent it in its proper light' (544). And because the American literati also looked deferentially to England to arbitrate in matters of literary accomplishment, even those American writers who did not actually move to Europe, as so many did, 'normally wait for England to approve [their] work' (544). The cumulative effect of such dependence and deference was that American writers were really a foreign 'English' enclave within their own nation. 'The only authors I recognize as Americans', Tocqueville concluded, 'are journalists, who are not great writers, but who speak the language of the country and make themselves understood. I consider the others to be aliens' (544–545).[8]

In Tocqueville's view, the crude and dependent state of nineteenth-century American letters was not to be attributed to democracy as such, but rather to the fact that American democracy had developed in the quite distinctive circumstances of a transplanted English colony governed by a formatively anti-aesthetic Puritan value system. Furthermore, this democracy was set in a vast and uncultivated continent without pre-established aristocratic institutions to check matters. In such circumstances, a preponderantly middle-class society given to unfettered pursuit of commerce and individual self-advancement offered a particularly stark example of what the long-term future of modern democratic culture would look like. Despite the adverse conditions of the present moment and their complete dependence on English literary value systems, Americans, Tocqueville predicted, would eventually produce an American national literature of their own and the features of that literature would indeed be possible to forecast.

In aristocratic societies, the business of government is restricted to an aristocratic ruling class, and it is that class that also promotes intelligence and literature. Such societies by their very nature are hereditary minded and look to the conventions and rules of the past to serve as guarantors of good taste and high accomplishment in the present. Hence, the natural tendency of such societies was that: 'Style will appear almost as important as thought, form as content; the tone of writing will be polished, measured, and sustained. The mind will always move in a dignified manner, rarely at a frenetic pace; writers will concentrate their attention more on perfecting their work rather than simply writing for the sake of it' (546). The inherent danger in such societies, one in which both writers and their aristocratic patrons were largely detached from the wider populace, was that literature would become abstruse and formally so self-obsessed as to lose touch with nature and common sense. In democratic societies, in contrast, ruling elites are typically not drawn from men born to ancestral wealth and cultivation but rather from those who had risen to public prominence through the professions or commercial activity. Accordingly, the ruling elites in democracies would inevitably be more varied in their interests and activities than their aristocratic counterparts had been; matters of literature and intellect would form only one limited part of their concerns, and not usually the main one at that. As a result, the elites in an advanced democracy would naturally tend to view both literature and scholarship as matters for distraction and relaxation rather than as serious lifelong pursuits. Lacking the long-term leisure, stability, cultivation and refinement of their aristocratic peers, and being more accustomed to the practical tedium of business and politics, the elites in a democratic society would naturally value 'books which are easily available, quick to read, and which demand no learned research for their understanding' (548). Craving either entertainment, spectacle or violent escapism in the arts generally, the patrons of the arts in democratic societies would cultivate a literature that catered to such desires. This, combined with the commercial pressures and the need to meet the interests of a largely uncultivated and heterogeneous mass public mentioned earlier, would generate the conditions in which literature, taken in general, would inevitably become less specialized and less exacting in terms of its higher accomplishments. In short, the top-down pressures of a less cultivated class of literary patrons and the bottom-up pressures of an unevenly educated and cultivated mixed-mass public could only mean that the literatures of democratic societies would lack the refinements and subtleties of their aristocratic predecessors. Democratic literatures might prove more vitally innovative and energetic than their aristocratic counterparts, but they would also be more demotic and commercial in orientation and less rigorously intellectual. 'Democratic literature always teems with authors who see in letters a mere trade, and for each of the few great writers, peddlers of ideas can be counted in their thousands' (550). The literatures of aristocratic nations tended naturally to look to the past and to the supernatural world for inspiration; those of democracies are oriented towards the future and to material satisfactions and returns. The inevitable deficiencies of democratic societies could best be checked, Tocqueville asserted, by a 'persistent education in the classics alone' (551) and by the creation of '[a] few first-rate universities' that would exert a stronger influence on the ruling elites 'than numerous poor colleges where badly taught and superfluous studies obstruct the establishment of necessary ones' (552).

Remarks on American literary underdevelopment and dependence on Great Britain of the kind outlined in *Democracy in America* were a European commonplace of the nineteenth century, and many American literary nationalists largely agreed with such assessments even if they deplored the situation and struggled to change it.[9] However, the thrust of Tocqueville's work had far more drastic implications for American literary nationalism than did the observations of those Europeans or Americans who simply dismissed the United States as a vulgar frontier society composed of puritanical-minded Yankee businessmen and unlettered backwoodsmen.[10] Against those who argued that America was too young and crude to support a strong indigenous literature, it was always possible to assert that this was a temporary retardation, and that, as the United States became wealthier and more educated, it would reduce its intellectual and literary indebtedness to England and Europe. By the same accumulative process, its national literature would, in the natural course of things, become riper. But the real gist of Tocqueville's argument was not that American culture was crude because America was a rude frontier society, a situation that would eventually pass. Rather, his argument was that the cultures of democracies generally – of which the United States was an adumbration but for which it was not by any means to be taken as the universal model or archetype – might be expected to be of lesser distinction than those of the old aristocratic societies of Europe. Thus, the whole logic of *Democracy in America* was to suggest that the development of American capitalism and democracy and the refinement of American culture and letters would, at best, remain in permanent tension with each other. At worst, the advancement of American capitalist democracy and the hope for a great national literature equal to that of the aristocratic European nations might always remain mutually thwarting ambitions.

In short, as the United States became more modern and democratic, its national literature would, like those of democracies generally, always prioritize speed, sensation, energy, accessibility and market value over polish and sophistication. The ceaseless flux and mobility of democracies were such, Tocqueville held, that they could seldom or never sustain any strong sense of tradition from one generation to the next, and without tradition the inherited knowledge on which all refined literary sensibility thrived could not be expected to prosper. By this logic, the United States might well in time become an extremely powerful, wealthy and admirably democratic society in some senses, but in a society in which even the ruling elites would be permanently in flux from one generation to the next there could be little expectation of the stability and continuity conducive to

aristocratic distinction in the arts. And because this condition of permanent flux was even more aggravated at all other levels of society, the only
check, if any, would be the cultivation of a restricted educated elite with
enough freedom from the ordinary commercial and political pursuits of
democratic society to develop the classical and traditional-minded sensibility that would serve to counter, even if never fully to remedy, this
condition. The cultures of the Greek and Roman and early modern
European republics had all been dominated by the cultivated taste of the
elites; in the new democracies foreshadowed by the United States,
Tocqueville claimed to discover a situation in which a common mass
culture might eventually overwhelm everything else, reducing to minority
subcultures anything opposed to its own mediocrity.

The limits of Tocqueville's framework are clear enough and have provoked much comment. *Democracy in America*, as Sheldon Wolin sums up,
'employs interchangeably "democracy" and "equality" to describe the new
cultural formation and "aristocracy" and "freedom" as the terms of contrast
that serve as controls delimiting the meaning and significance of democratic
beliefs and behavior'.[11] The conflation of 'democracy' and 'equality' in this
way obviously points up the lack of any developed analytics of capitalism,
class or class struggle. As such, the likely long-term deleterious effects of
democracy and capitalism meld indistinguishably for Tocqueville. One
might conclude that the real enemy of cultural ambition or value is some
chimerical 'equality' of social conditions rather than the capitalist subsump-
tion of everything into its commodifying processes. Moreover, in
Tocqueville's schema the deficiencies of democratic capitalism are formally
offset against its totalized opposite, an 'aristocracy' that tacitly claims, as
Wolin puts it, not only 'a superior understanding of egalitarianism because
aristocracy's own self-consciousness, even its power, had – unlike democracy – depended on the presence, rather than the elimination of its
opposite' (310). Moreover, this aristocracy, although not itself subjected
to a sociological analysis, has ascribed to it a level of cultural refinement and
subjective freedom that is offered as a universal criterion for such things. Its
real function in Tocqueville's work is to act as a given contrast to the
democratic system.

Nevertheless, it is hard to disagree with Wolin when he says that,
whatever its limits, what stands out in *Democracy in America* are not the
defects but the 'boldness' of Tocqueville's analysis, 'his attempt to offer a
theory of a unified culture that was far more than an inventory of topics,
such as literature, art, theater, rhetoric, science, education, manners, and
beliefs' (316). By attending to these interlocking aspects of modern

bourgeois democratic society, Tocqueville set a precedent for totalized socio-cultural analysis that would not be matched in marxist criticism until Lukács, the Frankfurt School and Antonio Gramsci.[12] And while Tocqueville's preference for aristocratic and elite cultures will inevitably seem conservative and provocative to those who assume democracy to be an unsurpassable good in every domain, it is the case, as Wolin again remarks, that in every department of culture 'Tocqueville's unvarying prescription was for uplift, for setting higher aims than democratic impulses aspired to' (320). In their different ways, the early twentieth century high modernists and, later, the Frankfurt School and Gramscian marxists would share precisely this ambition for uplift.

## III

Like Tocqueville, Matthew Arnold was much concerned with the cultural, intellectual and artistic debilities to which modern democracies appeared to him prone; much of his work was also devoted to advancing measures that would help to check or overcome these debilities. Arnold developed his ideas about such topics in his capacity as an educational expert and as cultural and social critic. In 1861 he published a report on French schools that was prefaced by an essay that he subsequently reprinted under the title 'Democracy', one that openly acknowledged its Tocquevillian pedigree. Published nearly thirty years after the second volume of the Frenchman's *Democracy in America*, Arnold's lectures on Celtic literature, delivered in Oxford in 1865 (the year of Yeats's birth) and 1866, as part of his programme as Professor of Poetry, were published as *The Study of Celtic Literature* in 1867. The Celtic literature lectures thus belong to the same period as his essays on democracy and on the function of criticism and on education and the state – these works share overlapping themes. Written, like *Culture and Anarchy* (1869), against the backdrop of Fenian dynamite campaigns in England, Arnold's essays on Celtic literature are informed by an anxious Victorian liberalism. Looking back to the work of Edmund Burke, he pleads the case for an English conception of Ireland, and of England's other Celtic regions, that would be informed by sentiments of sympathy and understanding rather than by the arrogant sense of imperial dominion and Protestant Anglo-Saxon supremacy that, in Arnold's view, dominated and degraded English Victorian public life. Taking issue with those who thought of modern English culture as wholly Teutonic, who dismissed the Celtic languages as merely 'the badge of a beaten race, the property of the vanquished', and as impediments to the Anglicization and by extension to the material and civil progress of the Welsh or Gaelic speakers, Arnold urges the study of Celtic literatures to his readers not only because this will help Englishmen to better know their fellow peoples within the Union but because it will also help the English to understand themselves better.[13]

Arnold's difficulty with English scorn for all things Celtic, a scorn he allows that his own father had exemplified, is not simply that this is conducive to bad relations between the peoples of the United Kingdom – though such arrogant attitudes certainly aggravate the Fenian agitation. The problem with English Teutonic supremacy, then, is not just that it alienates the United Kingdom's Celtic peoples, but that it expresses that sense of self-satisfied moral complacency and lack of intellectual self-criticism that is so reprehensible a feature of English national culture.[14] 'My brother Saxons', Arnold drily comments, 'have, as is well known, a terrible way with them of wanting to improve everything but themselves off the face of the earth' (14). *The Study of Celtic Literature* is patently not a work on the same scale as Tocqueville's *Democracy in America*, nor one so central to Arnold's own larger body of writing. Nevertheless, its consequence for late nineteenth- and early twentieth-century domestic and international conceptions of Irish culture was ultimately almost as far-reaching as was Tocqueville's study for American culture.

Drawing heavily on European philology and ethnology, and on more popular discourses of national and racial character, Arnold stresses to his readers that the Celts are not a race alien in blood, language and religion to the English because Celt and Teuton are both part of a vaster Indo-European linguistic and cultural civilization. Moreover, he asserts, the English themselves are not in any case a purely Teutonic people but a composite of Saxon or Germanic, Celtic, Norman French and Latin elements. Conceding that the dominant element in this mix is Germanic, Arnold nevertheless insists that the Celtic peoples of Britain conquered by the Saxons had never been entirely extirpated, and English national character, therefore, has a Celtic substratum. In keeping with contemporary discourses of national character, Arnold believes that language and literature are the vital clues to the specific genius of peoples and thus much of *The Study of Celtic Literature* takes the form of an elaborate inventory of the virtues and defects of the various national elements that comprise the modern United Kingdom.

The dominant traits of the modern English character, Arnold insists, are *'energy with honesty'*, qualities he offsets against a lesser Germanic *'steadiness with honesty'* (81, all italics here and to follow appear in the original).

English honesty, he suggests, has its root in the Germanic element of the English national genius, but much of the energy and liveliness of the people derives from the Latin elements introduced during the period of Roman imperial rule and later again by the Latinized Normans as well as by contact and intermingling with the Celtic peoples of the region. Germanic steadiness had given the English most of their cardinal achievements – a capacity for good government, their sturdy self-dependence and liberalism, their talents for industry and material progress, their practical and scientific qualities, their lack of flightiness. But were one to subtract energy from that steadiness the result, in Arnold's view, would be that stolid and dull flatness that could be observed in the weaker aspects of German culture: 'The universal dead-level of plainness and homeliness, the lack of all beauty and distinction in form and feature, the slowness and clumsiness of the language, the eternal beer, sausages, and bad tobacco, the blank commonness everywhere, pressing at last like a weight on the spirits of the traveller in North Germany, and making him impatient to be gone' (82).

The Celtic peoples, Arnold notes, were deemed by Ernest Renan, a Breton, to be a shy and retiring race. Even if the Welsh might seem to confirm this, the voluble, high-spirited, pugnacious Irish did not. For Arnold, 'sentiment', rather, was the key attribute of the Celtic genius just as 'steadiness' was of the Teutonic. By 'sentiment' Arnold means: 'An organization quick to feel impressions, and feeling them very strongly; a lively personality therefore, keenly sensitive to joy and to sorrow; this is the main point' (84). Volatile and vivacious – even the famous Celtic melancholy was but a reflex downswing of a spirited temperament, restive with restraint and ardent for life and new impression – the quick-witted, impetuous Celt was inclined to despise 'the creeping Saxon' (92) as dull-witted and phlegmatic, just as the latter was disposed to disdain the flighty, mercurial Celt for his want of discipline and resolution. For all its admirable energy and vitality, then, the Celtic temperament was deficient, especially in practical affairs of business and government in which the Teutonic excelled: 'The Celt, undisciplinable, anarchical, and turbulent by nature, but out of affection and admiration giving himself body and soul to some leader, that is not a promising political temperament' (91). The same want of application and industry meant that the most unalloyed of the Celtic peoples, the Irish, had utterly failed 'to reach any material civilisation sound and satisfying', something which the contemporary state of Victorian Ireland, a country always 'out at elbows, poor, slovenly, and half-barbarous' (88), made all too obvious.

The strengths and weaknesses of these national temperaments were as manifest, Arnold held, in their respective artistic achievements as they were in the social sphere. The same want of steady application that made the Celts unsuited to commerce or self-government also prevented them from achieving real greatness in the architectural or plastic arts, and in such disciplines they lagged behind even the Saxon English, who in turn lagged behind the Greek and Latin or German races in these arts. Checked and impeded by the Celtic strain in their otherwise predominantly Germanic temperament, the modern English generally lacked, he argues, that quality of *architectonicé*, or rigorous and elevated sense of compositional structure, necessary to produce a Raphael, Rubens or Dürer or a Bach or Beethoven. Nevertheless, even in the highest products of German genius there was a 'want of quick instinctive tact, of delicate, sure perception' (124) that disposed it to a humdrum heaviness or to clumsy infelicities of style of a sort that the quicker, surer English, enlivened by their Latin, Norman and Celtic elements, were temperamentally better equipped to avoid. Hence, because of an innately prosaic element detectable even in their best poetry, the Germans had never matched the poetic achievements of Pindar, Virgil, Dante, Shakespeare or Milton; likewise, the old German *Nibelungen* lacked the imaginative fire of the Icelandic Eddas or the ancient saga literatures of the Welsh and Irish. Even Goethe confirms this: 'Goethe, with his fine critical perception, saw clearly enough both the power of style in itself, and the lack of style in the literature of his own country; and perhaps if we regard him solely as a German, not as a European, his great work was that he laboured all his life to impart style into German literature, and firmly to establish it there' (116).

But if the Germans singularly lacked style, '[t]his something in *style*' was exactly what the Celts have 'in a wonderful measure'. Indeed, '[s]tyle', Arnold avers, 'is the most striking quality of their poetry' (121). In fact, he added, there was a direct ratio between the Celts' lack of capacity for worldly business and government and their exceptional talent for poetry and keen feeling for style: 'Celtic poetry seems to make up to itself for being unable to master the world and give an adequate interpretation of it, by throwing all its force into style, by bending the language at any rate into its will, and expressing the ideas it has with unsurpassable intensity, elevation and effect. It has all through it a sort of intoxication of style' (121). Unable to produce anything major in the fields of architecture, the plastic arts or even prose on a scale equivalent to the epic attainments of the Greeks, Romans, Germans or English, the Celts cast all their genius into poetry and cultivated a Pindaric 'intoxication of style'. This 'Titanism in poetry' (127) was exemplified by James Macpherson's *Ossian*, a Romantic epic inspired by the Ossianic poetry of ancient Ireland. *Ossian*'s imaginative, ethereal, otherworldly yet above all defiantly rebellious Titanism, Arnold noted, had captivated Napoleon and Goethe alike and represented a modern eruption of primitive inspiration that stimulated a wave of emulation 'like a flood of lava through Europe' (127). Nevertheless, despite Europe's enthusiastic reception of *Ossian*, 'no nation of Europe so caught in its poetry the passionate penetrating accent of the Celtic genius, its strain of Titanism, as the English' (129). The greatest poetry of English literature from Shakespeare and Milton through to Byron displayed a quickness and nobility of style and a 'power of rebellious passion' (131) that no other European or purely Germanic literature had matched, and this could be attributed to English literature's long contact with or assimilation of the Celtic substratum in its national mixture.

More openly polemical than *Democracy in America*, *The Study of Celtic Literature* had a more immediate impact than did Tocqueville's work. In Arnold's view, English contempt for the cultures of the Celtic peoples of the United Kingdom was as much a danger to the stability and long-term interest of the British state as the insurrectionary anarchy of its Fenian antagonists; these disruptive elements aggravated one another. Because the English, he observed, lack either the strongly centralized and assimilative impetus of the French state or the sociability of the French, qualities that allow the latter to bind their minorities to them, a belligerent assertion of Teutonic superiority flies in the face of the English state's self-interest. Hence, England needs to be able to make good what it lacks in terms of centralization or sociability by way of cultural amity and co-optation. English superiority rests on a history of conquest, but the fact that the Englishman's 'Welsh and Irish fellow-citizens were hardly more amalgamated with him now than they were when Wales and Ireland were first conquered' (xiv) was proof enough that coercion alone could never produce a secure and confident state or a cohesive national unity. But since 'the skilful and resolute appliance of means to ends which is needed both to make progress in material civilisation, and also to form powerful states, is just what the Celt has least turn for' (88), there could be no valid argument for any separatist independence for the Celtic peoples. These peoples, to the contrary, had every reason to be grateful to the English who excelled in such matters, and thus the Irish and other Celts must inevitably remain securely with the Union and contribute to it.

Nor, for that matter, had Arnold any sympathy with movements for the preservation or revival of Celtic languages: 'The fusion of all the inhabitants of these islands into one homogeneous, English-speaking whole, the breaking down of barriers between us, the swallowing up of separate provincial nationalities, is a consummation to which the natural course of things irresistibly tends; it is a necessity of what is called modern civilisation, and modern civilisation is a real legitimate force; the change must come, and its accomplishment is a mere affair of time' (10). In that respect, Arnold allowed, '[t]raders and tourists do excellent service by pushing the English wedge farther and farther into the heart of the principality [of Wales]; Ministers of Education, by hammering it harder and harder into the elementary schools' (10–11).

Thus, Arnold's empathy for things Celtic in no way diminishes his British unionism. Despite his apparent enthusiasm for the Welsh Eisteddfods, he cannot even find sympathy for 'the literary cultivation of Welsh as an instrument of living literature' (11) and concludes that: 'For all serious purposes in modern literature (and trifling purposes in it who would care to encourage?) the language of a Welshman is and must be English' (11). The aggressive note of imperial and state assimilationism is pronounced here, as is Arnold's insistence that that the natural medium for any modern literature of the Celtic regions must be English. Nevertheless, the English must for their part, Arnold contends, begin to appreciate that no material services they could confer on their Celtic co-nationals 'can surpass that which the Celts can at this moment render England' (x) by communicating their qualities. For the negative side of English material progress and prosperity was cultural coarsening and gross worldliness – a middle-class philistinism that showed itself as aesthetic vulgarity, self-flattering moral complacency and spiritual and intellectual superficiality – to which the Celtic feeling for style and otherworldliness was the necessary antidote. And since the English national character had in any event innate Celtic as well as Germanic and Latin strains, to disown that Celtic element as alien would merely make the English unharmonious and eccentric, out of proper balance with themselves. Hence, for the good of their own psychological equilibrium as well for the greater cohesiveness of the state and the proper integrity of the national culture, the peoples of the United Kingdom needed to learn how to put their mutually complementary best qualities productively to work with each other. In this view of things, the best future open to the Celts was not the political one of national sovereignty argued by the republican-minded Fenians nor even the devolution argued by the constitutionalist Irish Home Rule party, but rather an intellectual and cultural project 'for renewing the famous feat of the Greeks, and conquering their conquerors' (x).

However different their objects and modes of enquiry, there is considerable convergence between Tocqueville and Arnold on the issue of modern culture and literature. For both thinkers, the key feature of the modern era is that the long history of the great European aristocracies is nearing its close and a new era of middle-class democracy is emerging in its place. For both, the expansion of capitalist industry and the loosening of traditional forms of authority by means of this extension of democracy seemed likely to lead to a coarsening of both civic culture and the fine arts. Tocqueville detects this coarsening in an American culture that has plenty of vim and vigour but suffers from a lack of distinction, formal rigour and inherited tradition; Arnold detects it in the vulgar materialism and often boorish aesthetic and intellectual standards of English Victorian public life. Himself of middle-class origins, Arnold may be rather more caustic about the aristocracy than Tocqueville, and his characterization of them as 'Barbarians' in *Culture and Anarchy* emphasizes the defects as much as the virtues of that class. There, the aristocracy is convicted of a 'White Jacobinism' or reactionary individualism and anti-intellectualism every bit as socially destructive as that of the 'Red Jacobinism' of the radical democrats who always stress citizens' rights but never responsibilities. Nonetheless, Arnold shares with Tocqueville the conviction that the model version, if not always the actuality, of the aristocracy and of the great ecclesiastical institutions of Europe had 'undoubtedly for centuries served as ideals to ennoble and elevate the sentiment of the European masses'. Thus, when the grand cathedrals and ancient palaces of these authorities disappeared as 'a beacon to the imagination of thousands', European life would inevitably be the poorer.[15]

In Arnold's view, in sum, the splendours of the great European churches and aristocracies had, if nothing else, 'preserved these masses from any danger of over-rating with vulgar self-satisfaction an inferior culture, however broadly sown, among them, by the exhibition of a standard of dignity and refinement still far above them' (169). The slackening of that check incurred by the decline of aristocracy and the loss of religious faith would almost certainly augment modern cultural vulgarity. Without any exterior standards by which to measure its own attainments, middle-class self-satisfaction and arrogance would increase and the general level of middle-class culture deteriorate. For Arnold, 'the great American people' exemplified this tendency and showed the dangers that lay ahead in the future. Their country having grown up without the 'salutary standards' that Europe had inherited from the feudal ages, and having no aristocracy and no august history in either church or state, Americans were consequently 'accustomed to see everywhere a certain mediocre culture diffused with indisputable breadth', and to regard this 'with a sense of perfect self-satisfaction, which is deteriorating' (169-170). The American people, he ventured, 'offers a spectacle full of interest, indeed, but inspiring the most grave reflections; – the spectacle of a people which threatens to lose its power of intellectual and moral growth' (170).

In *The Study of Celtic Literatures* Arnold looks not to the preservation of an English aristocracy as such, but rather to the assimilation of the non-industrialized and essentially non-modern Celts to redress the defects of an English culture dangerously loosened in sinew by democracy and coarsened in grain by modern industrial materialism. The Celts and the aristocracy are not exactly equivalent because the Celts, given their supposedly temperamental lack of application, have bequeathed to Europe no grand monuments to match those of the aristocracy. Nevertheless, despite such differences, there are more telling correspondences because, for Arnold, the Celts are a people that have been overwhelmed, as have the aristocracy, by modern progress and whose civilization has been shattered beyond recovery in any political sense. Like the aristocracy too in this more positive sense, the Celts have, for Arnold, an innate feeling for style, a love of poetry, a disposition *'always ready to react against the despotism of fact'* (85), and a quickness of imagination and sociability that could only leaven an English middle-class culture so stupefied by its own success and so consistently agitated by its noisily schismatic Protestant sects as to reduce civic life to a quarrelsomely philistine factionalism. However, the products of Celtic literature were habitually imbued with 'the secret of natural beauty and natural magic', and it was this 'same sensibility [which] made the Celts full of reverence and enthusiasm for genius, learning, and the things of the mind; *to be a bard, freed a man,* – that is a characteristic stroke of this generous and ennobling ardour of theirs, which no race has ever shown more strongly' (91). And if the Celts, even more than the aristocracy, were given to love of the mind, genius and learning, then their assimilation into British public culture could only be to the advantage of an England whose chief vice was to overvalue its worldly achievements and material progress and to underestimate its need for cultural elevation.

In these diagnostics, the cultural tendencies of the nineteenth-century United States and Ireland threaten to be realized in diametrically opposed ways. For Tocqueville, the United States is an outgrowth of English society, but lacks any leavening tradition of an English aristocracy, and not only exemplifies the great vigour and energy of an emerging democracy but also a kind of worldliness, commodifying mania, materialist acquisitiveness and social formlessness that may well prove inimical to the creation of a New World high culture equivalent to that of Old Europe. The conditions of industrialized society are such, he avers, that labour will inevitably become increasingly specialized in a manner that refines the skills of the workers but reduces their humanity ('as he, the workman, improves, so does he, the man, lose his self-respect. [. . .] The craft makes progress, the craftsman slips backwards' (645–646)). Industrialism will also create business operations of such grand magnitude that they will inevitably summon into being a new managerial class so wealthy, so habituated to command and so elevated above the working class as to become a new kind of industrial manufacturing aristocracy. Although this extravagantly wealthy class will acquire many of the mannerisms of the old aristocracy, modern commercial society is so volatile in nature and so dependent on cyclical acquisitions and losses of fortunes that a capitalist aristocracy can never, for all its titanism, acquire the integrity or dynastic coherence of a hereditary class: 'In fact, although there are rich men, richer classes do not exist, for the wealthy do not share a common spirit or objective or traditions or hopes; there are individual members, therefore, but no definite corporate body' (647–648). Moreover, an 'aristocracy' of industry does not physically settle itself among the workers nor is there any inherited moral economy to bind it to that working class, and its ultimate purpose is not even to govern the workers but to exploit them for profit. Hence, it might well be the case, Tocqueville observed ominously, that 'the industrial aristocracy which we see rising before our eyes is one of the most harsh ever to appear on the earth' (648).

America emerges in Tocqueville's work as a byword for democracy, modernity, material progress and a worldliness marred by an attenuation of human roundedness and by a prospective coarsening of high artistic achievement. It stands in polar contrast to Arnold's Ireland with its outmoded addiction to charismatic or aristocratic leadership, wretched poverty and backwardness, redeemed nevertheless by an imaginative unworldliness, an intellectual ardour and a quickness and delicacy of sensibility that are badly needed in an increasingly materialistic age. The Gaelic languages may be 'the badge of a beaten race' (5) and quite unfit in Arnold's view for the practical affairs of modern business or government that will inevitably be transacted entirely in English. Still, Gaelic should not be merely abandoned but retained at least for antiquarian study, and *The Study of Celtic Languages* concludes therefore with Arnold's exhortation that Oxford establish a Chair of Celtic literatures for such a purpose. As he nears the end of his treatise, Arnold lifts his eyes from England and

Europe to take in America. He observes that if the English race continues to insist only on its Germanic or Teutonic qualities, 'we ride one force of our nature to death; we will be nothing but Anglo Saxons in the Old World or in the New; and when our race has built Bold Street, Liverpool, and pronounced it very good, it hurries across the Atlantic, and builds Nashville, and Jacksonville, and Milledgeville, and thinks that it is fulfilling the designs of Providence in an incomparable manner' (147). The English radical Richard Cobden, Arnold muses, had been wont to recommend to Englishmen the study of the United States and had urged that the youth of Oxford should be taught 'a little less about Ilissus, and a little more about Chicago' (148). Chicago had its claims on English attention, Arnold concedes, but they were not the most urgent because 'our American brothers themselves have rather, like us, to try and moderate the flame of Anglo-Saxonism in their own breasts, than to ask us to clap the bellows to it in ours. So I am inclined to beseech Oxford, instead of expiating her over-addiction to the Ilissus by lectures on Chicago, to give us an expounder for a still more remote-looking object than the Ilissus, – the Celtic languages and literature' (148). In any event, what appeared remote in one respect, he concluded, might not really be so in another. With the sole exception of Brittany, England and its empire now contained all that was left of 'the shrunken and diminished remains of this great primitive race' and, he adds, 'we have Ireland, the Scotch Highlands, Wales, the Isle of Man, Cornwall. They are a part of ourselves' (149).

Unless and until it could bring this inherited prodigal Celtic element into harmony with its Germanic and Latin or Norman elements, the English character would always be out of proper harmony with itself, as would its extended Anglo-Saxon cultural offshoots across the empire and the United States.[16] Tocqueville had recommended to America the establishment of a small number of elite universities that would inculcate the Greek and Latin classics as a means to check modern democracy's tendency to cultural speed, shapelessness and subjectivism; in *On Translating Homer*, published in 1861, the same year that he published his 'Democracy' essay, Arnold followed a similar line, arguing the usefulness of the Greeks especially as a counter to the indiscipline of European Romanticism and as a means to Hellenize an excessively Hebraic and philistine England.[17] In *The Study of Celtic Literature*, the literature of the Celts, displaying a similar sense of remoteness or distance from the modern world yet having the advantage of actually 'belonging' to the English state, is recruited to essentially similar ends, despite the Celts' innate propensity to indiscipline. For Tocqueville classicism, for Arnold classicism and Celticism are necessary tonics to check the baser tendencies of modern culture.

In sum, then, Tocqueville and Arnold share not only common classical liberal anxieties about the capacity of modern industrial democracies to nurture high cultures equivalent to those of the past, but also a similar discursive standpoint, a disposition to speak as reasoned intermediary. Tocqueville addresses his readership as a coolly composed liberal mediator between Old World *ancien régime* and New World democracy, between a fading but cultured aristocracy and a rising but still-uncultivated bourgeois middle class. Arnold likewise situates himself as a rational and ironic intermediary, poised between the zealous extremes of Saxonism and Celticism, between uncompromising Teutonist British Unionist and Celtic Fenian nationalist fanatic. Crucially, for both Tocqueville and Arnold, modern democracy must appropriate to itself estranged and aristocratic cultures that already largely belong to the past as correctives to the deficiencies of the modern present and antidote to worse futures. The European aristocracy and the Celts had each been vanquished in the long march to modernity, but something of their spirit must be preserved and cultivated if the culture of modernity was not to be too crassly commercial, utilitarian, philistine and plebeian. The agenda here might be melioratively reformist in tone, but the sense that liberalism, democracy and high cultural attainment were temperamentally out of kilter with each other is a shared refrain in the works of both thinkers.

That fundamental diagnosis would hold for future generations, long after the more prescriptive solutions proposed by Tocqueville or Arnold had faded. Even so, the prescriptive elements in their works were not without issue. Arnold's lectures on Celticism bore their first institutional fruit in England with the establishment of a Chair in Celtic at Oxford in 1877. Across the Atlantic, Harvard University began its teaching in Celtic studies in 1896 – one year before Barrett Wendell taught that institution's first course in American literature – and there were at least eight Celtic studies programmes in the United States by 1915.[18] In Ireland, meanwhile, a post-Famine political and cultural nationalist resurgence turned Arnold's Celticism to very different purpose. Where Arnold had diagnosed an inability in the Celt to recognize the despotism of fact as the reason the union of Ireland and Britain had to be maintained, the Irish dissidents saw in Arnold a characteristic English refusal to recognize the fact of despotism in the asymmetric political and economic union of Ireland and Britain which they were determined to dissolve. For both parties, Celticism remained a cultural instrument and a political weapon; that weapon became more potent as the nineteenth century came to its close. Within a generation of Arnold's lectures, Celticism was already a key element in the Irish literary 'renaissance', and that Irish 'renaissance' found its call and response in American 'renaissances' across the Atlantic. These 'renaissances' in turn merged to lend impetus to 'modernist' ambitions.

## IV

Tocquevillian and Arnoldian conceptions of America's and democracy's deficiencies are recurrent topoi in the works of those who became America's great modernist expatriates and clearly shaped their understandings of their vocations. Henry James's study of *Hawthorne* (1879) is a famous and controversial example. Commenting on the debilities Hawthorne had had to overcome, James expressed what appears an almost hyperbolically Tocquevillian sense of all the things that the United States lacked necessary to the creation of a refined literature:

> If Hawthorne had been a young Englishman, or a young Frenchman of the same degree of genius, the same cast of mind, the same habits, his consciousness of the world around him would have been a very different affair; however obscure, however reserved, his own personal life, his sense of the life of his fellow-mortals would have been almost infinitely more various. The negative side of the spectacle on which Hawthorne looked out, in his contemplative saunterings and reveries, might, indeed, with a little ingenuity, be made almost ludicrous; one might enumerate the items of high civilization, as it exists in other countries, which are absent from the texture of American life, until it should become a wonder to know what was left. No State, in the European sense of the word, and indeed barely a specific national name. No sovereign, no court, no personal loyalty, no aristocracy, no church, no clergy, no army, no diplomatic service, no country gentlemen, no palaces, no castles, nor manors, nor old country houses, nor thatched cottages nor ivied ruins; no cathedrals, nor abbeys, nor little Norman churches; no great Universities nor public schools – no Oxford, nor Eton, nor Harrow; no literature, no novels, no museums, no pictures, no political society, no sporting class – no Epsom nor Ascot! Some such list as that might be drawn up of the absent things in American life – especially in the American life of forty years ago, the effect of which, upon an English or a French imagination, would probably as a general thing be appalling. The natural remark, in the almost lurid light of such an indictment, would be that if these things are left out, everything is left out.[19]

Some critics have wondered whether James is not being parodic here and affecting a spoof Arnoldianism, ironically ventriloquising the condescending English viewpoint rather than expressing it as his own.[20] Yet there is little doubt that this was the view straightforwardly taken by James and others on various occasions. A similar sense of America's deficiencies is voiced, sometimes more vehemently, in the writings of the expatriate generation that came to Europe in James's wake. Pound's excoriations of American provincialism, puritanism and inability to produce anything other than a crassly middlebrow magazine literature are (as will appear below) also conveyed in recognizably Tocquevillian and Arnoldian terms. In accord with this are T. S. Eliot's insistence on the importance of 'tradition' in 'Tradition and the Individual Talent' and his advocacy of the classical temper in letters as a corrective to the egoistic subjectivism and spurious self-sufficiencies of English Romanticism or American Pragmatism.

Likewise, Tocqueville's contention that 'strictly speaking, the inhabitants of the United States have not yet gained a literature' would find repeated echoes in the writings of the earlier American modernists. Pound's critique of American critics who suffocate American literature by simply ratifying the verdicts of third-rate English or French critics offers a judgement that is itself, ironically, merely a second-hand repetition of Tocqueville's observation that Americans take all their literary standards from England. So too is John Dos Passos's lamentation in 1914 that 'American literature is a rootless product, a cutting from England's sturdy well branched oak tree, nurtured in the arid soil of the New England colonies and recently transplanted to the broad lands of the Middle West'[21] or T. S. Eliot's 1919 assertion that 'Hawthorne, Poe and Whitman are all pathetic creatures' and that the world of nineteenth-century America was generally too 'thin' and 'secondhand; it was not original and independent – it was shadow'.[22] Early poems like 'Aunt Helen', 'Cousin Nancy' and 'Mr Apollinax' make related dry fun of prim American cultural aridity. Amy Lowell offered a similar verdict in 1917 when she indicted even her own distinguished ancestor with other earlier American writers, remarking '[g]ood poetry, if not strikingly great poetry, marked the epoch of Whittier, Bryant, Emerson, Lowell, Longfellow, and Holmes. They were English provincial poets, in the sense that America was still a literary province of the Mother Country'.[23]

In late nineteenth-century Ireland, the same spell of Paris and London and the same dependence on authoritative French and English conceptions of Irish culture are also discernible, but so too is the quickening summons of some burgeoning peripheral national 'renaissance'. In George Moore's early *Confessions of a Young Man* (1886 in French; 1888, English), his rhapsodies about the magnetic spell of the Parisian artistic and literary world are redolent of those of the young Henry James for Paris and

London. And in both writers, the same urgency to escape one's backward country of origin for an artistic apprenticeship in some foreign artistic capital is evident. However, despite his attraction to Paris and London, Moore could not resist, for a time at least, the lure of the Irish Revival, and in 1901 he returned to Ireland and involved himself energetically in the Dublin literary scene before eventually returning to London in 1911. Yeats, coming after Moore, cultivated in his early career (as Moore had done) the disposition of the artist as dandified aesthete and natural aristocrat, though Yeats's commitment to Celticism, Irish mythology and Revivalism was far more fundamental than Moore's. Even the lower-middle-class Joyce, persistently sceptical of both Celticism and Yeatsian Revivalism and always diffident in his response to both Moore and Yeats, betrayed similar early tendencies to affect a scorn for the masses and for the backwardness of his own country and its art and politics. 'The Day of the Rabblement' (1901), one of Joyce's earliest published pieces, excoriates Yeats and the Irish Literary Theatre for 'making terms with the rabble-ment' by producing Douglas Hyde's Irish-language play *Casadh an tSúgáin* (*The Twisting of the Rope*) and Yeats's and Moore's *Diarmuid and Gráinne*, a play based on ancient Irish legend. To stage such works was, in Joyce's view, to concede too much to the domestic nationalist 'multitude' and to break faith with the more cosmopolitan European agenda that the Literary Theatre had initially set itself. 'No man', Joyce's essay opens, citing the heretic Giordano Bruno, 'can be a lover of the true or the good unless he abhors the multitude; and the artist, though he may employ the crowd, is very careful to isolate himself.' By conceding to middle-class taste in drama Yeats had failed, in the young Joyce's view, to maintain the hauteur and distance requisite for the genuine artist and thus had made the Irish Literary Theatre the 'property of the rabblement of the most belated race in Europe'.[24] After Joyce went into lifelong 'exile', his later works, includ-ing *Dubliners* (1914) and *A Portrait of the Artist as a Young Man* (1916), display a much more complex sense of the relationship between the provincial and the cosmopolitan, or between the demotic lower classes and high art. Yet Joyce's decision never to return to Ireland tells its own story; in this respect at least, he is similar to his American contemporaries, Pound and Eliot. In *Ulysses* Joyce parodies the Hiberno-Arnoldian idea of 'Hellenizing Ireland', but even in this most iconic of all high modernist texts the Arnoldian dichotomy of Hebrew and Hellene operates as a central and familiar organizing device.

In sum, in the cases of Moore, Yeats and Joyce, as in that of their American contemporaries, the nineteenth-century sense of metropolitan

European cultural superiority and of the masses as the vulgar enemy of genuine artistic ambition retains its force, however much that conception of things might cohabit with a new sense of national self-assertion and literary opportunity. Still, the crucial difference between Tocqueville and Arnold and the Irish and American modernists cited here is that the former pair belonged to an era when French and English power was still at a meridian whereas the latter group belong to a time in which that ascendancy, though still formidable, was becoming more fragile. The defeat of the French by the Prussians in 1871, the challenge offered by the Boer Republics to the British Empire in 1899–1902, and the Japanese victory over the Russian Empire in 1904–1905, were all signs that the world system long guaranteed by British and French power had wobbled and entered a period of serious challenge. Even earlier than this, the Irish Famine of the late 1840s and American Civil War of the early 1860s had been volcanic events, cataclysms nearly as convulsively traumatic for their respective societies as World War I would soon become for Europe generally. However, the effect of these mid-century convulsions and ruptures was to accelerate the momentum of new nation-building drives, these naturally taking different forms variously for the Irish and for white Americans and African Americans, not to mention Germans and Italians. The Irish and American high modernists – many like Stein, Joyce, Eliot or Pound born in the 1870s or 1880s – were born close enough to their domestic national cataclysms to be shaped to some extent by their reconstructive reverberations. They came into their professional primes during the European catastrophe that shook the world from 1914 to 1918 and most would live long enough to witness a further catastrophe in 1940. Connoisseurs of chaos indeed, their careers were lived as episodes chequered by catastrophes domestic and European.

Still, it was World War I that most directly exposed the fragility of the Anglo-French domination of the world order and the fatal interdependencies of a system that never recovered from the sudden and shocking disappearance of the Habsburg, Ottoman and Romanov empires. The West as once known was certainly in decline, as Otto Spengler's famous book announced. Welcomed by some, lamented by many, the aftershocks of the collapse continued throughout the period between the world wars. Yet it must be remembered that the writers who later became the Irish and American modernists also came of age in an era after which their own societies had already passed through major purgatorial watersheds. Accordingly, though they might still draw on the second-hand Tocquevillian or Arnoldian terminologies that had saturated

Anglo-American and European cultural criticism the better to castigate the social and cultural inadequacies of their own nations, the modernists were also undoubtedly galvanized (however indirectly) by the ways in which the crisis of World War I had brought their own countries onto the world stage as never before. It might even be said that because of their respective mid-nineteenth-century national histories, the Irish and Americans hailed from countries that had already witnessed the savagely destructive sides of modernity – and had assimilated the dialectics of Enlightenment – in ways that would fully come home to Western Europe more widely only after 1914. Moreover, as the world order shook and tilted in new directions, Tocqueville's work might be said to have set the Americans a civilizational challenge: as the United States now felt itself on the way to becoming the world's most prosperous society and a great superpower, its men of letters wondered whether America could produce a sophisticated high culture to match these roles or whether the debilities that Tocqueville had earlier diagnosed would continue to mar twentieth-century national cultural production and render it inferior. For his part, Arnold, however unintentionally, had given the writers of the Celtic nations a sense of mission, a conquered 'Greek' vocation to redeem the philistine imperial 'Roman' culture of the Teutonic or Saxon peoples. The challenges that confronted the Irish and the Americans were not therefore exactly the same. For the Americans, the pre-eminent task was to overcome not only their long-standing literary dependence on England but also the supposed debilities of advanced democratic culture more generally; for the Irish, it was to rescue themselves from the backwardness and disorder apparently innate to the Celt while simultaneously redeeming Saxon England of its grossness.

In the early writings of all of these Anglophone modernists, the conception of a new literary and cultural 'renaissance' (whether conceived in national or internationalist terms) is consistently yoked in various ways to a sense of British and of French literary 'decline'. We can observe this most clearly in the pre-war writings of Yeats and Pound, the two most formidable organizers of their respective national literary vanguards. Even as a relatively young poet in the 1890s Yeats had already taken up the theme of London's literary decline and had linked it to a sense of Irish literary emergence. In his article 'Hopes and Fears for Irish Literature', published in *United Ireland* in October 1892, Yeats opens with the comment that every time he crosses the Irish Sea between London and Dublin he is struck by the differences between the cultivated peoples of either place, a difference so pronounced that the milieux 'could not differ more if they were divided from each other by a half score of centuries'.[25] But this is no plaint about Irish peripheral laggardness. What Yeats wants to underscore for his readers is his sense that '[i]n England amongst the best minds art and poetry are becoming every day more entirely ends in themselves', while in Ireland there prevails the contrary belief that 'literature must be the expression of conviction, and be the garment of noble emotion and not an end in itself' (248, 249). The commitment to art for art's sake observable in London is attributable, Yeats says, in large degree to the 'influence of France' and the 'Decadants' [sic] and is 'every year pervading more completely English literary life' (248). This is the literature of an age that 'is getting old and feeble' and represents what he calls 'a school of the sunset' (249, 248). There is much to be said for the art for art's sake doctrine, Yeats allows, because it stimulates writers to see literature not as 'the handmaid to humanity' but rather 'a terrible queen' to be served for her own sake, thus releasing writers from bowing to 'the prejudices of the multitude' (248). However, the doctrine is not one Yeats can embrace since his own conviction, as he recalls telling an uncomprehending audience of young English writers in London, is that the very highest literature and art depend 'upon conviction and upon heroic life' (248). In Ireland, he continues, this sense of the heroic, nurtured by a collective interest in the nation's ancient history and legends and in its contemporary struggle, is a vitalizing force. Although Irish writers have as yet been too crude and careless of their art to refine that sensibility into the highest literature, their basic creative impulse is more vital than that of their English or French counterparts: 'We [Irish]', Yeats asserts, 'have the limitations of dawn. They have the limitations of sunset' (250).

By May 1893, as though his mind were following the seasonal changes, Yeats had developed these crepuscular musings into an elaborately cyclical sense of literary evolution, one that would remain key to his whole vision of the Irish Revival. In a lecture given to the National Literary Society in Dublin, he set himself the task of establishing 'in what stage the literature of England is, and in what stage the literature of Ireland is'.[26] As his address was reported in *United Ireland*, Yeats contended that in order to make such assessment it was necessary to look beyond both countries to discover more general laws of literary development. Comparing such development to cellular evolution that runs from simple to complex organisms, Yeats invokes an idea of literature as unfolding like a tree, which in its youth is a simple shoot, in its developed state a complicated thing of many branches, and in its maturity yields a great luxuriance of flowers and fruit. Literature, Yeats suggests, follows a like trajectory. It begins with a period of narrative poetry, epic and ballad, that takes collective national history and mood as its theme; then it advances to a dramatic stage concentrated not on the whole collective but on great personages or 'isolated colossal characters' (270); later, it moves into a lyric phase, the characteristic preoccupations of which were introspective siftings of mood or psychology. Greece, Yeats contended, had passed through these three stages and could go no further and 'when the barbarian had defeated them into silence there came a long blank' and things had to wait on another creative cycle 'when the literature of England arose and went through the same stages' (270).

England's literature, too, he asserted, had waxed and was now waning: beginning with Mallory's legends of Arthur and the bustle of national life in Chaucer, developing into its dramatic phase in the Renaissance and marked by Shakespeare's focus on great tragic characters, and then ripening into the lyric phase of the Romantics, a phase that failed to achieve dramatic verse but still produced a fine harvest in the poetry of Byron, Shelley and Keats. Afterwards, the thrust of English literature was increasingly on the internal as opposed to external world and it had evolved towards ever greater complexity of thought and language as evidenced by Browning and Tennyson. What was true of England, Yeats reasoned, was also true of all the major literatures of Europe: they had reached an autumnal moment of great flowering but also of imminent decline:

> [T]he older literatures of Europe are in their golden sunset, their wise old age [and thus] we here in Ireland who, like the Scandinavian people, are at the outset [of] a literary epoch, must learn from them but not imitate them, and by so doing we will bring new life and fresh impulse not only to ourselves but to those old literatures themselves. But are we really at the outset of a literary epoch? or are we not, perhaps, merely a little eddy cast up by the advancing tide of English literature and are we not doomed, perhaps, to its old age and coming decline? On the contrary, I affirm that we are a young nation with unexhausted material lying within us in our still unexpressed national character, about us in our scenery, and in the clearly marked outlines of our life, and behind us in our multitude of legends. Look at our literature and you will see that we are still in our epic or ballad period.
>
> (273)

Four years later, in 1897, Yeats returned to this topic and took up Arnold more directly in 'The Celtic Element in Literature', an article in which he did not dispute the great Victorian or his French counterpart, Renan, so much as, in his own words, 'restate a little' their terms.[27] Concurring with these authorities that a distinct feeling for nature and '"natural magic"'

(130) and melancholy were the keynotes of Celtic literature, Yeats added that the study of folk belief had advanced greatly in the interim and thus 'I do not think [Arnold] understood that our "natural magic" is but the ancient religion of the world, the ancient worship of Nature and that troubled ecstasy before her' (130).

Celticism, in this Yeatsian revision, becomes not only part of the ancient heritage of the British Isles, as Arnold had proprietorially positioned it, but is folded into the great river of primitive religions and cultures of Indo-Europe. Conceived in these wider spatio-temporal dimensions, Celticism becomes a reservoir of an ancient or non-modern *mentalité* that is practically global in its reach, one that had moreover seemed on the verge of disappearing in the course of Europe's advanced modernity but was now being called on to renew the world once again as modern Western civilization began to run down. Whatever Celticism surrenders here in terms of local geographical definition, it more than recoups by joining forces with a primordial non-modern sensibility of universal extension and in so doing acquires a vocation not just to leaven English philistinism but to redeem a depleted modernity *tout court*. Arnold had noted *Ossian*'s power to release a romantic spirit that had flowed 'like a flood of lava through Europe', but Yeats's vision expresses a 'Titanism' of vision and ambition and a primitivist and anti-modern thrust well beyond anything that Arnold might have contemplated or countenanced.

What lends Yeats's vision for Celticism its plausibility is his capacity to connect it to wider late Romantic and proto-modernist literary currents then emerging all over Europe:

> In our own time Scandinavian tradition, because of the imagination of Richard Wagner and of William Morris and of the earlier and, as I think, greater Henrik Ibsen, has created a new romance, and, through the imagination of Richard Wagner, become all but the most passionate element in the arts of the modern world. There is indeed but one other element as passionate, the still unfaded legends of Arthur and the Holy Grail; and now a new fountain of legends, and, as I think, a more abundant fountain than any in Europe, is being opened, the fountain of Gaelic legends [. . .] 'The Celtic movement', as I understand it, is principally the opening of this fountain, and none can measure of how great importance it may be to coming times, for every new fountain of legends is a new intoxication for the imagination of the world. It comes at a time when the imagination of the world is ready as it was at the coming of the tales of Arthur and of the Grail for a new intoxication. The reaction against the rationalism of the eighteenth century has mingled with a reaction against the materialism of the nineteenth century, and the symbolical movement, which has come to

perfection in Germany in Wagner, in England in the pre-Raphaelites, in France in Villiers de l'Isle-Adam, and Mallarmé, and in Belgium in Maeterlinck, and has stirred the imagination of Ibsen and D'Annunzio, is certainly the only movement that is saying new things. The arts by brooding upon their own intensity have become religious and are seeking, as I think Verhaeren has said, to create a sacred book.

(137–138)

For all its appearance of hesitancy ('as I think' is repeated three times and appears with another 'as I understand it'), this passage gathers towards a vision of exceptional ambition. Beginning at the outer rims of Europe with Scandinavian and Gaelic legends of the far north and extreme west, Yeats's prose moves centripetally inwards to the metropolitan cores of Germany, England and France. What the peripheries possess, in Yeats's account, is a trove of premodern legend, rejuvenating 'fountains' of inspiration from which their modern literatures may take force, and when that inspiration finds expression in artists of genius such as Ibsen, Wagner or Mallarmé it can then reshape the imagination of a whole continent as well. 'Passion' and 'intoxication' are the valued qualities of this new literature, one renovated ironically by contact with the ancient and primordial, and these qualities find a responsive audience not just in Europe's peripheries but also in its core literary nations where the latter, precisely because they represent the most advanced but also exhausted stages of modernity, have grown weary of the rationalism and materialism of which so many of their own modern intellectuals have complained.

As Yeats constructs it, Celticism thus acquires a literary pedigree that is very old (Scandinavian, Arthurian and Gaelic legend) but issues nonetheless in a literature that is also distinctly modern and even avant-garde (Wagner, Maeterlinck, Mallarmé, D'Annunzio). It is attached to Romantic critiques of the Enlightenment and to materialist critiques of modern capitalism, the right- or left-wing pedigrees of which are not specified, though the vocabulary of the passage tells its own story. Despite Yeats's late Romantic idioms, this conception of literature is both forward-looking in its ambitions (Yeats's essay closes with the hope that that even as Irish legends 'move among known woods and seas' they nevertheless 'have so much of a new beauty that they may well give the opening century its most memorable symbols' (138)) and fundamentally modernist in its conception of literature as a 'sacred book' that can redeem a troubled materialistic modernity. The redemptive aesthetic mission that Yeats ascribes to Celticism here was already present in *The Study of Celtic Literature*, though in far more modest, meliorative and carefully circumscribed terms in Arnold's case. Yeats, however, detaches Celticism from Arnold's preoccupations with university programmes and endowed chairs, as well as from the classical liberal idioms of English-centred social and cultural reform, and lends his own version a more messianic, visionary cast. In the passage between Arnold and Yeats, in other words, the language of a culturally supremacist liberal imperialism, working to strengthen the imperial authority of the British state, is re-worked in the direction of a radical anti-liberal, anti-imperial and anti-modern agenda with ambitions to rejuvenate modernity and modern literature *tout court*. Yeats's ambition is astonishing in its extravagant 'titanism', but in the final analysis what gets carried over from Arnold is the ambition to create a more cultivated and balanced social order than that represented by modern liberal, industrial capitalist and imperial England. For Arnold, that ambition always required the English people and imperial state to work to perfect themselves the better to rule the world with greater sophistication and refinement. For Yeats, it requires the overcoming of almost everything England stands for – not only its industrial capitalism and imperialism but also its secular and staid middle-class liberalism.

Like Yeats's 'The Celtic Element in Literature', Pound's *Patria Mia* wrestles with and overturns inherited metropolitan intellectual authority to articulate a highly ambitious idea of a literary 'renaissance', but remains conceptually enmeshed in what it overturns. Though Tocqueville is never directly mentioned, the shadow of *Democracy in America* slants across the pages of *Patria Mia*. 'America, my country', Pound writes in his treatise's opening line, 'is almost a continent and hardly yet a nation, for no nation can be considered historically as such until it has achieved within itself a city to which all roads lead, and from which there goes out an authority.'[28] The concern with the United States' lack of a European-style literary capital was a familiar one in American letters; the dilemma of a society grown to the size of a whole continent yet running the risk of becoming gelatinous for lack of the normal supports of a conventional (European) nation-state was, as we have seen, one that agitated many Americans besides Pound. A few paragraphs later, the Tocquevillian note is sounded even more strongly when he comments that Americans 'waste no time in philosophic speculation. Among them understanding is of no repute. Any intelligence which cannot express itself is apt to be afflicted, and that which cannot do something obviously to immediate advantage is despised' (24). This re-echoes Tocqueville's observation that American society was so given to utility and innovation that it set far more value on the application of science than on the contemplation of philosophic or scientific first principles. However, whereas Tocqueville worried that this might

ultimately lead to a fatal stagnation of knowledge, Pound is more ambivalent because, as we will see, the restless energy of American society is for
him also one of its most promising features.

When it comes to American literature, Pound is even more
Tocquevillian: for the most part, he argues, those who cultivate literature
in America are so pretentiously imitative of French and English letters and
their imitations are themselves so second-rate, so lacking in any sense of deep
tradition, so out of contact with the rude Elizabethan or Rabelaisian vigour
of American life, as to be deservedly ignored. Because '"art in America"',
writes Pound, using scare quotes to signal the inauthenticity of the very
term, has so little application to American life, '"the American" cannot be
expected to take it seriously, and [this is] why it is left to the care of ladies'
societies and the "current events clubs"' (36). Though those who belong to
this effete world profess the conventional disdain for commercial literature,
there is, Pound avers, more originality in American advertisement literature
than in genteel American literary productions: '[I]n the composition of
advertisements there is some attention paid to a living and effective style'
because '[w]herever there is an immediate ratio between action and profit
the American will at once develop his faculties' (36-37).

Nevertheless, if American advertisement has at least the virtue of not
being locked in a deadly recirculation of second-rate European idioms and
retains some sort of energizing contact with everyday American life –
Tocqueville had said as much of American journalism – the overall effects
of the capitalist market and the profit motive on letters are still utterly
deleterious. The sheer vitality of American capitalism may serve as a rough
stimulus of sorts, but the attempt to subordinate literary production to the
dictates of market production destroys any chance of genuine literary
achievement: 'The serious artist does not play up to the law of supply
and demand', Pound remarks, but in America '[a]s the factory owner
wants one man to make screws and one man to make wheels and each
man in his employ to do some one mechanical thing that he can do almost
without the expenditure of thought, so the magazine producer wants one
man to provide one element, let us say one sort of story and another
articles on Italian cities and, above all, nothing personal' (39–40). For
Pound, in sum, American capitalism attempts to apply the same Fordist
logic to literary production that it does to automobile production, but the
specialism, mechanism and impersonality that serve the purposes of car
manufacture are precisely what prove most deadly for the creation of any
worthwhile ambitious literature. This subjugation of culture to a middlebrow levelling of taste and to the commodification of the mass market was

precisely the antinomy earlier diagnosed by Tocqueville; the purpose of *Patria Mia* is to resolve that antinomy.[29]

Pound's way to tackle this problem is to declare his faith in the possibility of a great American literature and the imminence of an American Renaissance. The United States currently, he acknowledges, must recognize that it is in the condition of the European Dark Ages, but just as in Europe that medieval darkness was made to give way to the Renaissance so too must America be readied for its new age. So, just as Yeats had created a sense of Irish opportunity by stressing the debility of English society and letters, Pound too contrasts American youth and vitality to European disease and degeneration. Though America's current inability to support any really ambitious first-rate literature sends its writers into exile to Europe, nevertheless, '[t]o return to America is like going through some very invigorating, very cleansing sort of bath. [. . .] There may be evil in the country, but the odour of the rottenness is not continually obtruded upon one' (55). Because Northern Europe in general and England in particular (from where Pound is writing his tract) epitomize this stench of decay, Pound goes to great lengths to insist that America is not an Anglo-Saxon country and even to detach it geographically from its usual sense of origins:

> The Englishman, in dealing with the American, forgets, I think, that he has to do with a southerner, a man of the Midi. He thinks, erroneously, that the United States, once a set of his colonies, is by race Anglo-Saxon. New York is on the same parallel with Florence, Philadelphia is farther south than Rome. It is certain that climate has about as much to do with the characteristics of a people as has their ethnology. And especially if the race is mongrel, one stock neutralizing the forces of the other, the climate takes up its lordship and decrees the nature of the people resulting.
>
> (24–25)

This climacteric insistence on the southerly character of the United States is motivated by Pound's desire to get round the arguments of those like Tocqueville and Arnold who had insisted that because America was essentially a colonial offshoot of England it was therefore heir to all the modern industrial vices of its parent country or that it displayed those vices in even grosser form. Thus, whereas Yeats's strategy in countering Arnold is to reverse the positive and negative valences of Saxon and Celt, and to position the two as intrinsically antagonistic rather than complementary forces, Pound's is to substitute an environmental in lieu of a racial determinism.

Even as he works to de-Anglo-Saxonize America, however, the grip of racial thinking is not entirely released; rather, it is transferred into the medicalized terminology of degeneration and eugenics. What we get in the process is a southern or Mediterranean America that possesses an aggressively Italianate or Roman imperial vigour and potential that contrasts positively with the diseased and atrophied world of Northern Europe. Himself a product of the Dark Age of medieval America he repudiates, Pound can nonetheless see in New York portents of a better America to come:

> Having been brought up in the American mediaeval system, I see also a sign in the surging crowd on Seventh Avenue (New York). A crowd pagan as ever imperial Rome was, eager, careless, with an animal vigour unlike that of any European crowd that I have ever looked at. There is none of the melancholy, the sullenness, the unhealth of the London mass, none of the worn vivacity of Paris. I do not believe it is the temper of Vienna.
>
> (26–27)

These lines were penned in the years leading up to World War I, the chaos and carnage of which can only have confirmed Pound's sense of the essential accuracy of his estimates.

Pound's de-Anglo-Saxonized America allows him to take a broadly positive approach to immigration, the bugbear of most of his white 'nativist' American contemporaries because an inflow of mixed races had seemed to the latter to fly in the face of any possibility of an organic society or coherent national culture and to be an impediment to American cultural refinement. However, for Pound this immigration is another sign of American vitality: Hungarians, Swedes, Croats, Slavs, Czechs, Italians, Irish and Russian Jews all flood into America, he observes, and, '[w]e get from every village the most ruthless and the most energetic. The merely discontented stop in England' (22). The problem is, he allows, that all this raw immigrant energy is devoted only to one end, making money, and thus its usefulness for a cultural renaissance remains nugatory. One looks at these Seventh Avenue crowds, he muses, and knows that they are not Anglo-Saxons, and that they have the pagan energies of imperial Rome, but also that 'they are the dominant people and that they are against all delicate things. They will never imagine beautiful plaisaunces. They will never "sit on a middan and dream stars", as the Irish peasant said to Joseph Campbell' (27). Pound, in other words, has succeeded to his own satisfaction in de-Anglo-Saxonizing America, but nevertheless he cannot Celticize it as Yeats did Ireland. Insofar as America has escaped its Dark Age, the United States has done so in its cities, in New York especially, and it cannot therefore claim the lyrical Celtic imagination of the non-modern aristocrat and peasant that the Irish Renaissance was claiming for the Irish. An American renaissance will have to find some other footing.[30]

Try as he might, Pound struggles to get beyond the assertion that the United States is on the verge of a renaissance and the stubborn difficulty remains as to how to translate that potential into actuality, especially in the case of the literary arts. Nevertheless, he can declare with confidence his faith in the potential of such a renaissance, though he prefers the terms 'American Risorgimento' (41) or '*Risvegliamenti*' (86), presumably to suggest a shakeup more than exclusively artistic. In any case, the first great sign of a new American art for Pound is not literary but rather architectural. In its skyscrapers at least, New York has finally 'put forth its own expression. The first of the arts arrives. Architecture that has never wholly perished from the earth, that has scarcely ever slept for so long a period as the other arts, has appeared among us' (27–28). There are resonances here of Yeats's Irish 'renaissance' or re-awakening of a distant past, but Pound's idiom is in contrast futuristic and Italianate rather than Northern European and primitivist. In *Patria Mia*, the same New York skyscrapers that had rendered Henry James aghast in *The American Scene* (1904) because they had seemed so brutally indifferent to all earlier ambient architectural tradition and so unapologetically celebratory of capitalism, excite Pound because in these buildings at last 'the mire of commerce has fostered the beautiful leaf' (28). And as architecture is a public art it has the educative and propagandist value that every cultural renaissance needs to launch itself:

> And in our architecture the artist may set his hope, for after a people has learned a fineness of beauty from good buildings, after it has achieved thus the habit of discrimination, it will not be long patient of unsound and careless production in the other arts, and the intellectual hunger for beauty, which is begotten of comparisons, will not rest content with one food only.
>
> (28)

America's architecture, in short, is deemed promissory to the future because it educates American public taste and creates a hunger for beauty that will eventually help to ripen the other American arts also. When this happens, New York will not just 'uccede Lundun' in some giganticist sense that would satisfy only the vulgar; it will become lovelier than London also.

Still, if architecture is the first beautiful leaf flowering from the mire of American commerce, it is also an applied art and thus qualitatively different to the visual or literary arts, which are not. However, in literature and painting too, Pound argues, there have been promising auguries, above all in the figures of Whitman, James McNeill Whistler and Henry James. Whistler has proved that 'being born an American does not eternally damn a man or prevent him from the ultimate and highest achievement in the arts' (51). To know James 'one must know both Continents' and though the 'core of his work is not limited by America, yet no one has better understood the charm of all that is fine in American life' (48). For his part, poet 'Whitman established the national *timbre*' and 'goes bail for the nation' by clarifying that 'being born an American is no excuse for being content with a parrochial [*sic*] standard' (64). If these John-the-Baptist-like artists testify that American culture can one day produce greatness to match Europe's, the mistake, Pound believes, is to assume that they stand proof for the furthest reach of American achievement rather than being, like architecture, testament merely to its first beginnings. The challenge, then, is how to create in America more than a few exceptional or anomalous figures and to cultivate the kind of critical mass of first-rate artists and intellectuals that had ignited the fifteenth-century Italian Renaissance.

This returns Pound to the subject of capitalism and *Patria Mia* asks whether that system will prove the ruination of American literature – by subjecting all creativity to Fordist modes of standardized production that by their very nature thwart higher achievement and by reducing every product to a commodified mean in order to accommodate the widest middlebrow audience – or might not be somehow made to serve as its saviour. Capital can never hope to convert literature into one of the applied or productive arts in the same way as architecture because the a priori conditions for great literary and intellectual achievement are leisure, contemplation and experiment, precisely the things to which capitalism's restlessly busy ethos is most hostile. Even so, Pound speculates, despite that ethos, Americans seem desperately hungry to support the arts: 'The profits of monopoly after monopoly have been poured into the endowments of universities and libraries, and into the collection of works of art' (79); so indiscriminate is this hunger in fact that 'any hoax that is even labelled "culture" will sell like patent medicine' (79). However, even if the American addiction to collecting and displaying art from all over the world is currently mostly indiscriminate, the mere possession of collections eventually teaches greater discrimination. And just as the rich collectors of Rome had once sent out their agents to indiscriminately collect art from all over Greece and the East, so too the wealthy American collectors may sow the seeds of a higher general civilization by eventually cultivating 'that discrimination between the sham and the real which is essential to the fostering of all art worthy of the name' (70).

In all this turning over of possibilities and means, Pound's instinct is on some level democratic and even civic republican. He chides, for instance,

the American universities because '[i]t is lamentably true that the colleges
and universities talk democracy and breed snobbishness, and that they lean
toward petty monopoly' (80). He allows, too, that '[a]ll the fine dreams of
empire, of a universal empire, Rome, the imperium restored, and so on,
came to little', whereas 'the free cities [of the Italian republican city-states]
now here, now there, contrived to hold out against the feudal system and
are become the model for our present constitutional governments' (69).
These lines suggest a preference for the competitive fertility of small
republics over big imperial states. But because he seems convinced that
the education of the masses will inevitably be a long, slow process or that
securing popular agreement is always difficult, whereas the wealthy have
more agency to act without endless consultation, and because what is most
immediately needed is the investment to seed the great artistic capitals or
super-universities required to kick-start an American renaissance, Pound
turns to the American capitalist plutocracy as a modern equivalent of the
Medici whose wealth nurtured the Italian Renaissance.

Acknowledging that this is to defer to the same capitalist system he
holds accountable for so much of America's literary and cultural ills, and to
propose a feudal model of patronage at odds with his desire to lift America
out of its current Dark Ages, Pound persuades himself that this will be a
temporary or holding arrangement only. We may believe, he says, 'that the
millionaire is no more a permanent evil than was the feudal overlord' and
even that his 'predominance may be of shorter duration' (69). Meantime,
there seems no reason why the capitalist magnate 'should not confer upon
society, during his reign, such benefits as he is able' (69) and thereby
become like the Medici munificent sponsors of the arts, the latter now
remembered less for their corruption than for their patronage. 'Die he
must', writes Pound of the millionaire, 'and he may as well leave gifts,
lest people spit upon his tomb and remember him solely for his
iniquities' (70).

These prescriptions contain a good deal of self-conscious bravado. Once
Pound has peremptorily ruled out socialism and utopian schemes to effect
any more radical post-capitalist change, and accepted the premise that
'[t]here need be little actual change even in the existing [social] machinery'
(79) of America to furnish the start-up momentum for his Risorgimento,
he has effectively settled for a 'revolution' against the existing status quo in
the American arts world that actually depends on retaining the socio-
economic status quo. He readily accepts, he declares, that this makes
him 'an opportunist' (69) rather than a real revolutionary, but the compromise is one that he is willing to make.[31] Tocqueville, it will be

remembered, had anticipated that the American capitalists would one day become a kind of aristocracy in their own right ('one of the most harsh ever to appear on the earth'), but had suggested that because in such a changeable society fortunes would always be rising and falling that it was doubtful that this capitalist class could ever acquire the sense of caste solidity, tradition and acquired taste possessed by a hereditary aristocracy. Pound recognizes this is a problem and acknowledges that America's contemporary ruling class has little of the broad cultivation of Renaissance popes or princes, but his renaissance needs money to get itself started and so he turns for funding to the most immediate sources he sees to hand.

And what is it that Pound hopes to do with the financial support of the American millionaire elites? His immediate aim is that they should provide the patronage to support 'a class of artist-workers free from necessity' (97) that would have the means and time to cultivate itself to a level where it might be expected to produce great works. Still, because he attributes the poverty of American culture to the pedantic dullness and low standards of higher education offered by the existing American universities, especially in the humanities,[32] and to the Fordist commodification of literature enforced by the commercial publication industry, his more far-reaching ambition is to radically reconfigure the relationship between 'the universities and the arts and the system of publication linked together for some sort of mutual benefit and stimulus' (61). The problem for American art, as Pound sees it, is that its artists must either go abroad to Europe in search of tradition and higher artistic levels of taste and ambition or remain at home to cater to the fungus of the literary magazines and their genteel publics. To remedy this, he proposes the idea of a 'super-college' (93) where writers, scholars, reviewers and artists of many sorts would be clustered to create a catalyzing situation in which they would all challenge each other to greater levels of ambition:

> On the whole, the professors would shine [in the super-colleges], for they have at least some hoard of knowledge to bank on. The professor who couldn't manage the normal literatist would be a fairly poor lot. But on the contrary, when a seminar managed to hit on an artist of parts, the debate would be enlightening to both the faculty and to the students. New life would be infused into the study of letters. Literature would come to be regarded as something living, something capable of constant transformation, and rebirth.
>
> The effect on writers would be even more worthwhile, for the normal magazinist, confronted for once, at least, in his life, with the array of past achievement, or drubbed by what he would regard as a fossil, might be

driven to consider art as an art. He might on being invited into debate be brought for once to question himself about his reasons for existence. In fact, the whole outrageous scheme would stir up more than a few backwaters of mental stagnation.

(87)

Pound is anticipating here the rudiments of what Mark McGurl would later label 'the program era' in American culture, though in Pound's 'super-college' the creative writers and scholars would not be hived off into separate zones of activity, but would instead collaborate, debate and dynamize each other.[33] For Pound, these super-colleges would ideally be adopted by great cities, which would add to the vitality of both college and city and aggrandize the latter's reputation by so doing. Finance is vital to all this: '[I]f America has any desire to be a centre of artistic activity', Pound writes, 'she must learn her one lesson from the Ptolomies. Art was lifted into Alexandria by subsidy, and by no others means will it be established in the United States' (73).

The challenge to London and Paris in this is clear. 'If any great city in America', Pound writes, 'would tether a hundred young artists, chosen for their inventive faculties and not for their capacity to agree with contemporary editorial boards, that city could within two decades become the centre of occidental art' (95). 'A hundred men, in New York or Chicago, kept to work at painting, sculpture, architecture, musical composition and all branches of literature, and any other art one might happen to think of later, would be a reasonable beginning' and show reasonable intent to 'make some sort of a centre' (93).

On the face of it, *Patria Mia*'s 'super-colleges' might seem a mere throwback to Tocqueville's *Democracy in America*, which had argued that '[a] few first-rate universities would be more effective' (552) than a wide network of inferior colleges in developing the knowledge of the classics so that the latter might act as brake on the tendential slovenliness of the literary arts in a democratic age. But Pound's idea is far more forward- than backward-looking, more avant-garde than purely classicist. He believes that American artists need to be schooled in the classics and the great traditions, but he is also looking to invention, collective criticism, something more laboratory-like and livelier than the scholasticism of the universities, the commercialism of the literary magazines and publishing houses, or the charlatan anti-intellectualism of the unschooled writers and artists. What has changed in the interval between Tocqueville and Pound is a new sense of American possibility. For Tocqueville, writing in the 1830s, there is little sense that America can hope anytime soon to compete with Europe in literary or artistic terms; his recommendations are offered with a view to saving the society from its own worst tendencies and excesses. For Pound, in contrast, America is a new Rome on the verge of world power, but one that has yet to achieve its renaissance. The United States, in Pound's estimation, has the vitality that Europe has lost even if it has not yet acquired that sense of tradition that Europe once possessed. However, because Europe or England appear no longer to be able to sustain that tradition, the possibilities for radical change, in Pound's view, are opportune and immediate. Having contemplated the night-time sky-line of New York from the harbour in the company of the Irishman who surmises that 'it uccedes Lundun' and having himself deemed it already nearly the most lovely of the world's cities, the Pound persona closes the passage in question with a reference to Venice:

> The Irishman thought of size alone. I thought of the beauty, and beside it Venice seems like a tawdry scene in a play-house. New York is out of doors.
> And as for Venice; when Mr. Marinetti and his friends have succeeded in destroying that ancient city, we shall rebuild Venice on the Jersey mud flats and use the same for a tea-shop.
>
> (33)

In this boast, the United States will assimilate that sense of millennial tradition and deep history that Europe's futurists foolishly and arrogantly discard. But the gesture will be more than merely imitative appropriation; Americans will take over Europe's unwanted Venices but will also rebuild them to its own enormous size and titanic ambition so that even fabled Venice will seem a mere teashop once the American Renaissance has done its work.

## V

What appears clear here, I hope, is the degree to which the languages of metropolitan decline and decadence and those of peripheral renaissance and rejuvenation, those of cosmopolitan condescension and provincial self-assertion, dialectically provoke each other. Even as they take up the idioms made familiar to the nineteenth century by Tocqueville, Arnold and others, writers like Pound and Yeats consistently worry those terms, turn them terminologically over and redeploy them to their own advantages. The conceptions of Irish or American 'renaissances' they thereby developed represent in some respects at least rather magnificent repudiations of conventional nineteenth-century British and French conceptions of Ireland and the United States.

Even when they are at their most complimentary and generous minded, metropolitan thinkers like Tocqueville or Arnold are invariably condescending towards Irish and American cultures. Nevertheless, in the hands of Pound or Yeats, and many others of their era, these received idioms and analyses are put to several new uses: if, on the one hand, the works of these august metropolitan critics can be deployed to castigate domestic Irish and American letters for their persistent lack of accomplishment, they are also cited as warrants to spur the peripheries to greater ambitions, to urge new opportunities and grander visions. In short, the acts of modernist self-fashioning primed by Yeats and Pound and other contemporaries take Tocqueville or Arnold and their ilk at their word when they want to distance themselves from the assumed deficiencies of their countries of origin, but this doesn't mean they by any means genuflect to Paris or London in some deferential sense. Instead, they seize on the language of 'decadence' to suggest that even if their own natal countries remain backward in some respects, they have also funds of qualities that can become resources to reinvigorate European metropolitan societies and literatures now past their meridians and sinking into the insolent slovenlinesses of advanced capitalist commodification or establishment complacency.[34] Culturally poor though Ireland or the United States might be deemed to be in many respects, then, that poverty is never judged unalloyed: ancient Irish treasuries of myth, legend and folktale, Celtic asceticism and visionary imagination, early Christian ages of saints and scholars, youthful American energy and vigour, America's provincial hunger for culture, its vast wealth – these can all, Yeats and Pound declaim, become assets and turned to advantage. Moreover, such assets must be put to use not only to redeem Irish or American national cultures, but to save Western civilization more generally from its own increasing senescence.

Pound's or Yeats's grand manners can be florid and fantastical, but this boosterism must be viewed against a longer historical context of metropolitan condescension. After his own fashion, each writer deploys the language of 'revival' or 'renaissance' or 'Risorgimento' as a deliberate tactic, a calculated posture adopted to repudiate the long-standing sense of deference to English culture habitual to the local American and Irish cultural establishments in which they had been formed. In other words, the swagger or swank of Pound's or Yeats's esoteric claims is not simply or not only the mark of their grandiose personal temperaments (though it may be that, too). Rather, just as the styles of Tocqueville and Arnold, with their rhetorics of cool detachment, mandarin impartiality and classical decorum, are supported by that confident sense of French or British metropolitan superiority that comes with belonging to nations already acknowledged everywhere as cultural world leaders, so too Pound's pugnacity and Yeats's hauteur are the reflex corollaries of their determination not to be intimidated or constrained by their status as laggard provincials in Europe's cultural capitals. The aggressive insistence on English 'decline', things already detectable in the early manifestoes of these impresarios of American or Irish 'renaissance' even before World War I, became even more strident after the appalling carnage of that European-centred war. But the confidence of Pound or Yeats that the contemporary generations of Irish and American writers for which they spoke were at least as capable of greatness as any of their metropolitan counterparts resident in Paris or London would also grow commensurably after 1918. The 1920s after all would launch *Ulysses*, *The Waste Land*, *A Vision*, *The Tower*, *The Making of Americans* and the earliest publication of *The Cantos*.

Though the rivalry with London is clearly marked in even the early texts by Yeats and Pound discussed above, the intention from the outset is never simply to match London. The ambition is always much greater, 'to uccede'. In Yeats's early essays, his hopes for an Irish literary and artistic renaissance are woven into his vision of a wider series of peripheral revivals coming into their own on the margins of Europe and in India, China, Japan and the United States. In Pound's case, the desire is not just that America will become a cultured nation equal to the greatest European ones, but that it will become a great world centre in its own right, thus remaking the established order of things and opening up a whole new era for literary and cultural production. For both writers, that is, the goal of rejuvenating Irish or American national cultures is significant, but not a sufficient end in itself; such rejuvenations are conceived rather as a necessary stage on the way to remaking what we might now call the world literary system more generally. When Pound thinks of New York as a modern Rome or of some future New Jersey so wholly transformed as to make Venice seem unremarkable by comparison, or when Yeats remarks that London and Paris are in the decadent hour of their cultural sunsets while Ireland feels within itself the first stirrings of sunrise, they perform a rhetoric of radical rupture and of transnational as well as national renewal – gestures that would soon come to define 'high modernism' more generally.

What is equally significant is the way in which the rhetorics of 'renaissance' once set in motion reverberate and multiply elsewhere, triggering new versions among writers from other backwater communities with sometimes far greater claims to subaltern status. As well as the Irish and American 'revivals' and 'renaissances' in this period, we also have the Negro

Renaissance, later termed the Harlem Renaissance, which forked across the Atlantic via Caribbean literary migrations to New York, London and Paris. Later, the 'Southern Renaissance', as well as various American city-identified counterparts, the Chicago or San Francisco renaissances, followed. Whether one or other of these served as precedent to the rest – did Emerson, Thoreau, Whitman, James and the nineteenth-century 'New England Renaissance' inspire Yeats and the Celtic Revival or was the latter trigger for its twentieth-century American counterparts? – seems less significant than what they share in common: similar rhetorical tactics, similar senses of historical injury and recovery, shared competitive rivalries with more industrially advanced and established centres, a common messianic sense of the redemptive capacities of the arts and literature.[35]

As Michael Soto has argued, 'Renaissance rhetoric', in this era, 'signals a self-conscious emergence from colonial dependency to postcolonial sufficiency and even supremacy' (59). Certainly, as Soto shows, the Irish Revival found warm receptions in the United States, among both elite white cultural nationalists and the emerging Harlem intellectuals and writers. There, the combination of Philo-Celtic societies from the 1870s, the Celtic Studies programmes expanding across American universities from the 1890s and the Irish American and Catholic presses were all in situ to nurture this Irish reception, to promote and propagandize for it. But without the stirrings of its overlapping American counterparts could the Irish Revival have attained in its own right its wider significance?

If the Irish Revival travelled westwards, so too the American 'renaissances' travelled eastwards across the Atlantic, as first white Americans and then their African American and Caribbean successors migrated to Paris and London. 'Nobody in England ventures to speak of a poetic renaissance', declared Valéry Larbaud in 1921, adding, '[i]n the United States people do'.[36] Larbaud needed to be no great prophet to notice this. By 1921 the Irish and Americans were already about to release works in Paris and London that would change the face of twentieth-century literature. Whatever the new 'Renaissance' signified, a rupture with the old literary order was soon to be commonly dated to 1922.[37]

Still, while there might be much to admire in the chutzpah of these peripheral insurgencies, the reactionary tendencies in some versions of the literatures they promoted are evident. Yet when contemporary liberal critics bemoan the reactionary nature of some of the major Anglophone modernists, they should remember that the origins of that reaction may be traced not only to the right- or left-wing extremes of twentieth-century European post–World War I politics such as fascism or communism but also to nineteenth-century French and British classical liberalism. As noted above, even in the case of relatively moderate figures such as Tocqueville or Arnold, the extension of democracy was regarded as bringing with it immense dangers both political and cultural. Moreover, the liberalism of both thinkers, like that of so many of their nineteenth-century contemporaries, was perfectly compatible with a conviction in the rightness of the French and British empires and the conviction that opposition to empire in the colonies or any radical working-class dissent at home should be forcibly quelled and by the severest measures where necessary. Nineteenth-century classical liberalism, in other words, was a cosmopolitan ideological placeholder for the established world system and for the ruling classes in the hegemonic states that supervised that system, and the classical liberal commitment to democracy was as such typically circumscribed by the imperatives of Europe's leading nations.[38] Liberalism was always as much or more fearful of the tyrannies of the masses than of the masters.

Culturally speaking, therefore, the more reactionary elements of Yeats's or Pound's modernisms owe at least as much to classical liberalism, and in Pound's case to Jeffersonian republicanism, as to its overt repudiation or to the embrace of newer 'savage gods' by Yeats and Pound in their maturities. Fearing that the democratization of education might not lead to a general advancement of learning but rather to a downward levelling of education for everyone, Tocqueville had recommended that to check this the Americans should cultivate the development of a few elite universities that would undertake to produce a refined ruling class, while technical colleges would best serve the needs of the greater mass of society. Whether or not he had read or recalled Tocqueville on such matters, it is to some form of 'super-college' too that Pound looked in *Patria Mia* to nurture the critical mass of artists necessary to generate an American cultural renaissance. In similar measure, when Yeats affiliated himself to the Irish national movement and lent his cultural credit to the Irish struggle for self-determination, but simultaneously aligned himself with the culture of the Big House and championed a Protestant elite that had always given Ireland intellectual leadership, he was acting in consistency with a classical liberalism that regarded a patrician check on democracy as indispensable to its proper functioning. Though both Pound and Yeats would attribute the downfall of Europe during and after World War I to a long history of materialism and to a weak-kneed middle-class liberalism, and though both would look to varying extents to strongmen like Mussolini to check that decline, they were thinking as much in the spirit of Tocqueville's or Arnold's classical liberalism as against that tradition when they formed such views. Or, to put matters another way, their mutual misgivings about the character of modern society owed a great deal to classical liberalism's own internal contradictions on such matters. While it might be argued that a reading of Nietzsche, Spengler, Major Douglas or others had pointed Pound, Yeats and others in authoritarian directions, there was much in the classical liberal tradition that had always pointed that way anyway.

The great ambition of modernist literature is hard to separate off, therefore, from the inherent and inherited contradictions of classical liberalism, and modernism's elitism has classical liberal origins even if some versions of modernism also repudiated liberalism precisely because its contradictions had become by the early twentieth century so acute. Determined to challenge the backwardness and provincialism of their own societies and to produce a literature equal to if not greater than anything produced in metropolitan Europe, determined equally not to kowtow to the regnant artistic arbiters of taste in London or Paris, determined, finally, to resist the concessions to middlebrow levels of taste towards which the capitalist cultural market impelled artistic production at home as much as abroad, the Irish and American modernists were at once defiantly rebellious against the existing order of things and recalcitrantly, unapologetically mandarin in temper. Combating, as they saw it, the provincialisms and philistinisms of centre and periphery alike, as well as striving to retain for, or restore to, art a sense of high vocation to which liberal-capitalist modernity was tendentially hostile, the modernist, whether an exile like Eliot or Pound, Joyce or Stein, or a more stay-at-home figure like Yeats or William Carlos Williams, Jean Toomer or William Faulkner, was self-constitutively an embattled figure.

However, to be embattled in this manner was nevertheless not to be merely a victim or an abjectly outmoded figure – a poète maudit, a dandy, an outcast, a bohemian. By aligning themselves with tradition and the greatness of the disappearing past, or with the avant-garde and the prospects of a transformed future, or in some instances with both, the modernists fashioned the image of the artist more as cultural grandee than hapless victim of the times. However much they might differ from each other in other respects, it is this elevated sense of the artist and the artistic vocation that gives the Anglophone 'high modernist' generation of Pound, Yeats, Eliot, Joyce, Stein, Fitzgerald, O'Neill and others its coherence. It may also be what distinguishes this generation from the later, perhaps more humbled by history, European modernist generations that came after World War II when such militantly defiant poses or outsized ambitions for literature were harder to sustain.

Tocqueville might not have been surprised by modernism. The transition from aristocratic to democratic cultures, he argued, was likely to be gradual and marked by myriad subtle changes. In the course of such transitions, 'there almost always occurs a moment when the literary genius of democratic nations will vie with that of aristocratic nations, both wishing to establish their joint sway over the human mind'. Such clashes appear as 'brief but brilliant periods, when creativity avoids ebullience and liveliness avoids confusion' (549). Eighteenth-century French literature was Tocqueville's touchstone for such brilliance. As Moscow and New York emerged to challenge Paris and London, and as London found itself reckoning with literary and artistic 'renaissances' in New York and Dublin, the Frenchman might have recognized in modernism repetition with difference.

## CHAPTER 3

# 'The Insolence of Empire': The Fall of the House of Europe and Emerging American Ascendancy in The Golden Bowl and The Waste Land

As matters stand, I think we may reasonably ask whether the Americans 'most prominent in cultivated European opinion', the Americans who 'live habitually out of America', are not less exiles than advance agents of the expansion now advertising itself to the world. They may be the vanguard of the great army of adventurers destined to overrun the earth from these shores, and exploit all foreign countries to our advantage.

William Dean Howells, 'American Literature in Exile', *Literature and Life*, 1902.[1]

Is it too huge a conception, too inordinate an idea to say that the American conquest of England is but an incident of the Greater Invasion, an affair of outposts preparatory to the real manoeuvre that shall embrace Europe, Asia, the whole of the Old World? Why not? And the blaze is ahead of us, and every now and then from afar off there in the countries that are under the rising sun we catch the faint sounds of the skirmishing of our outposts. One of two things invariably happens under circumstances as these: either the outposts fall back upon the main body or the main body moves up to support the outposts. One does not think that the outposts will fall back.

Frank Norris, 'The Frontier Gone at Last', 1902.[2]

## I

American literary expatriates provoked considerable anxiety in nationalist literary circles in the late nineteenth and early twentieth centuries, for they suggested that the United States still lagged culturally behind Europe. In the passage cited above, William Dean Howells calmly deflects such anxieties. The country's literary exiles, he suggests, are best understood neither as escapees from American society's putative materialism nor as evidence of some unpatriotic Europhilia. Rather, these exiles are 'the vanguard of the great army of adventurers destined to overrun the earth from these shores, and exploit all foreign countries to our advantage'.

Whatever their conscious intentions, the long-term historical consequence of the American exiles, he claims, is that they will have become agents of some wider American destiny to enrich itself from the cultures of the world. Norris's article, coming in the wake of Frederick Jackson Turner's famous 1893 Chicago address on 'The Significance of the Frontier in American History', predicts an ongoing march of American progress beyond the United States' eastern and western shores. The country's 'epic of civilization' (1189) will continue, Norris suggests, until American supremacy, 'whether of battle-ship or bridge-building', has translated itself into a single planetary patriotism, 'the brotherhood of man' (1190). Despite their different idioms, Howells and Norris share a common confidence that despite the closing of the Californian frontier, the United States' transcontinental world career in literary and other matters is only beginning.

Until the 1920s at least, London remained the primary Mecca for America's 'passionate pilgrims'.[3] In 1896, a financially strapped Mark Twain left Connecticut and settled with his family for a period in London to restore his depleted fortunes. American writers and artists already living in London in that period included Pearl Craigie, Stephen Crane, Bret Harte, Harold Frederic, Frank Harris, Henry James, James McNeill Whistler and John Singer Sargent. In 1908, Ezra Pound arrived and decided to settle there. Hilda Doolittle (H.D.) arrived in 1911. In 1912, Robert Frost came to the city travelling there via Glasgow from Boston. In 1914, T. S. Eliot began to make London a more permanent home. Amy Lowell also arrived in 1914, determined, during her visit, to recruit Imagist talent for American publication. An unknown figure when he sailed for Glasgow in 1912, Robert Frost published his first volumes of poetry in London and returned to America in 1915 already with a considerable reputation. Some, like Lowell or Frost, became important figures in twentieth-century American letters, but few who returned to the United States in the early part of the century attained the levels of literary fame or notoriety acquired by those, like James, Eliot and Pound, who stayed in London. Pound eventually cast off London in 1920, first for Paris and then for long-term residence in Rapallo, but in the early twentieth century George Moore's old quip that 'Henry James stayed in France and read Turgenev and Flaubert, Mr. Howells returned to America and read Henry James' still carried weight.[4]

Those Americans who remained in Europe in the early twentieth century might seem perfectly to embody Pascale Casanova's conception of the 'assimilated writer'. As used by Casanova, the term refers to those émigré writers who settle permanently in more culturally prestigious metropolitan capitals, where they adapt to the social and literary mores of their host society 'and begin by almost clandestine means to appropriate the literary heritage of the centers for themselves'.[5] However, in other ways the American exiles stretch Casanova's category to breaking point. For Casanova, literary assimilation represents 'the lowest level of literary revolt' (207) and is typically practiced by writers who migrate to foreign capitals from colonies or former colonies with little cultural capital of their own, although she does allow that this kind of adaptive career has also been followed by many writers from countries that have accumulated considerable cultural resources. In any case, in Casanova's schema the assimilated writer is essentially a submissive type who adheres to established metropolitan literary tastes and forms. For her, such writers lack the system-disruptive attributes of either 'rebel' writers, who remain at home to advance their own peripheral national literatures or 'revolutionaries', meaning those writers who also move to the metropole but there become aggressive innovators who shatter the prevailing norms and forms of both their home and host societies.

The difficulty with Casanova's work in this regard is that some of the émigré writers in London in this early twentieth century who appear to be almost ideal types of the assimilated writer on one level can simultaneously be, in her terms, 'revolutionary' figures on another. Oscar Wilde, the Irishman who worked hard to shed his debasing Irish accent and cultivated the persona of a very dandified English gentleman and crafted outwardly conventional English comedies of manners for the London stage, appears to epitomize the 'assimilated writer' on several levels. Yet despite Wilde's conformity in these respects, he was a flamboyant outlaw to convention and an avant-gardist in most other respects, particularly in his very French and scandalous *Salomé*. Wilde's countryman George Bernard Shaw seemed in his public persona to be the very model of the English Fabian liberal rationalist; but as dramatist and critic, Shaw was the pioneer of the new Ibsenite drama in London and made an international literary career, as Wilde had done, by satirizing the cultural mores of his adoptive home. Henry James's assimilation into English high society culminated in 1915 in his wartime embrace of English citizenship. His career is a triumph of metropolitan adaptation, yet few writers can have teased out the tortuous dialectics of the expatriate condition with more subtlety than he did. T. S. Eliot, prissily respectable in his banker's pin-striped suit and bowler hat, ostentatiously converted Anglican-Catholic and royalist conservative, eventually business partner in Faber and Gower, could seem so over the top in his adaptive Englishness that Virginia Woolf would invite her brother-in-law to come to dinner to see Eliot 'in a four-pieced suit'.[6] A hyper-assimilated writer in his public persona, Eliot nevertheless is, in his art, far closer to Casanova's category of the 'revolutionary' iconoclast who breaks the received moulds of both domestic and metropolitan culture to create something strange and new.

Casanova's schema, then, may be too rigid to capture the nuances of the adaptations of these American and Irish expatriates to a literary London that was in a moment of acute transitional flux. Certainly, at least until the end of World War I, London remained internationally powerful enough to compel cultural assimilation – hence Eliot's complaints about the difficulties of assimilation and the more abrasive Pound's sense of resentment of English complacency and his eventual departure. In *The Education of Henry Adams*, published in 1907, Henry Adams, commenting on a meeting with Kipling on a voyage to America, noted that 'Kipling and the American were not one, but two, and could not be glued together'. He attributed their social awkwardness to the assumed superiority of the English and the interiorized diffidence of the American in the face of such assumption. Hence, presumably, why Americans, in Adams's view, 'felt it little if at all, with Celts'. 'All through life', Adams concluded, 'one had seen the American on his literary knees to the European; and all through many lives back for some two centuries, one had seen the European snub or patronize the American; not always intentionally, but effectually. It was in the nature of things'.[7] Neither he nor Kipling could overcome this intangible order.

Adams was older than Wilde or Shaw and belonged to a different generation to Pound and Eliot, and by the time *The Education of Henry Adams* was published things were already changing. The fact that the Irish interlopers, Wilde and Shaw, were able to assume the very highest positions in London theatre and that the Americans, Henry James, Pound and Eliot, were soon recognized as the best practitioners of the novel, poetry and criticism in 'English' was an early warning sign of how unstable the English literary capital had become. Americans might have been for centuries on their 'literary knees' to things European, but that was about to change. Had London adopted James and Eliot or had 'The Master' and 'The Pope' come to govern it?

The ways in which Henry James and T. S. Eliot negotiated their American backgrounds and English acculturations are well-developed critical topics and will be touched on here only in passing.[8] Instead, my primary concern will be to show how major works by each of these authors – namely, *The Golden Bowl* (1904) and *The Waste Land* (1922) – may be conceived as complex deliberations on and expressions of the shifting balance of world power as Western European global supremacy began to wane and the United States commenced its ascent to world power. My argument is not that *The Golden Bowl* and *The Waste Land*, two formally very different kinds of texts, offer direct thematic reflections on the transfer of global hegemony from Europe to the United States, though this changing of the transatlantic order of things is indeed an overt concern in James's novel. My proposal, rather, is that we can detect in these works an anxiety about what the declining condition of Europe, including that of Great Britain and its empire, means for the future. In each work, we can see determined salvage operations that involve taking European culture and tradition into American charge in an attempt to rescue them and recover their coherence.

Readers will not find in James's or Eliot's writings the brash, often triumphalist, American tones that distinguish so many of the works in this period that reflect on the United States' future destiny in a changing international order.[9] Nevertheless, what I have in mind here is the case made by Giovanni Arrighi in *The Long Twentieth Century* when he argues that to attain global supremacy a new superpower must exercise something more than military muscle, economic clout or political force to attain its end. To consolidate itself internationally, Arrighi says, the new hegemon must also display a formidable restructuring resolve, a can-do capacity to steady the collapsing structures of the old world system, and the organizational nous to remake a new world system on new terms. That new system, Arrighi suggests, will serve the emerging hegemon's own advantage obviously, but will also operate to the more general (however unevenly distributed) benefit of all its major constituents.[10]

On some level, I want to propose, *The Golden Bowl* and, in a different manner, *The Waste Land* offer intimations of this process of American assumption of control of the world system, something that would politically come to full fruition only several decades later after World War II. Taking William Dean Howells at his word when he proposes that America's exilic writers, whether they know it or not, march out in advance of the American flag and demonstrate by their cultural appropriations how Americans will sooner or later overrun the globe and in so doing learn how to 'exploit all foreign countries to [US] advantage', I will show that there is in James and Eliot a tentative, sceptical, but nevertheless remarkably confident disposition that displays itself prepared to step in and assume control of a rickety world order that has lost its bearings and thus seems ripe for American management and re-structuration. In their different ways, *The Golden Bowl* and *The Waste Land* are texts about breaking civilizations, civilizations badly splintered in the former case, shattered to fragments in the latter one. As such, these works may be read as semaphores for the felt weakening of British and European ascendancy in this era. However, as aesthetic objects, James's oblique and exquisitely managed novel and Eliot's encyclopaedic-cum-orchestral poem are not just documents of disintegration, but works also of reconstitution or new totalizations on new architectonic principles. In their respective treatments of shattering, salvage and re-composition, these works point to horizons beyond their own moment, to new world orders still only partially emerging into view during the decades before and immediately after World War I.

## II

Though the general idea for *The Golden Bowl* was initially sketched as early as 1892, James's last major work did not get underway until summer 1903 and it was finally published on 10 November 1904. Some months earlier, in February 1904, Roger Casement had published his famous account of Belgian atrocities in the Congo. In April of that year, the United Kingdom signed the *Entente Cordiale* with France, formally coming to a modus vivendi with its long-time imperial competitor, while in May US military engineers commenced work on the Panama Canal. On 8 November 1904, two days before James's novel appeared, Theodore Roosevelt was re-elected president of the United States for a second term. The Boxer Uprising in China, 1899–1901, and the Second Boer War, October 1899 to May 1902, occurred in the years just before James began work on *The Golden Bowl*, while the Russo-Japanese War, beginning in February 1904 and not ending until September 1905, overlapped with its conclusion. These events – the Boer War, widely regarded as a serious embarrassment to British imperial supremacy, and the Japanese victory over Russia, the first time a major modern European power was defeated by an Asian opponent – were straws in the wind, intimations of an increasingly shaky balance of international power. American involvements in Panama and Roosevelt's election signalled a new flexing of American overseas might and the Japanese victory highlighted not only an ominous assertion of Japanese militarism in Asia but also, from a British perspective, a worrying weakening of Tsarist Russia that augured poorly for the long-term stability of the European balance of powers.

On 14 October 1904, less than a month before *The Golden Bowl* appeared, Joseph Conrad published *Nostromo*, his panoramic tale set in the fictional South American republic of Costaguana, a narrative that bore the obvious impress of Panamanian events. In *Nostomo*, Holroyd, the San Franciscan financier, tells Charles Gould, the English mine owner, that European capital has been thrown into South America in all sorts of 'fool investments' whereas a shrewder American capital can afford to bide its time, step in at the proper moment and reap the rewards. 'Of course', Holroyd pronounces, 'someday we shall step in. We are bound to. But there's no hurry. Time itself has got to wait on the greatest country in the whole of God's Universe. We shall be giving the word for everything: industry, trade, law, journalism, art, politics, and religion, from Cape Horn clear over to Smith's Sound, and beyond, too, if anything worth taking hold of turns up at the North Pole'. 'And then', Holroyd prophesizes, 'we shall run the world's business whether the world likes it or not. The world can't help it – and neither can we, I guess'.[11]

Despite their proximate publications, *Nostromo* and *The Golden Bowl* are seldom linked and perhaps for obvious reasons. *Nostromo* combines the generic conventions of the historical novel and adventure tale, its plot narrates the opening up of a backward agrarian society to international capital and involves an arabesque sequence of coups, restorations and impending revolutions. *The Golden Bowl*, in contrast, is an indoors novel in which a series of amorous dramas and battles of will are enacted at the level of interior consciousness. *Nostromo*, in sum, is a distinctly 'out of doors' political narrative with an openly imperial theme whereas *The Golden Bowl* is patently not that kind of fiction. Set largely in London high society and dealing with the intricate marriage and adultery plots typical of the domestic novel, its interests appear more moral and psychological than political, and commentary on *The Golden Bowl*, therefore, has focused mainly on James's explorations of interior consciousness, his elaborately turned ironies and the hallmark complexities of his late style.

Still, if we can get beyond the fact that these are different kinds of novels, the correspondences between the two texts are compelling. With its large, multinational cast of characters, mainly of European, South American and American background, *Nostromo* has a more epic, transatlantic sweep than any of Conrad's other novels. *The Golden Bowl*, too, though restricted to a much smaller and more tightly knit upper-class constellation of American, Italian and British leading figures, possesses a capacious transatlantic vision. Adam Verver, James's massively wealthy magnate and devoted art collector whose treasuries of art objects seem to be gathered in from all over Europe and the Orient is a different kind of American to Conrad's Holroyd. Holroyd is a figure drawn from a conception of American puritanism, the Calvinist severity of that country's colonial beginnings and primitive accumulation now ripening, in Weberian fashion, into a messianic capitalism that will not rest until it has subordinated the whole world to its rule. Adam Verver, in contrast, is a cosmopolitan and cultured European-facing American who appears all refinement and gentility where Holroyd is bombastic and evangelical. Holroyd waits patiently for the hour when American capital will 'give the word' for everything from religion to business to art; Verver has ambitions to marry his daughter into the remnants of the old Italian nobility and wants to elevate the American Midwest by having his lavish art collections shipped there to furnish the great museum that he has funded in some eponymous American City. Conrad's figure offers an image of a blatantly supremacist muscular Americanist imperialism of the kind many might associate with Roosevelt or American evangelicalism; James's Verver, on the other hand, represents the way in which the grossness of capital accumulation might try to put itself to the service of ennobling people and lifestyles. For all the obvious differences between the two novels and their leading American figures, it is clear that Verver's civilizing vision is as grandiose in its own way as Holroyd's. And despite working with such very different materials as they do, Conrad's and James's novels are equally attentive to the dynamics of commodification and reification and to the ways in which socio-historical contradictions can frustrate American visions.[12]

The Golden Bowl is divided into two volumes, 'The Prince' and 'The Princess'. Volume One opens with Amerigo, impoverished elder son of a once-powerful aristocratic Italian family, wandering distractedly through London's Bond Street, still dazed with the realization that he has just signed an engagement contract to Maggie Verver and thus become heir to the fabulous Verver fortune. For Amerigo, the sensation of the hour is intensified by his delight in the English capital, a city where he can relish the sense of an 'Imperium' that had once belonged to ancient Rome but can now be felt much more vividly by the Thames than by the Tiber.[13] Buoyed by the extraordinary good fortune of the hour and in flâneur-like fashion sensually relishing the many rich objects on display in London's department store windows – where they are paraded 'as if, in the insolence of Empire, they had been the loot of far-off victories' (5) – Amergio is at once radiantly happy and yet not entirely without misgivings. Aware of his imperfect character, which is apparently not only his own but also that of his class, race and religion, he cannot help wondering whether he can really conduct himself with the fastidiousness that the Ververs expect of him. He is troubled, too, by a vague undercurrent of resentment, feeling himself to be, like Adam Verver's art objects, an expensively purchased commodity. 'You're a rarity', Maggie had bantered with him during their courtship, 'an object of beauty, an object of price', one that can only be had in Europe and if not 'perhaps absolutely unique [. . .] you're so curious and eminent that there are very few others like you' (12).

Over the course of Volume One, narrated from Amerigo's point of view, these early anxieties slowly accumulate into a corruption that seems fated. When he visits his friend Fanny Assingham, who has helped broker this marriage, Amerigo learns that Charlotte Stant, a beautiful and intelligent woman of no fortune with whom he was once in love, is returning from the United States to London to attend Maggie's wedding. Thrown together again on the eve of his nuptials, Amerigo and Charlotte go shopping together in secret to buy Maggie a wedding present. On this excursion, they consider a golden bowl offered to Charlotte by a Bloomsbury antiques dealer but decide to abandon it as an ill-omened gift when the Prince detects that the gold-inlaid crystal bowl conceals a flaw. Under its magnificent veneer, the bowl is cracked. However, the significance of that flaw ramifies and signals an imperfection not only in the ornamental bowl but also in the whole web of the intimate human relationships that constitute the story. Maggie and the Prince marry and she bears a son, and, after a time, Adam Verver marries Charlotte, their union conceived as a solace to him for the loss of his daughter's companionship to Amerigo. To all outward appearances, these domestic arrangements seem perfect: they allow Maggie and her father to preserve the Edenic contentment of their pre-marital familial intimacy and Charlotte and the Prince to resume the earlier friendship broken off by their respective financial necessities. Adam and Maggie are socially retiring and keep increasingly at home after their marriages; this allows Amerigo and Charlotte to fulfil many of the social obligations the Ververs relinquish. In time, however, that post-marital friendship ceases to be chaste and Amerigo and Charlotte, though zealously careful not to disturb the tranquillity of their spouses, enter into a dangerous adulterous liaison.

If 'The Prince', a title that inevitably recalls Machiavelli, is about the tactics and expectations that go into the making of a grand marriage, and those that enable a covert adultery, 'The Princess', narrated entirely through Maggie's consciousness, is essentially about the even wilier tactics necessary to salvage a faltered marriage. Once Maggie begins to intuit her husband's and friend's infidelity, and has that foreboding confirmed when she learns from the Bloomsbury antiques dealer that the two had secretly visited his shop together to purchase a wedding gift for her, the period of her spousal innocence is irreparably shattered. The familial arrangements that had seemed so exquisite had all along concealed a flaw or perhaps many flaws. Contemplating her situation, Maggie comes to an awareness not only of the treacheries of the Prince and Charlotte, but also of the nearly incestuous intimacy of her own filial relationship with her father, Adam; the Ververs' mutual self-sufficiency, she now realizes, had rendered Amerigo and Charlotte almost redundant to their happiness. Essentially, what Maggie discovers in Volume Two is that if she is to save her marriage and everything she cherishes, then she must exercise a singleness of purpose and a self-discipline even more subtle and severe than those needed by Amerigo and Charlotte for the conduct of their illicit but circumspect affair. Were she to cry out in spontaneous protest at her betrayal, Maggie would destroy the serenity of her father's marriage, mortify her husband's sense of dignity and her own, create an ugly scandal and shatter the whole edifice of the elaborately refined but faulty world that she and Adam have constructed.

Deciding to forgo the satisfactions of spontaneous outrage and revenge for coolly meditated stratagems, Maggie does just enough to convey discreetly to the Prince that she has divined his deceit and then manages things with such expert tact that he then silently distances himself from Charlotte. Later, in a climactic encounter near the end of the novel, Maggie also confronts Charlotte on the terrace as the others play cards inside. Carefully evading anything that might trigger blustery accusation or angry confession, she keeps her rival suspended to the end in an agony of unknowing about what has caused Amerigo to detach himself from the affair and return to his wife. When Charlotte, trying to draw out Maggie, remarks on a change in Maggie's attitude and asks her friend if she has cause to complain of her, Maggie sidesteps the question, replying evasively, 'I accuse you – I accuse you of nothing' (486). Charlotte never quite knows exactly how her rival has outplayed her because Amerigo has refused to disclose to her his knowledge of Maggie's knowledge. Amerigo's circumspection, which wears the air of an integrity that owes everything to the corruption that preceded it, silently expresses the tacit compact with Maggie by which he decides to become faithful again to his wife, leaving an uncomprehending Charlotte with no option but to perform the part of the devoted wife of Adam. Charlotte knows that Maggie has triumphed over her, definitively, and has managed this by a forever-elusive subtlety she cannot penetrate. To prevent any repeat of earlier follies, Adam and Maggie also reach a tacit agreement to sacrifice their own intimacy the better to protect their marriages. To ensure this, Adam and Charlotte will leave England forever to live in American City, where Charlotte will preside over her husband's grand art museum, while Maggie and the Prince will remain in London.

A difficulty with *The Golden Bowl* is that any summary such as this risks trampling on precisely those kinds of adroit perspectival shifts, obscure motivational complexities, elliptic uncertainties and arabesque sentences torqued to the point of obscurity that seem fundamental not only to the novel's plot but also to James's extraordinarily dexterous management of his narrative. Like many of James's works, *The Golden Bowl* – the title has biblical and Blakean resonances – is about the dialectics of innocence and experience and about the responsibilities and consequences of not knowing and knowing. At the core of the work, there is what one critic has described as a terrific competition of female intelligences.[14] On the one side, there is the worldly intelligence of Charlotte, a woman without inherited fortune educated by experience to know that she must depend only on her own wits if she is to survive in a world that has allowed her little room for manoeuvre. On the other side, there is Maggie's more protected intelligence, which events must waken from its sleep to break through her initial innocence. When that innocence is punctured, it soon becomes clear, however, that Maggie is possessed of her own immense resources of active intelligence, self-discipline, shrewdness and strategy.

In Volume One, we might say, Charlotte makes her way bravely in the world by knowing how to bear her inherited disadvantages without complaint but also by knowing how to recoup what she can, when she can, by means of shrewd risk-taking and canny assertiveness. In Volume Two, the awakened Maggie finds that she too must suffer excruciating losses without clamant protest but has also to learn how to rouse herself to assertiveness and to out-Machiavel her Machiavellian frenemies and to do so with such delicacy that they will have little option left but to keep their silence, maintain appearances and respect the proprieties essential to this well-mannered, upper-class world. What precise acts of muted communication pass between Maggie and the Prince, such that he knows that she knows of his affair, but that she can nevertheless also convey to him that she wishes him to acknowledge her knowledge but not to confess his trespass outright in such a way as to embarrass them both? How much exactly does Adam Verver know or guess of Maggie's suffering or of Charlotte's and the Prince's duplicities? To what extent does Adam recognize or acknowledge the Ververs' culpability for their spouses' duplicity? And by whose lead, or by what cross-currents of muted understandings between father and daughter, is it agreed at the end of the novel that they must separate forever, he to keep his distance in the United States, she to stay in England? At what point does Maggie's apparently magnificent sangfroid, that quality that serves somehow to win the day for her while still preserving everyone's dignity, start to shade into a sinisterly manipulative will to dominate everything? Is the reader supposed to applaud her final victory over Charlotte as moral, magnificent and magnanimous? Or, is it to be considered the wintry triumph of a self-controlled and obsessively all-controlling ice queen? Has Maggie finally outgrown the solipsistic domestic circle of the father-daughter-centred relationship that dominates Volume One to enter into a more heteronormative marriage at the end of Volume Two or only replaced one selfishly enclosed solitude *à deux* with another? What are readers to make of the elusive Adam, American businessman in his first career, leisured art collector and amateur connoisseur in his second, whose vast fortune is the foundation on which all of these marriages and fates ultimately rest? To what extent are readers expected to assent to the resolutions of Volume Two as a morally just sorting out of everyone's proper rewards? Do readers identify with Charlotte and the Prince as representatives of a passionate human vitality instinctively pressing to loosen the golden shackles of money and marital morality that attach them to the reified roles of splendid spouses acquired to furnish out the wealthy world of the Ververs? Or, should readers deplore rather the scheming duplicity of Amerigo and Charlotte, their desire to have their rich cake and yet to eat it? Having knowingly entered into the marriage contracts that allow them the enormous comforts of the Ververs' wealth, don't they doubly compromise themselves when they violate those contracts freely entered? Should readers, therefore, sympathize with Maggie and Adam, who find themselves wronged yet nevertheless coolly and calmly correct their erring partners without loss to their dignity? Or, is the apparent high-mindedness of the Ververs in this regard only a higher form of humbugging? These sorts of questions have long animated critics of *The Golden Bowl*, but part of the pleasurable frustration of James's work is that it handles matters so delicately as to disable definitive answers to such inquiries. In a novel where card playing and the cool shrewdness it requires is a central trope, James manages his own cards with such dexterity that admirers of his novel are as likely to applaud that skill as to demand that everything be explained to them.[15]

We will return to these matters later, but it needs also to be said that part of *The Golden Bowl*'s accomplishment is the way in which it balances its chiaroscuro subtleties with the broad allegory of the international scene. If readers become too enmeshed in the finer points of the work's many technical or verbal subtleties, they tend to lose sight of the larger framing international allegory; but if, on the other hand, they attend only to that allegory, they risk seeing that at the expense of all else. Still, if one stands back a little from the intricacies of plot, psychology, tone and irony – as Maggie stands back from the household bridge game in the climactic scene on the terrace just before she confronts Charlotte – what is striking is how much of the contemporary political world James manages to accommodate in this novel. Like earlier works, *The Golden Bowl* is based on a marriage of convenience between American wealth and European breeding, an alliance rendered from the opening pages through the Prince's inner consciousness and which therefore launches the novel with a nearly giddy sense of finding all the wealth and ease of the world more or less at one's disposal. This rich sensation of wealth and power is nevertheless agitated by a nagging undertow of anxiety. What nags the happy Prince at the start of the novel is whether he, blessed with such astonishing fortune, has the ability to manage it successfully or whether this extraordinary affluence will inevitably beget its own laxities, corruptions and consequent undoing, thus visiting on London a fate that had once befallen Rome. Does he possess or is he possessed? Has he the status of an object, a commodity in a world of commodities, but the awareness of a subject?

This story of a merger between American money and European aristocracy implies the possibility of a perfect congruence and of a threatening calamity. Tocqueville and Arnold had asked whether a capitalist society, defined by wealth making, restless acquisitiveness and a republican-democratic polity committed to ideals of civic engagement and equality, could ever match the high form and cultivation of aristocratic society. It is clear that the European aristocracy in *The Golden Bowl* is an exhausted class whose day is already past and which must accommodate itself to the changed circumstances of a new era. Amerigo's family has had a long Italian history quite Gothic, luridly Jacobean even, in its colourfulness; but its present condition is defined by mortgaged properties and chronic indebtedness. In *The Persistence of the Old Regime*, Arno Mayer argues that even as it was overtaken in the nineteenth century by the industrial middle classes, the European aristocracy remained a vital force in several departments of European society – especially in higher politics, the military, diplomacy and the patronage of culture and the arts – until the losses incurred by World War I and increased post-war taxes on property and inheritance finally terminated it as a social force.[16] In *The Golden Bowl*, Amerigo knows himself from the start to be a '*morceau de musée*' (12) so impoverished as to be extremely lucky to be rescued as a collector's item by an American connoisseur of rarities. The challenge that confronts him, therefore, is how he will manage to adapt himself to this new world. Will he, as Fanny Assingham muses, steer his ship safely to port in the Golden Isles of the Verver fortune and be able, like his Vespucci forerunner, to successfully attach his old family name to the new continent? When he has made his self-reifying but still rather magnificent bargain with present realities, will the Prince be satisfied to merely act the consort's part to ornament a marriage or will he take on the more active responsibility of infusing some genuinely admirable old-world qualities into the new world onto which he is grafted?

Moreover, it is evident from the opening chapter that it is not only Europe's traditional ruling class that has almost literally reached its sell-by date, but that the European empires are now also past their meridian. In the first paragraph of the novel, we are told that the Prince 'had strayed simply enough into Bond Street' (5), and that he likes to saunter there because the thrill of empire may be felt in London far more intensely than in Rome, the latter city now become as much an archaic museum piece as the Prince himself. However, the westward course of empire and wealth that had once shifted the world's centre from Rome to London is now patently moving it on again to the United States where Europe's classical and imperial art treasures are already being shipped like pirates' loot to American City by Adam Verver. But Rome, once a great republic and then a great empire and finally only a corrupted prize for barbarian invaders, has always been a byword for hubris to its Western successors, a reminder that present republican virtue or imperial splendour may be mere preludes to imminent decline and fall.

The phrase 'the insolence of Empire' (5), sounded in the same paragraph that sees Amerigo stray distractedly into Bond Street, suggests the dangers that await a complacent contemporary Europe and its empires as well as its once-powerful, now-diminished aristocracies. Indeed, though the novel is set in London, none of the major characters in its inner circle, almost Racinian in its tightness, is English. In Lady Castledean, its most aristocratic English figure, the reader is offered a portrait of a grand lady compromised in a shabby affair with the much younger and common-sounding Mr. Blint. That unattractive couple act at first as a negative foil to the luminous Prince and Charlotte, but the contrast dims as the latter embark on their adultery at Matcham. Later, the high-sounding but low-acting English Lady Castledean will prove no match for virtuous American Maggie. Likewise, in the comically named Colonel Bob Assingham, the English figure who comes closest to the Roman American inner circle of the novel by way of his shrewder Jewish American wife, and whose first spoken words are 'I don't quite see, my dear' (49), we catch glimpses of a once-great British Empire already on its way to becoming useless and obtuse. Assingham sports moustaches 'worthy of Attila the Hun' (52), but he is nevertheless now a retired and slippered colonel and he is so spectrally gaunt that his clothes hang loosely on him. Though he retains something of 'the habit of tropic islands, a continual cane-bottomed chair, a governorship exercised on wide verandahs' (51), he is really only ever wholly at home with the world in his London club. Narratively speaking, Colonel Bob's main function in *The Golden Bowl* is to try to bring his bluff English common sense to bear on James's elaborately elusive plots. However, because he requires many of the obscurer things in the novel to be explained to him by his wife, Fanny, he serves as a useful aid to the struggling 'common reader' who also needs many things to be made intelligible if he or she is to catch up with what is going on. Thus, in a work so much about the intricacies of diplomacy and quickness of intellect and insight, of cognition, knowing and 'seeing', Colonel Bob's dimness is at once a narrative device and a damning judgement.[17] To need in James's world to have everything explained to one is a decided disability.

What we get in *The Golden Bowl*, then, is an England that is not yet quite become Hugh Kenner's 'sinking island' or even sinking empire – London is allowed some of its lissom evening grandeur – but that is nonetheless past its best, and the attentive reader can easily find intimations of its diminished future. At any rate it is evident that, the Prince possibly excepted, real wealth and active intelligence in the novel are almost wholly American. The Ververs, the very name suggests some mix of energy and *élan*, represent this American ascendancy as it comes near to its hour of world domination and the fundamental question with which the novel wrestles is how well the United States might meet that destiny and what challenges it must confront and what costs incur to do so.

However, as many critics have noticed, despite its centrality to the narrative and the various visits that some of the leading figures pay to the country, the United States as such remains largely an abstraction in *The Golden Bowl* and Adam Verver, the diminutive billionaire who epitomizes a titanic American ambition, is one of the most elusive riddles in the work.[18] An entrepreneur or financial speculator in his early career, there were times in his past when Adam had liked or 'had believed he liked transcendent calculation and imaginative gambling all for themselves, the creation of "interests" that were the extinction of other interests, the lived vulgarity of getting in, or getting out, first' (109). This sounds like vulture-fund speculation, but James does not offer his readers much with which to speculate about Adam's early life. Now, his toils over and fortune made, Verver has in any case put that ruthless ugliness behind him and can dedicate his second career to a new imperial mission. Unlike its British or French predecessors, Adam's mission is not to 'civilize' distant peoples of the earth, but to civilize his fellow Americans and to create of them almost a new race. The museum in American City, the apotheosis of Verver's mission, is described in prose at once so heightened and hypotactic that it is hard to know whether the stress should fall on the fineness or folly of this Adamic ambition:

> He had wrought by devious ways but he had reached the place, and what would ever have been straighter in any man's life than his way henceforth of occupying it? It hadn't merely, his plan, all the sanctions of civilisation; it was positively civilisation condensed, concrete, consummate, set down by his hands as a house on a rock – a house from whose open doors and windows, open to grateful, to thirsty millions, the higher, the highest knowledge would shine out to bless the land. In this house, designed as a gift primarily to the people of his adoptive city and native State, the urgency of whose release from the bondage of ugliness he was in a position to measure – in this museum of museums, a palace of art which was to show for compact as a Greek temple was compact, a receptacle of treasures sifted to positive sanctity, his spirit to-day almost altogether lived, making up, as he would have said, for lost time and haunting the portico in anticipation of the final rites.
>
> (109–110)

This 'museum of museums' is represented in a straitened, somewhat jagged purple prose that merges idioms of industrial and finance capital (forging and sweating, calculation, interests), Christianity (a house on a rock open to grateful and thirsty millions, treasures sifted to positive sanctity), Mosaic liberation (releasing the masses from the bondage of ugliness) and Hellenic aestheticism (a museum compact as a Greek temple). Indeed, in combination these idioms add up to some virtually new communion in its own right: when Adam contemplates his grand plan, he envisages 'a monument to the religion he wished to propagate, the exemplary passion, the passion for perfection at any price' (110). Needless to say, the subaltern class perspective of the thirsty millions condemned to 'the bondage of ugliness' whose plight the museum is to soften, does not actually appear anywhere because *The Golden Bowl* is restricted to the vantage point of the highest elites. The crude American crowds exist for it only as the intended beneficiaries of Adam's munificence. Art figures in Verver's mind not so much as the antithesis of the religion of capital as its complementary cultural correction and completion.

For all of James's sub-clausal scrupulosity and tonal sarcasms, the redemptive idea of art sketched here begins to look very like what will later come to be known as 'modernism' and remarkably like the religion of Americanism that emerged more or less concurrently. What binds the two is the idea that once the United States had surpassed every earlier civilization in wealth and might, it remained only for it to catch up culturally and intellectually, to match or surpass its antecedents also in social refinement and cultural sophistication, the very qualities that by common consensus nineteenth-century America singularly lacked. Only when it had put its fantastic wealth to work to cultivate itself could the United States leave behind the 'barbaric yawp' of its crude colonial settler capitalist adolescence to give a lead to the world in 'the higher, the highest knowledge' as in everything else. In short, to be a world power America needed not only to accumulate wealth, but also to educate itself into a more refined worldliness. Whatever *The Golden Bowl*'s hedging about the likely long-term success of this Ververian ambition, it seems clear that there can be no absolute distinction between James's own sense of mission and Adam's. After all, the novel is for James more or less what the museum is for Adam: an international bridge to connect new civilizations and old, the looser artefact of a democratic age with ambitions to preserve the best the aristocratic epochs had had to offer, a civilizing vehicle of education, cultivation and discrimination quickened by 'the passion for perfection'. All this might appear at odds with the capitalist laws of the marketplace that are content to set their store by profit and loss and are burdened by no such lofty ambitions for universal cultivation. However, the animating passion at the heart of both Verver's and James's grand designs is that a surplus of wealth might yet create a new elite with sufficient cosmopolitan sensibility and sophistication of intellect and *savoir faire* as to be able to save American capitalism from its own grosser tendencies.

Still, while there is no absolute distinction between Verver's and James's ambitions to cultivate publics in need of cultivation, neither do they exactly coincide. Verver may be a cosmopolitan and Europeanized American abroad, but he is devoted to a fixed purpose, to send his art treasures home to help cultivate the United States. He is, therefore, included within his creator's wider literary ambition to cultivate both American and European reading publics but he is ironized by his assumption that the civic or elevating value of these activities is self-evident. In contrast, *The Golden Bowl* keeps matters of reification, commodification, of iron and gilded cages, too vigilantly before the reader to warrant any such easy assumption about the compatibility of great wealth, refined sensibility and mass cultivation. Indeed, in all of those critical scenes in which the golden bowl appears – when Amerigo and Charlotte first inspect it in the Bloomsbury antique shop, when the Jewish vendor returns to Portland Place to confess to Maggie the flaw in the crystal, when Fanny Assingham dashes it to pieces on Maggie's hard but polished floor, when Maggie handles the broken pieces before Amerigo – the whole stress falls on the imperfection of the eponymous artefact. This gilded-over flaw refers, as already mentioned, to Maggie's marriage and to the ampler illusion of the exquisitely arranged familial relations she had initially relished. Beyond that again, it bespeaks the difficulty, even the impossibility, of binding together the wider transatlantic civilizations, the crystal and the gold, or the radical speciousness of the ambition to do so. One of the things that the blemished bowl reveals to Maggie is that she has been complacently trapped in the beautiful delusion of a perfection already attained when that elusive perfection still needed to be harder won.

To the reader, what this suggests is that there are cracks in everything, including even *The Golden Bowl*. The novel itself is divided or cracked into two volumes, each one monopolized by a spousal consciousness, neither in perfect accord with the other (unless perhaps at the very end, maybe not even then). Perfection (whatever that may be), this implies, has actively to be created and may even then always remain a beautiful fiction, an ideal with a sense of public obligation attached, or a sense of mission that takes the form of an ideal. Adam Verver's conviction that capitalism may be rescued from its own aboriginal ugliness and restlessness by the aesthetic cultivation that wealth can support is peculiarly his. However, this is only one of the novel's thematics. The marriage of Old and New Worlds, European aristocracies of blood and American aristocracies of industry, passions for wealth and aesthetic accumulation, and perfections of form and substance are not to be had as readily as Adam Verver imagines. Nonetheless, the desire for such marriages, such convergences, is both imperative and potentially destructive, and Maggie has to absorb this duality and survive. If the Verver 'passion for perfection at any price' and the ambition this underwrites is to be rescued, only Maggie, and not her father, can do it. And to acknowledge the cracks, not miss or gild them over, is the necessary first step in her undertaking. 'It will be *she* who'll see us through. In fact, she'll have to. And she'll be able' (208, italics in original), declaims Fanny Assingham, who on this occasion at least gets things right.

It is widely agreed that what distinguishes Maggie, even in the throes of her mortification and abjections, is the remarkable self-composure and 'heroic lucidity' (460) that she maintains and that enables her to steer through the wretched imbroglios in which she finds herself immersed. Confronted with the svelte and solicitous treacheries of her husband and Charlotte, with Fanny Assingham's partial complicities in their deception of her, and with her father's apparent innocence to the attendant dangers, Maggie restrains a spontaneous urge to express her outrage. Instead, heroically containing her anguish, she bides her time until she can weigh the situation fully. Furthermore, despite the felt sting of the injustices done to her, she acknowledges to herself that she has been at least a passive accomplice to the adultery by failing to see how she had neglected her husband to retain her accustomed intimacy with Adam. She concedes, further, that she had counted too unthinkingly on the happiness of Charlotte's marriage to her father because that arrangement had so well suited her own needs. Finally, Maggie, even when most abject, realizes the value of what she already has, however flawed, and decides not to surrender the blemished goods for the dubious and transient gratifications that outrage would yield.

To give vent to what she feels, Maggie decides, would be to unleash a salacious public scandal and bring the world of Eaton Square, Fawns and Portland Place down in ruin. This triumph of the will over the instinctive desire to lash out emerges from a titanic inner struggle. While she watches all those closest to her companionably play bridge together, Maggie thinks how easily she could, so to speak, bring down the whole house of cards on this splendid scene of apparent innocence and ease: 'it was a scene she might people, by the press of her spring, either with serenities and dignities and decencies, or with terrors and shames and ruins, things as ugly as those formless fragments of her golden bowl she was trying so hard to pick up' (476). Above all else, what this climactic scene at Fawns stresses is how the disciplining of one's own passions and the sure knowledge of one's own interests are essential prerequisites to the skilful rule of others. As she steels herself mentally for the long-anticipated confrontation with Charlotte, Maggie has first to wrestle terrifically with herself before she can do so with her rival:

She continued to walk and continued to pause; she stopped afresh for the look into the smoking-room, and by this time – it was as if the recognition had of itself arrested her – she saw as in a picture, with the temptation she had fled from quite extinct, why it was she had been able to give herself from the first so little to the vulgar heat of her wrong. She might fairly, as she watched them, have missed it as a lost thing; have yearned for it, for the straight vindictive view, the rights of resentment, the rages of jealousy, the protests of passion, as for something she had been cheated of not least: a range of feelings which for many women would have meant so much, but which for *her* husband's wife, her father's daughter, figured nothing nearer to experience than a wild eastern caravan, looming into view with crude colours in the sun, fierce pipes in the air, high spears against the sky, all a thrill, a natural joy to mingle with, but turning off short before it reached her and plunging into other defiles.

(476–477, italics in the original)

In this much-cited passage, Maggie feels the surges of her entitlement to 'the straight vindictive view, the rights of resentment, the rages of jealousy, the protests of passion', but she nevertheless always takes the higher view both of herself and of those whose fates are now at her disposal. She reminds herself that 'for *her* husband's wife, her father's daughter' to openly indulge her keen sense of 'innocence outraged and generosity betrayed' (477) would be disastrous because to do so would be to succumb to chaotic passions figuratively associated here with a wildly Oriental, Dionysian barbarism. The 'wild eastern caravan' is one in a thick seam of Asiatic (mainly Chinese) references; it recalls some of the purpler passages in Nietzsche's *The Birth of Tragedy* (1872) and anticipates their echoes in Thomas Mann's *Death in Venice* (1912). Although the passage offers only a loose version of the Nietzschean combat, Maggie, who is no unimperilled Apollonian, can be read as exercising a rational will that saves her from the fatal Dionysian impulses to which Mann's Aschenbach and so many later modernist protagonists succumb.[19] Is it her aristocratic or republican *pietas*, her sense of being wife to *this* husband, daughter to *this* father – the spouse now takes precedence in the passage cited above – or some achieved combination of the two that allows Maggie to steel her dignity and steady her virtue to vanquish Charlotte by refusing to be goaded into open conflict and by giving away absolutely nothing that she does not want to impart? Amerigo is a Roman aristocrat with, as we know from the opening paragraph, a relish for the sense of '*Imperium*'(5), but he lacks Maggie's American and therefore probably more republican-minded self-discipline and active virtue. Certainly, by the end of the novel it is clear that it is Maggie, not he, who governs their future.

In the later stages of the novel, once she has awakened to the reality of her situation, Maggie comes to realize that the beauty of social 'forms' is likely to seduce only to deceive, unless that beauty becomes active in positive deeds. Amerigo is all stereotypical graceful social charm, sincerely attentive to everyone else's ease as well as his own, but his essential passivity is always perfectly clear. He has an attractively easy grace, but he is all ease without active energy. We see this at Matcham, where it falls to Charlotte to study the train schedules that will take the lovers to Gloucester Cathedral and from there to the consummation of their affair; her practical genius for arrangement on this occasion is attributed to her 'Anglo-Saxon blood' (269). And Amerigo's mute passivity and proper sense of dignity, his willingness not to confide Maggie's discovery of their secret to Charlotte, are again all that are called for when Maggie undertakes the work of re-establishing their marriage. Maggie makes the journey in the novel from an indulged passivity to a reawakened activity. Amerigo does not; he falls more deeply into his racially conceived role. The Ververs, unlike Amerigo, come eventually to suspect that the remarkable ease and social passivity of their lives might be its own undoing. At one point Adam asks Maggie:

> There seems a kind of charm, doesn't there? on our life – and quite as if just lately it had got itself somehow renewed, had waked up refreshed. A kind of wicked selfish prosperity perhaps, as if we had grabbed everything, fixed everything, down to the last lovely object for the last glass case of the last corner, left over, of my old show. That's the only take-off, that it has made us perhaps lazy, a wee bit languid – lying like gods together, all careless of mankind.
>
> (368)

After she has discovered her husband's affair Maggie can no longer afford to be so languidly superior. She has to exert exceptional powers of emotional forbearance, active powers of observation or surveillance, and knowledge of herself and others to save her own marriage and her father's. What this means, among other things, is that to escape the dangers that surround her, to re-establish things once more, she has to sustain the gracefully established old social forms even as she quietly but busily goes about rearranging things on an entirely new footing. To accomplish this, she first has to quell her own 'rights of resentment' and 'rage of jealousy', second, to pretend to perfectly unperturbed ease and happiness in her marriage so that her father will not inquire too deeply into it and so that Charlotte will remain confounded by not knowing how all this has been managed or why Amerigo has recommitted to Maggie. Last, it becomes clear to her that Charlotte and Adam must be sent to the United States so that old temptations cannot possibly be renewed. What all of this requires from Maggie, in sum, is a kind of extraordinarily suave and canny capacity for tactful or even manipulative manoeuvres such that, while all the time seeming merely to preserve the usual order of things, she actually reconstructs that order more firmly than before, though now on revised terms, her terms.[20]

An appealing analogy between the salvaging of Maggie's marriage and the working out of James's 'international theme' is to be found in Giovanni Arrighi 's *The Long Twentieth Century*. There, Arrighi contends that a would-be superpower can only restore a shattered world system by providing the singularity of will and leadership as well as the tremendous resources of wealth and force necessary to found that system anew in ways amenable first of all to itself but also in a manner that is plastic enough to serve other contending parties in the system, at least sufficiently so to secure their consent. After World War I, Arrighi argues, there was a struggle for governance of the world system between the *conservative* forces of the British and French, who wanted to return as much as possible to the pre-World War I imperial order of things, the Soviets, pressuring for a *revolutionary* remaking of the system, and the United States, which wanted to *reform* the system, meaning neither simply to rehabilitate the old order as it was nor to revolutionize its structures entirely.[21] Transposed to this analysis, Maggie's mission is clearly essentially reformist. The Ververs may fret that the charm and privilege of their lives are secured by a 'wicked, selfish prosperity', but Maggie's whole bent in the final stages of the novel is to rearrange things so that that charmed life will be as little discomfited as possible or only as much as is absolutely required to preserve it from further threat. All her powers of knowledge, ingenuity and diplomatic skill are devoted to reform, not radical change: her triumph will be to keep the forms of marriage, to preserve the proprieties of wifely decorum, to maintain Amerigo's dignity, to circumvent any ruinous prospect of chaos or public scandal. This cannot be had without exacting its price – the removal of Adam and Charlotte to American City – but in the end hers is a triumph of rearrangement and restoration, nothing more radical. Indeed, the motto of *The Golden Bowl* might well be that of another famous reformist, Giuseppe di Lampedusa's Tancredi in *The Leopard* when he pronounces that: 'If we want things to stay as they are, things will have to change'.[22]

This analogy between restored marriage and reformed international order is strengthened in the light of that scene at the start of Book Fifth, in which Maggie, conscious that she must now rely only on her own resources to manage everything, decides that she cannot lean any further for support even on Fanny Assingham, 'this good friend's presence having been doomed to become, with that climax of their last interview in Portland Place, a severely simplified function' (456). In the early parts of the novel, Fanny, as matchmaker, had played a considerable supervisory role in the diplomacies that brought about the marriage of Amerigo and Maggie, then that of Charlotte and Adam. It was to Fanny, too, that Maggie had turned to confide her first suspicions of the troubles in her marriage and to her that she had disclosed her certainty that those suspicions were confirmed. Now, though, all Maggie wants from Fanny is for her to keep up appearances, to maintain 'their general sign of unimpaired beatitude' (456) with whatever effort this requires. Maggie wonders if Fanny really has the fortitude for this, but when Fanny arrives at Fawns for an evening's company Maggie finds herself reassured by the latter's ability to carry things off:

> She treated her young friend meanwhile, it was to be said, to no betrayal of such wavering; so that from the moment of her alighting at the door with the Colonel everything went on between them at concert pitch. What had she done that last evening in Maggie's room but bring the husband and wife more together than, as would seem, they had ever been? Therefore what indiscretion shouldn't she show by attempting to go behind the grand appearance of her success? – which would be to court a doubt of her beneficent work. She knew accordingly nothing but harmony, she diffused restlessly nothing but peace – an extravagant expressive aggressive peace, not incongruous after all with the solid calm of the place; a kind of helmeted trident-shaking *pax Britannica*.
>
> (456, italics in the original)

This is a knotty passage to parse because the free indirect discourse and slippery pronoun references make it hard to tell when 'she' refers to Fanny or to Maggie. What we can say, though, is that the passage expresses Maggie's, not Fanny's, interior consciousness and mental strivings. Having reassured herself that Fanny has the ability to act up her part and not give herself away by indiscretions, Maggie relaxes a little and decides that 'she', meaning Fanny or herself or both, 'knew accordingly nothing but harmony'. Strikingly, this harmony is imaged in remarkable terms as 'an extravagant expressive aggressive peace' monitored by 'a kind of helmeted trident-shaking *pax Britannica*'. That adjectivally enjambed triad, 'extravagant expressive aggressive', that prefaces 'peace' captures exactly that combination of Machiavellian diplomacy and steely determination to keep Charlotte and the Prince locked in their separate cages of ignorance that

Maggie displays so consistently as she moves towards final triumph. The 'peace' she wins at the end is secured above all by her strength and resolution, and if the passage calls up an image of a feminine 'helmeted trident-shaking *pax Britannica*' this is precisely because the pacific- and feminine-looking Britannia always comes spiked with martial helmet and trident, her matronly benevolence braced by military might. But Fanny and Maggie are both Americans, not Britons, and the victory envisaged at the end of *The Golden Bowl* is not the repair of some cracked Great Britain but something that portends a new and wider-reaching *pax Americana*.

Critics interested in the allegory of 'the international scene' in *The Golden Bowl* debate whether James's loyalties lean more towards the European or the US side of the Atlantic.[23] The fact that Prince, Princess and Principino remain in London whereas childless Adam Verver and Charlotte are sent off to American City, a fate that has the appearance of a sentence of doom, tends to tip matters towards those who believe that James's Europhile, aristocratic preferences outweigh his American repub- lican allegiances. Maybe, maybe not. The more significant point, it seems to me, is not where exactly the balance of James's sympathies lie, but rather that *The Golden Bowl* is above all committed to the idea that what is nowadays called 'hard power' is always best kept subordinate, where possible, to 'soft power', that domination is never more firmly secured than when leavened into a hegemony. For Conrad's *Nostromo*, the figure of an unapologetic American international ascendancy is Holroyd, an unap- pealingly puritanical male and a bombastically evangelical banker. In the case of *The Golden Bowl*, however, the ultimate victory goes to the 'timid tigress' (308), Maggie, who wants above all to sustain her marriage to the Roman Prince but who never ceases to cooperate dutifully with her father, entrepreneur, aesthete, art collector, connoisseur, museum builder. Historically speaking, the end of the nineteenth century and the beginning of the twentieth was indeed a great age of American art collecting and museum and gallery construction as well as the era in which the United States first flexed its international imperial muscle.[24] As it went on to become a new world power and eventually the guarantor of the capitalist world system, the United States' capacity to be both a great cultural powerhouse as well as military-industrial titan would be essential to its global self-assertion. The fact that Maggie's stays on one side of the Atlantic, therefore, and integrates into her marriage the finer aristocratic and American virtues, and that Adam and Charlotte are transferred to American City, there to redeem the ugliness of capitalism by the elevating graces of art, may not require any choosing of sides. Taken together, the couples suggest an ambitious vision of some new transatlantic elite with the will to reconstruct things in Europe and America by knowing how to blend the 'feminine' soft strengths of diplomacy, the arts, high culture and easeful living, with the more 'masculine' activities of money and militarism.

## III

'These fragments I have shored against my ruin'.[25] In *The Golden Bowl* the cracks that mar the would-be wedding gift are nearly imperceptible, tiny slivers visible initially neither to Charlotte nor Maggie but only to the Prince's finer connoisseurial eye. Indeed, even after the bowl has been shattered and the fragments laid before Amerigo, Maggie can still muse that '[t]he split determined by the latent crack was so sharp and so neat that if there had been anything to hold them the bowl might still quite beautifully, a few steps away, have passed for uninjured' (435). Ultimately, though, there is nothing to hold the bowl together except for 'Maggie's hands' (435) and ingenuity. And it is never clear, even at the end, if the golden bowl – 'as it *was* to have been', '[t]he bowl without the crack' (462, italics in the original) – might ever again become whole or whether flaws must be acknowledged as the ordained nature of things, something needing to be recognized, mended and mastered.

In T. S. Eliot's *The Waste Land*, cracks come before the reader quite differently: now, not as scarcely noticeable hairline flaws concealed behind some outwardly beautiful order of things but rather as part of an already thoroughly fissured world for which ruins, shards, wreckage, heaps of broken images are the only given. For James, the task of re-totalization is strenuous, requiring determined decision, purposeful vigilance, composed intelligence, discipline and tact. For Eliot, the cracks have become so all-pervasive, the task of reconstitution so arduous, the odds against reintegration apparently so daunting, that any real hope for totalization seems chimerical, and the labour required so enormous as to inspire only a sense of fatigue and futility. In *The Golden Bowl*, once Maggie discovers the flaw in her marriage and order of things, she must decide if she wishes to repair her marriage, and once her decision is made it is steelily pursued, though in James that 'decision' and its ramifications are couched in terms so subtle as to make them almost imperceptible. In *The Waste Land*, on the other hand, we are in a world beyond finer things – a world of lust rather than marriage, of superstition rather than religion, of literature reduced to litter, of coldness instead of feeling. This world is also beyond the kind of moral decision crucial to James's fiction. Or, rather, decision survives in Eliot's poetry only as a kind of dithering questioning without resolution: 'What shall we do tomorrow? What shall we ever do?' 'What should I resent?', 'what have we given?', 'Shall I at least set my lands in order?' (41, 46, 49, 50) Jamesian scrupulosity of manner and style suggests a world where everything depends on fine discrimination and careful decision; Eliotic self-interrogation implies ethical choice dithered to neurotic indecision and chronic vacillation.

The obvious explanation for this difference would appear to be historical. James completes his career before the great European landslide; Eliot's gets properly underway afterwards. *The Golden Bowl* was published in 1904 and may be read as an early anticipation of incipient European imperial decline. *The Waste Land* was composed shortly after World War I when Europe's descent into chaos was already an accomplished fact. That unexpected catastrophe's ramifying consequences in death tolls, epidemics, starving populations, mourning families, collapsed states, revolutions and unrest were everywhere evident. Between 1914 and 1918, the forces of disorder, occasionally to be glimpsed through the thickets of baroque syntax in James's later works yet always narratively contained by his formal fastidiousness, had been unloosed. Eliot and 'the men of 1914', therefore, inherited a civilizational mess almost unimaginable to those whose careers were made before the great catastrophe. Like *The Golden Bowl*, *The Waste Land* has been interpreted in recent decades in the light of the cultural politics of colonialism and empire. Many of these readings are illuminating, some powerful, but it seems fair to say that the stress generally has fallen heavily on decline: *The Waste Land* is read, that is, as a culminating achievement in a longer history of French and English decadent poetics or as one of the many masterpieces of the period prognosticating apocalypse now. Read thus, critics add the decline of Europe and the fall of empire to the more familiar list of overlapping crises – sexual and marital, religious, philosophical – long acknowledged to have personally afflicted Eliot and to have nurtured his poetry and criticism in this period.[26]

There is much to be said for this way of reading Eliot. However, I want to suggest that to stress the sense of breakdown and desolation in *The Waste Land* at the expense of that work's reconstructive will to salvage and shore up what is broken misses much about how the poem works as form and about its larger place in the history of empire and Euro-American relations. To say that the decade after 1918 was one of intense crisis for Europe generally and for Eliot particularly is to repeat a well-established fact. World War I ended with the signing of the German Armistice on the eleventh hour of the eleventh day of the eleventh month in 1918. However, the collapse of the Austro-Hungarian Empire (Hungary became an independent Republic five days after the Armistice), the consolidation of the Bolshevik Revolution in Russia, and the entry of the United States into the war in 1917, together with Woodrow Wilson's commitment to the rights of nations to self-determination, changed the landscape and terms of international politics forever. In December 1918, the Sinn Féin party won a landslide victory in national elections in Ireland, rendering the more moderate devolutionary Home Rule party obsolete, and this set the United Kingdom on course for three further years of internal warfare that would lead in 1921 to the first territorial shrinkage of Great Britain since the Tudor era. In 1918–1920, a global flu pandemic infected somewhere in the region of 500 million people around the world and resulted in 50 to 100 million deaths. For Eliot, too, these were years of regular crisis – his father, Henry, died in January 1919; marriage and health problems intensified; 'He Do the Police in Different Voices' remained 'a sprawling chaotic poem';[27] in 1921 an exhausted, overworked Eliot famously had to take leave from Lloyd's Bank to recover his health at Margate and Lausanne.

Nevertheless, as some Eliot scholars have pointed out, their general grimness notwithstanding, the years between 1918 and 1922 when *The Waste Land* was finally published were also ones of exceptional if incremental achievement for Eliot. When he took up his position with Lloyd's Bank in 1917, Eliot's home letters record an upsurge of energy and purpose due to the new work and better pay. Later, when Woodrow Wilson visited London in late December 1918, Eliot and his wife went to see the first American president to visit England pass in procession to Buckingham Palace and Eliot wrote enthusiastically to his mother of the 'streets all hung with American flags' and commented: 'It was really an extraordinary and inspiring occasion. I do not believe that people in America realise how much Wilson's policy has done to inspire respect for America abroad. I think that *all* the nations, allied, hostile, and neutral, *trust* us as they trust no other'. About current British politics, described as 'in complete chaos at present', Eliot declared himself pessimistic, but he still looked forward 'to see the satisfaction of the peace negotiations along Wilson lines'.[28] Eliot's work in the Colonial and Foreign Office of Lloyd's brought him something of an insider's insight into the Parisian peace negotiations, and this eventually caused him to conclude that Clemenceau had outmanoeuvred all other leaders and that 'Wilson went down utterly before European diplomacy' and had 'made a grave mistake in coming to Europe' ('Letter to his Mother', 2 October 1919, 336–337, 337). Taking his cues perhaps from John Maynard Keynes's *The Economic Consequences of the Peace*, which famously described Versailles as 'a Carthaginian peace', Eliot had decided by then that the European settlement was 'a bad peace, in which the major European powers tried to get as much as they could, and appease or ingratiate as far as possible the various puppet nationalities which they have constituted and will try to dominate' (337).

However, even as Eliot's political hopes rose or fell back, his career edged forward. In 1917, he became associate editor of *The Egoist* and *Prufrock and Other Observations* appeared that year with *The Egoist*. In the same year he wrote an essay on 'Turgenev' for *The Egoist*, noting of the Russian that: 'Turgenev was, in fact, a perfect example of the benefits of transplantation; there was nothing lost by it; he understood at once how to take Paris, how to make use of it. A position which for a smaller man may be merely a compromise, or a means of disappearance, was for Turgenev (who knew how to maintain the rôle of foreigner with integrity) a source of authority, in addressing either Russian or European, authority but also isolation'.[29] The applicability of these remarks to Eliot's sense of his own position in England and 'how to take' London needs little stressing. In 1919, he published *Ara Vos Prec* with Ovid Press and *The Egoist* published 'Gerontion' and 'Tradition and the Individual Talent', and the Hogarth Press published *Poems*. In 1920, Eliot published *The Sacred Wood*, his first essay collection, and *Poems* with Knopf in the United States.

Thus, by March 1919, Eliot's letters to his mother record an increasingly assured sense of satisfaction with his advancing role in English letters: 'There is a small and select public which regards me as the best living critic, as well as the best living poet, in England'. His role as reviewer, he adds, enhances his authority and 'I can have more than enough power to satisfy me'. He concludes: 'I really think that I have far more *influence* on English letters than any other American has ever had, unless it be Henry James' ('Letter to his Mother', 29 March 1919, 279–281, 280, italics in the original). All this 'sounds very conceited' (280), Eliot concedes, but in the following month he wrote to his Harvard professor, J. H. Woods, remarking: 'As to America: I am a much more important person here than I should be at home. I am getting to know and be known by all the intelligent or important people in letters, and I am convinced that I am more useful in the long run by being here' ('Letter to J. H. Woods', 21 April 1919, 284–286, 285). To whom exactly he was 'more useful' in London Eliot does not explain, but the correspondence, as well as his comments on Turgenev's bilateral authority in both Europe and Russia, hints at national as well as personal literary achievement and ambition. Wilson might have proved no match for the Europeans in Versailles, but, his multiple crises notwithstanding, this particular overseas American was being outmanoeuvred by no one in London.

On a personal level, Eliot's decision to remain in London and abandon a Harvard academic for a poetic career had been a bitter disappointment to his father, and the son's anxious stress on his achievements is sometimes accounted for in this oedipal light. However, the other Henry that recurs frequently in the letters of these years is Henry James, and with this paternal literary predecessor Eliot is also in this period clearly keeping accounts.[30] In 'On Henry James', a witty essay published in the *Little Review* in August 1918, Eliot complained that James's importance had 'been overlooked on both sides of the Atlantic' and paid warm tribute to his countryman. 'It is the final perfection, the consummation of an American to become', he quipped, 'not an Englishman, but a European – something which no born European, no person of any European nationality, can become'.[31] James's international novels, Eliot continued, had cast a caustic eye on the 'vices and absurdities' (112) of his countrymen, something that to many Americans seemed scandalous, yet had British readers been able to read James better they would have found themselves depicted no less severely. 'Henry James's death', Eliot remarks archly, 'if it had been more taken note of, should have given considerable relief "on both sides of the Atlantic", and cemented the Anglo-American entente' (112).

I have been stressing the twin elements of acute crisis and increasingly confident ambition in Eliot's career leading up to 1922 because each seems essential to *The Waste Land* and to the wider historical moment into which the poem so successfully tapped. The sense of European disintegration that followed World War I was patently devastating, but this breakdown provoked in turn ambitious reconstructive attempts to re-establish the international world system, to reconstitute the British Empire and, in the case of the United Kingdom, to cauterize the disintegrative consequences of the Anglo-Irish War of 1918–1921. The Paris Peace Conference and the Versailles Treaty of June 1919, the establishment of the League of Nations in January 1920, the Locarno Treaties of 1925, the Anglo-Irish Treaty of 1921, in which the term 'the British Commonwealth of Nations' replaced for the first time the term 'the British Empire' in the controversial Oath of Allegiance to the British Crown and the 1926 Imperial Conference, which first established the British Commonwealth of Nations, are just some of the landmark attempts to remake the world system after the international order held together by the *pax Britannica* had vanished. Further, in Eliot's sally in 'On Henry James' that it was the ultimate consummation of an American to become not English but a European, something that no European-born national could do, because to be rooted in any one nation was to be too local and limited to see things whole, there is the imputation, however tongue-in-cheek, that European letters too need to be taken into charge and that Americans might be best placed to do this. The whole point of Eliot's James essay, in short, is that both British and American societies have their inherent debilities and parochialisms – these chastened in James's fiction – and that only a *'metoikos'* (a resident alien) like James, or like Eliot himself, could ever hope to be sufficiently citizens of the world to see matters whole again.

When he became editor of *The Criterion*, the first issue of which appeared in London in October 1922, and carried in its pages *The Waste Land*, itself famously a work scissored by Ezra Pound from the mess of 'He Do the Police in Different Voices', Eliot had finally attained both the vehicle and cultural authority to promulgate his vision. Published with European contributions translated into English in London and managed by an American expatriate editor, *The Criterion* was self-consciously international in scope and reconstructive in vision. Europe had plunged itself into a disastrously disintegrative war of nations; *The Criterion*'s mission was to re-connect Europe's 'men of letters' through a new comity of literary and intellectual exchange, and in so doing to re-found the 'republic of letters' that the war and post-war bitterness threatened to wreck. As Jason Harding remarks, Eliot's new journal from the start sought close links with cosmopolitan European periodicals such as *Nouvelle Revue française* and with like-minded European intellectuals, most notably Ernst Robert Curtius and Hugo von Hofmannsthal, the latter credited with popularizing the term 'conservative revolution' in 1927, a phrase that captures *The Criterion*'s tendencies generally between 1922 and 1939.[32] Brought up in the south of the United States in the era just after American Reconstruction, Eliot could now hope, the success of *The Waste Land* to hand, to reconstruct English and European letters by stimulating, as he retrospectively put it, 'that circulation of influence of thought and sensibility between nation and nation in Europe, which fertilises and renovates from abroad the literature of each one of them' and by bringing 'into public view those works of literature which are not only of local, but of European significance'.[33]

Set in this wider socio-historical context, it is striking how finely *The Waste Land* is pitched between its disintegrative and reintegrative tendencies. On the one hand, an insistence everywhere in that work, already familiar from Eliot's earlier poetry, on desiccation, drought, desolation and the death drive, registering a shrivelled world trapped as much in timorousness as sordidness; on the other hand, an inarticulate yearning or tremulous groping for some form of renewal that might lead beyond modernity's mess and morbidity. Compositionally speaking, *The Waste Land*'s form suggests a magpie makeshiftness and a rickety provisionality and yet at the same time its five-section structure, embellished by Greek epigraph and distinguished by Roman numerals, is indicative of a classical, or at least distressed-classical, tact. At some level, this form seems slackly open-ended. After all, mightn't Pound have made further cuttings or saved some lines from the earlier drafts without damage to the music or meaning of the whole? Would inserting another well-curated line or passage from another dead poet alter anything much one way or another? And yet this plasticity may equally represent a cardinal virtue, sign of an elastic totality that does not repress or coerce its particulars but confers on them, rather, an unusual element of play or autonomy. If this is a work expressive of a broken civilization with scarcely enough will left even to contemplate renewal, then its morbidity is nevertheless strangely musical – so many styles, poetic metres and rhythms, and lines in several languages, are gathered in from across so many centuries and civilizations to fugue into what is acoustically at least more a baroque than a classical requiem. Beginning with the spent Sibyl's exhausted '*apothanein thelo*' ('I would like to die') (37) in the opening epigraph, concluding with 'Shantih, shantih, shantih', translated for us in the notes as 'The Peace which passeth understanding' (50, 55), *The Waste Land*'s general trajectory might suggest some onerous but not wholly unfruitful working through of crisis. Or, it might do so were it not for the fact that the particularly polyvocal, opaque and fragmented last stanza checks any confidently consolatory conclusion and sustains the work's oscillatory swings between hopeless regression and possible renewal to the last.

Given their common concern with issues of fragmentation and reintegration, it will be instructive to set *The Golden Bowl* and *The Waste Land* alongside each other to see what this discloses. In James's fiction, 'the international theme' is typically focused on the relationship between American wealth and cultural aspiration on one side and English or European aristocracy and cultural inheritance on the other. The 'theme' is never exclusively fixed on Euro-American national connections; more complex equations, fertile to permutation, between money, leisure, culture, sensibility and morality, are also always involved. Generally, the Jamesian

world is outwardly refined, cultured and humane, its surreptitious vicious-
ness brought only gradually and discreetly into play. In Eliot's case,
however, scenarios of this kind typically appear rather in grotesque caricature. As Eric Sigg has noted, Eliot's early poetry, like much late nineteenth-
century American aestheticism, habitually pits two Americas against each
other: 'an older, "politer" American confronted a younger, "cruder" one,
with all of the attendant religious, ethnic, occupational, and value-oriented
conflicts. To be placed in either camp entailed consequences harmful to
national (and personal) coherence: history constrains and enfeebles one
group, while the other, having rejected gentility and history alike, explodes
in a raw, highly suspect energy'.[34] This force field gives us crude Apeneck
Sweeney versus effete Prufrock, prissy Aunt Helen versus her forward
footman, the swampy hippopotamus versus the True Church, or what
Sigg calls '[a]rtless life and lifeless art', each vacuous (123). Transposed
onto Europe, the same aesthetic gives us Eliot's 'Burbank with a Baedeker:
Bleistein with a Cigar' or Burbank, representing masculine Chicagoan
wealth, and Princess Volupine, prostituted European aristocratic feminin-
ity – the Jamesian transatlantic encounter reduced by Eliot to Hogarthian
cartoon. Here, capital too is entirely corrosive, its grossness accentuated by
anti-Semitic inference, but culture is no more reassuring, Canaletto's fine
Venetian views regarded now by '[a] lusterless protrusive eye' that '[s]tares
from the protozoic slime'.[35] In *The Waste Land*, too, memories of aristocracy flit across the poem. They appear in the opening stanza in the voice of
Maria and her central European childhood memories of the archduke, her
cousin; in the figures of Cleopatra and Ophelia and their hysterical modern
counterpart, the upper-class lady (reminiscent of his 1915 poem 'Portrait of
a Lady') in 'A Game of Chess'. Later, they recur in the Elizabeth and
Leicester passages of 'The Fire Sermon' or the allusions to the overthrow of
the Winter Palace ('Prison and palace and reverberation') at the beginning
of 'What the Thunder Said' or to 'a broken Coriolanus' towards that
section's end (47, 49). Nevertheless, what we get in *The Waste Land* –
whether in their classical, Renaissance, or modern European iterations – are
faded ghosts of aristocracy, not the thing itself, and the emphasis, as in the
legend of the Fisher King, is on impotence and neurosis, nothing
redemptive.

   Like European aristocracy, the other half of the Jamesian equation,
American affluence and cultural hunger or culture-vulturing, has also
receded, at least overtly, in Eliot. We know that the facsimile version,
'He Do the Police in Different Voices', opens in a blowsy American voice
recounting a drunken night in Boston, taking readers slumming into a

louche lower world familiar from 'Sweeney Erect' and 'Sweeney Among the Nightingales'. However, Pound, not without reason, excised this lumpy American opening, confining *The Waste Land* to one city, and Eliot himself eliminated his initial title for Section Two, 'In the Cage', with its references to James's novella of that name and also to *The Golden Bowl*, and replaced it with the Middletonian 'A Game of Chess'. These changes further occluded American reference and thickened the Renaissance English layerings, pushing the poem generally further back in time.[36] The long Dry Salvages sailing scenes that front 'Death by Water' in the facsimile original fell also to Pound's cutting-room floor, leaving only the eleven-line 'Phlebas the Phoenician' section we now have. Yet, though fiercely pruned, the United States' presence is not wholly excised. It still resonates in the muffled allusions to Whitman, in Eliot's jazzy rhythms and capricious syncopations, in 'the dark rankling of passions inhibited' by the 'fear of life' and 'fear of vulgarity' that Edmund Wilson felt to be what Eliot shared most conspicuously with Henry James and the American tradition running back to Hawthorne.[37] Perhaps America remains visible most of all in Eliot in the lust for cultural collecting and agglomeration; this is as evident in *The Waste Land*'s teeming allusions to other works as in Adam Verver's piratical mania for art acquisition.

In the end, then, *The Waste Land* leaves us with only hallucinatory after-images of a mainly feminized – plaintive and helpless – European aristocracy and with a United States that has been scraped from the poem's canvas or painted over and remains on in the work only subcutaneously, available more to the intelligent ear than to the protrusive eye. 'Burbank with a Baedeker: Bleistein with a Cigar' may offer us what one critic has called 'a sort of Henry James novel in miniature',[38] but in *The Waste Land* there is no obvious transatlantic allegory and the Jamesian impetus to stage transcontinental encounter or integration as fine moral drama has no place. In a world without even the appearance of grandeur, where scenes ancient and modern counterpoint each other to neither's advantage, where everything has been reduced to rubble, ambitions to connect, integrate or re-totalize must be differently pursued.

A second, even more telling difference is that *The Waste Land* provides its readers with no intelligent, probing, reconstructive consciousness of the kind that James offers to his readers in the figure of Maggie Verver in *The Golden Bowl*. This difference cannot simply be attributed to a distinction between poetry and novel; many dramatic poems achieve coherence with the help of a supervening consciousness, and Eliot's critics have much debated whether *The Waste Land* might be read as the expression of a single unifying consciousness or dispenses with any coherent subjectivity altogether. There seems little to warrant the notion of a single consciousness in *The Waste Land*. However, if we take cracks and fragmentation, or disintegration, as a common element in both James and Eliot, clearly the reconstructive will to re-totalization is embedded in James's text primarily in the figure of Maggie and in the self-disciplining and mental labours she performs to recover her marriage. For reasons outlined earlier, *The Golden Bowl* is an extremely difficult text to read and the struggling reader, regularly perplexed in any case, would be entirely baffled were it not for the light offered by Maggie's own baffled struggle to make sense of and to overcome her predicament. Maggie, in short, serves in *The Golden Bowl* as a kind of sleuth (with Fanny Assingham as her Watson) and as such serves both the interpretative and reintegrative functions performed by such figures. By contrast, the absence of any equivalent diagnostic and connecting consciousness in *The Waste Land* means that this labour of decoding, linking and re-ordering, or piecing things together, devolves directly onto the reader, who finds herself thrust into what seems a bizarrely disordered universe without any assistance to make sense of it. Another way to say this is that *The Waste Land*, on first readings at least, presents itself as a chaotic poem whose topic may also be chaos, and which immerses its readers in the cognitive experience of chaotic confusion without offering them any obvious means to overcome this situation.

What is to be done? It seems only modestly helpful to the reader to say that the poem's abrupt transitions and flagrant discontinuities, dissonant voices, multiple languages and meters, heaped fragments and broken images all reproduce Eliot's sense of a world that lacks any kind of organic coherence or religious, political, ethical or cultural order. This is patently true, but it is also like throwing a non-swimmer into turbulent seas on the advice that this is the only sure way to discover for herself the real sensations of drowning. The reader will surely submit to such threatening experience only if there is some sense that persistence with what looks like a meaningless poem will eventually yield some higher sense. Otherwise, likely reader responses, all familiar enough to anyone who has taught *The Waste Land*, include bewilderment leading to indifference. Or else bewilderment leading to a kind of muddling through towards only very generalized levels of meaning ('the poem is about Eliot's personal distress and search for faith' or 'it expresses a morbid post-World War I *Weltanschauung*'), or, for the more intrepid, to a higher kind of source-hunting and allusion-chasing. The latter kind of reader, encouraged by Eliot's Notes, may all too enthusiastically take on those detective functions, more commonly performed by a Marlowe- or Maggie-type participant narrator or protagonist. Bewilderment, muddling through, source-hunting and clue-solving are all conditions or activities that must be negotiated in any serious engagement with Eliot's poem. However, in a work that relies so much on more intangible connective tissue, such as aural resonance or verbal under-patterns, even the really committed reader is still likely to feel deprived of the satisfaction of conclusive 'coherence'.

'We can only say that it appears likely that poets in our civilization, as it exists at present, must be *difficult*'. This, Eliot explained in 'The Metaphysical Poets' (1921), was because contemporary 'civilization comprehends great variety and complexity, and this great variety and complexity, playing upon a refined sensibility, must produce various and complex results' so that '[t]he poet must become more and more comprehensive, more allusive, more indirect, in order to force, to dislocate if necessary, language into his meaning'.[39] The 'dissociation of sensibility' (64), commencing in the seventeenth century, detaching intellect and passionate feeling to their mutual cost, and becoming ever more acute since then, created this necessary 'difficulty' because what had been so long separated could only be reconnected with great ingenuity and effort. Nevertheless, that it was the business of the poet to connect is clear: 'When a poet's mind is perfectly equipped for its work, it is constantly amalgamating disparate experience; the ordinary man's experience is chaotic, irregular, fragmentary. The latter falls in love, or reads Spinoza, and these two experiences have nothing to do with each other, or with the noise of the typewriter or the smell of cooking; in the mind of the poet these experiences are always forming new wholes' (64). Poetry's function is to make of disaggregated experience 'new wholes'.

Two years earlier in 'Tradition and the Individual Talent', Eliot had insisted that to attain a mind 'perfectly equipped for its work' the poet would have to do much more than rummage in the storeroom of his own 'personality', an individualist fallacy come to baneful flower in the Romantics and persisting in the Victorians. In Eliot's estimate, this rummaging issued in a reflective, ruminative poetry on one hand, and a much smaller body of intellectual verse on the other hand, but no unified sensibility (though in Shelley there are still 'traces of a struggle towards unification of sensibility' ('The Metaphysical Poets', 65)). The corrective to this over-bloated fetish of self and self-expression is tradition and its concomitant, 'the historical sense', and Eliot's conception of tradition therefore sounds like some kind of structuralist historicism. He considers tradition here, in sum, as a kind of comprehensive and transhistorical but adjustable system in which new works agitate the overarching constellation that precedes them. Thus, by assimilating these new works, the system itself is reconfigured. However, the reordering process triggered by the insertion of new works is imagined not as radical epistemic break or as the slow formation of some new totality, but essentially in terms of reorientation and ongoing continuity:

> [W]hat happens when a new work of art is created is something that happens simultaneously to all the works of art which preceded it. The existing monuments form an ideal order among themselves, which is modified by the introduction of the new (the really new) work of art among them. The existing order is complete before the new work arrives: for order to persist after the supervention of novelty, the *whole* existing order must be, if ever so slightly, altered; and so the relations, proportions, values of each work of art toward the whole are readjusted; and this in conformity between the old and the new. Whoever has approved this idea of order, of the form of European, of English literature will not find it preposterous that the past should be altered by the present as much as the present is directed by the past. And the poet who is aware of all this will be aware of great difficulties and responsibilities.[40]

As in 'The Metaphysical Poets', a heavy stress falls here too on 'great difficulties'. In this instance, it falls on the poet's need for the kind of extraordinary receptivity that will allow him to write with a feeling in his bones not just for his own generation but with the sense that 'the whole of the literature of Europe from Homer and within it the whole of the literature of his own country has a simultaneous existence and composes a simultaneous order' (38). Eliot declares himself alive to the protest that attends such encyclopedic, hyperbolic ambition: 'The objection is that the doctrine requires a ridiculous amount of erudition (pedantry), an objection which can be rejected by appeal to the lives of the poets in the pantheon'. 'It will even be affirmed', he continues, 'that much learning deadens or perverts poetic sensibility'; to this, his reply is that, having made due allowance for the 'necessary receptivity and necessary laziness' (40) essential to poetry, it is still essential that the poet must labour a lifetime to internalize the tradition that will eventually absorb (if he is worthy enough) him in turn. To accomplish this, the poet will have to aim far higher than mere university education or general social cultivation – 'it is not desirable to confine knowledge to whatever can be put into useful shape for examinations, drawing-rooms, or the still more pretentious modes of publicity' (40) – because tradition, he insists, 'cannot be inherited, and if you want it you must obtain it by great labour' (38). To those

like Shakespeare, gifted with exceptional receptivity, and who could therefore acquire 'more essential history from Plutarch than most men could
from the whole British Museum' (40), this assimilation of tradition might
come easily enough, but whereas '[s]ome can absorb knowledge, the more
tardy must sweat for it' (40).

These essays, written before *The Waste Land* was completed, serve,
better than the 'Notes' that follow it, to communicate the ambition and
operative logic of that work. To the very receptive reader, one possessed of
a unique mind like Shakespeare's perhaps, *The Waste Land* might communicate its meanings telepathically as it were, but for the tardier non-
elect rest there is no option but to 'sweat for it'. Even then, mere 'sweating'
may take us only so far because, as Eliot proposes in 'The Metaphysical
Poets', the dissociation of sensibility means that to rely solely on intellect is
to fly on one wing only. There are obvious differences between *The Waste
Land* and 'Tradition and the Individual Talent'. The critical essay presents
'tradition' in conceptual grandeur as a systemic totality, assimilative and
adjustable, capable of revealing relations between part and part, part and
whole; the poem, on the other hand, presents us with the same European
tradition in terrific tatters, and in this instance the poet, whose business it
is to connect, can 'connect / Nothing with nothing' (46). For the poem to
do its work, the reader must be willing to recognize something of the
former splendour of what is available now only as wreckage and yet at the
same time be prepared to concede the astonishing degree of its current
dereliction. The act of reading this assumes requires as its corollary not
only considerable humility – otherwise why not treat the wreckage merely
as so much antiquated dross? – but also some sense of reintegrative
purpose: a willingness like that of Maggie Verver when she handles the
pieces of the golden bowl to explore whether that shattered object might
yet be refurbished to its former wholeness (never perfect). However, given
the sheer extent of brokenness – of sensibility, of civilizational resolve, of
poetic form – in *The Waste Land* it must soon be clear that no matter how
much 'sweat' the reader is willing to commit to it the poem proposes no
final coherence. Still, a stubborn willingness to search for this lost coherence might at least be a kind of training for some strenuous eventual
recovery.

However, for the reader without Greek or Latin, the sense of mortification begins in *The Waste Land* before the very portals of the poem
because without those languages the Petronian epigraph must remain
unintelligible. The much-discussed substitution of the original
Conradian epigraph ('the horror, the horror' passage) does not only cut

away the savagery of empire from *The Waste Land*. The replacement of an epigram in English by one in Latin and Greek quietly underscores the thinness of twentieth-century cultural levels generally, which is another kind of modern savagery: throughout his career, Eliot laments the declining status of classical European languages in modern education, asserting in 1925 that '[n]eglect of Greek means for Europe a relapse into unconsciousness'.[41] The Anglophone monoglot reader who skips round the Sibyl's unintelligible Greek cannot play truant for long: the Dantean tribute to Pound ('*il miglior fabbro*') immediately follows Petronius, and the first section, 'The Burial of the Dead', then faces the reader with three separate snatches of German and concludes with Baudelaire's French ('You! hypocrite lecteur! – mon semblable, – mon frère!' (39)). The midsections of *The Waste Land* remain mostly in English, but the foreign European languages re-enter again, much more forcefully in 'What The Thunder Said', and towards the very end when they too are interrupted by Sanskrit. But even if the English monoglot dismisses all of these foreign borrowings as excrescences to be bypassed or checked in a glossary, the pile-up of English metres and passages from across so many centuries is likely to expose the foreignness of English culture to itself, highlighting its historical shifts and idiomatic debts – biblical, classical, continental, imperial. In short, then, for anyone not already extremely erudite, to read *The Waste Land* is to oblige oneself to go to school in a catholic curriculum that vastly exceeds what F. R. Leavis would later call 'The Great Tradition', a tradition essentially novelistic and modern and reaching back only to Shakespeare.

At the same time, though, the reader is compelled to see that vaster but shattered tradition stretched, as Eleanor Cook has proposed, across three superimposed imaginary maps – one of London city, a second of imperial Rome, and a third world atlas extending from the Christian Mediterranean to Buddhist or Sanskritic Asia.[42] However conservative and patrician Eliot might be, *The Waste Land*'s frame of reference is neither insularly nationalist nor wholly modern in any abbreviated sense. Rather, its imaginative reach is across centuries and continents, and if it cannot 'connect' its elements comfortably or elegantly in any inherited form this is because what it wants to connect is so prodigious and conceived against such a vast and tattered canvas as to make connection a matter of fantastic ambition. Nonetheless, for the reader willing to 'sweat for it' and take on the 'ridiculous amount of erudition (pedantry)' required to master the poem, the reward no doubt is a corresponding enlargement of imaginative vision, a deepening of cultural sensibility and historical sense, and some appreciation of the enormity of the task of reconstruction that 'men of letters' everywhere felt they now confronted.

In a letter written to his mother on 28 April 1918, Eliot complained that to judge by American newspapers sent to him, the war in Europe did not seem to have affected America 'very seriously yet'. He contrasted American wastefulness with European economies of paper and noted that: 'I don't mean that [the war in Europe] is not the chief subject of interest, but that it is *simply* the chief subject of interest, and not the obsessing nightmare that it is to Europe':

> And we can't make you realise three thousand miles away all that that means. Even with all your privations and difficulties. Your papers talk about the 'fight for civilisation'; do they realise either what civilisation means or what the fight for it means? We are all immeasurably and irremediably altered over here by the last three years.
> ('Letter to His Mother', 28 April 1918, 229–230, 230. Italics in the original.)

The letter conveys Eliot's sense of how little of 'the horror, the horror' of the European situation had penetrated American culture despite the United States' involvement in the conflict for over a year when this was written, as well as his estimate of how fundamentally the war had altered everyone in Europe. What the letter expresses most of all is a vexed scepticism about how little Americans might appreciate what 'civilisation' means and therefore what the 'fight' for it means. Eliot does not dismiss the word 'civilisation' as of dubious usage nor slight the 'fight for civilisation' as wartime propaganda. His complaint, in essence, is that the American understanding of both 'civilisation' and the 'fight' for it remains superficial and that the war has in any case so pulverized things as to alter 'immeasurably and irremediably' the Europe Americans like to think they are rescuing. Eliot's gist, in sum, is that Americans have taken on a task beyond their understanding and for which they may not at all be equipped.

Though both James and Eliot are concerned with the business of connecting and recovering to the extent possible that which has been cracked or broken, the crucial difference between *The Golden Bowl* and *The Waste Land*, finally, is that in James's pre-war novel both Europe and America, however flawed each may be separately, have their greatness, abstract though America's may be. Crucially, in Eliot's post-war poem, however, America appears only as muted whisperings in the wider European echo chamber and his Europe is in smithereens. In *The Golden Bowl*, the Prince may be passive and imperfect, but he seems tractable and open to correction. Maggie may be too culpably closeted and unworldly to begin with, but she proves a terrifically quick learner and expert diplomat. Whether Adam's art collections will really civilize American City may be an open question, but that vast ambition may not be entirely without merit. For James, *some* quality of the heroic is still attached to the project of connecting European and American civilizations, however pricked by ironies that enterprise may be. One can see what Pound meant in his 1918 essay on James when he insisted that though the latter's novels might be set in drawing rooms and not drawn on large historical canvases, they 'treat of major forces, even of epic forces'.[43] In this view, James belongs to an American epic tradition, not a minor novelistic one.

For Eliot, working in a lower mock-epic register, the question, however, is not so much how to integrate Europe and America, but whether either has a 'civilisation' healthy enough to save or integrate in the first instance. In one instantiation, the United States may be over-cultured but desiccated, in another primitive and vital, more savage than cultured. America is taken to be generally too youthful historically and too rawly democratic to have ever become fully 'civilised'. Eliot's England suffers its own worsening dissociation of sensibility and complacent parochialisms, and Europe generally has collapsed into splintered parts in the Great War. Hence, *The Waste Land*'s task, in contrast to that of *The Golden Bowl*, is not to discover how to conjugate the finer elements of the United States and Europe and to discipline the worst, but to recover some sufficiently serious, as opposed to newspaper-level, conception of their common mother 'civilisation' adequate to save it. The reader who struggles with *The Waste Land* undergoes training from the very start to recognize the enormity of the reconstruction task involved and to confront her own deficiencies in the cultural and historical equipment needed to meet this task. However, by engaging that epic struggle at least, the reader also leaves behind the merely superficial sense of the 'fight for civilisation' that Eliot ascribes to American newspapers and can start to acquire some more robust and forbidding sense of what that 'fight' must mean.

A key thing to note here about the Europe offered to the reader in *The Waste Land* is that it comes in unassembled parts (like a contemporary IKEA pack) and that it is overwhelmingly a *literary Europe*. The poem has its significant and obvious religious and anthropological layerings (where the Cumaean Sibyl, Buddha, Ezekiel, Christ, Augustine, Madame Sosostris, Jessie Weston and James Frazer all keep company), one or two English architectural references (to Sir Christopher Wren; perhaps one should also include Nicholas Hawksmoor's St Mary Woolnoth, or Lord Holford's London Bridge), one note to an English historian (James Anthony Froude), and, more surprisingly, given Eliot's academic training, only one reference, also in the Notes, to a philosopher (the Englishman F. H. Bradley). *The Waste Land* has its own unique music, but it mentions only one European classical composer, Wagner, though some have found possible suggestions of Richard Strauss's *Salomé,* and there are also the Ziegfeld Follies. Source hunters will find more oblique references perhaps than those in the Notes, but it is perfectly clear nonetheless that *The Waste Land*'s pretensions to historical depth and geographical extent, impressive though they are, rest primarily on its overlapping strata of literary allusion and not on allusions to other arts or disciplines. Ultimately, it is its capacity to somehow accommodate Homer, Ovid, Petronius, Virgil, Dante, Chaucer, Kyd, Shakespeare and the Jacobeans, Spenser, Donne, Milton, Marvell, Goldsmith, Gay, Baudelaire, Laforgue, Verlaine, Dickens, Huxley, Hesse, Joyce and Pound, and a steady subterranean susurrus of several others not listed here, that allows *The Waste Land* its epic and encyclopaedic resonances.

In reality, though, with its some 434 lines (not counting the Notes) that work is at best a pocket-epic or epyllion. For its terrific compactness of form, the work is better considered alongside modernist novellas like *The Heart of Darkness, Death in Venice, The Metamorphosis* or *The Great Gatsby* than with works of truly epic and encyclopaedic scope such as *Ulysses, A Vision, The Cantos, Doctor Faustus, The Magic Mountain* or *The Death of Virgil.* None of this is to enter into old disputes as to whether Eliot's learning is merely showy and bogus or exceptionally impressive. Nor is it necessarily to agree with those critics, mostly English perhaps, who aver that there is something distinctly American in Eliot's whole conception of tradition as something that must be earned by a sweaty lifetime's bookishness: after all, the aristocratic conception of tradition was precisely that it *was* inherited and more to be associated (as with Amerigo in *The Golden Bowl*) with gentlemanly cultivation and easy and gracious deportment than strenuous studious effort.[44] Even for an English poet younger than Eliot like W. H. Auden, Eliot's insistence on this determined acquisition of tradition through diligent homework was something 'that I do not think any European critic would have said just this'. The European would agree, Auden opined, that 'every poet must work hard', yet balk at the suggestion 'that no sense of tradition is acquired except by conscious effort'.[45] The fact, however, that *The Waste Land* could offer its readers such a formidable challenge in terms of mastering tradition and the task of putting that broken tradition together again, and yet be tightly compact enough as to make this seem much more manageable than mastering great sprawling epics like *The Cantos* or *Ulysses*, is surely part of its astounding success.[46]

The stronger point finally to make here, I think, and the most telling correspondence between James and Eliot, is that in this moment Americans feel themselves able, and have the determination and the confidence, to take charge of Europe's affairs. When Eliot says in 'On Henry James' that it is the consummation of the American not to become English but European, when he insists in 'Tradition and the Individual Talent' that the serious poet must be able to write with the feeling that 'the whole of the literature of Europe from Homer and within it the whole of the literature of his own country has a simultaneous existence and composes a simultaneous order' (38), when he displays a tatterdemalion and fallen Europe that needs like Humpty-Dumpty to be re-collocated in *The Waste Land*, or invites in *The Criterion* Europe's 'men of letters' to help him restore 'the idea of a common culture of western Europe',[47] he sounds neither American nor English exclusively. Rather, he sounds like some mandarin intellectual version of Maggie Verver and the Prince rolled into one, polished sophisticate and diplomat extraordinaire combined. As Eliot may possibly have intuited from the Versailles Treaty onwards, his ambition to restore 'the idea of a common culture of western Europe' was against the odds, even doomed; by 1939, when *The Criterion* wound down, he knew it conclusively to be so, for the moment at least. After the second plunge into catastrophe that came in 1940, what became known as 'Western Europe' would indeed require American rescue, both militarily in the war and economically afterwards in the form of the Marshall Plan. However, in many respects Eliot may be seen in retrospect to have been well ahead of that great game since the 1920s and he might well claim that in *The Waste Land* and *The Criterion* he had already attempted something like his own literary version of the Marshall Plan, a rescue mission to save literary Europe from its internal dissensions and 'strange gods', and especially, though not only, from communism.

Yet for all its polyglot variety, *The Waste Land* is finally not a European but an English-language poem, one in which other languages play important but obviously subordinate parts in the composite whole. Indeed, in Eliot's hands here English engorges other languages, and renders them minor to it, just as 'global English' would do as the century proceeded and as France and French lost their earlier European supereminence. The dominance of English indeed is already such that any quotation in any language, even Latin, no matter how trite, seems impossibly learned and esoteric. For all its catholicity of language and ideas, *The Criterion* was likewise, as Eliot readily acknowledged, a London-based, English-language periodical within whose pages other European languages were translated into English. Eliot's poetic formation may have been Anglo-French, his disposition European, classicist and Dantean, his politics oscillating between English Tory and French Maurrasian, and in these respects he was indeed as much or more 'European' than he was either American or English. Nevertheless, his literary achievements were written in English, of course, and remained fundamentally Anglo-American. Thus, however 'European' it may look, *The Waste Land* anticipates the Anglo-American domination of Western Europe to come and the subordination of French and German to what we now call 'global English'. After World War II and the second shattering of Europe within a generation, it was the United States that was readiest to own and reclaim that expatriate accomplishment.

## IV

When World War II ended in 1945, Eliot found himself in circumstances of continental collapse somewhat like those that had obtained in 1918. Now the young avant-gardist making his way in London had become an internationally celebrated establishment poet and critic. In the earlier post-war aftermath, he had written *The Sacred Wood* and begun to assert himself as rival and successor to Matthew Arnold as poet-critic and then sealed this success with *The Waste Land*.[48] In this second post-war period, a major work, *The Four Quartets*, was already in circulation; it was published in book form in 1943. The honours ratifying his achievement rolled in: he received an honorary degree from Harvard in 1947, the Order of Merit in January 1948, the Nobel Prize in November 1948. From this period onwards, Eliot's most significant works are in drama and prose, no longer poetry. In many respects, though, what is remarkable is how consistent Eliot's preoccupations and prescriptions remain in these respective aftermaths to war: in both periods, the breakdown of Europe and Western civilization and the urgency of the need to reconnect and reconstruct dominate his thoughts. But in other ways what is more important is not simply how much Eliot's circumstances have changed, but how much the relative positions of the United States and Europe had shifted and to what effect.[49]

In an article published initially in Norway and then in *The Sewanee Review* in summer 1945, 'The Man of Letters and the Future of Europe', and in a series of radio broadcasts to Germany (these appearing first in German translation in 1946 and later collected as a single piece in English in 1948 as an appendix, titled 'The Unity of European Culture', appended to *Notes on the Definition of Culture*), Eliot reprised and reiterated his own commitment to European letters. That commitment, evident from the foundation of *The Criterion* in 1922, remained steadfast, but Eliot set out what he now considered the chief difference between the earlier moment and the present one. The passage from 'The Man of Letters and the Future of Europe' is worth citing to clarify Eliot's position in 1945:

> The primary aim of politics, at the end of a great war, must be, of course, the establishment of a peace, and of a peace which will endure. But at different times, different notions of what conditions are necessary for peace may prevail. At the end of the last war, the idea of peace was associated with the idea of independence and freedom: it was thought that if each nation managed all its own affairs at home, and transacted its foreign political affairs through a League of Nations, peace would be perpetually assured. It was an idea which disregarded the *unity* of European culture. At the end of this war, the idea of peace is more likely to be associated with the idea of *efficiency* – that is, with whatever can be *planned*. This would be to disregard the *diversity* of European culture. It is not that 'culture' is in danger of being ignored: on the contrary, I think that culture might be safer if it were less talked about. But in this talk of 'culture', the notion of a European culture – a culture with several sub-divisions, other than national boundaries, within it, and with various crossing threads of relationship between countries, but still a recognizable universal European culture – is not very prominent: and there is a danger that the importance of the various cultures may be assumed to be in proportion to the size, population, wealth and power of the nations.[50]

Eliot went on to cite Great Britain as analogous to Europe in that it offered in microcosm 'the problem of regional diversities of race and culture within one nation' (337), but declared his confidence that this friction, while it might result in ultimately greater political autonomy for Scotland or Wales, was culturally fructifying. Repudiating Nazi attempts to produce a completely unified German national culture and a corresponding over-confidence in centralized planning, Eliot went on to declare that the 'cultural health of Europe, including the cultural health of its component parts, is incompatible with extreme forms of both nationalism and internationalism' (338). The essay stresses the inherent tendency of both industrialization and state capitals to homogenize culture into a single administered uniformity, and thus Eliot advocates 'regionalism' (335) – within Europe as a whole and within its component states – as a counter to this centripetal uniformity. Culture, Eliot declared, was poorly amenable to social engineering, and therefore '[t]he union of local cultures in a general culture is more difficult to conceive, and more difficult to realize' (335) than commonly allowed, and needed to be acknowledged and treated as such. The article concludes with an appeal to European men of letters, whatever their political views, which needn't concur with Eliot's, to recognize that the issue of getting some balance between whole and part was of common European concern. 'Such agreement', he asserted, 'would give more content to the phrase "the republic of letters." The "republic" or (to use a stronger term) the "fraternity" of letters does not, fortunately, demand that all men of letters should love one another – there always have been, and always will be, jealousy and intrigue among authors: but it does imply that we have a mutual bond, and a mutual obligation to a common ideal; and that on some questions we should speak for Europe, even when we speak only to our fellow countrymen' (342).

These 1940s writings challenge the idea that Eliot's career follows some simple line from early 1920s high modernist metro-cosmopolitan to eventual Little Englander. Indeed, in many respects they situate Eliot instead in the company of a wider host of European intellectuals and politicians who, from World War I onwards, had been deliberating the idea of some kind of European federation, conceived as a bulwark against the Soviet Union's communist materialism to the east and the capitalist materialism of the United States to the west.[51] These writings also display certain affinities (and differences) between Eliot's thought and that of German thinkers such as Theodor Adorno (whose reflections on the totally administered society and the 'culture industry' were also appearing in this period) and Erich Auerbach (whose anxieties converged with Eliot's when he contended that the real obstacles to a future 'world literature' would not be the enormous diversity of cultures but rather their reductive standardization and Anglicization).[52] In 'The Man of Letters and the Future of Europe' and 'The Unity of European Culture', the problem that Eliot worries at continually is how to articulate a comprehensive idea of Europe that would be coherent and yet sufficiently diverse to allow Europe's plurality of nations, regions and localities to retain their cultural particularities. This is essential to him because the ongoing exchange between parts and whole is vital to their mutual fertility. Formally, then, the governing challenge is the same as that which agitated *The Waste Land* decades earlier: how to find a composite whole pliable and resilient enough to contain without overly coercing its parts; how to keep those centrifugal parts from rendering the whole incoherent and collapsible.

Ultimately, Eliot's answer to both the aesthetic and political questions came back to the same thing: Christianity. No aesthetic, as he had long argued against both Matthew Arnold and I. A. Richards, can be expected to supply the socially integrative and spiritual functions supplied by religious belief and orthodoxy. Similarly, as he made clear in 'The Unity of European Culture', '[t]he dominant force in creating a common culture between peoples each of which has its distinct culture, is religion' (126). Europe might share a common literary heritage in 'the literature of Rome, of Greece and of Israel' (116), but none of these of course were Christian, and 'Israel' (the more familiar term 'Hebrew' might have been expected here; 'Israel' was not yet a state in 1946, but was just becoming so in 1948 when the lectures were published in English) belonged to Arabia or Asia rather than to Europe proper. As he pondered the question of 'Asia' culturally in these broadcasts, Eliot declared that 'I do not want to give the impression that I regard European culture as something cut off from every other' (117), and acknowledged the important contributions of translations from Asia's 'great poetry' and 'very difficult metaphysics' (116) to European culture generally and to modernism, including his own studies in 'ancient Indian languages' (116). Nevertheless, despite this apparent openness, Eliot finally insisted that these classical and Asian arts had been taken up by and filtered through a Europe that was millennially Christian in its legal systems and common faith. In this account, Enlightenment and anti-Enlightenment Europe is reduced to a single sentence – '[o]nly a Christian culture could have produced a Voltaire or a Nietzsche' (126) – and conceived as negative reactions to a larger abiding Christianity. Thus, Eliot was adamant:

> If Christianity goes, the whole of our culture goes. Then you must start painfully again, and you cannot put on a new culture ready made. You must wait for the grass to grow to feed the sheep to give the wool out of which your new coat will be made. You must pass through many centuries of barbarism. We should not live to see the new culture, nor would our great-great-great-grandchildren: and if we did, not one of us would be happy in it.
>
> (126)

This sentiment recalls Henry James's comment on Hawthorne: 'it takes a great deal of history to produce a little literature', and also that passage in *The Golden Bowl*, cited earlier, when Maggie repudiates the violent passions associated with Oriental caravans. His convictions about Christianity were enough for Eliot finally to separate Europe more definitively from Asia – '[i]f Asia were converted to Christianity tomorrow, it would not thereby become a part of Europe' (126) – and to encourage it to close up its cultural frontiers. This conception of Europe would become in time standard Christian Democrat Europhile orthodoxy and remains today a guiding principle of the European People's Party, the largest party in the European Parliament since 1999. Likewise, questions of how to integrate part and whole, center and periphery, nation and confederation, remain as fundamentally critical and vexatious for the European Union today as for Eliot in the 1940s before that body had ever come into existence.

Meanwhile, however, as intellectuals in a shattered Europe were contemplating different recoveries for that continent, real initiative had passed to the United States. There, the United States' university system was undergoing the most rapid expansion it its history and preparing a more generally educated populace and training the new elites, scientific and humanist, necessary to America's now consolidated global hegemony. Eliot's Harvard degree of 1947 and the *Time* magazine cover and feature of 6 March 1950 may be taken as general markers of Eliot's repatriation into American patrician and middle-class cultures. Valuable work has appeared in recent years on the take-up of a modernism, which had often been dismissed in earlier decades as effetely European and un-American, by the big commercial magazines such as *Time* or *Life* in this early Cold War period and about the re-positioning of Eliot especially as a symbol of American internationalism rather as a renegade son.[53] Some tentativeness still remains in the laconic *Time* portrait of the artist, which notes Eliot's 'bookish pallor', fondness for hearty English breakfasts and the 'impeccable dark blue suit' and the 'tightly rolled umbrella' that he carries on his way to Faber and Faber – shades here still of Virginia Woolf's quip decades earlier about over-the-top assimilation into Britishness. Nevertheless, this English Eliot is now checked by another more American self that had been prepared to do military service for the United States in World War I and retained a fondness for bourbon and American popular song. So, when it comes to the crunch question – 'why should Americans bother about this Missouri-born American who talks like an Englishman, has not lived in the U.S. for the past 36 years, and gave up his U.S. citizenship to become a British subject?' – the answer came readily enough: 'Perhaps the simplest answer is: Because T. S. Eliot is a civilized man. He is more; he is a commentator on his age who is considered by some more important than Gabriel Heatter or Walter Winchell – or even Walter Lippmann'. The obvious inference here was that if Eliot was a civilized man then perhaps America itself might be deemed civilizing internationally, its long-standing anxieties on that score abated. Furthermore, if the expatriate poet was as much a 'commentator on his age' as radio-broadcaster Heatter, muckraking newspaper columnist and J. Edgar Hoover- and Joseph McCarthy-supporter Winchell, and Lippmann, journalist and author credited with writing a foundational book on American media studies as well as coining the term 'Cold War', then Eliot's writings must be, whatever their difficulty, significant indeed. As one of several nice touches, the *Time* article noted that as Eliot made his way to work: 'He left his flat in Cheyne Walk, Chelsea (Expatriate Henry James used to live in the flat just below)'.[54] At this flourish William Dean Howells might have been permitted a told-you-so smile and Eliot himself must have relished that here he was positioned above James, the admired literary countryman-and-predecessor with whom he was as a young man so mimetically competitive.

Still, it would be too simple to see this post-war moment only as one when modernism went masscult in the United States. As Geoffrey Galt Harpham recounts in *The Humanities and the Dream of America*, a Harvard University committee published its document *General Education in a Free Society* in 1945, and this wartime document, soon generally termed the Redbook, was designed by a 'committee [that] fully understood that the United States was about to become a global power, a dominant but far from unopposed nation whose fundamental principles were about to be tested in the same way as its military capabilities had been tested during the war'.[55] I. A. Richards had a significant role in writing this report, which, according to Harpham, was instrumental in making English and the humanities de facto 'as the first among equals in the divisions of knowledge' (157) in this programme for higher education that would reshape university teaching for several decades to come. However, as Alex Beam has also shown, the attempt to disseminate the values of 'Western civilization' now also extended its reach well beyond Harvard or Ivy League walls. In 1952, the University of Chicago and *Encyclopedia Britannica* combined to launch the 54-volume *Great Books of the Western World*, a 32,000-page, small-print compendium that compressed the literary, philosophical and scientific achievements of that civilization into 443 exemplary books. The British consul general H. A. Hobson attended the official launch of these volumes at the Waldorf-Astoria Hotel, and a complimentary set was to be sent to Queen Elizabeth; a few months later President Harry S. Truman received his *Great Books* at the White House.[56] *Britannica*'s salesmen would push the set to socially aspiring middle-class American homes. One year later, in 1953, Leon Edel published the first volume of his mammoth five-volume biography of Henry James. America's literary sons were being repatriated, Anglo-American cultural bonds cemented and an idea of the United States as inheritor and senior custodian of 'Western Civilization' generally consolidated. [57] None of this is to say that everything that had been shattered in World Wars I and II was now being re-sutured in Chicago or Harvard or in the *Great Books* sets, and that Europe and the United States, capitalist commodification and high culture, Christianity and modernity, had finally attained concord. But the United States, Hiroshima serving as token of its determination to dominate, was finally setting out to equip itself with a stronger sense of 'civilisation' than Eliot had felt it had possessed in 1918 when he wrote to his mother to ask if his countrymen knew what either 'civilisation' or 'the fight' for it really meant.

'London Bridge is falling down falling down falling down' (50) is one of the easier rhymes to recall from the last stanza of *The Waste Land*. In 1967, the Common Council of London placed that bridge on sale. Robert McCulloch of McCulloch Oil bought it on 18 April of that year for nearly $2.5 million. It was then dismantled brick by numbered brick, and shipped via the Panama Canal to California, and finally trucked to Lake Havasu City, Arizona, where it was rededicated on 10 October 1971. [58] In the same year that McCulloch bought London Bridge, Eliot's memorial plaque was installed in Westminster Abbey. In 1971, some months before the bridge was reopened in Arizona, the facsimile version of *The Waste Land* was published, to great academic interest. These may be no more than whimsical anecdotes, but they chart something of the complex crosscurrents in Anglo-American capital and culture, matters on which James and Eliot were both such shrewd observers. They remind us how much by the 1970s the one-time great empire and mother-culture head-quartered in London had become if not wholly a vassal, then certainly an economically weakened and more tractable tutee to its erstwhile colony, itself long since grown into a new Rome.

# Contesting Wills: National Mimetic Rivalries, World War and World Literature in Ulysses

The tercentenary of Shakespeare's death is at hand, but no hint has reached us that Dublin intends to take any formal notice of it. The proper celebration would be, of course, a week of Shakespearean drama, performed by a good company, at one of our principal theatres. [...] It is quite probable that the tercentenary of '*unser* Shakespeare' will be celebrated in Berlin [but not] on the boards of any theatre in Ireland. [...]

At this time, the whole Empire is fighting for ideals that Shakespeare, more than any other human being, helped to shape and glorify. Irish soldiers are bleeding and dying for those ideals. Is it wholly impossible that at such a time we in Dublin should render thanks to Shakespeare, on the three hundredth anniversary of his death, by a worthy performance of his greatest play? One thing, at any rate, is certain, if in 1916 Shakespeare would 'spell bankruptcy' in a British capital, while Mr Charles Chaplin earns £130,000 a year, we must, for very shame, cease to sneer at Germany's title to the possession of Shakespeare. She is acquiring him, as the lawyers say, by right of *usucapio*.

'Shakespeare in Dublin', *Irish Times*, 24 March 1916.[1]

And at the end of it all, it must have seemed to [Joyce] that he held English, his country's spiritual enemy, in the hollow of his hand, for the English language too came at his call to do his bidding. [...] This language found itself constrained by its new master to perform tasks to which it was unaccustomed in the service of pure literature; against the grain it was forced to reproduce Joyce's fantasies in all kinds of juxtapositions, neologisms, amalgamations, truncations, words that are only found scrawled up in public lavatories, obsolete words, words in limbo or belike in the womb of time. It assumed every intonation and locution of Dublin, London, Glasgow, New York, Johannesburg. Like a devil taking pleasure in forcing a virgin to speak obscenely, so Joyce rejoiced darkly in causing the language of Milton and Wordsworth to utter all but unimaginable filth and treason.

Such is Joyce's Celtic revenge ...

John Eglinton, *Irish Literary Portraits*, 1935.[2]

Fair indeed is the crown, and the fight for fame well worth the
winning, where even to be worsted by our forerunners is not
without glory.

Longinus, 'On the Sublime'.[3]

# I

If one had to choose a year when modern Irish literature won recognition
within the wider field of 'world literature' then it would have to be 1922,
with the foundation of the Irish Free State and the publication of *Ulysses*.
Valery Larbaud's introductory lecture on *Ulysses*, delivered to a packed
audience in Adrienne Monnier's La Maison des Amis des Livres on
7 December 1921, was the critical initial moment of Parisian consecration.
Larbaud, comparing what Joyce was doing for Ireland to what Ibsen had
done for Norway, Strindberg for Sweden, and Nietzsche for Germany,
declared that with Joyce's epic novel 'Ireland is making a sensational re-
entrance into the first rank of European literature'.[4] Two other, more formal
consecrations followed quickly: the Nobel Prize in Literature was awarded
to William Butler Yeats on 10 December 1923, and George Bernard Shaw
was conferred with his Nobel award for 1925 on 11 November 1926. In his
Nobel acceptance speech, Yeats noted that he had been greatly indebted to
Scandinavian literature because his lifelong fascination with William Blake
had compelled him to study Swedenborg, and then went on say that that he
did not think 'our Irish theatre could have ever come into existence but for
the theatre of Ibsen and Bjørnson'. Yeats stressed that his own achievement
was part of the larger collective endeavour of the Irish Revival. 'Thirty years
ago,' Yeats remarked, 'a number of Irish writers met together in societies
and began a remorseless criticism of the literature of their country. It was
their dream that by freeing it from provincialism they might win for it
European recognition'. Acknowledging those who had laboured alongside
him, Yeats concluded, 'when I return to Ireland these men and women,
now growing old like myself, will see in this great honour a fulfillment of
that dream'.[5]

Larbaud's *Ulysses* lecture and Yeats's Nobel acceptance speech both rest
on unspoken assumptions inherent to processes of consecration into world
literary status. Both make clear that 'world literature' in this period
remained fundamentally European centred. The arbiters of distinction
are French or Swedish and Yeats conceives of his award as the culmination
of a thirty-year-long collective effort to rid Irish literature of its 'provincialism' so that it might eventually earn 'European recognition'. For a

writer from a literary periphery to be accepted into the front ranks of European literature is to become a figure of truly international distinction, and thereafter he or she (there were two women Nobel Prize winners in the period 1920–1930) can simultaneously exemplify and transcend their national status. Prizewinners from the core or established European literary nations like France, Germany or England are not usually expected to have to work for thirty years to deprovincialize their literary traditions nor are their literatures usually thought to have to make a 're-entrance' into literary modernity as Larbaud thought Ireland's did with *Ulysses*.

Nevertheless, while the 1920s brought conspicuous international recognition to Irish literature, something that was of real importance to the new Free State as it attempted to consolidate itself in the unstable post-war interstate system, the success was not without ironies. Unlike the United States, for which Henry James, Eliot, Stein, Pound and others were winning a similar distinction, Ireland was not on the verge of becoming a great world power. Politically and economically, the country remained heavily dependent on Great Britain for most of the twentieth century; the Free State became a Republic in 1949, but it was not until its entry, along with that of the United Kingdom, in 1973 into the European Economic Community (later the European Union) that this damaging dependency began to be reduced. In this sense, Irish literary modernity served as a kind of premature and compensatory modernity that leaped ahead of social modernization and could do little to alleviate ongoing Irish subordination to greater powers. This anticipated the South American literary 'Boom' of the 1960s and 1970s when, despite its ongoing economic underdevelopment, the region produced a literature whose innovative panache won metropolitan esteem. The Cuban Revolution's challenge to the political domination of the United States was a prelude to this remarkable release of energy, just as the Irish political revolution unleashed by Easter 1916 undoubtedly lent real charge to Irish modernism. Nevertheless, when Joyce, Yeats and Shaw won recognition in Europe through Nobel Prizes or other consecrations, the process involved as much Anglicization as Europeanization. The Revival had set out to de-Anglicize Ireland and to create a new national literature in Gaelic or at least to encourage a bilingual literature, yet all of the Irish writers in the 1920s who won most international acclaim wrote in English. Their successes might have boosted Ireland's literary profile and increased its cultural capital, but they also inevitably further consolidated the long-standing ascendancy of English in nearly all areas of Irish society. The attempt by Yeats, Synge and others to steep Irish literature in English in the vats of Irish mythology, folklore and dialect, or those of Joyce and O'Casey to draw on the lower-class idioms of urban Dublin, were never more than compensatory gestures of differentiation. Anglophone writers in the Caribbean, Africa and India, where other local languages and literary traditions remained in far sturdier conditions than was the case for Irish in early twentieth-century Ireland, conducted similar strategies of indigenizing English, but the most famous writers in these regions were soon ingathered into 'Commonwealth' or 'Anglophone world' literary canons. It was possible to distinguish one's national or regional literature from English or British literature, but at the same time to add to the increasing international prestige of an 'English literature' now apparently uncoupled from English national territory or Empire. In this sense, Ireland's triumphant 're-entrance into the first rank of European literature' also represented a significant moment in the expansion of literary 'global English'. This was not the kind of outcome for which Douglas Hyde and the Gaelic League had hoped. Nor would Yeats or Joyce, those who did most for that expansion, have wholly relished the prospect.

As noted in Chapter 1, Hugh Kenner has described the modernist moment as one in which the singular entity of 'English Literature' split into the 'three provinces' of British, American and Irish literatures. Before this rupture, Kenner contends, 'if you were not one of them [the English] and chose to write in English, you either courted assimilation, like Washington Irving, or remained a barbarian, like Herman Melville'. Afterwards, however, 'England's literature became a special case, the literature of one province among several. It is all like the separation of French and Spanish literatures from Latin, which in turn mutated in its homeland into Italian'.[6] Possibly, but Kenner assumes a continuing and deepening divergence of 'Englishes' over time and discounts the possibilities of any new convergence. Yet if it took Yeats's fiercely willed conception of Ireland as an antique land all at war with a contemptible modernity, Synge's attempt to turn English towards Irish, Joyce's ever-more-extravagant linguistic avant-gardism, and, to a lesser extent, Wilde's and Shaw's satirical assaults on British literary pieties to achieve this ruptural breakup of a previously more London-dominated 'English Literature', it still remained questionable if the smaller Irish literary province, once established, could remain viable for long. Could a country with a population smaller even than that of many single English shires really be expected to be able continuously to reproduce the collective efforts of differentiation represented by the Revivalists generally or individually by the extraordinary ambitions of Yeats or Joyce? And, if not, what was there to prevent Irish literature in English from becoming in time only a minor variant of English literature again, one that would eventually be returned to the British mainstream? Paradoxically, as Ireland became less 'backward' and as Irish social circumstances became closer to those in the United Kingdom or the United States, the effort to sustain some sort of distinguishable Irish literature might well become ever more demanding. Once Irish living standards and everyday ways of life converged more closely with those in other advanced capitalist societies, what exactly would remain to differentiate Irish writing from these other metropolitan Anglophone literatures? Did Irish literature thrive on Irish backwardness, or on the struggle to overcome backwardness, for its distinctiveness? And, if so, would it lose much of its distinctiveness if Ireland finally 'caught up' with the United Kingdom and the United States?

Furthermore, if the world literary system, as Pascale Casanova has argued, emerged from a repetitive process of national literary rivalries – whereby the English and Germans competed with the French for literary distinction, and the colonies of the British, French, Spanish or Dutch empires and so on have then competed in their turn with the European metropoles to fashion their own indigenous national literatures – then this means that a mimetic impetus is one of the dynamos of literary production generally.[7] Writers and nations compete to distinguish their works from those of earlier predecessors even as they also try to copy the successes of those they contest. Hence, the conviction that American or Canadian literatures, say, have some saliently different features to English literature and to each other, but hence also the obvious fact that, however different they think themselves to be, 'national literatures' as such are in effect modular. They all make largely the same claims to express something of the particular character or history of the people for which they speak; they all have their canons of greater and minor figures; they frequently deploy rather similar periodization strategies; and so on. In other words, the generative mimeticism that seems essential to the creation of both 'national literatures' and 'world literature' involve processes of copying or simulation as well as those of differentiation. At the level of content, all national literatures claim to be distinguishable in some important respects to others; however, the actual concept of a 'national literature' is a replicable type to which all nations or nation-states lay similar claim.[8]

In the case of a small island like Ireland, so geographically close to Britain, part of it even yet a part of the United Kingdom, the last polity to be included within and the first to leave the Ukanian state, the dynamics of this mimetic process of emulation and rivalry can be expected to be especially intense. It is easy to dismiss this whole enterprise of literary nationalization as merely a narcissism of small differences. Yet because that enterprise cannot be separated from broader histories of colonization, struggles for political sovereignty, or the official recognition or neglect of particular languages, the forging of national literatures is hardly an inconsequential matter. Nevertheless, despite the extensive debates that have emerged around various concepts of 'world literature' (however conceived) in recent times, there has been remarkably little reflection on the concept of mimetic rivalry as such, even though national rivalries are readily acknowledged to be crucial motivations for the creation of national literatures and world literary systems. Harold Bloom's *The Anxiety of Influence: A Theory of Poetry* (1973) remains a formative study of literary rivalry; René Girard's conception of mimetic rivalry, first outlined in *Deceit, Desire, and the Novel: Self and Other in Literary Structure* (1961, translated 1965), and then elaborated across several humanities disciplines, is another.[9] In Bloom's view, only the most robust poetic talents can ever overcome the weight of their forebears to forge truly original literary works, styles and identities of their own; even then, for Bloom, triumph exacts its price as the energies of poetic sons are sapped by unshakable anxieties about ongoing indebtedness to fathers however much the latter are overthrown. Mimesis for Bloom is violent and domineering; it is about emerging poets wresting authority and voice from precursors. Yet as literary latecomers attempt to transform a debilitating belatedness into a creative strength rather than mere affliction, the agon as such is unavoidable and productive.

In Girard's study, the novel from Cervantes to Dostoyevsky reveals the unrecognized truth of mimetic desire: namely, that desire originates spontaneously neither in the instincts of the desiring subject nor in the intrinsic qualities of the desired object but is always something mediated to us by others. For Girard, in short, we learn to desire by taking our leads from prestigious models. These models may take either the form of 'external mediators', who as gods, aristocrats or heroes enjoy a status far above that of the emulating disciple, or of 'internal mediators', who are much closer in status to the emulator and who may therefore generate a more toxic and vicious, because proximate, rivalry. In either case, for Girard, the value of the object of desire, whether that be a material thing or an erotic love object, derives not from the object itself but from the external or internal mediator who prizes it. The subject needs mediators to assure him that the object is worth his desiring even though mediators can then become tormenting rivals for the object, thus producing an intimate dynamic of emulation, envy, *ressentiment*, competition and revenge. For Girard, naive 'romantic writers' create under the misconception that desire is spontaneous and has its origins in the desiring subject, but the greatest 'anti-romantic' writers intuitively grasp the truth of mimetic desire, and in their most accomplished works disclose the triangulated neuroses that govern relationships between model, rival and object.[10]

Both Bloom and Girard have written on the 'Scylla and Charybdis' episode of *Ulysses* that will be a key text for this chapter. However, neither critic has engaged with national as opposed to personal literary rivalries between individuals. Nor does either critic have any conception of 'world literature' as a larger system that might require such rivalries for its operative logic. For Bloom and Girard, in short, mimetic desire is viewed as a struggle between competing individual ambitions or as something whose operations can be disclosed by exceptional literary works; viewed in Casanovan light, mimetic desire has to be considered in more systemic terms as something intrinsic to the creation of 'world literature'. Moreover, even for their time, Bloom's and Girard's works are remarkably male centred. For Bloom, the stress falls always on individualized agons between canonical Western male predecessors and canonical latecomers; for Girard, it falls on an equally Western canon of great works that expose the putatively fundamental operations of mimetic desire as he understands that concept. Bloom's and Girard's works both have a conservative impetus. In Bloom's, for instance, modern latecomers always seem to be at an overwhelming disadvantage compared to classical or early modern predecessors against whose castrating power they struggle mightily but in an agon that is often debilitating. Likewise, most of Girard's work assumes the overwhelmingly toxic nature of mimetic desire and stresses especially the dangers stemming from those forms of desire regulated by 'internal mediation' in more modern democratic or socially levelled societies. In other words, Girard considered the more productive or creatively generative aspects of mimetic rivalry only very late in his long career, and that perception was then awkwardly retrofitted to his prior theoretical schemas.[11] That said, the stress in Bloom's and Girard's theories on the destructive aspects of mimetic desire generally might well serve as a useful foil to the more positive conceptions of personal and national competitions for prestige inherent in the work of Pascale Casanova and others. Indeed, there are ways in which the works of all three critics might serve as useful correctives to one another and help to produce some more dialectical conception of national literary rivalries and authorial contests than is offered by any one theory singularly.

This chapter will propose that Irish writers in the Revival and modernist periods had a finely developed sense of the vicissitudes of mimetic rivalry.

This consciousness was sharpened by their collective will to fashion a new literature for Ireland that would become something more than merely a minor tributary to English literature. That national literary ambition was in turn greatly overdetermined by the heated intensities of the ongoing Irish nationalist struggle against British imperialism, and the Irish national struggle was itself enacted and reconfigured within and by the context of a catastrophic European war that had been ignited by nationalist-imperialist rivalries. National and world power rivalries, in short, were rife at the time. That Irish-English agon, I will suggest, impelled individual Irish writers in this era to try their strengths against English precursors in qualitatively different ways and with quite different models of how rivalry worked. Not surprisingly perhaps, Shakespeare and English Renaissance writers appear as inevitable forebears to the Irish Revival (or 'Irish Renaissance' as it was more commonly called in the period); they therefore serve as model for and rival to early twentieth-century Irish literary endeavour. The Irish Renaissance, in other words, felt itself a belated successor to the English Renaissance, and its self-articulation for this reason required some kind of a negotiated relationship with early modern English writers and especially with Shakespeare.

However, it would be wrong to think of the literary production of the period exclusively in terms of an Irish-English contest. The Irish Renaissance was itself a fractious affair that pitched Irish writers of different religions, classes, genders and political convictions and with very different ideologies of the aesthetic against each other. George Moore's satirical depiction of Revivalist Dublin in *Hail and Farewell!* or Æ's (George Russell's) characterization of the Revivalist literary movement as 'five or six people who live in the same town and hate each other cordially' is enough to remind us that Irish writers were at least as fiercely competitive with each other as they were anxious about English literary influence.[12] British-Irish national rivalries and intra-Irish Revivalist rivalries were in turn much complicated by the fact that Catholic-separatist nationalist and Protestant-imperial loyalist attachments in this period produced conflicting conceptions of 'Irishness'.

*Ulysses*, the single most ambitious prose work to emerge from this larger context, internalizes these intra-national and international rivalries and makes them part of its fabric. The 'Scylla and Charybdis' episode raises the whole question of literary rivalry to an extraordinary metacritical and dialectical level. Stephen's wrestling with Shakespeare before a doubtful audience in the National Library acts out an anxiety of influence and the mimetic rivalry it incites; it subjects these to sustained general reflection on the nature of literary production and national and international literary competition. This episode, as we will see, compresses a whole compendium of earlier strong Irish misreadings of Shakespeare into Stephen's performance and it also transacts Joyce's ongoing rivalry with his own Irish contemporaries, all articulated in a doubled time frame that pits the 1904 Dublin of the novel's setting against the 1922 Paris of *Ulysses*'s eventual triumphant publication. In this reading, even though 'Scylla and Charybdis' obviously performs a contest between Joycean and Shakespearian personae, it knowingly wages and stages that contest against the backdrop of three wars: the Second Boer War (1899–1902), a conflict still fresh to recent memory in the recreated Dublin of 1904; and World War I and the Irish War of Independence, events of equally recent memory at the time when *Ulysses* was published. Set in these two overlaid 1904 and 1922 contexts, 'Scylla and Charybdis', I suggest, satirizes the liberal humanist sentimentalism of the Goethean concept of *Weltliteratur*. In the light of Stephen's much-heralded and hostilely or mockingly received interpretation of *Hamlet*, we see how tangled personal, national and international literary rivalries can be and that they cannot easily be extricated from the more catastrophic conflicts of the political world order. In Joyce's imagination, Goethean *Weltliteratur* may profess its high-minded supranational transcendence of unseemly personal and vengeful national rivalries, but it is nevertheless out of such base stuff that 'world texts' are created and from which they can never wholly be purged. *Weltliteratur*, in *Ulysses*, consecrates the texts it elevates into a cosmopolitan supranational system that claims to be neutrally above the conflicts of nations and their melancholy obsessions; yet world literature also requires nations and national rivalries and, even when they are elevated to 'world classics' or 'great books', canonical literary texts are always made to serve some political purpose or other.

## II

'Shakespear, for instance, is to me one of the towers of the Bastille, and down he must come'. So wrote George Bernard Shaw to Ellen Terry on 27 January 1897, explaining the 'capers' with regard to 'Shakespear', English Bardolatory and the conventions of Shakespearian theatrical production that Shaw would repeat across his career. 'In any language of the world', he wrote in an article in *The Saturday Review* a year later, 'Brand, Peer Gynt, and Emperor or Galilean prove their author a thinker of extraordinary penetration, and a moralist of international influence.

Turn from them to To be or not to be, or, The seven ages of man, and imagine, if you can, anybody more critical than a village schoolmaster being imposed on by such platitudinous fudge'. To compare Ibsen and Shakespeare, he insisted, chastising William Archer who had done so, is mistaken because '[f]rom such a test Ibsen comes out with a double first-class: Shakespear comes out hardly anywhere'.[13]

Some three decades later in a collection of essays titled *Literary Blasphemies*, Ernest Boyd, the Irish-born author of *Ireland's Literary Renaissance* (1916), one of the earliest books about the Irish Revival, blasted English literary pieties in terms that might even have made Shaw blanch. 'Nowadays', Boyd wrote in 'An Address to the Indignant Reader', 'we should have no hesitation in pointing out that Milton was a psychopathic Puritan' and 'an undersized man with the pigmentation of an albino'. 'There is evidence suggesting', he added, that 'his mysterious affection of the eyes was the result of hereditary syphilis'. 'Milton', Boyd contended, 'remains as a sacred relic of the belief that Puritanism and literature can be harmoniously reconciled'. The fact that his work now relied so heavily on scholarly annotators illustrated, Boyd proposed, 'more perfectly than any other the process of artificial respiration whereby classical literature is kept alive', whereas to the average reader Milton, like all Puritans, had managed only to make 'the Devil irresistibly attractive'.[14] In the Shakespeare essay that opened his volume, Boyd cited, without endorsing, Voltaire's assessment of *Hamlet* as the work of a 'drunken savage' and Tolstoy's verdict that Shakespeare's works satisfied neither the demands of art nor morality. He also recalled the estimates of several British critics, from David Hume to David Garrick, of the Bard's intellectual imperfections and took issue with what he considered the absurdly sentimental conceptions of the English Renaissance rehearsed from Charles Lamb or Algernon Swinburne to T. S. Eliot or Rupert Brooke. Then he gave his own verdict:

> That 'golden age' of British theater was actually a period when the foul, the extravagant, and the horrible flourished – thanks to the hocus-pocus of blank verse, in which the record of bombastic futility was achieved. It was a period when the British theater was in a state of barbarousness compared with which the theater of France and Spain stood in the same relation as the American bathroom to a Tudor cesspool. It was, however, into this uncouth society of ranters and brawlers that Shakespeare came to learn his trade as playwright and from which he was gradually to emancipate himself – though never entirely.[15]

In Boyd's assessment, Shakespeare might be an incomparable master of English, but he was a genius 'handicapped by the conventions and conditions of an age when brawn was more respected than brains', and his work 'does not open up the glorious world of Elizabethan literature but rather closes it by showing us the best that the times could produce'. Shakespeare, Boyd asserts, surely echoing Shaw here, 'has no message for mankind' and '[i]f he is irresistible it is because he is a musician of words so lovely that the English tongue is forever illuminated by his use of it'.[16]

In his epilogue to *Shakespeare and the Victorians*, Adrian Poole writes that '[t]he best way of marking an end to Victorian Shakespeare is to look towards Dublin'.[17] True, but in some ways Dublin had also done much to produce the venerated Victorian Shakespeare, especially in the work of Edward Dowden (1843–1913). Holder of the first Chair of English at Trinity College Dublin, and author of a steady flow of works on the English playwright, including among many others *Shakespere: A Critical Study of His Mind and Art* (1875), *Shakespeare Primer* (1871), *The Sonnets of William Shakespeare* (1881) and *Introduction to Shakespeare* (1893), Dowden did much to consolidate the late Victorian conception of Shakespeare as a solidly professional man of letters. Dowden's Shakespeare therefore makes a marked contrast to that of his French contemporary, Hippolyte Taine's 1863 version of Shakespeare as a man of extravagantly passionate and impulsive genius.[18] Instead, Dowden offers a distinctly un-French and un-Celtic Shakespeare who was a 'prudent, industrious and economical' writer exemplified by his '[e]nergy, devotion to the fact, self-government, tolerance' and '[s]uch habits of thought and feeling [as] are those which belong more especially to the Protestant ideal of manhood'.[19] Yet even as Dowden, who was also president of the English Goethe Society, worked industriously to secure this upright Protestant Shakespeare, successive generations of Irish writers were also working hard to overthrow that icon.

Oscar Wilde could speak humorously of being as an Irishman 'condemned by the English to speak the language of Shakespeare'. In 1888 Wilde praised Shakespeare at Stratford-upon-Avon in conventional Victorian tones as one of the many great English poets who had helped to create 'the same eloquent tongue' that sustained 'this great empire – the greatest empire the world had certainly yet seen'. Even so, Wilde was also happy to chip away at the Christian Shakespeare a year later in 'The Portrait of Mr. W. H.' (1889) by creating a homosexual Shakespeare infatuated with a boy actor.[20] Shaw's early career as a reviewer and a champion of Ibsen triggered a lifelong series of volleys against Shakespeare, starting with the above-mentioned article in *The Saturday Review* in March 1898 when he berated William Archer for classing

Shakespeare as a thinker equal to Ibsen. Shaw reiterated this charge in 1905 when he claimed that 'Shakespear's weakness lies in his complete deficiency in the highest spheres of thought, in which poetry embraces religion, philosophy, morality, and the bearing of these on communities, which is sociology'. Shaw's campaign against Bardolatory persisted in one mode or another for some sixty years, yielding several comparative assessments of his own merits versus those of the English precursor, including the essay 'Better than Shakespear?', printed as the preface to his *Caesar and Cleopatra* (1899, preface 1901), and the puppet-play 'Shakes versus Shav', produced in 1949.[21]

In March 1901, as Shaw's move-Shakespeare-out-of-my-way crusade was getting underway, Yeats visited Stratford-upon-Avon to view the history plays. That visit yielded 'At Stratford-on-Avon' (1901), an essay later published in *Ideas of Good and Evil* (1903), which registered Yeats's decisive break with Dowden. Scorning the Victorian utilitarianism that ran from George Eliot to Dowden and that honoured a Shakespeare who supposedly preferred the practical and worldly Henry V to the deposed dreamer Richard II, Yeats argued that this was essentially to assess Shakespeare's art by the mentality of 'a Municipal Councillor weighing the merits of a Town Clerk'.[22] For Yeats, Shakespeare was not Dowden's practical-minded middle-class man of the modern world but, rather, a last survivor of the Middle Ages who had had unfortunately been forced to take his work from European Renaissance materials because he lived in an era of 'the great famine, the sinking down of popular imagination, the dying out of the traditional phantasy, the ebbing out of the energy of race'. Depicting an English Renaissance that looked uncannily like his own conception of the Irish Revival, and a Bard that resembled Yeats himself, Yeats declared that 'Shakespeare wrote at a time when solitary great men were gathering to themselves the fire that had once flowed hither and thither among all men, when individualism in work and thought and emotion was breaking up the old rhythms of life, when the common people, no longer uplifted by the myths of Christianity and of still older faiths, were sinking into the earth'.[23] In 1909, the Irish American Frank Harris, later biographer to Shaw and Wilde, published *The Man Shakespeare and His Tragic Life-Story*. Harris portrayed the Shakespeare of the early comedies as a wild, high-living young sensualist whose coerced and bitterly unhappy marriage to Anne Hathaway forced him to flee to London. There, Harris contended, Shakespeare suffered another unhappy love affair, this time with a handmaid to Queen Elizabeth, Mary Fitton, an event that transformed the playwright into a disconsolate nihilist whose personal torments nevertheless yielded the darkly passionate tragedies and the sombre late problem plays.[24]

Viewed against this Irish backdrop, it seems fair to say that whatever else they might be, the young James Joyce's championing of Ibsen over Shakespeare or the famously iconoclastic take on *Hamlet* that appears in *Ulysses* is not particularly original in tenor. On the contrary, by the time *Ulysses* appeared in 1922, an Irish literary irreverence for Victorian Shakespearian pieties was well established, even conventional. 'The bard's fellow countrymen', John Eglinton remarks dryly in the course of Stephen's perorations on *Hamlet,* 'are rather tired perhaps of our brilliancies of theorizing'. Eglinton's comment is taken up by Best who insists that the most brilliant of these 'theorizings' is Wilde's 'The Portrait of Mr. W. H.' and in the course of Stephen's performance Best had already reminded the company that 'we ought to mention another Irish commentator, Mr. George Bernard Shaw. Nor should we forget Mr Frank Harris. His articles on Shakespeare in the *Saturday Review* are surely brilliant'.[25] Joyce, then, self-consciously situates his own irreverent take on Shakespeare in 'Scylla and Charybdis' within an archive of earlier Irish subversive takes on the English Bard. In other words, when Stephen conducts his baroque interpretation of *Hamlet* in the National Library, he is fully conscious of the fact that he is a latecomer to these inventive Irish acts of Bardocide and that his own performance will have to compete with many entertaining precedents.

Still, these iconoclastic Irish constructions of Shakespeare are nevertheless only one part of the story, and Stephen's version of Shakespeare has to confront also the quite different Shakespeare of other Irish adversaries. The Shakespeare of Wilde, Shaw, Yeats, Boyd and Harris, in other words, always ran alongside a doughtier Irish Shakespeare, the cherished icon of an embattled loyalist Ireland whose loyalism became ever more intense as the Irish Home Rule campaign threatened to undo the union with Britain and World War I threatened to undermine British imperial hegemony internationally. Dowden's work, which offered the Elizabethan playwright as epitome of manly English Protestant value, was itself part of a larger unionist and imperialist commandeering of Shakespeare that was also gathering pace in these decades as the British state began to feel its domestic integrity and global supremacy threatened. Thus, against the kinds of irreverent or Hibernicized Irish Shakespeares cited earlier there was also a series of turn-of-the-century national/imperial campaigns designed to promote the playwright not only as the greatest of English writers but also as a world figure without compare. In 1901, for example, the same year that Yeats visited Stratford-upon-Avon, the British Empire Shakespeare Society (BESS) was founded to promote Shakespeare's work across the empire by way of dramatic readings, scholarly editions, discussion circles and commemorations; that society's official gazette ran from 1915 to 1939. In 1907 the Dublin branch of BESS was established, its inaugural meeting presided over by the famous Trinity College classicist, John Pentland Mahaffy, erstwhile tutor to Oscar Wilde, and future scoffer of *Ulysses* as evidence that a separate Catholic university ought never to have been established for the 'aborigines' of Ireland. Mahaffy's presidency of BESS was assumed in 1908 by Dowden, erstwhile friend to Yeats's father, John Butler Yeats, though the Yeatses were cultural nationalists and Dowden was adamantly not.[26] From the late 1880s onwards, Dowden had in fact lectured at public meetings to maintain the union with Britain, assisted as secretary of the Liberal Union, led the Irish Unionist alliance and had even requested from Swinburne (a figure also invoked in the opening of *Ulysses* and in the 'Scylla and Charybdis' episode) a unionist song. That song, 'The Commonweal: A Song for Irish Unionists', had appeared in *The Times* on 30 June 1886, Gladstone's association with Charles Stewart Parnell denounced there in the line 'See the man of words embrace the man of blood!'[27]

As the 1916 tercentenary of Shakespeare's death approached, BESS and the Shakespeare Tercentenary Society tried to promote a global Shakespeare by having his work commemorated on every continent. The outbreak of World War I complicated these plans, but as late as 1913 the then president of the German Shakespeare Society, Alois Brandl of Berlin University, delivered a British Academy Annual Shakespeare Lecture on the topic of 'Shakespeare and Germany', at which stage he could still look forward to a common British and German celebration of the tercentenary. Nevertheless, Brandl, not without a hint of German-British rivalry, went on to claim in his lecture that Shakespeare was currently more widely performed in Germany than in England and that German culture in some respects enjoyed a greater affinity with Shakespeare than did his native land. That sentiment was not unusual: by the early twentieth century there was a widespread feeling in both England and Germany that Shakespeare had been appropriated by German scholarship and positioned in the emerging national German literary canon as the nation's 'third German classic', alongside Goethe and Schiller. By 1916, two years into World War I, the British desire to repossess Shakespeare from the Germans, and to impress him on the Empire as icon of its greatness and symbol of its unity, had acquired a more perfervid quality.[28]

The 24 March 1916 *Irish Times* editorial, 'Shakespeare in Dublin', passages from which are cited at the head of this chapter, needs to be understood in this wider context.[29] The article laments the fact that the Shakespeare tercentenary is at hand, but that Dublin seems to be doing little to mark the occasion. The Bard's death, the article frets, will be better marked in Berlin than in Dublin because the Germans have long been taking custody of '*unser* Shakespeare'. To add insult to appropriation, American-style mass culture, represented by Charlie Chaplin, can command large commercial audiences in London that the Bard cannot. The editorial, in short, represents a perfect condensation of Irish upper-class unionist anxieties about the progress of the war in Europe, about Irish loyalty and lack of imperial patriotism and about the apparently declining capacity of Shakespeare to serve as a common cultural glue whether in London, where Chaplin commands bigger audiences, or in Dublin, where the English writer's tercentenary appears to be treated with indifference. Shakespeare's tercentenary by historical coincidence fell on Easter Sunday, 23 April 1916. When Patrick Pearse, James Connolly and the other leaders of the republican insurrection, several Shakespeare lovers among them, entered the General Post Office on Easter Monday, 24 April 1916, readers of *The Irish Times* must have felt that the newspaper's editorial writer's ominous sense a month before of Irish and German threats to the Empire had assumed an even more sinister form than they had feared.

## III

Urbane, to comfort them, the quaker librarian purred:
– And we have, have we not, those priceless pages of *Wilhelm Meister*. A great poet on a great brother poet. A hesitating soul taking arms against a sea of troubles, torn by conflicting doubts, as one sees in real life.

(*Ulysses*, 151: 1–4)

The 'Scylla and Charybdis' chapter, set in the National Library on the afternoon of 16 June 1904, opens *in medias res* with these words, a softly sibilant purr to a humanist conception of literature as the work of a benign transnational fraternity of great brother poets and as a testament to the great German Goethe's reverence for the even greater British Shakespeare, *primus inter pares* in all right-thinking literary hierarchies. Thomas William Lyster, director of the National Library and translator in 1883 of Heinrich Dünzter's *Life of Goethe*, speaks the lines. Lyster's companions include Richard Irvine Best, who as a young man had gone – as Stephen too has done – to Paris, though in Best's case to study Old Irish. Like J. M. Synge, whom he had befriended in Paris, Best had attended Henri d'Arbois de Jubainville's lectures in the Collège de France and on his return to Dublin he had translated Jubainville's *Le Cycle Mythologique Irlandais et la Mythologie Celtique* into English in 1903; in 1904 he became assistant director at the National Library. The third in this company is John Eglinton by penname, but really another William, William Kirkpatrick Magee, poet and critic, by 1904 author of *Two Essays on the Remnant* (1896) and *Literary Ideals of Ireland* (1899), the latter a friendly critique of what Eglinton felt to be the Yeatsian Revivalists' excessive reverence for Celtic mythology at the expense of modern intellectual ideas.

All three librarians share a common Irish Protestant heritage and membership in the Irish literary and scholarly establishment, the upper tiers of which were still strongly Protestant and unionist at the time. All three also had strong connections with both Dowden and Yeats. Lyster would later be remembered by Stephen Gwynn as 'Dowden's most ardent disciple';[30] Best was an admirer of Pater and Wilde and a friend of Dowden, his fellow Goethe enthusiast; in 1904, thanks to Dowden's support, Eglinton had been appointed to the National Library as librarian.[31] Also present when the episode opens is Æ, mystic, poet, leading Revivalist and Yeats's closest Irish associate. In the early twentieth-century Irish context, all four figures indicate how Protestant writers dominated both the nationalist cultural Revival, of which the most distinguished figure was Yeats, and Irish cultural unionism, for which Dowden was a key intellectual figurehead. In wider literary terms, these figures might also be considered lower-tier factotums to the operations of world literature: revering Goethe, so often associated with the origins of *Weltliteratur*, and even more so Shakespeare, the chief ornament of any world literature canon, they are – as poets, translators, editors, scholars, critics and librarians – bookmen professionally committed to the circulation of texts fundamental to Goethe's liberal humanist conception of world literature in terms of cosmopolitan intellectual exchange.

'Monsieur de la Palice, Stephen sneered, was alive fifteen minutes before his death' (151: 16–17). In this urbanely professional company of men of letters, Stephen Dedalus is a nettled outsider, a Catholic by background, conscious that, because of his drinking, consorting with prostitutes and constant indebtedness, he is a figure of disrepute among these well-respected Protestants. However, the episode is constructed so that its events are viewed from Stephen's perspective; we have access throughout his performance to his inner thoughts and responses to his interlocutors, but not to their inner reactions to him. Outwardly, Stephen speaks 'super-politely' (152: 56), at least to begin with, though inwardly he is mostly contemptuous, treating his interlocutors as pedants whom he must at once entertain and yet intellectually vanquish if his *Hamlet* lecture is to be a success and his intellectual superiority asserted. To Stephen, the librarians appear essentially as clerk copyists out of *Bouvard et Pécuchet* (1881), the *sottisier* novel for which Flaubert was reputed to have read 1,500 other books and which he wanted to be the greatest of his works, an unsurpassable masterpiece. That novel's recyclings of the verities of received nineteenth-century literary and scientific knowledge, and Flaubert's conception of it as an encyclopaedic farce that would give expression to his contempt for his contemporaries, has considerable significance for the 'Scylla and Charybdis' episode and indeed for that combination of epic, encyclopaedia and farce that is *Ulysses* more generally. Flaubert's work, however, unlike Joyce's, was never brought to a conclusion.[32]

Lyster's reverent invocation of Goethe's and Shakespeare's transnational literary brotherhood at the outset of the 'Scylla and Charybdis' episode reads very differently depending on whether readers view the library episode from the pre–World War I vantage point of 1904 or the post–World War I and post–Easter 1916 perspective of *Ulysses*'s publication. Pre-war invocations of fraternal German-British literary relations had done nothing to stop a disastrous European war; after World War I, writers like T. S. Eliot knew that it would take a great deal of effort to re-establish the 'republic of letters' that had broken down during the war years. In any case, despite this invocation of literary fraternity, it is immediately clear that the atmosphere in the National Library scene is generally one of bristling hostility barely repressed beneath well-mannered exchanges and intellectual badinage. Æ's and Eglinton's irritation seems to be founded on their disapproval of Stephen's earlier intellectual boastings and his customary air of superior hauteur and their ill feeling is aggravated by the fact that Stephen has sponged money from them. Like Best, Stephen is a returnee from Paris, and that city, where *Ulysses* will be published under the imprint of the American Sylvia Beach's 'Shakespeare and Company', impinges on the young writer's mind throughout this and other episodes. However, unlike Best, who has at least translated Jubainville, Stephen has published nothing noteworthy. Likewise, Æ is a recognized man of letters in Dublin, Eglinton a published critic, and Best and Lyster are translators; all are in solid professional employment whereas Stephen is merely an occasional but unhappy part-time teacher. Moreover, Stephen's consciousness of the sums he has borrowed from the individuals present, combined with his sense that he has been excluded from the Dublin literary establishment, whether in its Dowden and unionist or Yeatsian cultural nationalist-affiliated formations, lends edge to the proceedings.

Stephen's sense of exclusion is stressed throughout the episode. Æ, the most senior literary figure present, is openly antagonistic to him and leaves to return to his offices at *The Homestead* newspaper while homeless Stephen (and behind him exiled Joyce) is still only starting his performance. For Æ, Stephen's biographical approach to Shakespeare, 'this prying into the family life of a great man' (155: 181), is an ill-mannered display confirming Stephen's general impertinence. When Æ gets up to go and the others present gather ceremoniously round him, Stephen's ostracism could hardly be made plainer. John Eglinton reminds Æ that George Moore is holding a literary soirée that evening and begs Russell to attend; while others, including Buck Mulligan, have been invited, Stephen has not. To add insult to injury, Lyster announces excitedly that Æ 'is gathering together a sheaf of our younger poets' verses' (158: 290–291), and in the hubbub that follows we learn that works by Padraic Colum and James Starkey will appear in that collection, but nothing by Stephen.

As in 'Nestor' and 'Proteus', Stephen is painfully conscious throughout 'Scylla and Charybdis' that he exists essentially as unfulfilled potential. Teaching the history lesson in 'Nestor', Stephen ponders the 'infinite possibilities' foreclosed by actually realized historical events and wonders, 'was that only possible which came to pass?' (21: 50–52); in 'Proteus', he ruefully recalls his Parisian pretensions and the green oval-leaved books he was to bequeath 'to all the great libraries of the world, including Alexandria' where '[s]omeone was to read them there after a few thousand years, a mahamanvantara' (34: 141–143); in 'Scylla and Charybdis', he ponders again the 'possibilities of the possible as possible: things not known' (159: 349–350). From the perspective of 1904, Stephen is an envious and self-thwarted nobody venting his spleen on those who have already achieved some position in the world of letters. Read from the vantage of 1922, however, the figures he takes on in 'Scylla and Charybdis' will have been reduced forever by Joyce to bit-players in what was already becoming the legend of *Ulysses*. The reader's sense of whose potential has been fulfilled and whose unrealized or foreclosed looks very different whether the 'Scylla and Charybdis' episode is considered from a 1904 or 1922 perspective.

Nevertheless, though the rivalries between Stephen and his company are those of intimate enemies, they also have a larger national literary tenor. In an episode beginning with an invocation to Goethe and Shakespeare, John Eglinton's opening taunt to Dedalus is that he has never made good his student literary boast that he could produce an epic to rival Milton's English epic. 'Have you found those six brave medicals, John Eglinton asked with elder's gall, to write *Paradise Lost* at your dictation? *The Sorrows of Satan* he calls it' (151: 18–20). Like William Blake, who had also proposed to rewrite Milton's Biblical epic with Satan as hero, Stephen is pegged here as a figure of Luciferian ambition. But Eglinton is jibing at the gap between juvenile ambition and its later non-actualization. *The Sorrows of Satan*, Marie Corelli's 1895-published, Faustian-modelled novel, considered to be one of the world's first international best-sellers, mocks in its trashy popularity Stephen's juvenile aestheticist craving for literary greatness. Even as Stephen feels Eglinton's sting, 'He holds my follies hostage' (152: 34), the latter presses again and underlines not just Stephen's overweening adolescent pretensions but those of Irish literature more generally: 'Our young Irish bards, John Eglinton censured, have yet to create a figure which the world will set beside Saxon Shakespeare's Hamlet' (152: 43–44). The stakes are plain: despite his boasting, Stephen has not matched Milton, nor has the Irish Revival matched Shakespeare. Later, when Moore's literary soirée is being discussed, that lack is mentioned again: Lyster remarks, '[o]ur national epic has yet to be written, Dr Sigerson says. Moore is the man for it' (158: 309–310), and remarks that Moore and his friend Edward Martyn 'remind one of Don Quixote and Sancho Panza' (158: 308–309). To produce a national literature that will achieve world recognition, it is necessary to produce, as Shakespeare, Cervantes and Goethe have all done, a work that will be accepted everywhere as a great national epic. Greatness also is attained when authors create figures that acquire a life almost independent of their authors, as Hamlet, Falstaff, Milton's Satan or Don Quixote do. For Eglinton, for a literature to fall short of this is to remain minor, to lag behind Shakespeare about whom even the French and Germans will concede that, in Alexandre Dumas's words, '[a]fter God Shakespeare has created most' (175: 1028–1029).

Eglinton had in fact published an essay titled 'Irish Books' in 1911, which reappeared in *Anglo-Irish Essays* in 1917, where he had posed the question whether despite 'the voluminous literary activity of the last twenty years' the Irish had yet produced 'a Book [. . .] which Ireland seems likely to take to its affections permanently'. 'If a masterpiece should still come of this literary movement', he predicted:

we need not be surprised if it appears by a kind of accident and in some unexpected quarter, and we have a fancy that appearances in modern Ireland point to a writer of the type of Cervantes rather than to an idealising poet or romance writer. A hero as loveable as the great Knight of Rueful Countenance might be conceived, who in some back street of Dublin had addled his brains with brooding over Ireland's wrongs, and that extensive but not always quite sincere literature which expresses the resentment of her sons towards the stranger.[33]

When the 1911 essay was republished in 1917, Eglinton added a short coda retracting the severity of his earlier verdict with the remark that 'the collected poems of Mr. Yeats, AE, and others, Synge's plays, etc., will doubtless be called "books" by generations of Irish readers'. He noted, too, that in 1911 'Mr. James Joyce had not yet published his highly instructive studies in the life of those young men who have chiefly to be reckoned with nowadays in arranging or forecasting the future of Ireland'. Moreover, he concluded by observing that his Cervantean prediction, meaning a comic or anti-Romantic masterpiece, had since had 'a partial fulfilment in Mr. George Moore's *Hail and Farewell*.[34] Eglinton can be considered wonderfully astute in his forecasting that any really epic work that might emerge from Ireland would probably be mock epic rather than poetic and heroic, a Cervantean anti-romance rather than an idealizing Yeatsian romance. Nevertheless, he was also wide of the mark when he considered Moore's *Hail and Farewell* to be the predicted mock epic, though in 1917 he could hardly have anticipated *Ulysses*, the real fulfillment of his augury. Nor, of course, could Eglinton have anticipated the damning role that he himself would play in that Cervantean comic masterpiece when it did appear.

'See this. Remember' (158: 294). In the library scene, Stephen commits himself, in words that recall the Ghost's injunction to Hamlet to seek his revenge, to remember the sneers of those who dismissed him and Irish literature as merely fallow possibility, as unrealized and unlikely-to-be-realized potential. Within the immediate time frame of the chapter, Stephen submits these jibes to memory so that at some future point he may exact his revenge; within the larger frame of *Ulysses*, Joyce achieves this vengeance. Revivalists and Dowdenists alike had failed to recognize Stephen's youthful genius, but *Ulysses* now sentences the Dublin doubters to be recalled to posterity as eternal Rosencrantzes and Guildensterns of literary pedantry. In *Ulysses*, modern Ireland will find its epic, its work to rival Shakespeare and Cervantes, Dante and Goethe, and the other world masters, and it will not be George Moore who will be the man for it. Within the time confines of 'Scylla and Charybdis' itself, though, Stephen is forever doomed to remain a frustrated epitome of thwarted potential only. Even as he delivers his *Hamlet* reading, he comments superciliously on his own pretensions, and knows the performance to be a provocation, much of it merely improvised bravado cadged from fellow Irish commentaries on the English author or from the works of Georg Brandes, Simon Lee and others. 'A. E. I. O. U.', Stephen quips to himself early in his performance, thinking of the money he owes to Russell, but this 'I owe you' is readable here both as an acknowledgement of the sum due and also an 'I.O.U' or threat that he has scores with Russell yet to settle. Even as he muses on the unpaid financial debt, Stephen recalls that he 'spent most of it in Georgina Johnson's bed, clergyman's daughter' (155: 196–197), clearly relishing the fact that the bedded woman's father is a Protestant minister. For all its antic humour, there is no little Calibanesque venom in 'Scylla and Charybdis'.

Yet while 'Syclla' is certainly a Joycean revenge plot, it is also clearly something more. Æ and the Dublin librarians may be Stephen's (and Joyce's) immediate antagonists, but Stephen's engagements with them never amounts to much more than witty repartee and intellectual score settling, and beyond their proximate rivalry lies the more formidable, if ghostly, quarry that is Shakespeare and, beyond Shakespeare, general issues of international literary rivalries. For all its advertised ingenuity as described by Mulligan to Haines in the opening chapter, Stephen's representation of Shakespeare and *Hamlet* is reasonably straightforward. While still a callow adolescent, Shakespeare, or so Stephen has it, was seduced by Anne Hathaway, a twenty-six-year-old local beauty, more sexually experienced than he. This early baiting of the boy Shakespeare led directly to his unhappy marriage to Anne, but inflicted also a lasting sexual trauma from which William the conquered would never recover. As soon as his twins are born, an embittered Shakespeare forsakes Stratford for London where he has a successful theatrical career, though even that success can never erase from his memory his overthrow by Anne. *Venus and Adonis* is one of the earliest literary issues of this formative trauma and establishes Shakespeare's London reputation. Yet even if this work and his early comedies and *Romeo and Juliet* make the rising playwright's reputation as a flamboyant love poet, his sexual confidence, Stephen argues, can never again be wholly recovered because 'Belief in himself has been untimely killed' (161: 455–456):

He was overborne in a cornfield first (a ryefield, I should say) and he will never be a victor in his own eyes after nor play victoriously the game of laugh and lie down. Assumed dongiovannism will not save him. No later undoing will undo the first undoing. The tusk of the boar has wounded him there where love lies ableeding.

(161: 456–460)

*The Taming of the Shrew* vents, Stephen proposes, the younger Shakespeare's rage against women and represents his attempt to master in art what cannot be mastered in life. But when Shakespeare learns that Anne has committed adultery with Richard and Edmund, the two Shakespeare brothers who give their names to William's theatre's most heinous villains, his unmitigated rage against women and the foulness of usurping brothers become leitmotifs in all of his great works. That rage begets, in Stephen's account, not only the venomous *ressentiment* of Iago – 'His unremitting intellect is the hornmad Iago ceaselessly willing that the moor in him shall suffer' (174: 1023–1024) – but also the fury of the Ghost-father in *Hamlet* who upbraids his treacherous brother Claudius and Gertrude, his adulterous wife. In Joyce's reading, as in Frank Harris's *The Man Shakespeare and His Tragic Life-Story*, Shakespeare's creative fecundity or imaginative magnificence never allows him to overcome his traumas through cathartic sublimation: '[T]he theme of the false or the usurping or the adulterous brother or all three in one is to Shakespeare, what the poor are not, always with him. The note of banishment, banishment from the heart, banishment from home, sounds uninterruptedly from *The Two Gentlemen of Verona* onward till Prospero breaks his staff, buries it certain fathoms in the earth and drowns his book' (174: 997–1002).[35] As he reaches the end of his lecture, Stephen is insistent on this point: 'Man delights him not nor woman neither, Stephen said. He returns after a life of absence to that spot of earth where he was born, where he has always been, man and boy, a silent witness and there, his journey of life ended, he plants his mulberrytree in the earth. Then dies' (175: 1030–1034).

Within this larger construction of Shakespeare's life, *Hamlet* occupies a special place for Stephen, as that play is usually thought to be Shakespeare's masterpiece and the work most commonly used to convey the legend of 'Gentle Will', the great-natured Shakespeare of Goethe and Bardolatory. Critical to that legend is the idea that Shakespeare is most closely identified in *Hamlet* with Young Hamlet, the meditative prince of Goethean conception whose misfortune it is to be born into a world too brutal for his contemplative character and humanist spirit. Stephen upends this reading in several ways. His most obvious reversal is to insist, taking a lead from William Rowe, that Shakespeare had played the part in the original production of the play not of the youthful Prince, played by Richard Burbage, but of the vengeful Ghost of Old Hamlet railing against the sins of adultery and usurpation. Through the figure of the Ghost, Stephen insinuates, Shakespeare expresses his grief for his own dead son, Hamnet, and his unquenchable fury with his traitorous wife. Furthermore, Stephen's Hamlet is no shy sentimentalist or stranger to brutality, but is instead responsible for the corpse-strewn stage that ends the tragedy. He is anachronistically associated also with English excesses in the Boer War:

> A deathsman of the soul Robert Greene called him, Stephen said. Not for nothing was he a butcher's son, wielding the sledded poleaxe and spitting in his palms. Nine lives are taken off for his father's one. Our Father who art in purgatory. Khaki Hamlets don't hesitate to shoot. The bloodboltered shambles in act five is a forecast of the concentration camp sung by Mr Swinburne.
>
> (154: 130–136)

In this passage, author and character blend into each other, as do various British colonial atrocities. The legend that John Shakespeare, William's father, was a butcher is welded to Old Hamlet's smiting butchery of the Poles, and the phrase 'Khaki Hamlets don't hesitate to shoot' invokes the Irish slogan 'Don't hesitate to shoot' used to protest English coercion policies in the 1880s and again in the Boer War. That latter war begets the reference to Swinburne's 'On the Death of Colonel Benson', a vitriolic attack on Boer outrages against the British, considered by some Swinburne's apologia for the English concentration camps of that war.[36] Here, the bloodthirstiness of Shakespearian revenge tragedy finds its contemporary apotheosis in self-righteous Swinburnian bellicosity during the South African war, both hard to dissociate from the even more appalling 'bloodboltered shambles' of World War I during which 'Scylla and Charybdis' was being composed.

    In general, Stephen's Shakespeare hews far closer to that of his more 'realist' or 'rationalist' Irish or Irish American contemporaries such as Shaw, Harris and even Dowden than to the 'idealist' or 'romantic' Shakespeare of Goethe's *Wilhelm Meister* or of Yeats or his associate Æ in the library. Like Harris, Stephen insists on the unhappiness of Shakespeare's early marriage as a primal source for his creative life and that this marital bitterness was until the end unmitigated. Like Shaw and, in a different manner, Dowden, Stephen also stresses the entrepreneurial Shakespeare, the successful professional man of letters and shrewd businessman who rises swiftly from ostler to chief dramatist for the Globe and ends by returning in prosperity, if not happiness, to Stratford to live as a rich country gentleman. Stephen's Shakespeare is no feudalist of the kind that Walt Whitman had set himself to oppose or that Yeats's 'At Stratford-on-Avon' essay had embraced.[37] Yet though Stephen's entrepreneurial Shakespeare steers Joyce close to Dowden and away from Yeats, the crucial difference lies in their respective conceptions of capitalism and the English Renaissance. For Dowden, Shakespeare's business acumen is something approved and the English Renaissance, in conventional Victorian manner, is understood as a golden age of masculine Protestantism and English self-assertion. For Stephen, in contrast, that Renaissance is already decidedly capitalist and imperialist and displays all the signs of their corrupt excesses. '[A]n age of exhausted whoredom groping for its god' (169: 810), he calls it, and asserts that 'Sir Walter Raleigh, when they arrested him, had half a million francs on his back including a pair of fancy stays. The gombeen-woman Eliza Tudor had underlinen enough to vie with her of Sheba' (165: 628–631). This rapacious extravagance is also Shakespeare's: 'He was a rich country gentleman, Stephen said, with a coat of arms and landed estate at Stratford and a house in Ireland yard, a capitalist shareholder, a bill promoter, a tithefarmer' (167: 710–712). As such, his art, 'more than the art of feudalism as Walt Whitman called it, is the art of surfeit' (165: 625–626). And behind that surfeit lie all the vices of vicious capitalist avarice and relentless accumulation. 'The son of a maltjobber and mon-eylender', Shakespeare 'was himself a cornjobber and moneylender, with ten tods of corn hoarded in the famine riots' (168: 742–744). A usurer, Shakespeare 'drew Shylock out of his own long pocket' (168: 741–742) and 'sued a fellowplayer for the price of a few bags of malt and exacted his pound of flesh in interest for every money lent' (168: 745–747). Moreover, his drama plays to English populist sentiment. Shylock's pros-ecution in *The Merchant of Venice* panders to the persecutory climate surrounding the execution of Roderigo Lopez, a Portuguese Catholic and converted Jew convicted of plotting to poison Elizabeth. The lost Armada is jeered in *Love's Labour Lost*; *Hamlet* and *Macbeth* pay tribute to the coronation of the Scottish witch-hunter James I. *The Tempest* reflects Shakespeare's investments in English expansionism into the Americas and features 'Patsy Caliban, our American cousin' (168: 756–757).

In these passages, Stephen's Bardicide rhetoric becomes quite vitriolic and is lent added edge by his references to gombeens, famine-hoarding, Ireland yard, and the legal persecution of Catholics – terms that associate Shakespeare and early modern English capitalist imperialism with the ravaging of Ireland under British rule in phrases that seem expressly calculated to rile his Protestant audience. In other words, these passages pull out all the stops to disabuse any sentimental idea of Shakespeare or the English Renaissance, and Stephen's interpretative method has rightly been said to anticipate late twentieth-century New Historicist or postcolonial readings of Shakespeare.[38] Nevertheless, despite this sandblasting indictment of the English national writer, Shakespeare is never merely a foil to Stephen nor solely a figure of scorn. As many critics have noted, behind the figure of the cuckolded, unappeasably jealous Shakespeare it is hard not to see the Joyce who worked himself to fever-pitches of jealousy over Nora Barnacle's imagined affair with one of his Dublin friends; playing to that perversity, Nora addressed Joyce in some of her letters as 'Dear Cuckold'.[39] Moreover, Stephen's portrait also allows lyrically for Shakespeare's poignant grief for his dead son, a grief that syncopates with Stephen's own guilty grief, silently ruminated across the episode, for his dead mother. Stephen, Joyce and Shakespeare share in addition a common sense of being usurped – Shakespeare by his adulterous brothers, Stephen by the sycophantic Mulligan, Joyce by his fellow Irish writers and intellectuals – and the same plangently exilic 'note of banishment, banishment from the heart, banishment from home'. An intense rivalry with Shakespeare, then, does not preclude all sorts of identifications with him.

Most unexpectedly of all perhaps, given the English writer's long association with London, Stephen – in one of the few places where he converges with Yeats's Shakespeare – invokes a provincial Shakespeare, a rustic writer from the periphery who has to migrate to the literary capital to secure his fame. Recalling his own youthful literary ambitions in Paris, Stephen says of Shakespeare's move to the English capital that 'Elizabethan London lay as far from Stratford as corrupt Paris lies from virgin Dublin' (154: 149–150). Here, Stephen and Shakespeare are invoked as similar provincial aspirants or passionate pilgrims who must forsake their homes and become ghosts to their past lives to achieve a metropolitan fame. Where Stephen and Shakespeare differ most is in relation to the matter of debts: an emotionally mean-spirited and financially accumulating Shakespeare sues viciously to recover even his pettiest loans from his debtors; spendthrift Stephen, a squanderer like his father, Simon, is, in stark contrast, a debtor who never pays off his debts. Yet neither the Irish nor the English writer is so idealistic as to imagine art above or immune to commerce.

When Stephen's *Hamlet* performance is done, he offers to sell it as an article to an irate Eglinton for a guinea, Eglinton complaining that Stephen is 'the only contributor to *Dana* who asks for pieces of silver' (176: 1081). The rebuke implies that there is something mercenary and Judas-like in Stephen's approach to literature, but Stephen, like his Shakespeare, is an unsentimental materialist who knows that neither art nor the artist transcends the capitalist conditions that produce them. And, again, if we think of 'Scylla and Charybdis' not simply in terms of 1904 but also in terms of 1922, then the analogy between Joyce (as opposed to Stephen) and Shakespeare becomes deeply ironic indeed. At that point in his performance when Mulligan invokes Dowden on Shakespeare, and all three librarians prick eager ears to receive the admired professor's words, Stephen muses to himself, 'William Shakespeare and company, limited. The people's William. For terms apply: E. Dowden, Highfield House . . .' (168: 729–730). In light of Stephen's entrepreneurial Bard, the phrase 'Shakespeare and company' could refer to Shakespeare as intrepid literary businessman, but Stephen's 'For terms apply' also seems to have in mind Dowden's businesslike capacity to turn out Shakespeare criticism. However, 'Shakespeare and company' is also very obviously a reference to Sylva Beach's 'Shakespeare and Company', 12 Rue de l'Odéon in Paris, the expatriate American's bookshop that Joyce referred to as 'Stratford-on-Odéon', and that did so much to introduce Joyce to his French promoters and that eventually undertook the publication *of Ulysses*. The mauling of the English playwright in 'Scylla and Charybdis' involves, then, a very complex tangle of emulation and competition, of identification and differentiation, that allows for no easy severance of Joyce and Shakespeare, who appear here both as 'great poet on a great brother poet' and as national rivals. It is not Stephen only who must adroitly steer a fine course between the rocks and the whirlpool in his interpretative performance in this episode. So too must the readers of 'Scylla and Charybdis' as they navigate the intricacies of Joyce's complex relationship to his English predecessor and the Bard's many ghostly reincarnations in literary and critical afterlives.

'You are a delusion, said roundly John Eglinton to Stephen. You have brought us all this way to show us a French triangle. Do you believe in your own theory?' (175: 1064–1065). Stephen's discourse on *Hamlet*, in full flight, had a little earlier been temporarily derailed by the entry of Buck Mulligan, to whom the librarians, rubbing salt into Stephen's sensitivities, offer a warmer welcome than they had earlier offered to Stephen. When Lyster wonders if Mulligan likewise has 'his theory too of the play and of Shakespeare' (162: 504), Mulligan, reprising a witticism exercised earlier that morning on the hapless old milkwoman in 'Telemachus', when he pretended to have trouble understanding to whom she might be referring when she exclaims 'Glory be to God', now pretends not to recognize the name Shakespeare, creator of most after God:

> Buck Mulligan thought, puzzled.
>     Shakespeare? he said. I seem to know the name.
>     A flying sunny smile rayed in his loose features.
>     – To be sure, he said, remembering brightly. The chap that writes like Synge.
>
> (163: 507–511)

Mulligan's joke on Shakespeare, a name he pretends to recover from memory lapse only by association with Synge, the Irish Renaissance swan (or 'cygne') summoning to mind the almost-disremembered Swan of Avon, here offers a reversal of canonical Irish-English precedence more outrageous than Stephen's assault on *Hamlet* because the jest suggests a literary world where centre-periphery relations had been so reversed that English Shakespeare might be appreciated only because his work had anticipated Irish Synge's! On this occasion, though, when Mulligan's witty brio threatens to eclipse Stephen's flagging performance, it is actually Eglinton who saves the day for Stephen, ending the Mulligan interruption by insisting that Stephen resume his oration:

> – We want to hear more, John Eglinton decided with Mr Best's approval. We begin to be interested in Mrs S. Till now we had thought of her, if at all, as a patient Griselda, a Penelope stay-at-home.
>
> (165: 618–620)

Eglinton had earlier declared, angrily, that Anne Hathaway was of no interest to Shakespeare's art – 'She died, for literature at least, before she was born' (156: 216) – so the critic's newfound interest in 'Mrs S' (she still, however, has no separate identity for Eglinton) is at least a partial concession to Stephen, a nod that he has hooked his listeners more than they might wish. From here, Stephen proceeds to his presentation's climax with verve, running from the uncertainties of fatherhood to the fervour of Shakespeare's sibling rivalries until he finally turns to the question of creation – God's and Shakespeare's – and then on to Hamlet's railleries against marriage. It is at this point that Eglinton finally loses patience and brings Stephen to a sudden halt with his angry exclamations about French triangles. For Stephen, this bad-tempered interruption of his lecture at this moment suggests that he has touched on a raw nerve by stoking Eglinton's own anxieties about marriage and creation, or rather his lack of potential for either one:

– Those who are married, Mr Best, douce herald, said, all save one, shall
live. The rest shall keep as they are.

He laughed, unmarried, at Eglinton Johannes, of arts a bachelor.

Unwed, unfancied, ware of wiles, they [the librarians] fingerponder
nightly each his variorum edition of *The Taming of the Shrew*.

(175: 1059–1063)

The Stephen of 1904 like the rest of the company present is not married,
of course, but the Joyce of 1922, though still unwed, is a father of two
children and the creator, as he well knows, of a masterpiece. Eglinton, of
arts as well as wife a bachelor, has the last word in 'Scylla and Charybdis'
then, when he halts Stephen's oration, but in 1922 it is Joyce, the creator
who has turned irate Eglinton into a hapless creature of his own creation,
who has the last laugh.

## IV

The 'Scylla and Charybdis' episode dramatizes all sorts of rivalries on
several levels – Joyce's with Shakespeare, those of the Irish and English
Renaissances, Stephen's (and Joyce's) with Æ and (behind him) Yeats,
Joyce's with Eglinton and Dowden, Shakespeare's with Anne Hathaway
and his brothers – but what can we finally make of those rivalries? Is the
episode simply a belated Joycean settlement of bad debts with those literati
from his Irish youth whose actual loans he never repaid but who are paid
off here finally in different coin? And if Joyce subjects English Shakespeare
to some kind of charivari at Stephen's hands, what can this possibly yield?
Will a comic beating up of Shakespeare by Stephen really elevate Joyce or
merely enter him in a long list of rivals – from Whitman to Tolstoy to
Shaw – who have engaged in self-aggrandizing but ultimately quixotic
combats with him?

If we turn for answers to these questions to Bloom and Girard, two of
the most influential theorists of mimetic rivalry in modern literature, we
might arrive at different answers. Both critics are admirers of *Ulysses* but
Girard is more wholly approving because he finds in Joyce's work a
vindication of his own anti-Freudian readings of mimetic desire. Like
Shakespeare, Girard contends, Joyce intuits the significance of mimetic
desire everywhere, whether in life or art, and discloses the endless cycles of
aggressions that it unleashes. For Girard, biography may not give the clue
to the work of art, but neither can life and art be wholly separated from
each other in strictly formalist fashion. Thus, if Joyce and Shakespeare

share a common diagnosis of the workings of emulative desire, this is because they were both scrupulously attentive to the perverse dynamics of their own envies and rivalries. More than this, Girard's Joyce recognizes himself in Shakespeare's work: 'Behind [Joyce's] portrayal of a mimetic playwright writing highly mimetic plays, we can recognize the husband of Nora, a highly mimetic novelist writing highly mimetic novels'.[40] What wins Girard's approval above all in the 'Scylla and Charybdis' episode is that at one point in his discourse Stephen proves sceptical of 'a new Viennese school' (169: 780) whose conception of incest he considers less compelling than St. Thomas Aquinas's, the theologian viewing both financial hoarding and incest as forms of antisocial endogamy or refusals to share (money or daughters or sisters in marriage).

Girard, then, finds in Joyce a prestigious support for the French Catholic theorist's own rivalry with the German Jewish Freud: the rejection of Freud's Oedipal theory is crucial to Girard's conception of mimetic desire for which desire is not, *contra* Freud, formatively and instinctively aroused by the child's unconscious pre-Oedipal desire for oneness with the mother and Oedipal rivalry with the father, but emerges, in less parentally fixated manner, only later when the infant subject begins to desire objects (material or erotic) that are lent value by the fact that they are already desired by some prestigious other who shows what is worthy of desire. Hence, the fact that Stephen's reading of *Hamlet* identifies that play's author-actor with Old Hamlet rather than Young Hamlet, with the father rather than the son, Girard says, testifies to Joyce's repudiation of 'the unworkable Oedipal mythology' (257), or to the son's sexual desire for the mother and antagonism to the obstructing father, promoted by Freud. If Stephen's lecture grinds to sudden halt with Eglinton's outburst about 'French triangles', Girard contends, this is because Stephen's revelation of the perverse truths of mimetic desire will not be tolerated by a hostile audience. Stephen – much like, one suspects, Girard's conception of himself as neglected intellectual in France – is sacrificially silenced by his intellectual countrymen who prefer to cling to orthodox verities rather than to accept new truths. In any event, Girard suggests, Stephen has also exhausted himself because he knows that mimetic desire is by its nature impossible of real satisfaction and doomed to self-expenditure. 'In an ever-renewed effort to outmaneuver its own absurdity, [mimetic] desire becomes more and more absurd and self-defeating' and '[a]ll attempts to break out of the circle reactivate the circle' (259). Thus, though he repudiates his theory only momentarily in the face of collective pressure, returning silently to its further elaboration just moments after its apparent repudiation, Stephen never resumes his discourse, choosing silence in the face of audience intransigence. For Girard, the lesson Stephen learns is that if Shakespeare's life offered no escape from the tangles of mimetic desire then neither can the young Irish intellectual's own rivalry with Shakespeare or with his Irish interlocutors bring genuine satisfaction. Joyce, through Stephen, despairs of any serious recognition from the literary establishment of his own time, has his younger self, Stephen, commit to aloofly disgusted silence, and looks to the distant future as the only hope for recognition of his genius.

Like Girard in some respects, Bloom sees in Joyce an exemplum of agonistic struggles, the essential mechanics of which Bloom had already long since elaborated in his earlier works on the anxiety of influence. Curiously, Bloom too finds in Joyce an anti-Freudian: 'A better critic of *Hamlet* than Freud was', he avers, 'Joyce found no trace of lust for Gertrude or murderousness toward King Hamlet in their son'.[41] Crucially for Bloom, influence is not a matter of benign bequest passed down from forerunner to latecomer, but rather an oppressive precedence that for strong writers at least means they have to appropriate, rewrite or wholly subjugate through misreading their great forerunners if they are ever to become creative authorities in their own right. In Joyce's case, Bloom declares, it is Shakespeare's capacity to create characters who assume a life of their own and, above all, Shakespeare's mastery of language that Joyce envies, not Shakespeare the playwright. 'Shakespeare the man, the lord of language, the creator of persons, occupied [Joyce] more than Shakespeare the maker of plays', Bloom avers, citing Frank Budgen on the topic (386). This Shakespeare, Bloom believes, was Joyce's abiding obsession, the career-long adversary who led him to ever more daring if also increasingly desperate pursuits: 'Challenged by Shakespeare as by no other, not even Dante, Joyce hunts his rival down as Captain Ahab pursues the White Whale. No more than Moby-Dick is Shakespeare definitively harpooned by Joyce, but neither Milton nor Melville comes so close to triumph over the Leviathan of literature'.[42]

Here, we have the anxiety of influence as opera bouffe perhaps, but Bloom insists that both *Ulysses* and *Finnegans Wake* are concerned with containing Shakespeare by internalizing him, in the former work by making him a character, in the latter by trying to outmatch Shakespeare's linguistic fecundity with the *Wake's* own relentlessly punning riverrun of language. In *Ulysses*, Bloom believes, Joyce splits himself between Stephen and Leopold Bloom, versions of his older and younger self. The younger self, Stephen, takes on Shakespeare in the 'Scylla and

Charybdis' episode but is worsted in the struggle, and in the nightmarish 'Circe' episode a phantom-like Shakespeare returns to mock him for his failure. In 'Circe', according to Bloom, Shakespeare mocks Stephen-Bloom-Joyce, effectively saying: 'You stare in the mirror, trying to see yourself as me, but you behold what you are: only a beardless version, lacking my onetime potency, and rigid in facial paralysis, devoid of my ease of countenance'.[43] In short, the cuckolded Shakespeare who shows himself to Bloom and Stephen is their own image reflected back to them – the one cuckolded by his wife, the other always doomed to be preceded and overshadowed by William the Literary Conqueror. Undaunted, though, Joyce takes up the challenge to Shakespeare again in *Finnegans Wake*, there attempting nothing less than to take on his rival with a 'controlled aggressiveness' that openly displays 'a profound desire to play at replacing English with the dialect of the *Wake*' (398). Though Bloom allows the *Wake* its magnificence, the verdict goes, on points at least, to Shakespeare: 'Joyce, though he fights brilliantly, in my judgement loses the contest' (401). One of the reasons he loses, Bloom concludes, is that Shakespeare's works are less abstruse than Joyce's and therefore will always attract a wider audience. This envy of Shakespeare's vast reception or viewership makes the *Wake* a work of 'genial desperation' (399), 'a tragicomedy rather than the comedy that Joyce intended' (393). Only a few pages into 'Anna Livia Plurabelle' Bloom finds Joyce keening the want of '*a brandnew bankside*' (393) or a Liffey-bank theatre that might secure him the national audience and popular applause that the Globe had once won Shakespeare. 'Shakespeare', Bloom concludes, 'had the Globe Theatre and its audience; Joyce has only a coterie' (393–394). The modernist writer, in this reading, cannot hope to match the great early modern English precursor for immediate or mass appeal.

As flamboyant in their own ways as Stephen's lecture in the National Library, Girard's and Bloom's readings throw significant light on Joyce's contention with Shakespeare in *Ulysses*, but for all their suggestiveness – to which we will return – both theorists' works are static and ahistorical. Thus, for Girard, Joyce simply discovers in his own psyche and rivalry with Shakespeare a universal truth about the nature of mimetic desire that Shakespeare's works have also disclosed and that all great anti-romantic literature reveals. For Bloom, Shakespeare is assumed, with a certainty that Dowden or the Victorians might have envied, to be the absolute founder of the modern Western canon, the complete writer with whom to compete is always to be second best. Thus conceived, Bloom especially returns us to truisms about Shakespeare the creator without compare, the myriad-minded man, the lord of language and all those commonplaces of nineteenth-century Victorian criticism that Stephen's neurotically raging, entrepreneurial but stingy Shakespeare is designed to controvert. Moreover, while both Girard and Bloom celebrate Joyce's apparent anti-Freudianism and Stephen's supposed repudiation of Oedipal readings of *Hamlet*, it is hard not to dissociate this from their mutual adherence to obsessively masculine models of rivalry and mimesis, models in which rivalry – whether inscribed in great literary works or transacted between great writers – is invariably male. As such, their shared antipathy to Freud might be connected to a reluctance to acknowledge the primacy of motherhood that Freud at least partially acknowledges by way of the Oedipal complex.[44] It might be argued that this antipathy to mothers holds true, too, for Stephen's or Joyce's contentions with Shakespeare, yet in the library episode at least Stephen suggests that '*Amor matris*, subjective and objective genitive, maybe the only true thing in life. Paternity may be a legal fiction' (170: 842–844) and that 'Fatherhood, in the sense of conscious begetting, is unknown to man', a 'mystical estate, an apostolic succession' (170: 837–838). Part of the 'cunning Italian intellect' of the Catholic Church, Stephen asserts, is that it had elevated the Madonna to near but never equal status to the Holy Trinity, the veneration of mother-figure and Holy Family making the uncompromisingly paternalist fiction of that all-male Trinity more palatable to 'the mob of Europe' (170: 840).

Here, Joyce comes very close to suggesting that fatherhood, like male authorship, is never pre-eminent but always 'founded, like the world, macro and microcosm, upon the void. Upon incertitude, upon unlikelihood' (170: 841–842), and thus secondary to women's capacity to give birth. By this logic, Shakespeare's creative career, or Joyce's own, might be viewed as compensations for that primordial lack. Thus conceived, Shakespeare's whole creative career is generated from an envious rivalry with Anne Hathaway's capacity to give birth and to subdue both Shakespeare and his brothers to her sexual appetite. And whereas for bachelor Eglinton 'Mrs S' was always already dismissed as 'a patient Griselda, a Penelope stay-at-home' (165: 619–620), in Stephen's reading to be a stay-at-home woman is not inevitably to be a model of deferential feminine virtue. *Ulysses*, of course, ends with its own 'Penelope' episode, and whether we view this final chapter, as some feminist critics do, as evidence of Joyce's will to subordinate female sexuality and fecundity to his own all-totalizing mastership or, as other feminists insist, as a tribute to the inherent transgressiveness of feminine sexuality and creative capacity, it can scarcely be doubted that *Ulysses* is far more attentive to questions of motherhood as well as fatherhood, and to adulterated as well as legitimate successions, than are the works of either Bloom or Girard for whom male lineages alone ever really matter.[45]

Still, whatever their shortcomings, Girard and Bloom have the critical virtue of taking literary rivalry seriously. Indeed, were we to read Bloom and Girard with rather than against each other, we might even conclude that 'the Western canon', as conceived by Bloom, if it is to be taken seriously, relies precisely on a mimetic model of desire. That is to say, what makes literary greatness seem a prize worth the huge efforts necessary to attain it is precisely the assurance of external mediators: in other words, it requires the continual sanction of previously canonized writers and the confirmation of illustrious critics that that elusive object – greatness, the glory it brings – is something tangible, provable, certifiable. Or, to put matters another way, to strive as Stephen would strive for greatness, or as Joyce behind Stephen also labours to produce his Homeric-Hibernian epic, when he might much more lucratively have turned his hand to lesser tasks like the writing of some or other version of Corelli's *The Sorrows of Satan*, depends on an act of faith that the works of Homer, Dante, Milton, Shakespeare and others represent some indisputable value, some literary gold standard worth emulating. It was indeed because *Ulysses* so obviously exhibited such vast ambition yet seemed so satirically demystifying of so many Western styles as it subjected them to its scurrilous *imitatio*, that even critics as cosmopolitan and urbane as Erich Auerbach in Western Europe or Georg Lukács in the Soviet zone could conceive of *Ulysses* as essentially a Mephistophelian work, a canon-negating rather than canon-confirming masterpiece.[46]

This Mephistophelian capability too was what John Eglinton stressed when he came to review Joyce's career in *Irish Literary Portraits* in 1935, and where he – in the second passage cited as epigraph to this chapter – anticipates Harold Bloom by arguing that Joyce's most fundamental adversary was not so much Shakespeare the man as the English language. For Eglinton, English is, for Joyce, 'his country's spiritual enemy', and something over which the Irish writer therefore wanted to acquire absolute control, this in order to hold the language 'in the hollow of his hand' so that it would docilely 'do his bidding'. Once Joyce had that command, Eglinton concludes, he was determined with satanic glee to make English utter all sorts of uncleanness and foulness against its own nature: 'Like a devil taking pleasure in forcing a virgin to speak obscenely, so Joyce rejoiced darkly in causing the language of Milton and Wordsworth to utter all but unimaginable filth and treason. Such is Joyce's Celtic revenge'.[47]

Now that *Ulysses* in our time enjoys the same reverential sanctity that Shakespeare enjoyed in the Victorian era, Eglinton's judgement may seem hysterically exaggerated. But 'Scylla and Charybdis' certainly suggests that literature, even great literature, is not always born of elevated motives. For Stephen, Shakespeare's art may be majestic but an unappeasable masculine rage and desire for revenge also go into its making as does the national chauvinism of an early modern English capitalist expansionism. And what holds for Shakespeare holds also for *Ulysses*. If rivalry and a competitive will to mastery born out of personal and national rivalries can be a goad or spur to greatness, then it is hard to know how either the writer or the work could ever purify that creative mimicry of its darker impulses or break out of all those cycles of mastery and slavery, repression and retaliation, that go into the making of the 'nightmare' of history (28: 377) from which Stephen would wish to be liberated.

Yet, where both Bloom and Girard think of mimesis essentially in terms of individual relationships – that is, in terms of rivalries between various authors or mimetic relationships disclosed in narratives like *Hamlet* or *Ulysses* – neither critic deals with those forms of mimesis that structure the institution of literature as such and that are fundamental to those competitive national bids for prestige from which 'world literature' issues. As noted earlier, Pascale Casanova argues mimetic rivalry is central to modern literary production: in simple terms, writers not only compete with their national contemporaries for personal recognition but are also compelled to operate within a world state system for which nations and national literatures and the rivalries they motivate are, whatever the writer's personal disposition, inescapable givens.

As we have already seen, 'Scylla and Charybdis' opens with Lyster's reference to 'the priceless pages of Goethe's *Wilhelm Meister*' and to the fraternal amity between Goethe and Shakespeare, 'a great poet on a great brother poet' (151: 2–3). But in 1922, when Europe was still reeling from the convulsions of World War I, and when T. S. Eliot was establishing *The Criterion* to restore the European literary and intellectual traffic that had been interrupted by the Great War, the invocation of the fraternity of Goethe and Shakespeare rings hollow or sounds rather sentimental. Only a few years earlier, British and German critics had been clasping Shakespeare to their respective nations in the most belligerent terms. The playwright Gerhart Hauptmann, whom the young Joyce admired, declared, for example, that Shakespeare's soul had merged with Germany's and 'though he was born and buried in England it is in Germany that he is truly alive'. So, too, the poet Hans Fulda wrote in 1916 that should Germany 'succeed in vanquishing England in the field, we should, I think, insert a clause into the peace treaty stipulating the formal surrender of William Shakespeare to Germany'.[48] In England, these German claims were responded to in like mode by Henry Arthur Jones, for example, writing from the Battle of Verdun and advising his countrymen to prepare for an announcement in Berlin on 23 April, Shakespeare's tercentenary, 'of the final or complete annexation by Germany of William Shakespeare, with all his literary, poetical, philosophical, and stage appurtenances'. 'By what insolent egotism, what lust of plunder, or what madness of pride, Germany dares add to the hideous roll of her thieveries and rapes this topping impudence and crime of vaunting to herself the allegiance of Shakespeare?'[49] Lyster is depicted in 'Scylla and Charybdis' as conciliatory and well intentioned, and the library episode in *Ulysses* is set before World War I provoked such intensities of rhetoric. Yet even in the sanctuary of the pre-war library, Lyster's conciliatory efforts are ineffectual: the much sharper intellects of Stephen and Eglinton are pitched against each other, quite bitterly, and Stephen and Mulligan display satirical qualities that relegate Lyster and Best to the role of sideline onlookers in the intellectual engagements. Quakers, or the Religious Society of Friends, are known for their liberal philanthropy and pacifism, but in the National Library intellectual hostilities are the order of the day. The fact that the 'quaker librarian' appears actually to have been a member of the Church of Ireland and not in fact a Quaker, even though the word 'quaker' is repeated thirteen times in 'Scylla' (and with an unmannerly lower-case 'q'), only underlines the degree to which peacemaking and antagonism are Joyce's concerns in this chapter.[50]

Still, as the constant sexual punning on 'Wills' should alert us, William Shakespeare is not the only rival William in Joyce's sights in 'Scylla and Charybdis'. 'Gentle Will is being roughly handled, gentle Mr Best said gently' as Stephen holds forth on Shakespeare's tight-fisted attitude to both his debtors and wife, a Will-fondling peroration to which Mulligan replies, 'Which will?' (169: 793–794). Indeed, the episode as a whole pits Stephen against not one but three Williams. The first is Shakespeare obviously, but there is also Goethe's *Wilhelm Meister*, the classic European *bildungsroman* in which young 'Master Will' has to struggle to become Wilhelm Meister. Offstage, but a ghostly presence throughout, mainly in the form of his associates, is William Yeats – that Irish William the Conqueror whose own anti-Dowdenite version of William Shakespeare in 'At Stratford-on-Avon' is indebted to the sentimental idealization of *Hamlet* and its author that was nurtured by the tremendous cachet that *Wilhelm Meister* enjoyed among the German Romantics such as Schlegel and Tieck and which was then taken up in England by Coleridge.[51] Stephen at one point refers to Shakespeare's 'trinity of Black Wills' (172: 911) – meaning Iago, Richard III and Edmund, all projections of the Bard's own darker self – but it seems to be the case that Joyce too has in Shakesepare, Goethe and Yeats such a trinity: if he is to become a world writer to match his precursors, he must somehow contain and internalize them, while also elevating himself by meeting them on their own grounds – the theatre, poetry, criticism, the novel. In the composite form of *Ulysses*, which subsumes all of these literary modes into itself, Joyce attempts precisely this cannibalization and overcoming. Yet in its Latinized Greek title his work sidesteps all of the modern national geniuses listed in 'Scylla' – Dante, Shakespeare, Cervantes, Goethe, Whitman, Yeats – doffing its cap only to Homer. Still, even as Joyce pays homage to Homer's great post-war epic, that work too is travestied by transferring its mythic peregrinations into Dublin's bars, newspaper offices, libraries, hospitals, churches, bedrooms, privies and brothels.

Yet if *Ulysses* lampoons the follies of national literary rivalries and the vanities of literary fraternities, this does not mean that Joyce or his work can ever really transcend the dynamics of national rivalries constitutive of the world literary system. National literary renaissances are typically linked with actual or imagined moments of national emergence, the latter often scripted in national myth-making or literary history (the two not always dissociable) in terms of conflicts with larger superpowers that have to be taken on as cultural and intellectual as well as political rivals for the emergent nation to express itself. As Barbara Fuchs has noted, the canonization of the English Renaissance in this manner began early: for her, Ben Jonson's ode of 1623 to Shakespeare, 'To the Memory of My Beloved, the Author William Shakespeare, and What He Hath Left Us', is a foundational text in this regard. In that ode, Fuchs contends, Jonson first accords Shakespeare pre-eminence among his own literary country-men, but then elevates him also above 'all that insolent Greece or haughtie Rome / Sent forth; or since did from their ashes come', this transcendence leading to the bragging conclusion: 'Triumph, my Britaine! Thou has one to showe / To whom all scenes of Europe homage owe. / He was not of an age, but for all time!' As Fuchs also notes, this ascription of all-conquering literary authority to Shakespeare cannot be divorced from a cocky English sense that an emerging Britain might finally tri-umph over the once-great Spanish Empire:

Particularly striking in this construction of the Elizabethan moment is its pugnaciousness, the sense that the literary excellence of England depends upon its besting someone else. Given England's sustained attempts in the period to emulate Spain, in the literary and imperial spheres, Spain becomes an obvious antagonist in this somewhat belligerent construction of a national canon, and both Elizabethan privateering and the 1588 defeat of the Armada are analogized to the cultural dynamics of the period.

During the Elizabethan era, [English] translators from the Spanish turned repeatedly to an aggressive metaphorics that equates *imitatio*, or translation, with forcible taking.[52]

It would be easy to trace similar pugnacities and forcible takings and remakings in the American Renaissance – Whitman's or Melville's appropriations of Shakespeare are obvious cases – or in the rather different context of the Irish Revival as it developed alongside the Irish struggle for national independence from Britain; as was noted at the outset of this chapter, that Revival too was marked by a considerable pugnacity towards Shakespeare. There is every reason to agree with Fuchs, then, that '[l]ike the central figures that animate them, periods have afterlives that colonize and constantly reformulate them, often in relation to new international pressures' (326). Thus, for example, Cervantes' influence on English literature is generally considered enormous, yet that influence has rarely been acknowledged for the English Renaissance period itself. And by the nineteenth century the author of *Don Quixote* had actually come to be equated in English letters with the end of the Spanish Renaissance and the decline of the Spanish Empire, even as Shakespeare was aligned with the by then world-spanning British Empire.[53] It was in this spirit that Byron could write in *Don Juan*:

> Cervantes smiled Spain's chivalry away;
> A single laugh demolish'd the right arm
> Of his own country; – seldom since that day
> Has Spain had heroes. While Romance could charm,
> The world gave ground before her bright array;
> And therefore have his volumes done such harm,
> That all their glory, as a composition,
> Was dearly purchased by his land's perdition.
>
> (13.11)[54]

For Byron, England rose as Spain fell and Cervantes's anti-romance marked or maybe even caused that Spanish decline by debunking the romantic heroic spirit on which Spanish greatness depended. Fanciful as this might be, the conscription of great works to tales of national becoming or overcoming has a long history.

Joyce was a thoroughgoing reader of Jonson as well as Shakespeare, and Stephen's construction of the English Renaissance in 'Scylla and Charybdis' allows that era its pugnacity but offers it to the reader, from an Irish Catholic and republican perspective, in a much less roseate light. Does this mean that in showing the darker sides of the English Renaissance and belittling the Irish one – mocking its literary lions, 'the tramper Synge' (164: 569), that 'old hake Gregory' (177: 1158–1159), and what Mulligan calls the toadying 'Yeats touch' (178: 1161) that likens Gregory's minor work to Homer – *Ulysses* offers itself instead as the only champion work of the Irish Renaissance, the belated fulfilment of the Irish national longing for a modern epic? The answer in one sense is an obvious yes. *Ulysses* makes good the lack of an Irish epic with which Eglinton taunts Stephen in the episode's opening. However, to answer only yes to this question would be to assert that Joyce does not just dramatically display these literary rivalries but also endorses them, something that a contrapuntal tendency to lampoon them in 'Scylla and Charybdis' and the Cervantean anti-romantic and mock-epic nature of *Ulysses* as a whole controverts.

For Dowden, as we have already seen, Shakespeare is the very embodiment of English Protestant modernity; for Yeats, a belated medieval mind and a romantic anti-modernist. However different their Shakespeares, Yeats and Dowden nevertheless both concur on the English Bard's quintessential Englishness; Yeats, as noted earlier, even laments his European borrowings and wishes Shakespeare had had a more purely native mythology on which to nurture his imagination. 'He was made in Germany, Stephen replied, as the champion French polisher of Italian scandals' (168: 766–767). What Stephen offers here instead is a non-national Shakespeare, or at least one who can never be wholly cleared of foreign debts to become purely national only: here, Shakespeare is a Europeanized writer who borrows his sources from the Italians, brings to them an added French sophistication or polish, and whose reputation was 'made in Germany', not England. In this account, Shakespeare the man-author is never the whole story; Shakespeare the world literary figure is an international construction, one who owes more to Goethe and German Romantic and later scholarship than to his own countrymen.

But what is true for the literary lion of the English Renaissance is no less true of the Irish Renaissance. In his 1907 lecture, 'Ireland: Island of Saints and Sages', Joyce had remarked:

> [I]t cannot be denied that these learned Germans were the first to present Shakespeare as a poet of world-wide significance, before the amazed eyes of his compatriots (who up until then had considered William as a person of

secondary importance, a decent devil with a nice bent towards lyric poetry, but perhaps a bit over-fond of English beer). Similarly, it was those very same Germans who troubled themselves with the languages and histories of the five Celtic nations.

> The only Irish grammars and dictionaries that existed in Europe until a few years ago, when the Gaelic League was founded in Dublin, were works by Germans.[55]

If Shakespeare-the-world-writer was elevated to that stature on the back of German scholarship, then so, too, Joyce suggests, was the Irish Renaissance indebted to Germany, neither one nor the other an autonomous national construction. And if the Irish Literary Renaissance was founded on nineteenth-century German philology, its contemporary flowering likewise depends on other non-national supports. Early in his library performance, Stephen, remembering a conversational snatch in 'Aeolus', recalls that 'A. E. has been telling some yankee interviewer' and muses 'Wall, tarnation strike me!' (152: 54–55). According to Gifford and Seidman, the reference here is to Cornelius Weygandt, professor of English at the University of Pennsylvania, enthusiast of the Revival and mentor to a young Ezra Pound; Weygandt had interviewed Æ on a trip to Ireland, and later published *Irish Plays and Playwrights* (1913), mentioning Joyce's name there in passing.[56] The 'Wall, tarnation strike me!' is surely a mimicry of the colloquial Yankee idioms with which Pound peppered his letters to friends. A few moments later, thinking again about Swinburne's 'On the Death of Colonel Benson', Stephen further muses: 'Between the Saxon smile and yankee yawp. The devil and the deep sea' (154: 139–140). As he listens to his interlocutors chatter happily about the Irish national epic and Moore's soirée, Stephen catches the phrase '[w]e are becoming important, it seems' (158: 312–313). If the Irish Revival is becoming important, one of the signs of its success is that it has won the attention both of an Oxonian and Arnoldian English Celticist enthusiast like Haines, too anxious to purchase a copy of Douglas Hyde's *The Love Songs of Connaught* to wait for Stephen's Shakespeare improvisation, and American devotees like Weygandt, or his pupil Pound, who did so much to promote both Joyce's and Yeats's careers. 'Between the Saxon smile and the yankee yawp' might refer to many things, from Arnold's benevolent but sinuously British unionist philo-Celticism to Whitman's bullishly world-embracing democratic Americanism, but for Stephen Saxon and Yankee represent the difficulty of steering between English and American benefactors who might equally represent the snares of Scylla and Charybdis, 'the devil and the deep sea'.

If there is no way, then, for Irish literature to completely repudiate or repay its debts and dependencies on others, no way to wrestle wholly free from its inscription in the international rivalries of either the political world or the world literary system, then the only thing to do is to own those debts even if one has no intention of repaying them. After all, if the Irish Revival boasts its resurgent Irishness but can only become a noteworthy international phenomenon by way of British and American promotions, then this is just as true of *Ulysses*. As the slyly knowing reference to 'Shakespeare and Company' in the library episode indicates, Joyce was conscious of his own supporters, too, literary as well as financial. When *Ulysses* eventually appeared in 1922, it did so, famously, with a great deal of help from an American-born bookseller of Presbyterian background and a French printer, Maurice Darantière, and with the selfless assistance of several young Frenchwomen and an English patroness, suffragist and later communist, Harriet Weaver. Famously, the book was launched on the world with the help of Valery Larbaud, writer, critic, translator and enthusiast of American literature, and would soon receive generous notices from Eliot and Pound.[57] Paris, the city that would make Joyce famous, shadows 'Scylla and Charybdis' and *Ulysses* in the form of Stephen's recurrent memories of that capital. Yet it is not always recalled flatteringly. 'Paris: the wellpleased pleaser' (157: 268), Stephen muses at one stage, the reference alluding to the judgement of Paris that awarded the crown of beauty to Aphrodite and in so doing won the awardee the favour of Helen that in turn triggered the war that led to the Greek destruction of Troy, Paris's home.

Does this mean, then, that collaboration trumps rivalry and that transnational exchanges and cooperations are finally more significant than rivalries in *Ulysses*? Hardly. '*The sentimentalist is he who would enjoy without incurring the immense debtorship for a thing done*' (164: 550–551, italics in original); Stephen's telegram to Mulligan, the line cribbed from George Meredith, is one of many reminders of the ubiquity of indebtedness in the library chapter and an injunction against the assumption that things are to be had for free. Cooperations and exchanges have always been part of literary production, but they are the counterpart of national and international competitions, not their negation. As his sardonic reference in a letter of December 1928 to Harriet Weaver concerning his bemusement at the enlistment of his own 'magic flute' into 'Pound's big brass band' indicates, Joyce was well aware that collaborations were commonly strategic ways of recruiting coteries of writers to serve particular purposes. Pound, Eliot, Larbaud and others championed *Ulysses* in just such manner to advance the cause of a modernist literature against its Victorian-minded detractors.[58]

*Ulysses*, as its Homeric borrowings would indicate, always seems all too aware that if 'Western literature' or 'European culture' has any unity, that unity does not emerge from some putatively common Hellenistic origins: the Irish epic's Latinate title reminds us that the Greeks come to us largely through their Roman conquerors. Nor was 'European culture' consolidated by some shared Christianity, the latter visible in the Irish novel largely through its bitter Catholic and Protestant animosities, with Bloom's Jewishness there to remind us of the scapegoats sacrificed to such animosities. Nor was any European unity consolidated by means of some shared heritage of liberal humanism, that latter mocked in the opening purrings about the 'priceless pages' of great poets paying fraternal homage to great brother poets and in the Quaker librarian's earnest certitude that Shakespeare's plays breathe '[t]he spirit of reconciliation' (160: 396). Ironically, what, if anything, unites Europe is the long history of its rivalries and struggles, these for Joyce recently made catastrophically visible by World War I and, more immediately, by one of that war's ragged tail ends being played out in Ireland as he composed his epic. The history of European literature, so much of which Joyce manages to compress into the pages of *Ulysses*, might not simply be reducible to war by other means, but in a world of inter-imperial aggression, vying nation-states and relentless capitalist competition, neither does literature float free above all this into some uncontaminated realm where those antagonisms might be forgotten.

It is against this context that we must return to Stephen and to the final sections of 'Scylla and Charybdis'. For all that Joyce deploys Stephen to demolish the sentimental conception of the Shakespeare so dear to the Victorian imperialist and unionist imagination, it remains the case that Stephen is allowed in that episode no final grand triumph over his English adversary, no loud crow of intellectual achievement surpassing that of Europe and the ages such as Ben Jonson claims for Shakespeare in 'To the Memory of My Beloved, the Author William Shakespeare, and What He Hath Left Us'. When an irascible Eglinton erupts with his angry expostulation about the 'delusion' of Stephen's Frenchified and farcified Shakespeare, Stephen is finally silenced and momentarily at least recants his theory. However, some moments later he is tempted, as Girard points out, to resume – 'Afterwit. Go back' (177: 1137) – but decides against it, led away reluctantly with Mulligan to go drinking: 'Swill till eleven. Irish nights entertainment' (176: 1105). It is in this downcast, stymied diminuendo of an ending too that Mulligan, insinuating himself in Stephen's good graces, chidingly reminds him of his dismissive review of the work of 'that old hake Gregory' (177: 1158–1159) and wonders why Stephen cannot for diplomacy's sake flatter her: 'Couldn't you do the Yeats touch?' (178: 1160–1161). The insults to the Yeatsian coteries in the Revival continue to fly then even after Stephen leaves off his performance, but Stephen at least has had enough. At the end of the 'Scylla and Charybdis', we find him still pondering the contest of wills in which he has engaged and feeling some sense of dejected futility or perpetual standoff: 'My will: his will that fronts me. Seas between' (178: 1202) – a phrase where the contesting 'will' might as well apply to William Yeats and Joyce separated and unreconciled by the seas that divide Paris and Dublin as to Joyce and Shakespeare sundered by centuries and the Irish Sea. As he exits the library for Kildare Street, Stephen bids himself to '[c]ease to strive' (179: 1221) and ruminates on the Celtic Druid priests making sacrifice in *Cymbeline*, the Shakespeare play in which the Celtic Britons triumph over imperial Rome, only to submit to Roman rule, in any event, in the interests of peace.

It is this downbeat denouement that sanctions critics like Harold Bloom or William Schutte, who are convinced that Stephen is worsted in 'Scylla and Charybdis'. It has also become a truism in contemporary criticism more generally to say that in this episode the unreconciled young artist is finally displaced from the centre of Joyce's work, just as he is earlier ejected from Mulligan's tower or excluded from Moore's soirée. After 'Scylla', so such arguments run, Joyce sidelines Stephen and gives over the novel to the more mature Blooms, Leopold and Molly, each offering after their own manner an affirmative 'yes' to the modern world in all its imperfections. From Richard Ellmann to Declan Kiberd, this serves as interpretive warrant for an affirmative humanist reading of *Ulysses* in which the novel endorses a peaceable Bloomian acceptance of urban modernity and a pragmatic and tolerant liberalism over Stephen-style recalcitrance and disaffection.[59] However, a standoff is not necessarily a defeat and there is little evidence here or later in the work that Stephen 'ceases to strive' or that Joyce's work can be summed up by latter-day Lysters in terms of 'the spirit of reconciliation' any more than can Shakespeare's. As *Ulysses* moves onwards from 'Scylla and Charybdis', the transfer of attention to Bloom is real enough, but even as this takes place the formal demands of the work become more, not less, intellectually strenuous, and the reader is certainly not allowed to 'cease to strive'. In fact, to borrow a phrase from Eliot cited in Chapter 3, to navigate *Ulysses* all the way, the reader has to 'sweat for it' even more than in *The Waste Land*. The mounting difficulties of reading the novel's final nine episodes, in short, require a very un-Leopold-like reader even if Bloom as character becomes their presiding figure.

During the remains of the day in 1904, Stephen does fall into ever greater despair till the reader eventually finds him drink-sozzled and grief-stricken in 'Circe's' brothel where he is worsted, now not by Shakespeare, but by British soldiers. Nevertheless, the young aspirant remains intransigent, refusing in the end Bloom's offer of a home for the night, just as he inwardly dismisses also his rescuer's homely common wisdom. It makes more sense, then, to see Stephen not as a repudiation of some too-fixed, intransigent younger self cast off by his wearied author, but rather as Joyce's determination to retain in his Ulyssean orchestra that refractory, non-co-opted note of dissonant negativity. As Theodor Adorno argues, this negativity became indispensable to a modernist art determined to remain true to its vocation – neither to sanction an aestheticist art for art's sake retreat from a world so full of exploitation and injustice nor to offer readers reassuring affirmations that modernity's catastrophes might easily or ever be ended. In this Adornean view, at that moment in history when capitalist society had created a deformed second human nature, functionally adapted to serve its coercive market logic, modern literature had no option, were it to safeguard some sliver of art's promise of happiness, but to turn against its own affirmative nature.[60] Correspondingly, Stephen's 'no', his impenitent *non serviam*, is as essential to *Ulysses* as Leopold's peace-loving diplomacy or Molly's orgasmic 'yes', each the corrective of the other, though no synthesis can ever reconcile them. In short, Stephen's stubborn 'no' is as necessary to the meaning of *Ulysses* as is Molly's 'yes'.

In Stephen's performance, Meister Wilhelm Shakespeare may be a callow peripheral writer who, like Stephen's author, makes a journey from the provinces to the literary capital where he eventually actualizes his great potential and who then, in this rages-to-riches tale, gets to return to Stratford, at last, unhappy and at home. For Stephen, as for Joyce, there will never be such final homecoming. As Stephen's anti-Shakespearian Shakespearian tale and Joyce's anti-Homeric Homeric epic suggest, not every homecoming affords an end to rivalry and discord. We may read 'Scylla and Charybdis' as that chapter in *Ulysses* where Joyce allows his part-self Stephen a victory or half-victory at least over English Shakespeare – the bookish victory of the Irish James over William comically reversing the tragic historical one of the Protestant William of Orange over French-supported Catholic James Stuart – gleefully indulges his revenge on his erstwhile Dublin intellectual doubters, and triumphantly anticipates how the imminent publication of his epic will transform the received image of his disparaged younger self. Nevertheless, the episode also acknowledges that even as Joyce becomes a 'world writer', the

well-pleased toast of 'Paris: the well-pleased pleaser', his work will ultimately be fated to become part of the same merry-go-round and sometimes not-so-merry-go-round of national literary rivalries. Even if 'world
literature' is deemed transnational and above all such pettiness, the world
literary system requires national mimicries and competitions for prestige to
sustain itself. For this reason, even the greatest literary epics can never leave
the nationalisms of small nations or great superpowers wholly behind. The
accomplishments of Shakespeare and Goethe, Cervantes and Ibsen,
Whitman and Yeats have never escaped being pressed into such service,
and *Ulysses*, despite all of Joyce's proper scepticism about epic heroics and
American-conducted literary 'big brass bands', could not hope to be
exempted from such conscription either. Joyce's conception of the 'great
book', then, is considerably darker, and considerably more irreverently
comic, than the Mallarméan notion of the 'sacred text' or the American
perception of 'Great Books' into which canons *Ulysses* was nonetheless
recruited in the Cold War that followed World War II. Predictably, the
nightmare of history has the very last laugh.

# 'That Huge Incoherent Failure of a House': American Ascendancy and American Epic in The Great Gatsby and Long Day's Journey into Night

God damn the continent of Europe. It is merely of antiquarian interest. Rome is only a few years behind Tyre and Babylon. The negroid streak creeps northwards to defile the Nordic race. Already the Italians have the souls of blackamoors. Raise the bars of immigration and permit only Scandinavians, Teutons, Anglo-Saxons and Celts to enter. France made me sick. Its silly pose as the thing the world has to save. I think it's a shame that England and America didn't let Germany conquer Europe. It's the only thing that would have saved the fleet of tottering old wrecks. My reactions were all philistine, anti-socialistic, provincial and racially snobbish. I believe at last in the white man's burden. We are as far above the modern Frenchman as he is above the Negro. Even in art! Italy has no one. When Anatole France dies French literature will be a silly jealous rehashing of technical quarrels. They're thru and done. You may have spoken in jest about New York as the capital of culture but in 25 years it will be just as London is now. Culture follows money and all the refinements of aestheticism can't stave off its change of seat (Christ! What a metaphor). We will be the Romans in the next generation as the English are now.
– Letter from F. Scott Fitzgerald to Edmund Wilson, London, May 1921.[1]

*Interlude* got a bad spanking from the critical boys in Berlin. They say I have no roots (being a Yank!) except in Ibsen and Strindberg, forgetting that that, if true, is equally true of their own playwrights. One even objects to the play bitterly because I stole the aside from Shakespeare! It is all too damn dumb! [. . .] But the thing that makes me especially sick about the discussions of this production and that of *The Hairy Ape* in Paris is the evident fierce animosity to Americans as artists. They are forced to see our industrialism swamping them and forcing them to bad imitations on every hand, and it poisons them. They are bound they'll die at the post rather than acknowledge an American has anything to show them in any line of culture. It's amusing – and disgusting! – this clinging of theirs to their last superiority out of the past!
– Letter from Eugene O'Neill to George Jean Nathan,
Saint-Antoine Du Rocher, Indre-Et-Loire, 12 November 1929.[2]

# I

In the letter cited above, a twenty-four-year-old F. Scott Fitzgerald writes from a London hotel to Edmund Wilson anticipating, in terms then becoming increasingly common, the end of European world dominance and French literary preeminence: 'They're thru and done'. The letter divides Europe into a white north and a black and oriental south, Germany's defeat in World War I breaking the unity of the white races and therefore abetting the Mediterranean south's creeping infiltration of the Teutonic-Celtic north. This imagined defilement maps suggestively onto the United States. When Fitzgerald writes, '[r]aise the bars of immigration and permit only Scandinavians, Teutons, Anglo-Saxons and Celts to enter', he is referring not to Europe but to American immigration policies, advocating state controls to save the United States from the degeneration he sees in continental Europe. In this view, the presumptively white Americans are now as far above the French as the French are above the Africans, and New York will soon become the capital of the literary world as Paris once was before French literary decline set in and as London for now remains. 'Culture follows money', Fitzgerald declares, and no amount of 'the refinements of aestheticism' can prevent the American cultural ascendancy that will soon make New York 'the capital of culture'. The next generations of Americans will become what the English are at present and the Romans were once: guardians of world-empire, arbiters of the arts.

However, anxiety frets the braggadocio. If America succeeds Rome and England, and if Paris and London must surrender their role as world literary capitals to New York, won't the United States follow a similar trajectory of rise and decline? Doesn't the migratory creep of Africanoid southerners to defile the white north of Europe transpose the 'Great Migration' of rural African Americans into the industrial north of the United States onto Europe, thus figuring European Nordic defilement as an anticipation of white American defilement to follow? The letter's most self-conscious moment occurs when Fitzgerald acknowledges that his 'reactions were all philistine, anti-socialistic, provincial and racially snobbish'. Here, he concedes – brazenly or self-mockingly? – that his reactionary impressions may tell more about his American prejudices than European actualities. How was Wilson supposed to construe the sentence: 'I believe at last in the white man's burden'? As half-joking, all in earnest? Italy, France and Europe may be 'thru and done', and the Americans now above them, '[e]ven in art!' – the exclamation mark scoring the sense of audacity Fitzgerald feels in making such claim – but the letter's racist jokiness indicates that the excitements of American ascendancy are troubled by a sense of foreboding.

In Fitzgerald's case, the contemplation of would-be greatness and actual decadence are always hard to separate. Four years later in 1925, we find him, writing now from Paris to Marya Mannes, describing New York, the city he would do so much to capture for literature in *The Great Gatsby* published that year, in a manner that conveys far less assurance about American ascendancy:

> You are thrilled by New York – I doubt you will be after five more years when you are more fully nourished from within. I carry the place around the world in my heart but sometimes I try to shake it off in my dreams. America's greatest promise is that something is going to happen, and after awhile you get tired of waiting because nothing happens to people except that they grow old, and nothing happens to American art because America is the story of the moon that never rose.[3]

In the earlier letter to Wilson, France was saved from being a literary wasteland only by its last living great writer, Anatole France, but now the United States, without ever having achieved a literary greatness to match France's, is imagined as a wasteland too because it blights its writers before they can ever ripen to greatness. Continuing to Mannes, Fitzgerald adds, 'America is so decadent that its brilliant children are damned almost before they are born. Can you name a single American artist except James and Whistler (who lived in England) who didn't die of drink?'[4] If Europe for Fitzgerald represents a past splendour now corrupted to the point that the continent is become 'of antiquarian interest' only, in the United States decadence curiously precedes ripeness, making his homeland a cemetery of youthful promise unfulfilled.

Written to theatre critic George Jean Nathan in 1929, Eugene O'Neill's letter from France complaining of French and German theatre critics displays how American writers continued to feel that the European intelligentsia persisted in condescending to the United States despite the latter's increasing international importance. In fact, O'Neill suggests, as American power increases, European hostility to American literature becomes more, not less, entrenched. Europe is swamped by the products of America's 'industrialism' and forced to develop its own 'bad imitations' of those products and this, he surmises, makes European critics even more crassly assertive about the superiority of European and the deficiencies of American literature. His European critics, O'Neill believes, fault his work for merely being a bad copy of Ibsen and Strindberg, and for stealing from

Shakespeare, in other words for not being authentically American enough, even though they also associate 'America' with a lack of literary distinction.[5] In the same letter to Nathan, O'Neill reports that 'in Paris I saw my first "Talkie" – *The Broadway Melody* – and, think what you will of me, I was most enthusiastic!' (101). The new sound movies, he surmises, will not 'do away with the charm of the living, breathing actor' (102), and playwrights will not suffer by having to compete with this new medium. To the contrary: '"The play's the thing" and I think in time plays will get across for what their authors intended much better in this medium than in the old' (102). Indeed, he writes, he is already planning a work, once he has completed a theatrical trilogy now under way, in which 'a stage play combined with a screen talky background [will serve] to make alive visually and vocally the memories, etc. in the minds of the characters' (102). Here, American cinema and theatre promise to become one great art, the two mediums collaboratively working together. When O'Neill won for the United States its second Nobel Prize in Literature seven years later in 1936, the only Nobel ever won by an American playwright, he acknowledged his debts to the Scandinavian literary world even as the Scandinavians acknowledged American literature's increasing profile more generally. What is most interesting in this 1929 letter, though, is the glance it offers of the shifting cultural field the playwright occupied. Rapidly changing cultural technologies had positioned O'Neill in a volatile situation: he had to navigate between the old American commercial theatre, the new epic American literary theatre he was struggling to create and a cinema industry transitioning from silent to sound movies, these now converging in a world literary system where European and American conceptions of culture still vied uneasily with each other. In this conjuncture, O'Neill asserts, American literature is beginning, like everything else American, to dominate Europe, this provoking European resentment as the Europeans desperately cling 'to their last superiority out of the past!', their artistic superiority.

Between 1918 and 1945 when it fought, bought and bombed its way to becoming a world power, and became as well the custodian of a new version of world literature, the United States may have produced its own great national literature, but its greatest literary works could never wholly endorse the idea of American greatness. When new nations and especially new nation-empires come to power, they typically require 'world writers' or authors of great epic works to attest their greatness. In England's case, as we have seen in Chapter 4, Shakespeare's greatness had coincided with the period when England began its ascent to world supremacy, and these two forms of greatness, literary and imperial, had long been associated. Could the United States produce a great world writer of equal stature or a great epic to mark its moment of coming-of-age as a world superpower? If not, why not?

In the first half of the twentieth century, the United States certainly produced no shortage of works with epic ambitions. In the silent era and in its post–World War II moment, Hollywood turned out an array of such works. Some were biblical epics, like Cecil B. DeMille's *The Ten Commandments* (1923, remade in 1956), *The King of Kings* (1927) or *Samson and Delilah* (1949); others like William Wyler's *Ben Hur* (1959), Stanely Kubrick's *Spartacus* (1960) or Joseph Mankiewicz's *Cleopatra* (1963) engaged with classical or classical-and-Christian grand narratives. These monumental cinematic epics often functioned as allegories of American or 'Western' overcomings of tyranny and were hugely popular with American audiences, but they were too distant in time and location from twentieth-century realities perhaps to serve as properly modern 'American epics'. Works with epic aspirations that engaged directly with American history and landscape, such as D. W. Griffith's *The Birth of a Nation* (originally *The Clansman*, 1915), John Ford's silent-era *The Iron Horse* (1924), David O. Selznick's *Gone with the Wind* (1939) or John Ford's *How the West Was Won* (1962), were also hugely popular with American and international audiences. Yet none of these productions was ever consecrated as the American epic; some perhaps seemed too blatantly racist and white supremacist to be accepted as the epic of a whole nation, and cinema was probably considered too new, too 'populist', not yet a sufficiently 'artistic' medium to be the bearer of a national epic.[6]

In the high literary field matters were equally troubled. Ezra Pound's *The Cantos*, its earliest sections first published in 1922, though the overall work still remained incomplete when Pound died in 1972, is widely regarded as one of the greatest twentieth-century modernist long poems and might surely qualify as a great American epic achievement. However, Pound's endorsement of Mussolini and his anti-American and anti-Semitic broadcasts during World War II have made *The Cantos* at least as controversial as Griffith's *The Birth of a Nation*. Other American long poems, such as T. S. Eliot's *The Waste Land* (1922), were either located abroad and thus conceived as more 'European' than American in character or, like Charles Olson's *The Maximus Poems* (published in the 1950s and 1960s and modelled on *The Cantos*), were communist in sympathy and thus alien to 'American values'. If cinematic epics seemed too close to popular spectacle to qualify as serious epics, many of these poetic works were perhaps too arcane, too highbrow, to command the so-called common reader's affections as Shakespeare had once done or appeared to do. This same problem confronted novelists with the epic ambitions of John Dos Passos's *U.S.A.* trilogy (*The 42nd Parallel* (1930), *1919* (1932) and *The Big Money* (1936)) or William Faulkner's Yoknapatawpha County novels.[7] Moreover, if epics are about triumphal foundings of great new nations, empires or ages, many of the American literary would-be epics mourned the passing of an earlier American republic, or some imagined version thereof, rather than celebrating the imperial republic that succeeded it.

Thus, in the period of the United States' ascent to world power American writers and film-makers displayed in fact a prodigious epic imagination and produced a whole corpus of works that tried to encompass that continental state's enormous scope and ambition. Yet it would seem that no single work was able to oust all other contenders to secure for itself the kind of unassailable canonical centrality that Shakespeare assumed in early modern English literature. Some American epics seemed too popular or populist to carry the high distinction of classical epic; others did not lack literary distinction but seemed too far removed from the value world of popular American audiences to qualify as affectionately 'national'. Moreover, in an era when the USSR still seemed to represent a ruptural new beginning in history, the United States, even in the moment of its ascendancy, represented a rearguard defence of 'Western civilization' and Western capitalism rather than the opening up of some great new stage of history. On a deeper level, part of the problem stemmed also from the modernist literary revolution itself and from the new conception of 'literature' that it forced into existence and from the fissure between 'mass' and 'high' culture that that revolution had deepened. In the course of its ascent, the United States had done much to become not only a great economic and military titan but also a leading centre of the arts, a state now able to compete with Europe and the world in terms of national cultural achievement.[8] In the period after World War I, the American research university was greatly developed and after World War II its student body was hugely expanded, these developments producing the kinds of highly trained and highly ambitious elite readers and scholars that modernism by its nature demanded.[9] Moreover, as Fascist Germany and the Soviet Union excoriated various forms of avant-garde art as exemplars of 'Western bourgeois decadence' from the 1930s onwards, the United States was afforded further opportunity to present itself as a world patron of modernist literary innovation and freedom of expression. During the Cold War era, the US State Department itself took on the task of promoting at home and globally more modernist over more socially committed conceptions of art, thus hardening modernism into a kind of official state aesthetic ideology, the antithesis of everything represented by 'socialist realism' and the communist idea of the overtly engaged artist. In all of these ways, the United States became by the end of World War II one of modernism's major custodians.[10]

The fact that the United States became in this period the world guardian of capitalism even as it also tried to enhance its own national symbolic capital by becoming a producer and champion of the modernist arts as well as championing the new Hollywood medium of popular cinema produced a situation rife with contradiction. In the nineteenth century, the United States was widely regarded in Europe, and by the country's own literary elites, as too culturally backward to compete with European high culture; in the twentieth century, the United States struggled mightily to shed this reputation and to become a centre of high cultural production in its own right. However, as it did so it also became a manufacturer of a globally distributed popular culture industry that was, in terms of the new literary field that modernism had created at least, the essence of anti-art, an industrially produced, commodified, standardized and market-designed 'art' regulated from start to finish by the dictates of advertising, mass consumption and profit. Paradoxically, then, the United States might finally have constructed for itself in the early to mid-twentieth century the infrastructures and institutional complexes necessary to support its own American high culture, but it had simultaneously become identified with a Hollywoodization of culture that threatened to overwhelm real artistic achievement not only at home but across the world. Could the United States simultaneously be a bastion of elite 'high culture' and the world's greatest factory of 'mass culture' in an era when, from the modernist perspective at least, the latter represented not so much an inferior version of art as its very antithesis?

Despite this situation's contradictory complexities, two American writers came nearest to resolving this American dilemma.[11] Both, whether coincidentally or not, were Irish American. With the publication of *The Great Gatsby* in 1925, F. Scott Fitzgerald produced something like an 'American classic' novel. When it appeared, *The Great Gatsby* was greeted by Fitzgerald's distinguished émigré contemporaries like T. S. Eliot as a real advance for American fiction, and in time, though not immediately, it also came to be accepted by an American reading public as a national 'foundational fiction' when it became a high school and undergraduate syllabus favourite.[12] Like *The Waste Land*, a contemporary text to which it is indebted, *The Great Gatsby* is a short work readable in one or two sittings. In its compact brevity, at least, it is therefore quite unlike *À la recherche du temps perdu*, *Ulysses*, *U.S.A.* or *The Cantos*, or so many other gargantuan modernist masterpieces that make onerous demands on their readers because of their length or technical complexity. However, while it has *The Waste Land*'s compactness, *The Great Gatsby* displays little of Eliot's work's refractory difficulty. To the contrary, it retains many of the typical features of American popular romance – it is a glamorous love story, a tale of rags-to-riches success, a work focused on a charismatic and enigmatic personality – yet it would also come to be viewed in the Cold War era at least as a beautiful mini-epic that expressed something large and fundamental about an epoch and a national destiny.[13] In other words, unlike the works of Stein or Dos Passos, Pound or Eliot, Faulkner or Stevens, *The Great Gatsby* is able somehow to reconcile (or has been critically accepted to do so) the contradictory exigencies of the modernist 'art novel' and the more popular national romance or national allegory that can command a wide and affectionate readership. The fact that *Gatsby* lent itself well to cinematic reproduction also helped its success of course.[14]

Unlike Fitzgerald, Eugene O'Neill never quite captured the American popular or modernist imagination with any one single work. *Long Day's Journey into Night*, a play posthumously premiered in Stockholm in 1956, then produced in New York later that year, comes nearest to doing so, but in O'Neill's case his real legacy resides not so much in this single play as in his career-long struggle to create an American high cultural or literary theatre, a foundational feat at least as arduous and ambitious as that which Ibsen achieved for Norway, Strindberg for Sweden, or that Yeats, with less success, undertook for Ireland. In other words, it is O'Neill's 'titanic' career arc rather than any one talismanic work that has acquired something of the 'epic tragedy' quality that we might also associate with *The Great Gatsby*. Fitzgerald's novel and O'Neill's career legend both rehearse tales of vastly ambitious self-remaking with costly consequences that mix a tremendous sense of grandeur with anguished tribulation, and more than a hint of delusion, despair and failure. *The Great Gatsby* manages somehow to straddle, however hazardously, the antithetical exigencies of American high and mass cultural ambitions, but O'Neill's whole career enacts a trickily navigated passage between contrary literary domains with adverse value systems, and it is the conviction that he somehow wrested American literary-theatrical greatness from literary-theatrical poverty that has earned him a lasting centrality in the canon of American theatrical literature in the age of American world ascendancy. As we will see later,

*Long Day's Journey into Night* is a self-divided work that offers support for the critical legend that was to make O'Neill into a kind of twentieth-century American modernist Shakespeare. However, that play also offers a darker counter-narrative that interrogates, to a far greater degree than O'Neill scholarship has done, the standard critical accounts of American theatre's coming-of-age.

The *Great Gatsby* and *Long Day's Journey* are obviously quite different texts in style and genre, but they share some compelling features worth teasing out. Each work proffers a tale of male rags-to-riches success: James Gatz's remaking of his impoverished Midwestern self as the gorgeous Long Island millionaire Jay Gatsby; James Tyrone's climb from immigrant slum destitution in Buffalo to become the wealthy Broadway star-actor in *The Count of Monte Cristo*. In both works, though, that dazzling rags-to-riches 'success' turns out to be a counterfeit achievement leading to destruction, the rags-to-riches tale turning into a rags-to-riches-to-ruin narrative. In both cases, moreover, the upwardly mobile male gains possession of the white purity of virginal American womanhood, represented by Daisy Fay and Mary Cavan, respectively. These seductions initially set a seal on the male figures' 'success', but will also come to haunt both Gatsby and Tyrone as a magical moment of promissory bliss that somehow perished forever in the instance of its consummation. More significantly, in each work the most overtly 'literary' figure in the tale conducts an extended reckoning with a more potent male figure who displays in his prime at least an enormous glamour and vitality that the less splendid 'writer figure' cannot match. Nick Carraway may survive to tell or write Gatsby's story, but he himself is no Gatsby; Edmund Tyrone may have more literary sensibility than James Tyrone, but he is a consumptive who will never have his father's great vitality. In short, what we get in both Fitzgerald's and O'Neill's works are narratives in which 'high' and 'low', 'old' and 'new' cultural male protagonists come into some sort of catalytic contact with each other, the 'low' cultural character initially displaying a tremendous potency that attracts the 'high' cultural figure. Both works, then, offer tempting visions of class bonding in the marriage of upper- and lower-class men and women, and of 'high' and 'popular' cultural bonding through the friendship or father-son affections of male figures. However, in the end, no fructifying totalization succeeds; instead, things come apart, and these tales of epic overcoming become tragedies.

In their respective ways, I will argue, each of these texts offers an ambiguous testimony to the spellbinding seductiveness and potency of American 'low' culture, only then for the figure most associated with that culture to be exposed. In this narrative transaction, an enfeebled 'high' culture gets some sort of eventual upper hand over an initially more potent 'low' culture: it is as though these texts were conducting a symbolic contest between American mass culture and American modernism, one in which the latter attains a narrow and always uncertain narrative victory over its ostensibly more seductive rival. However, this needs qualification: to speak finally of 'victory' for either party in *The Great Gatsby* or *Long Day's Journey* is wrong because in both cases any such overcoming proves pyrrhic. Even if Nick Carraway lives on to escape New York and memorialize Jay Gatsby or if Edmund Tyrone proves more sympathetic to audiences than his aging tight-fisted stage-star father, James Tyrone, the 'victor' here is also always the loser because the two parties involved show themselves ultimately codependant. The collapse of one figure, Gatsby or James Tyrone, also leads to an exhausted diminishment of the other, Nick Carraway or Edmund. In the age of American ascendancy, these texts suggest, the sophistication of American high culture and the glamour of American mass culture can be neither easily separated nor satisfyingly sutured.

## II

Still widely considered the quintessential novel of the American 'Roaring Twenties', *The Great Gatsby* is in important respects a post-war novel of the 1940s, the period in which it was rescued from neglect and accorded its honoured place in the American canon. When first published in 1925, the novel was praised by T. S. Eliot as 'the first step that American fiction has taken since Henry James', and Gertrude Stein wrote to Fitzgerald praising it as 'a good book'.[15] Despite this, the novel received a much more mixed reception generally in the United States. Some reviews dismissed it as falling 'into the class of negligible novels', and H. L. Mencken, who admired its style, regarded it as 'in form no more than a glorified anecdote'. Other reviewers agreed and held that, despite 'the glittering surfaces', the characters 'remain types'.[16] Compared to the more commercially success-ful *This Side of Paradise* and *The Beautiful and the Damned*, *Gatsby*'s sales were disappointing from the start. In the years that followed publication, neither a movie version (now lost) made by Paramount in 1926, a French translation that year as *Gatsby le magnifique*, which won from Jean Cocteau the compliment that it was 'un livre *céleste*, chose la plus rare du monde',[17] nor a Modern Library edition reissued in 1934 rescued its fortunes. The novel always had a small band of admirers, but even critical interest was limited.[18]

The turning point really only began in the 1940s, when, in a rising chorus of commendations, John Dos Passos praised *The Great Gatsby* in *The New Republic* in March 1941 as 'one of the few classic American novels'. An even more decisive upturn came after the war when Edmund Wilson edited the essay collection *The Crack-Up* (1945) and William Troy's 'The Authority of Failure' in *Accent* pronounced *Gatsby* 'one of the few truly mythological creations in our recent literature'. In the same year, Lionel Trilling compared the young Fitzgerald with the young Goethe in *The Nation* and proposed that 'Gatsby, divided between power and dream, comes inevitably to stand for America itself. Ours is the only nation that prides itself upon a dream and gives its name to one, "the American dream."' In the *Kenyon Review* in 1946, John Berryman declared that *Gatsby* was 'a masterpiece', and 'better than any other American work of fiction since *The Golden Bowl*.[19] From the mid-1940s onwards, identifications of *Gatsby* and Fitzgerald with 'America itself' or 'the American Dream' become almost axiomatic, and since then Fitzgerald's reputation has never looked back. In this respect at least, *The Great Gatsby* really belongs less to the 'Roaring Twenties' than to the early summer of American global ascendancy after World War II.[20]

This is significant because the post-war period is also the historical moment when the American universities enter something like their 'golden age' of expansion and when, through their Great Books, Western Civilization and World Literature courses, they become custodians of both American Literature and World Culture. Courses of these kinds had been pioneered since the 1920s, and had introduced American students either to the Western classics generally, meaning to philosophical and intellectual as well as imaginative works, or to works of literature proper, these taught exclusively in English translation because most students involved had no foreign language training. However, it was the expansion of the American middle classes by mid-century, the large number of soldiers returning after 1945 entitled to higher educational access, and the United States' determination to promote the prestige of American culture abroad that lent new momentum to this high cultural drive. Thus, it is possible to think of this era as one in which a new conception of 'world literature' emerges that differed in some fundamental respects to its earlier European forerunners. As John Pizer and Sarah Lawall have variously noted, *Weltliteratur* as a discursive paradigm may have been most closely associated in the nineteenth century with Germany, but 'world literature' as a pedagogical practice or as an institutionalized higher-level induction to and sampling of the riches of a trans-historical array of multi-civilization classics is an almost exclusively American phenomenon.[21] Lawall has put it as follows: 'Courses in world literature are a uniquely American institution. World literature exists elsewhere as a scholarly topic or as the subject of ambitious global histories, but it is not an academic institution. Only in the United States do we find a systematic attempt to encompass the "world" (however defined) in literature courses'.[22] It is not simply, then, the rise of New York as a twentieth-century world city, significant though this is, but also the development of the continent-wide American university system and the latter's construction of its own version of 'world literature' that gradually reconfigured the Western (or non-Soviet) world literary system in the latter half of the twentieth century.

Though it undoubtedly benefitted from this moment of American self-assertion, *The Great Gatsby* nevertheless displays considerable anxieties about the nature of 'American culture'. Or, put more precisely, the novel hesitates as to whether American culture has the capacity either to shed its mimetic deference to European aristocratic notions of aesthetic taste or to create an American democratic mass or popular culture that would ever be anything more than a meretriciously glittering commodified spectacle. As noted in the opening chapters, these anxieties go back at least to that other 'American classic', Tocqueville's *Democracy in America*, a work that was itself indebted to Enlightenment republican fears that the expansion of a modern commercial society would inevitably corrupt both political virtue and cultural ambition. For Tocqueville, we may recall, the early nineteenth-century American literary elites looked to England especially and to Europe more generally for their conceptions of high cultural taste, while a more vigorous domestic American literature, nurtured on the American press's usages of English, might prove more popular and be more distinctively American. However, given the capitalist nature of American society and Tocqueville's doubts about democratic levelling, American culture would always run the inevitable risks, he suggested, of commercial standardization, bombastic grandiloquence and abstract universalism. For Tocqueville, American letters appeared likely to veer between high cultural pretensions to an elite sophistication that would retain an imitative second-order European quality and a more authentic American culture that would, in its typical manifestations at least, display an admirable vigour and grandeur but never be able to separate these from a trashy market-driven commodification. If *The Great Gatsby* is an 'American classic', its Americanness stems in large part from its nervous expression and precarious 'resolution' of such antinomies.

These matters are at work on several levels in *Gatsby*. The American moneyed elite's affectation for things European appears in obvious parodic form in Gatsby's status as 'an Oggsford man', something that greatly impresses Meyer Wolfshiem even as it bemuses Nick and appals Tom Buchanan. [23] Gatsby's ludicrously clichéd account of his early years when he lived abroad after World War I expresses this Europhilic fantasy in comically sentimentalized form. He tells Nick that he had lived then 'like a young rajah in all the capitals of Europe – Paris, Venice, Rome – collecting jewels, chiefly rubies, hunting big game, painting a little, things for myself only, and trying to forget something very sad that had happened to me long ago' (52). Gatsby's West Egg house is 'a factual imitation of some Hôtel de Ville in Normandy, with a tower on one side, spanking new under a thin beard of raw ivy' (8). This artificial aging provokes from Nick an anecdote about how its previous owner, a brewer, had built it 'in the "period" craze, a decade before' and to increase its sense of authenticity had offered to pay the owners of all the surrounding cottages to have their roofs thatched in straw. However, that offer was refused, Nick remarks acidly, because 'Americans, while occasionally willing to be serfs, have always been obstinate about being peasantry' (69). The interior of Gatsby's house is also European and so are his clothes. When he shows Daisy about on her fateful visit to his home, Nick recounts that 'we wandered through Marie Antoinette music rooms and Restoration salons' as well as passing through 'the Merton College Library' (71) – a room introduced earlier in the novel as 'a high Gothic library, panelled with carved English oak, and probably transported complete from some ruin overseas' (37). Even in that famous moment when Gatsby shows Daisy his wardrobe of 'his massed suits and dressing gowns and ties, and his shirts piled like bricks in stacks a dozen high', he underscores their foreign provenance, telling her 'I've got a man in England who buys me clothes. He sends over a selection of things at the beginning of each season, spring and fall' (72).

What is true of nouveau-riche Gatsby is equally true of the older-money Buchanans. When he first visits their East Egg mansion, Nick informs the readers that '[t]hey had spent a year in France, for no particular reason' (8–9), though later we learn that they had gone there to allow a scandal that involved Tom with a hotel maid to blow over, a flight repeated at the end of the story when Daisy kills Myrtle. Their house, 'a cheerful red and white Georgian Colonial mansion overlooking the bay' (9), has the same European pretensions as Gatsby's, featuring as it does a pastorally evoked 'sunken Italian garden' (10) and 'a line of French windows, glowing now with reflected gold, and wide open to the warm windy afternoon' (9). On his first appearance, Tom, the ex-footballer, now polo-player, appears to the reader as proud possessor of all this, but despite the latent aggressiveness of his body's 'great pack of muscle' he is dressed in 'the effeminate swank of his riding clothes' (9), the garb he and other East Eggers wear to appear as English country gentlemen. Indeed, Tom later brags that at a time when motor cars are replacing horses, he prefers to convert the modern to the feudal rather than vice versa: "I've heard of making a garage out of a stable', Tom was saying to Gatsby, 'but I'm the first man who ever made a stable out of a garage' (92). Modern American wealth and mobility requires, in short, an imposed Old World veneer to make it seem posh and prestigious.

If both new and old American wealth share Old World European affectations that are treated by Nick with a certain wry amusement yet allowed some considerable charm in Fitzgerald's lyrical prose, the American working class's pretensions to similar styles are afforded sharper treatment. When Tom brings his working-class mistress, Myrtle Wilson, to their Washington Heights love-nest, Myrtle's inflated self-importance is underlined. Before she even enters the building, she throws 'a regal home-coming glance around the neighborhood' and gathers 'up her dog and her other purchases, and went haughtily in' (25); later, when the sense of status afforded by her attachment to Tom becomes swollen by alcohol, Nick notes that her 'intense vitality' is 'converted into impressive hauteur' (26). Soon, this hauteur gets out of hand to the extent that Tom, unable to abide it, suddenly breaks Myrtle's nose. In this episode, the apartment is likewise furnished with things European, but in much more tatty and tasteless ways than in Tom's or Gatsby's mansion: 'The living room was crowded to the doors with a set of tapestried furniture entirely too large for it so that to move about was to stumble continually over scenes of ladies swinging in the gardens of Versailles' (25). Whereas Gatsby's house boasts an impressively elaborate version of a Merton College Library, Myrtle's apartment is strewn only with mass cultural dross – 'Several old copies of "Town Tattle" lay on the table together with a copy of "Simon Called Peter" and some of the small scandal magazines of Broadway' (25) – and ornamented with Mr. McKee's unimpressive photographic portraits. McKee informs Nick that 'he was in the "artistic game"' (26) and later tries to solicit his help in winning West Egg commissions. Depicting characters that are cheap, drunken, violent or mercenary, and an apartment so tacky and cluttered that even to move about it was to stumble over tapestried scenes 'of ladies swinging in the gardens of Versailles', this scene is a kind of kitschy anti-pastoral, a degraded petty version of the aery spaciousness of Tom's stately mansion or Gatsby's feudal-style pile.

Nevertheless, while *The Great Gatsby* has much fun with American high- and low-style imitations of Europe, at the level of form the novel has its own mimetic imitations. After all, this quintessential 'American classic' has taken some of its most commented-upon features from European modernist works. The observer-participant retrospective narrative technique whereby Nick posthumously recounts Gatsby's fame and fall is borrowed from Joseph Conrad's *Heart of Darkness*, and the famous 'valley of ashes' (21) scene is a transposition of T. S. Eliot's London in *The Waste Land* onto the New York landscape. Furthermore, the contrast between the upper-class Buchanan house where the women are bored and nearly hysterical with unhappiness ('Sophisticated – God I'm sophisticated!' Daisy thrills with self-mockery to Nick (17)) and the vulgar but predatory vitality of Myrtle is taken from *The Waste Land's* 'A Game of Chess' with its neurotically modern upper-class Cleopatra and its barroom Cockney working women. The mock-epic catalogues of the guests who attend Gatsby's parties are versions of Joyce's extravagantly expansive satiric listings in *Ulysses*. To observe this is not at all to diminish Fitzgerald's artistry but only to underline that nowhere is there any pristine 'America' in *The Great Gatsby*. Even in its remarkable valedictory closing passage, the one in which 'the inessential houses' (140) of Long Island fade away and Nick imagines that first 'transitory enchanted moment' when 'man must have held his breath in the presence of this continent' and was 'compelled into an aesthetic contemplation he neither understood nor desired, face to face for the last time in history with something commensurate to his capacity for wonder', this magical primal encounter with the 'fresh, green breast of the new world' is invoked by visualizing how all this might then have 'flowered once for Dutch sailors' eyes' (140). Dr. T. J. Eckleburg's eyes, Owl Eyes, Dutch sailors' eyes, Nick's narrative lens: whether in its enchanted primordial verdant pastoral or ashy wasteland modern manifestations, Fitzgerald's America, and the 'wonder' or horror it provokes, can never really retrieve any sense of original unmediated purity; everything comes to us through others' eyes. Whatever America's aboriginal pristineness might once have been, it was lost forever, the passage suggests, with European settlement, and American culture seems ever since to have remained in thrall to a Europe that the United States needs both to become and to overcome in order to be 'itself'.

It is only in Gatsby's parties, those other most memorable moments in Fitzgerald's novel, that we can glimpse some alternative conception of American culture perhaps, one less enthralled by mimetic deference to things European and aristocratic. What distinguishes 'those gleaming, dazzling' (140) parties is their extravagance, their openness, their orgiastic promiscuity. Unlike the parties of the elite, by invitation only, 'People were not invited [to Gatsby's parties] – they went there' (34). When Jordan meets Nick at the first of these events, she tells him 'Anyhow he gives large parties', adding, 'And I like large parties. They're so intimate. At small parties there isn't any privacy' (41), and this association of intimacy rather than alienated anonymity with crowds certainly upends one of the standard modernist tropes where the masses, as in *The Waste Land*, for example, are associated with a purgatorial loss of identity. Gatsby's parties have a throbbing wildness and a spacious out-of-doors summery grandeur that contrast positively with the private but claustrophobic and shabby Washington Heights apartment party where Tom breaks Myrtle's nose. The madcap sociability of Gatsby's extravaganzas contrasts too with the snootily upper-class New York Yale Club where Nick takes his solitary dinners ('for some reason it was the gloomiest event of my day') and then goes to its library to study 'investments and securities for a conscientious hour', secure in the knowledge that 'it was a good place to work' (46).

Moreover, Fitzgerald expends some of his most glittering writing on Gatsby's parties, the opening one in particular is granted a 'spectroscopic gayety' (37) that eclipses nearly everything else in the novel:

> By seven o'clock the orchestra has arrived – no thin five piece affair but a whole pit full of oboes and trombones and saxophones and viols and cornets and piccolos and low and high drums. The last swimmers have come in from the beach now and are dressing upstairs; the cars from New York are parked five deep in the drive, and already the halls and salons and verandas are gaudy with primary colors and hair shorn in strange new ways and shawls beyond the dreams of Castile. The bar is in full swing and floating rounds of cocktails permeate the garden outside until the air is alive with chatter and laughter and casual innuendo and introductions forgotten on the spot and enthusiastic meetings between women who never knew each other's names.
>
> The lights grow brighter as the earth lurches away from the sun and now the orchestra is playing yellow cocktail music and the opera of voices pitches a key higher. Laughter is easier, minute by minute, spilled with prodigality, tipped out at a cheerful word. The groups change more swiftly, swell with new arrivals, dissolve and form in the same breath – already there are wanderers, confident girls who weave here and there among the stouter and more stable, become for a sharp, joyous moment the center of a group and then excited with triumph glide on through the sea-change of faces and voices and color under the constantly changing light.
>
> Suddenly one of these gypsies in trembling opal seizes a cocktail out of the air, dumps it down for courage and moving her hands like Frisco dances

out alone on the canvas platform. A momentary hush; the orchestra leader varies his rhythm obligingly for her and there is a burst of chatter as the erroneous news goes round that she is Gilda Gray's understudy from the 'Follies'. The party has begun.

(33–34)

There is nothing like this in Conrad, nor in Eliot (think of the grim awfulness of *The Cocktail Party*), nor even in Joyce (the party in 'The Dead' has a morbid quality; the more ebullient drinking session in 'Cyclops' in *Ulysses* is a male-only and menacing affair). The bigness and multi-instrumentality of the orchestra, 'no thin five piece affair', reflects the commodious raucous vivacity of the gathering. Here, the high-society orchestra does not condescend to the young woman who, with Dutch courage, essays a version of Joe Frisco's 'black bottom' dance and who is mistaken for an understudy to Gilda Gray, the inventor of 'the shimmy'. Instead, the orchestra leader 'varies his rhythm obligingly for her', high and low cultural forms gracefully accommodating each other. The scene is at least as splendid as the novel's closing passage, but it is narrated in the present and present perfect tense ('the orchestra has arrived', 'The last swimmers have come in', 'halls and salons and verandas are gaudy', the girl 'seizes a cocktail out of thin air', 'The party has begun'). We find here none of the melancholy retrospect of the 'green breast of the new world' ending where the tense is mainly past or past perfect ('the trees that had made way for Gatsby's house, had once pandered in whispers to the last and greatest of all human dreams', 'He had come a long way to this blue lawn', 'He did not know that it was already behind him' (140–141)). In *Gatsby*'s lyrically wistful finale, things are weighed down with a sense of weary completion, but in the former scene where '[t]he party has begun', everything is vital with quick immediacy.

Between this opening glimpse of Gatsby's party and those that follow, the reader is introduced to Gatsby's library when Jordan and Nick search for their host. They do not find Gatsby, but only his library where a drunken Owl Eyes assures the couple with comic intensity that the shelves of books are '[a]bsolutely real – have pages and everything. I thought they'd be a nice durable cardboard. Matter of fact they're absolutely real' (38). This insistent realism is intensified or undercut or both by Owl Eyes's description of Gatsby as 'a regular Belasco' (38), a reference to Broadway director David Belasco's panache for realistic effects, though whether Belasco's grandiose will to mimetic fidelity and his over-the-top theatricality can be separated is doubtful. There is at any rate something patently parodic in Owl Eyes's surprise that this English-style library might have books with actual 'pages and everything' (38). Owl Eyes has after all 'been drunk for about a week now' and had only retired to this room, he says, because 'I thought it might sober me up to sit in a library' (38). This sobriety associated with libraries comically anticipates Nick's later retirement to the Yale Club's library where there were few 'rioters around' to disturb his 'conscientious hour' studying high finance. It is hard not to detect here also a sly mockery of that bookish banker, T. S. Eliot, and of the intensely bookish allusiveness of *The Waste Land* and its fetish for the classics of past centuries and its solemnly depressive rendering of present-day London.

From the English-style library, the scene then cuts back again to outdoors, where the party now is in even more exuberant swing:

> There was dancing now on the canvas in the garden, old men pushing young girls backward in eternal graceless circles, superior couples holding each other tortuously, fashionably and keeping in the corners – and a great number of single girls dancing individualistically or relieving the orchestra for a moment of the burden of the banjo or the traps. By midnight the hilarity had increased. A celebrated tenor had sung in Italian and a notorious contralto had sung in jazz, and between the numbers people were doing 'stunts' all over the garden while happy vacuous bursts of laughter rose toward the summer sky. A pair of stage 'twins' – who turned out to be the girls in yellow – did a baby act in costume and champagne was served in glasses bigger than finger bowls. The moon had risen higher, and floating in the Sound was a triangle of silver scales, trembling a little to the stiff, tinny drip of the banjoes on the lawn.
>
> (38–39)

The passage underscores not just the promiscuous mingling of the crowds (old men and young women, couples and single girls, the superior couples shunted to the corners) but also of instruments and arts. The guests borrow banjoes or traps from the orchestra and, as well as a celebrated high-culture tenor singing in Italian, there is low-culture jazz sung by a 'notorious contralto'. The evening reaches its height when the band at Gatsby's request plays the piece known as 'Vladimir Tostoff's Jazz History of the World' (41). This is only one of several occasions when Gatsby's extravagance acquires a 'world' quality. On another occasion, Nick, seeing Gatsby's whole house 'blazing with light' and 'lit from tower to cellar', tells its proprietor that '[y]our place looks like the world's fair' (64), and Gatsby, we recall, is also in league with Meyer Wolfshiem, 'the man who fixed the World's Series back in 1919' (58). The year 1919 marked the post-war moment when American dominance over Europe got underway in earnest, but here it also figures a moment when American innocence ended and consciousness of its corruptibility could no longer be averted.

Part of the excitement of Gatsby's parties, then, is that, at their best at least, they signal a new kind of democratically inclusive 'world' or universality and a new kind of culture as well. The elite WASPy East Eggers cannot resist coming to Gatsby's fantastic parties, but when they try to maintain their standoffish superiority in the throng, as Jordan's company does at the first party, their commitment to preserving 'a dignified homogeneity' merely assumes 'to itself the function of representing the staid nobility of the country-side' (37). When Tom Buchanan comes to the third party, he suffers serious social discomfit when Gatsby, despite Tom's abashed protests, introduces him to everyone as 'Mr. Buchanan –' and then, after a pause, 'the polo player' (82). In the riot of Gatsby's all-in party, Tom's equine Anglophile and aristocratic pretensions now seem as absurdly out of place as Gatsby's pink suit and claim to be 'an Oggsford man' had earlier appeared to Tom. Furthermore, at this later party the old East Egg WASP aristocracy is outshone by a new and more luminous aristocracy, that represented by film star celebrities. 'I've never met so many celebrities!' (82). Daisy exclaims in wonder, and Nick notes that for Daisy 'in the very casualness of Gatsby's party there were romantic possibilities totally absent from her world' (85). Towards the end of the evening, before her mood sours, Nick recalls too:

> Almost the last thing I remember was standing with Daisy and watching the moving picture director and his Star. They were still under the white plum tree and their faces were touching except for a pale thin ray of moonlight between. It occurred to me that he had been very slowly bending toward her all evening to attain this proximity, and even while I watched I saw him stoop one ultimate degree and kiss at her cheek.
> 'I like her', said Daisy. 'I think she's lovely.'
>
> (83)

This rapt moment, which soon provokes a rapt recall of the autumn evening five years earlier when Gatsby and Daisy had first kissed, transfers romance, wonder and luminous enchantment from the old money, European-oriented American 'aristocracy', represented by Daisy and Tom, to the new Hollywood-oriented upstart 'aristocracy' of the movies. The old East Coast would-be American aristocracy is already about to be eclipsed by a new West Coast celebrity. No wonder that Daisy's change of mood comes quickly after she acknowledges the movie star's loveliness:

> But the rest offended her – and inarguably, because it wasn't a gesture but an emotion. She was appalled by West Egg, this unprecedented 'place' that Broadway had begotten upon a Long Island fishing village – appalled

by its raw vigor that chafed under the old euphemisms and by the too obtrusive fate that herded its inhabitants along a short cut from nothing to nothing. She saw something awful in the very simplicity she failed to understand.

(84)

Disenchanted Daisy leaves almost immediately afterwards, Gatsby noticing sadly that '[s]he didn't have a good time' (85). At the start of the next chapter, Nick peremptorily tells the reader that the parties are ended, the house closed to a disappointed public, and its host's 'career as Trimalchio was over' (88).

For readers, the conundrum of the parties in *The Great Gatsby* is not to know what they represent but to decide how they are supposed to regard them. As noted already, their extravagance and exuberance generally contrast positively with the exclusivism and world-weary seen-it-all lassitude associated with old American 'aristocracy'. And the gaily colourful and carnivalesque quality of the Gatsby gatherings contrasts favourably too with the morosely literary 'universality' of, say, *The Waste Land* or the solemnly self-improving 'universality' of the Great Books and World Literature courses already beginning to be inaugurated in the American university system. In contrast to these Euro-American-looking elite cultures, Gatsby's parties connote a hurly-burly democratic or even republican-minded gate-crashing openness where many ethnicities and social types raucously commingle. That said, the parties are always mediated to the reader through Nick and are therefore filtered via his characteristic mix of supercilious drollery and awkwardly self-aware snobbishness. The much-discussed mock-epic guest catalogues make clear that the guests are not only associated with the newer non-WASP but nevertheless 'white' immigrant ethnicities, but also with the emerging American culture industries, whether theatrical, cinematic, sporting or entertainment:

> From West Egg came the Poles and the Mulreadys and Cecil Roebuck and Cecil Schoen and Gulick, the state senator, and Newton Orchid who controlled Films Par Excellence and Eckhaust and Clyde Cohen and Don S. Schwartze (the son) and Arthur McCarty, all connected with the movies in one way or another. And the Catlips and the Bembergs and G. Earl Muldoon, brother to that Muldoon who afterwards strangled his wife. Da Fontano the promoter came there and Ed Legros and James B. ('Rot-gut') Ferret and the de Jongs and Ernest Lilly – they came to gamble and when Ferret wandered into the garden it meant he was cleaned out and Associated Traction would have to fluctuate profitably next day.
> [...] Also from New York were the Chromes and the Backhyssons and the Dennickers and Russel Betty and the Corrigans and the Kellehers and the Dewars and the Scullys and S. W. Belcher and the Smirkes and the

young Quinns, divorced now, and Henry L. Palmetto who killed himself by jumping in front of a subway train in Times Square.

(50)

There are a lot of Irish- and Jewish-sounding names among the comic roll call here and the fantastical professional and ethnic mix suggests that sense of a world-turned-even-more-upside-down that Nick considers when, driving with Gatsby over the Queensboro Bridge, he sees 'three modish Negroes, two bucks and a girl' being driven in a great limousine 'by a white chauffeur'. This prompts Nick to surmise that anything can happen in New York, where '[e]ven Gatsby could happen, without any particular wonder' (55). All of these ascending new sorts – the movie people, Broadway people, boxing promoters, bootleggers, the Irish, the Jews, the Negroes – provoke for Nick a sense of astonishment at New York but, paradoxically, part of what amazes him is that in this strange new world their assertiveness is no longer 'any particular wonder'.

However, if Fitzgerald lavishes some of his finest writing on these parties and makes the spectacles they create part of Gatsby's enigmatic mixture of garishness and 'greatness', strains of the old Tocquevillian scepticism about democratic culture persist. Perhaps the greatest indictment of the parties is that despite their exuberant democratic vitality and raucous inclusivity, they are, for Gatsby, their Trimalchio, never more than an instrument to an end. For him, they serve one purpose alone – to lure Daisy back into his orbit, to recapture his earlier capture of the very incarnation of that old 'aristocratic' elite white purity that is the antithesis of the promiscuous parties. Gatsby himself always remains soberly aloof to the lavish revels he sponsors, and once he knows that Daisy disapproves of their extravagant splendour, he shuts them down instantly. The books in Gatsby's English-style Merton Library are real but remain untitled and undistinguished from each other except for 'Volume One of the "Stoddard Lectures"' (38), which recalls '"The Rise of the Coloured Empires" by this man Goddard' (14) that Tom had been reading when Nick first visits East Egg. Intellectual or literary high culture, then, is identified with both an un-party-like sobriety and the elitist apocalyptic pessimism that runs through so much modernism from Spengler to Yeats to Eliot, not to mention through Fitzgerald's own early impressions of Europe as recounted in the letter to Edmund Wilson cited at the head of this chapter. Books in Fitzgerald's novel have none of the spirited collective glamour of the party or orchestra; to the contrary, they suggest sober isolation rather than festive sociability, racist chiliasm rather than orgiastic inclusivity.

Ironically, then, *The Great Gatsby* tempts its readers to enjoy the grand spectacle of the more popular-democratic cultural extravaganzas represented by these parties, but the work seems also to have to repudiate them to become an 'art novel' or 'high literature'. Or, to put matters another way, there is a sense in which Fitzgerald, like Nick, the bemused writer or raconteur of Gatsby's tale, finds himself oscillating anxiously between the old European-mimicking American WASP pseudo-aristocracy represented by the Buchanans and the rawer magnetism of the new culture-industry extravaganzas represented by Gatsby, but can never really feel wholly at home in either world. Each of these two worlds is allowed its partial glamour, the criminality and corruption of each are also acknowledged, and it is as if to become a classic of 'American literature' *The Great Gatsby* has somehow to absorb the enchantment peculiar to each of these worlds – WASP aristocratic and mass cultural – into itself while simultaneously morally transcending them both. *The Great Gatsby*, in short, becomes an 'American literary classic' by playing off against each other both sides of Tocqueville's critique of American high and mass culture – the one too snobbishly elite and imitatively European, the other too crassly commodified and vulgar – and by positioning itself as the vanishing mediator between the two and thereby somehow above both. Thesis – American culture is imitatively aristocratic and derivatively European – and antithesis – American culture is energetically and engagingly democratic but shoddy and vulgar – confront each other without achieving dialectical sublation, except at the level of the novel's style and form.

At the level of plot, the novel seems unambiguously to exorcise the upwardly aspiring lower-class figures. The two working-class characters most hopelessly in thrall to their upper-class counterparts – Gatsby to Daisy Fay Buchanan, Myrtle Wilson to Tom – are dead by the end of the novel, Myrtle run over by Daisy, Gatsby's death achieved by Tom through George Wilson, who kills Gatsby and then commits suicide. By contrast, the upper-crust Tom, Daisy, Jordan and Nick all remain alive. Though she is allowed her huge 'vitality', Myrtle is never granted any of Gatsby's greatness; instead, she seems the 'feminine' or culturally coarse and acquisitive verso to Gatsby's more positively drawn 'masculine' assertive epic ambition and lavish patronage of his guests. Still, *The Great Gatsby* operates relentlessly by way of negations of negations. Thus, while all the principal upwardly aspiring working-class characters are eventually eliminated and 'even though "Jay Gatsby" had broken up like glass' in the critical contest 'against Tom's hard malice' (115) when Daisy declares that she has loved them both and confesses that '[e]ven alone I can't say I never loved Tom' (104), Gatsby's greatness is somehow consecrated despite his defeat. His misplaced valuation of Daisy, whose commitment to him never matches his absolute devotion to her, persists and retains its worth despite all exposures of her hollowness – her inability to wait for him when he was at war in Europe; her passivity when she lets him take responsibility for Myrtle's death. This sense of Gatsby's worth also somehow survives the disclosures of his criminality, his associations with Cody and Wolfshiem, his utter indifference to Myrtle's fate. Indeed, Nick's assertion, which comes the morning immediately after Gatsby's failure to win Daisy or vanquish Tom in the suffocating New York hotel – "'They're a rotten crowd," I shouted across the lawn. "You're worth the whole damn bunch put together"' (120) – awards Gatsby a verdict of final worth over all others.

This is a curious valuation to be sure because it is in the end only Nick's conviction of the utter worthlessness of the 'whole damn bunch put together' – meaning the fake-aristocrats represented by the Buchanans, the lower-class hangers-on who mobbed Gatsby's parties – that confers that valedictory vote of superiority to the otherwise defeated Gatsby. In sum, even Gatsby's 'greatness' seems to be founded not on anything intrinsic to his own character, but falls to him by default because all the others are even worse than he is. True, his 'romantic readiness' (6) is granted an epic grandeur, but 'readiness' is a curious word and denotes a condition of being open to experience, but of what kind? A big-spirited keenness for something, but for what? As we have seen earlier, American readiness or promise was questioned by Fitzgerald when he wrote, also in 1925, that 'America's greatest promise is that something is going to happen, but after a while you get tired of waiting because nothing happens to people except that they grow old, and nothing happens to American art because America is the story of the moon that never rose'. *The Great Gatsby* seems both a paean to the romance of abstract but epic possibility and yet also a melancholy eulogy for the vagueness of possibility. Gatsby's American greatness, in short, appears as a kind of emptied-out greatness always waiting for its Godot.

Nevertheless, though *The Great Gatsby* may be a curious tribute to Gatsby's enigmatic 'greatness', Nick is obviously the one who survives in the end and the tale in that sense is his. What form Gatsby's tale might take were it to be conveyed to readers in his own voice is hard to imagine. Would it be absurdly sentimental and romantic? Bombastically epic? It hardly matters because the tale we have is filtered through Nick's voice or rather through this habitual two-timer's double voice: one romantic, lyrically appreciative, hesitantly or ruefully hymnal; the other sardonic, humorously depreciative. This is a voice that can express 'an unaffected scorn' for everything Gatsby represents (6) and yet say only Gatsby 'was exempt from my reaction' (5), that reaction being a generalized disgust. Within Fitzgerald's narrative economy, which places this begrudgingly admiring narrator midway between Gatsby and the Buchanans, Nick stands for something like the self-compromised, rather stymied triumph of American high modernism over the two forms of American culture with which it had to contend: on the one side, an 'old money' American elite culture always looking deferentially to Europe for models of taste and value; on the other, an American mass culture with a brash energy and vigorous democratic glitter that the elite culture lacks but which itself lacks sophistication or distinction. Within the terms of the novel, neither of these competitor cultures is satisfactory. The 'old money' WASP elite culture is too casually brutal and pseudo-intellectual in its masculine version (Tom). And it is much too passively beautiful in its feminized form (when Nick first sees Daisy and Jordan, they are stretched out on a couch in a pose of such extremely aery lassitude that they appear 'as if they had just been blown back in [to the room] after a short flight around the house' (10)) to be impressive. The 'new money' non-WASP-dominated mass culture is altogether more vital and enterprising than this elite culture but in its feminized instantiation, represented by Myrtle, it appears tasteless and coarsely acquisitive while in its masculine manifestation, Gatsby, it possesses a grandness of ambition that can never be disassociated from its own delusions of grandeur and behind-the-scenes criminal thuggery.

Throughout the novel Gatsby is linked through his party-guests with the emerging American cinema industry, with Broadway's commercial theatre, with the entertainment industries of sports and gambling.[24] Indeed, the grand parties he throws are afforded something of that 'colossal' scope and sense of 'surge and splendor' that Vivian Sobchack rightly sees as crucial to the mass appeal of American early and mid-twentieth-century cinematic epics.[25] While Nick remains the poorer neighbour in the eyesore cottage overshadowed by the gorgeous occupant of the mansion next door lit up 'like the world's fair', he is always Gatsby's subordinate accomplice, essentially another hanger-on among many. It is only when Gatsby is killed off that Nick can assume the more active agency of tale-teller and thereby mediate between the departed competitors, Tom and Gatsby, old 'aristocratic' elite and new democratic-commercial cultures, and us, his readers. However, even then, Nick's is a precariously tentative triumph over these 'old money' and 'new money' or elite and mass cultural competitors, because once he has detached himself from the Buchanans and from Gatsby his only real role is that of a chastened memorialist. By leaving New York for the Midwest, he searches out, as always, some elusive, probably imaginary 'third way' between the options variously represented by the Buchanans and Gatsby. Nick's final Midwestern retreat is functionally similar to modernist 'autonomy' – it offers a rejection of both traditional high culture, supposedly tasteful and improving, and commercial mass culture, supposedly entertaining, which has to convert its own inessential superfluity, because it refuses to justify itself as either tastefully improving or entertaining, to the modern world into a necessary virtue.[26] Put briefly, like the autonomous work of modernist art, Nick has to withdraw from the world to survive, his withdrawal both a protective gesture and a sign of worldly powerlessness.

Nick may be the ruefully inhibited survivor-tale-teller, then, but in *Gatsby* primary and final agency always rests with money. Money allows the Buchanans their pretensions to superiority and ability to flee to France when Daisy kills Myrtle. It is what lends Daisy's voice its seduction and explains her cool beauty 'gleaming like silver, safe and proud above the hot struggles of the poor' (117). It affords Tom his strings of polo ponies, dispensable mistresses, private investigators and new garages converted into old stables. Gatsby's grand parties require a wealth in abundance. Nick trades in bonds on Wall Street and Gatsby's underlings peddle fake bonds to suckers. It is money, too, that allows the most ruthless lower-world figures, Cody, Wolfshiem and Gatsby, to rise up in the world; it is what lubricates the American World Series and allows it to be fixed. The real deities of this new American-run world are 'Midas and Morgan and Maecenas' (7), an alliterative trio that confers a glittering sheen to everything and whose magic fingers reach into the field of high culture as into all others. Gaius Maecenas was a Roman diplomat, patron of the arts and promoter of the works of Horace, Propertius and Virgil, epic poet of the Roman Empire. J. P. Morgan, who died in Rome in 1913, was one of the great bankers of the early age of American ascendancy but also a lavish patron of the Metropolitan Museum, legendary art collector and promoter of American high culture. Midas turned everything he touched to gold, a cursed gift that led to his death by starvation. 'Culture follows money', Fitzgerald, as noted earlier, remarked in 1921 to Edmund Wilson. For Henry James's Adam Verver in *The Golden Bowl*, the hope is that capital will finance the museum in American City that will purchase the art and culture needed to refine a money-making, money-mad society. For Fitzgerald in *The Great Gatsby*, the romance of money and culture continues to cast a spell but the marriage never quite comes off: that romance is a tragic affair.

Fitzgerald's difficulty was that the inverted economy of modernism, which professed to despise traditional nineteenth-century culture and mass culture, and to be indifferent to or scornful of the honours and commercial success that went with bourgeois literature, required the repudiation of what Midas, Morgan and Maecenas stood for, in the short term at least, in pursuit of some deferred higher prestige that presupposed the worthlessness of such validations. Within the economy of *The Great Gatsby*, Nick, former bond-trader and Wall Street banker turned tale-teller, is the voice of this superior repudiation of such things, though his loving gaze remains permanently fixated on the glamorous New York worlds forsaken for the ascetically melancholy Midwest from where he speaks or writes. Within the larger economy of modernism, *Gatsby* won Fitzgerald the one sure-prestige triumph of his career. To become one of the great 'American classics', however, *The Great Gatsby* would have to forgo before its consecration the things synonymous with prestige in the United States in its era of ascendancy: money, wealth, celebrity, glamour, mass appeal. Fitzgerald had known all these things, but in his own lifetime *The Great Gatsby* won him none of them, only the praise of peers like Eliot or Stein. Small wonder that Fitzgerald, golden boy of the Roaring Twenties, remained to the end of his short days baffled by the logic of this 'success'.

Seven months before he died in December 1940, we find Fitzgerald writing from Beverley Hills to Maxwell Perkins, the editor who had helped Charles Scribner's Sons to make the transition from publisher of the now-dated John Galsworthy, Henry James and Edith Wharton to the newer reputations of Fitzgerald, Hemingway and Thomas Wolfe. In that letter, Fitzgerald complains that Scottie, his daughter, will boast in a year or so to her friends that her father was an author and yet be unable to find his books on any shelves, and asks:

> Would the 25-cent press keep *Gatsby* in the public eye – or *is the book unpopular?* Has it *had* its chance? Would a popular reissue in that series with a preface *not* by me but by one of its admirers – I can maybe pick one – make it a favorite with classrooms, profs, lovers of English prose – anybody? But to die, so completely and unjustly after having given so much![27]

The nonplussed desperation here reminds us of Gatsby's astounded, 'You loved me *too?*' (103, italics in the original) at that moment of truth when Daisy confounds him by telling him that she can never say she did not love

Tom, but that she did, however, love Gatsby also. Can one love two such different things at once? Some economies are so tricky as to be incomprehensible. The answer to Fitzgerald's baffled query to Perkins as to what it would take to get *Gatsby* back into the public eye was that it would require a US victory in World War II, a Cold War, his own death and his country's need for a literary-prestigious but popular pocket-size American epic to mark its new global-dominion. Then *The Great Gatsby*, which at the level of style sutures the appeal of Old World aristocratic elite culture and demotic New World mass culture, yet at the level of plot shows the two to be irreconcilable, would find its moment of greatness.

## III

When Eugene O'Neill's last play was posthumously premiered in New York in November 1956, three years after the playwright's death, theatre critic Justin Brooks Atkinson wrote: 'With the production of "Long Day's Journey Into Night" at the Helen Hayes last evening, the American theatre acquires size and stature. The size does not refer to the length of Eugene O'Neill's autobiographical drama, although a play three and three-quarter hours long is worth remarking. The size refers to his conception of theatre as a form of epic literature'. Atkinson, who had reviewed the New York premiere of Samuel Beckett's *Waiting for Godot* for *The New York Times* in April that year, concluded: '"Long Day's Journey Into Night" has been worth waiting for. It restores the drama to literature and the theatre to art'.[28]

The association of O'Neill's career with huge epic ambition and the elevation of American 'theatre to art' are staples of O'Neill scholarship. O'Neill certainly had epic ambition. From 1927 onwards, when he first conceived of a 'vast symbolic play of the effect upon man's soul of industrialism', and especially from 1935 to 1939 when he began work on a nine- and eventually eleven-play Cycle dealing with a multigenerational history of the Harford and Melody families, he hoped to do for America what Shakespeare had done for England with his history tetralogies or Balzac for France with his *La Comédie humaine*.[29] Yet while Shakespeare's histories are usually thought to mark a triumphant if costly consolidation of the English nation under the Tudors and Balzac's interlinked novels are gathered under the term 'comedy', O'Neill's projected epic cycle was decidedly sombre. 'What will it profit a man if he gain the whole world but lose his own soul?' was to be his national epic's core question, its stress more Faustian than affirmative.[30] The great epic was never completed, and O'Neill's late works, *The Iceman Cometh, Long Day's Journey into Night* and *A Moon for the Misbegotten*, are the tragic shards salvaged from his thwarted epic labours.

In a caustic but suggestive account of O'Neill's canonization as the founding father of American literary theatre's coming of age, David Savran has argued that this process required a combination of factors that contributed to a larger reshaping of the American cultural field. One enabling circumstance Savran cites was the rise at the end of the nineteenth century of new printing technologies (linotype machines, high-speed printing presses and rotogravure) that paved the way for the spread of new art magazines, little reviews and newspaper arts supplements that facilitated the rise of a new 'generation of theatre critics, most of them Ivy-League educated, upper-middle-class men (and a few women) intent on discovering and promoting an elevated theatre that would provide an American answer to European modernism'.[31] O'Neill's success in the 1920s, Savran argues, would have been 'unthinkable without the support and adulation of critics like George Jean Nathan, Alexander Woollcott, and Brooks Atkinson', just as the reputations of these well-placed admirers in turn were confirmed by their early 'discovery' of O'Neill to be what contemporary critic Benjamin De Casseres hailed as 'the first true dramatic genius that America produced'.[32] For these critics and their readers, Savran contends, the revolutionizing of American theatre meant an aesthetic and quasi-religious, not a political, revolution, though the aesthetic transformation could appear to imply a radicalism equal to or even greater than a political one. Thus, the effort to create a respectable literary theatre required the latter to distinguish itself not only from 'the gewgaws of Broadway and Hollywood' (569) but also from the more committed forms of drama sponsored by left-wing playwrights or promoted by the Federal Theatre Project established during the Great Depression. The goal of the latter project was to establish a popular-democratic 'people's theatre' designed not to compete with Europe's great national theatres but to mobilize American theatre workers and audiences to confront the immediate crisis of the moment.[33] That these left-wing and popular-democratic ambitions for American theatre flourished in the 1930s when O'Neill practically withdrew from writing new plays, was awarded the Nobel Prize, and struggled without success with his epic-cycle is certainly suggestive.

For Savran, O'Neill's obvious debts to European drama from the Greeks through Shakespeare to Ibsen, Shaw and Strindberg made his work wonderfully exportable to Europe in the interwar years, though O'Neill, he notes, brought to his European models the kind of naturalist American idioms, meaning gritty depictions of urban alienation, then much favoured in Europe. Crucial also to O'Neill's canonization as 'America's leading playwright', Savran argues, was his reputation for suffering, something that allowed his early critics to fashion him, in true modernist style, as 'a kind of saint, a holy man of art, one whose agonies redeemed the American theatre from the tyranny of dreck' (570). To qualify for modernist sainthood, the essential requirement was not conviction, except in art, but doubt, 'one whose motto might be "the 'old God [is] dead' and a new one [is] not in sight"' (570). O'Neill's lapsed Catholicism and his much-advertised debt to Schopenhauer and Nietzsche, Savran concludes, positioned him from very early on as 'a man who renounced the God – and the theatre – of his father for the truth of art' (570) and set him up to become the messiah of a new American theatre of his own troubled creation.

There is much in *Long Day's Journey into Night* that lends itself to Savran's account of how O'Neill's was constructed as a suffering saint of American modernist theatre and as a soul-tormented doubter believing in nothing but the redemptive power of great art. Here, however, I want to see that last play not as a simple exemplification of Savran's thesis but rather as a more complex, hesitant, even self-critical reflection on that process of self-creation and canonization. To view the play in this way is to see it neither as confessional autobiography nor as a work that simply burnishes the O'Neill 'legend', but engage it rather as an antinomian drama that reckons critically with the costs of modernist 'success' specifically as well as with the costs of 'American success' more generally.

To outward appearances, the Tyrone family, which is the subject of *Long Day's Journey*, represents a successful story of Irish immigrant assimilation. James Tyrone, the paterfamilias, was born in squalor in a Buffalo slum, had become a successful Shakespearian actor, and then earned a fortune acting as the lead in *The Count of Monte Cristo*, using his wealth to buy a country house in New London, Connecticut. His sons, therefore, were reared in comfort and well educated; all of the Tyrones can boast artistic or intellectual ambition or achievement. Nevertheless, what the play most memorably offers its audience is a vision not of artistic attainment or pastoral New England comfort but of a whiskey- and opiate-saturated hell in which all of the misery-afflicted Tyrones are experts in mutual torture and self-destruction.

At one point in the play's climactic act, Jamie warns Edmund, his younger sibling and would-be poet, to beware of Jamie's nihilistic will to destroy everything he loves out of jealous rage at his own failure to make anything of his life. However, Jamie also boasts that Edmund is his personal creation, the living incarnation of the dead ambition Jamie could not himself achieve:

> I've had more to do with bringing you up than anyone. I wised you up about women, so you'd never be a fall guy, or make any mistakes you didn't want to make! And who steered you on to reading poetry first? Swinburne, for example? I did! And because I once wanted to write, I planted it in your mind that someday you'd write! Hell, you're more than my brother. I made you! You're my Frankenstein![34]

The stage directions that follow this speech indicate that Jamie is puffed up here 'to a note of drunken arrogance' and Edmund regards his elder brother's boasts that he had formed him with some amusement even as he concedes, 'All right, I'm your Frankenstein' (167). The reference to Mary Shelley's *Frankenstein; or, The Modern Prometheus*, a work born of a wager, might alert us to *Long Day's Journey's* attentiveness to the complexities of creation and to the mimetic rivalries from which creation so often stems. That reference invites us, too, to attend to the mix of shards from his earlier abandoned epic projects and the tissue of sources from other literary works from which, like Frankenstein's monster, O'Neill's last play is constructed. Were we to believe Jamie's assertion that he is Edmund's Victor Frankenstein, then Edmund, his 'creature', often taken as the proxy figure in the play for O'Neill himself, becomes the 'monster' who revenges himself on all those who created him. In Shelley's narrative, this destructive cycle ends with both the maker's and the monster's deaths and with Victor Frankenstein's famous admonition to mankind to '[s]eek happiness in tranquility, and avoid ambition'.[35] *Long Day's Journey into Night* is certainly a Frankensteinian play to the degree that from its opening stage directions onwards it self-consciously advertises the materials from which it is constructed. It is this reflexivity that allows us to see *Long Day's Journey* not so much, as Savran suggests, as a work in which O'Neill uncritically self-fashions his own lugubrious 'legend' as tortured father-creator of a new American theatre, but rather as a play that questions the ideas of 'success' fundamental to modernism and modern theatre more broadly.

The stage directions to Act One of *Long Day's Journey* stipulate that the play opens in the living room of James Tyrone's summer house in August 1912. Though the directions are detailed, the room lacks distinction except for the two bookcases that line its rear and side walls. The stage directions indicate that to the rear of the stage: '*Against the wall between the*

*doorways is a small bookcase, with a picture of Shakespeare above it, contain-*
*ing novels by Balzac, Zola, Stendhal, philosophical and sociological works by*
*Schopenhauer, Nietzsche, Marx, Engels, Kropotkin, Max Stirner, plays by*
*Ibsen, Shaw, Strindberg, poetry by Swinburne, Rossetti, Wilde, Ernest*
*Dowson, Kipling, etc.'* (11, italics in the original). Of the other larger
bookcase, we are told: '*Farther back is a large, glassed-in bookcase with sets*
*of Dumas, Victor Hugo, Charles Lever, three sets of Shakespeare, The World's*
*Best Literature in fifty large volumes, Hume's History of England, Thiers'*
*History of the Consulate and Empire, Smollett's History of England, Gibbon's*
*Roman Empire and miscellaneous volumes of old plays, poetry, and several*
*histories of Ireland. The astonishing thing about these sets is that all the*
*volumes have the look of having been read and reread*' (11–12, italics in
the original). What is the function of these books for the play to come?
Why do the assembled volumes seem rather random in some respects but
are nevertheless so specifically identified?

   The first bookcase, which we might loosely associate with the Tyrone
sons because Jamie and Edmund will recite from several of the poets listed
there later in the play, is obviously the more 'modern' of the two. It is
furnished with the works of major nineteenth-century French novelists,
German philosophers and political thinkers, as well as of the Russian
anarcho-communist Kropotkin, all of which challenged bourgeois society.
This list is rounded off with works by three leading European playwrights,
'Ibsen, Shaw, Strindberg', and several poets typically categorized as
'Decadents', as well as by Rudyard Kipling. The second bookcase, with
its Dumas, Hugo and Lever as well as its Hume, Smollett and Gibbon
volumes, seems less modern in literary terms, and the presence there of
'The World's Best Literature in fifty large volumes' might suggest a taste
attuned to more conventionally established though maybe dated notions of
greatness. This bookcase is sometimes associated with James Tyrone, born
into poverty and having left school at ten, but who has nonetheless
managed to become a renowned actor and who had a dream to be one
of the finest Shakespearian performers of his day before he began to act in
*The Count of Monte Cristo.* However we construe them, Shakespeare in any
event dominates both bookcases. His portrait sits over the smaller one and
faces out to the auditorium and there are three Shakespeare sets in the
larger bookcase. From the outset, O'Neill has organized things, then, such
that the Bard's gaze looks out to the auditorium throughout the play that
follows and the audience there must sometimes look back to the watching
Shakespeare over the heads of the actors performing on stage. Still, if the
English national writer presides over the scene, it is Dumas's *Monte Cristo,*

or at least the American stage version of it, that has made the Tyrone fortune and thus actually built the house that contains the Shakespeare image or shrine and that has paid too for the squandered college educations of the sons of the uneducated father and the books they read. There are no American authors in the Tyrone collections, and the several loosely specified 'miscellaneous volumes of old plays, poetry, and several histories of Ireland' never come to life in the action of the play as Shakespeare and some of the Decadents mentioned do.[36]

The greater enigma of these opening directions, however, is that for all the specificity of the listed authors it is difficult to tell what purpose the bookcases can really serve, because in most theatres audiences will almost certainly not be able to make out either the authors or their titles. These works may nod towards O'Neill's own intellectual formation, but what purpose can this possibly serve for a theatre audience to which the titles of the assembled works will be invisible and the volumes appear only as furniture, as props? The insistence that 'these volumes have the look of having been read and reread' (how is this to be achieved for the stage?) indicates that we are not at least in the world of Gatsby's impressive English-imitation library where the books are real but uncut and thus essentially for display. However, if the Tyrones have, as we are told, assimilated their European books (in a way that Gatsby has not), the play that follows does not bombard its audience with literary references in some Eliotesque or Joycean manner either. O'Neill's citations in *Long Day's Journey* are economically and cleverly deployed, and even if critics have disagreed – as we will see later – about their effects, it remains clear that the allusions to and borrowings from other writers in this play function quite differently to how those in a poem like *The Waste Land* or a novel like *Ulysses* do. In the case of Joyce and Eliot, the literary allusions are so many and so abstruse as to overwhelm even the most erudite reader and force them to search for concordances. For the theatre viewer in the auditorium, this is hardly an option and 'The World's Best Literature' must serve some other purpose.[37]

For much of *Long Day's Journey*, citations play only a relatively minor role. As befitting an actor, Tyrone likes to quote Shakespeare, though mostly he cites only commonplace tags from the Bard of the kind Shaw had liked to lampoon. Thus, it is only in the fourth and final act that the bookshelves really come alive on stage when, in a final grand crescendo of citation, Edmund and Jamie will recite extensively from Kipling and the Decadents especially. That is to say, it is only as the play reaches towards midnight, all the Tyrones by then nearly stupefied by alcohol, morphine and despair, that the books, or some of them at least, come off their shelves to become something more than inert props. When this happens, it is crucial to note is that they do so not because the books are read or because the audience puzzles out the references (as solitary readers might do with Eliot or Joyce) but because they are now rhetorically declaimed in an emotional rolling wave of set pieces that have to be delivered by actors with real oratorical skills if this play is to work well. In other words, *A Long Day's Journey into Night*, as its title suggests, may end in darkest despond emotionally, but as a stage performance it concludes operatically with all of the actors allowed tremendous closing rhetorical set pieces. If O'Neill's play opens with a dry listing of books lined up as so much naturalistic stage furniture, it closes with a grand finale in which the word lives again not on the page but on the tongue, not behind glass cases or in well-fingered rows of 'world classics,' but delectably declaimed from the mouths of stage actors.

It is tempting here to jump to the conclusion that O'Neill's work, so saturated in moods of melancholy, offers its audience an exemplary case of nostalgia for the putative priority and purity of speech over the written word, for presence over absence, for the grand Shakespearian stage over the Dumas stage-adapted novel or commercial theatre, and so on.[38] Because the play is set in 1912, it might seem that it looks back nostalgically, too, to a time before World War I and therefore to an era before high modernism's difficult textuality gained so much prestige in that war's aftermath. An interpretation on these lines might be bolstered by reference to Mary Tyrone, the only major woman character in the play, and the long-suffering wife to the would-be Shakespearian actor and mother to two alcoholic sons, one a cynical gone-to-seed actor, the other a consumptive and apparently dying would-be writer and poet. The male Tyrones are all associated in one way or another with the world of books and stage and they trade citations from Shakespeare and others more frequently with each other as the play progresses. By contrast, Mary is afforded no literary allusions and she blames all of her misfortunes on the isolation she suffered in her husband's touring theatre years. Though she is depicted as better educated in her youth than James because she has attended a wealthy girls' college near Notre Dame, Mary is nevertheless the least bookish character in the play. Throughout *Long Day's Journey*, what she most longs for is a return to the primal innocence of the all-female world of the convent of her youth, and to a time in which she still believed in the loving protection of the Blessed Virgin Mary, the solicitude of her convent mentor, Mother Elizabeth, and the distant benevolence of her absent father. Back then,

Mary had hoped to be a nun or a concert pianist, but her girlish dreams belong to a time that pre-existed the sin of copulation with James Tyrone and her fall into his male-dominated world of theatre.

Mary's longing for the pristine world of the convent – a world of 'praying and playing the piano' (139) that Tyrone warns Edmund has been remembered more romantically than it ever was and is largely a figment 'put in her head by the nuns flattering her' (140) – becomes more acute as she slips towards the end of the play into her deepest daze of morphine addiction. Indeed, *Long Day's Journey* draws to its climax when Mary finally enters on stage all dishevelled, causing Jamie to remark: 'The Mad Scene. Enter Ophelia!' (174), to offer her most pitiful lament for this lost world of girlish innocence. Commanding centre stage and watched aghast by her three silenced menfolk, Mary is granted a closing soliloquy that recalls her convent adolescence, the religious vocation never realized, the faith lost forever. Her threnody of vast regret brings down the final curtain with the lines: 'That was in the winter of senior year. Then in the spring something happened to me. Yes, I remember. I fell in love with James Tyrone and was so happy for a time' (179). If on one level, then, books come off the shelf in Act Four when they take oral life as the declaimed speech of the Tyrone menfolk, this indicating the vitality of the spoken word over the written text or of the theatre over the library, on another level for Mary the theatre itself is equated not with life but with a fall, with a false promise that ended in delusion. Mary falls, in other words, from the Edenic female world of the convent into the male world of the theatre, where she 'was so happy for a time', before that momentary paradise showed itself only a hell. If this seems to suggest a nostalgia for not just a pre-textual but also a pre-theatrical world, for the kind of absolute oneness of word and world that only religion and not 'culture' in any of its media can represent, then this has to be set against the fact that Mary too, of course, is an actor and so belongs to the theatre world she hates. By the time she delivers her soliloquy, she is in any case lost in a delirium of morphine, the medical drug and religious opiate collapsing into each other.

Were Mary's closing soliloquy to be taken as a definitive final statement, then *Long Day's Journey* would come close to expressing an Eliotesque version of modernism that acknowledges that literature or 'culture' can never properly substitute for religion and that art's ambition to serve as a second-order religion for modernity was itself a kind of tragic overreaching, a wrong-turning. In Eliot's view, the mistake of Matthew Arnold and of many of Eliot's fellow modernists was to think that modernity might preserve the substance of Christianity, its capacity to give meaning to life, its sense of the ineffable, by transferring these things to 'culture'. However, it is hard to square this Eliotesque conviction with O'Neill's play because Mary's religious longing is so much associated with morphine and a regressive longing for infantile innocence. It would seem more accurate to say, then, that even if in this work O'Neill shares Eliot's conviction about the incapacity of 'culture' or 'art' to substitute for religion in the modern world, he does not share Eliot's belief that a return to religion is either possible or desirable. Mary's desperate desire for her lost faith is just that in the play: an inconsolable ache for something that, were it ever possessed to begin with, cannot now be recovered.

The presiding 'cultural' figure that looms over the play, of course, is not God but Shakespeare, and his votary in the work is James Tyrone, Mary's husband. In simplistic readings of *Long Day's Journey*, Tyrone tends to be dismissed as a hack, his sense of literature antiquated, his business shrewdness as a man of the theatre the very thing that has caused his downfall. To his family, his definitive vice is his stinginess, this a traumatized response to the poverty he suffered as a child and the fear of dying in a poorhouse he inherited from his Famine-fleeing Irish mother. That formative Irish immigrant experience has also bred in James a reflex antipathy to the English, this disdain transferred to the New England Yankees among whom he has nevertheless settled in Connecticut. Early in the day, Tyrone is pleased when his sons relate to him an anecdote about how Shaughnessy, one of Tyrone's Irish tenants, gained the upper hand through Celtic verbal flair over Harker, a Yankee 'Standard Oil millionaire' (23). However, that response to the Shaughnessy story also shows how self-conflicted Tyrone is, how much his rise from slum squalor to compulsive property investor and New England landlord has rendered him thwarted with himself. On the one hand, Tyrone's sense of antipathy to things English means that he cannot conceal his delight that the Irish peasant Shaughnessy has 'won a glorious victory' (23) over the Yankee Harker. On the other hand, as a New England landlord himself, he identifies with the propertied class and must disown this instinctive delight in the tale of his uppity 'wily Shanty Mick' (22) tenant; when his sons interpret the event in terms of class rather than Anglo-Celtic conflict, Tyrone sourly responds: 'Keep your damned Socialist anarchist sentiments out of my affairs!' (26). Tyrone's veneration for Shakespeare, a Bard-worship that causes him to believe that his idol has already said everything to be said in literature and to deprecate the nineteenth-century writers his sons prefer as purveyors by comparison of 'Morbid filth!' (136), conflicts with the actor's otherwise strong antipathy to things English, a contradiction he tries to resolve for himself, to his family's amusement, by insisting that Shakespeare, like the Duke of Wellington, was 'another good Irish Catholic!' (129).

The Shaughnessy anecdote and Tyrone's conviction that one only has to look to Shakespeare's plays to find proof for his Irishness associate Irishness with a natural Celtic eloquence or verbal fluency, the verso of which was an empty blarney, a common trope for much of the nineteenth and twentieth centuries. The negative version of Irish eloquence appears also in *Long Day's Journey* through Mary's complaints about the loquacity of Bridget, the off-stage servant who outwits Mary by telling never-ending tales of her relatives until the latter so wearies that she abandons any attempt to discipline her domestic. Irishness, in other worlds, is equated in O'Neill's play with linguistic excess, whether in the form of high eloquence or blarney, and Tyrone is the figure who has made his career of this talent. The opening stage directions underline this: '*He is by nature and preference a simple, unpretentious man, whose inclinations are still close to his humble beginnings and his Irish farmer forebears. But the actor shows in all his unconscious habits of speech, movement and gesture. These have the quality of belonging to a studied technique. His voice is remarkably fine, resonant and flexible, and he takes great pride in it*' (13, italics in the original). Unpretentious and humble by nature despite his wealth and success, Tyrone's greatest pride, then, is the well-trained voice that might have allowed him to become America's greatest Shakespearian actor were it not for that other vice, miserliness, that made the money-making Broadway play (never named in *Long Day's Journey* as *The Count of Monte Cristo*) irresistible to him.[39]

Tyrone's distinction between his commercial Broadway career playing romantic melodrama and the artistic-career-that-might-have-been as a great Shakespearian creates the impression that Shakespeare represents in *Long Day's Journey* an old early modern European 'high culture' that contrasts with the contemporary – to 1912 – European 'high culture' of Edmund and Jamie, the lovers of Baudelaire, Dowson, Swinburne, Wilde and other Decadents. This is an impression reinforced not only by Tyrone's remorseful sense of what might have been had he remained true to the promise Edwin Booth found in his early acting, but also by the contrast between sickness and health attributed to both character and literature running across O'Neill's play. Tyrone, we learn again from the stage directions, 'is sixty-five but looks ten years younger' and '*[h]e has never been really sick a day in his life*' (13, italics in the original). Jamie, his son and namesake, by contrast is an ominous *'thirty-three'* and *'lacks his father's vitality'* and thus *'the signs of premature disintegration are on him'* (19, italics in the original). Likewise, a death sentence of consumption hangs over ill-looking Edmund (the name of O'Neill's dead brother that he affixes to his own counterpart self in the play; the name may also evoke the vengeful bastard Edmund in *King Lear*). This contrast between old Tyrone's waning vitality and the younger and more modern sons' degenerative dispositions is transferred to their respective literary tastes so that Shakespeare is associated with Tyrone's robustness, and the Decadents with the sickliness of body or spirit of the Tyrone sons.

However, if this might seem to highlight a straightforward contrast between an Old World when the 'high culture' incarnated by Shakespeare was robust and a modern 'high culture' that has become feeble, Lawrence Levine's work complicates any such assumption. Levine shows that 'Shakespeare' in nineteenth-century America had never in fact belonged exclusively to a world of refined 'high culture' or transcended the commercial stage; rather, his works were most often performed in the rowdier 'low cultural' field of popular theatre. As Levine points out in a famous essay, Shakespeare was staged even in the most uncultured places of nineteenth-century North America, but '[e]verywhere in the nation burlesques and parodies of Shakespeare constituted a prominent form of entertainment', these generally far more widely enjoyed than Shakespeare performed whole or straight.[40] Travesties of *Hamlet*, Levine tells us, were especially popular: 'Audiences roared at the sight of Hamlet dressed in a fur cap and collar, snowshoes and mittens; they listened with amused surprise to his profanity when ordered by his father's ghost to "swear" and to his commanding Ophelia, "Get thee to a brewery"; they heard him recite his lines in black dialect or Irish brogue and sing his most famous soliloquy, "To be or not to be", to the tune of "Three Blind Mice"' (141). 'In one New York production starring first-rank Shakespearean actors', Levine adds, 'a stuttering, lisping Othello danced while Desdemona played the banjo and Iago, complete with Irish brogue, ended their revelries with a fire hose' (141). In this raucous theatrical milieu, Levine concludes, Shakespeare was loved above all because he could still be integrated into a world of entertainment and 'the art of oratory':

> The same Americans who found diversion and pleasure in lengthy political debates, who sought joy and God in the sermons of church and camp meeting, who had, in short, a seemingly inexhaustible appetite for the spoken word, thrilled to Shakespeare's eloquence, memorized his soliloquies, delighted in his dialogues. Although nineteenth-century Americans stressed

the importance of literacy and built an impressive system of public education, theirs remained an oral world in which the spoken word was central.

(156)

It was only with the transformation of the field of American culture production in the late nineteenth and early twentieth centuries, the era of an emerging modernism, when the division between popular entertainment and the polite arts was more firmly drawn, that Shakespeare, along with Italian opera, ascended into 'the elevated circles of elite culture' (170). 'By the twentieth century', Levine concludes, 'art could not have it both ways: no longer could it simultaneously enjoy high cultural status and mass popularity. Shakespeare is a prime example. He retained his lofty position only by being limited and confined to audiences whose space was no longer shared with, and whose sensibilities were no longer violated by, the bulk of the populace' (171).

Levine's vista of Hamlets speaking in brogue or banjo-playing Desdemonas seems much closer to the burlesqued Shakespeare that we encounter in Joyce's rambunctious 'Scylla and Charybdis' or 'Circe' episodes than to the sanctified Shakespeare who appears like a religious icon above Tyrone's bookcases of great literature. If Levine is right, then the theatre world that Tyrone might have occupied as a great Shakespearian actor and the world he actually lived in as star of *The Count of Monte Cristo* were never so cleanly separated as either Tyrone or O'Neill's audience might like to imagine. This inevitably complicates, too, the legend of Eugene O'Neill as an American Shakespeare who finally wrested a world-class high theatre from a wretched theatre of dramatic dreck because Levine suggests that the real source of Shakespeare's strength was that he combined high and low cultural appeal, whereas O'Neill's achievement was to separate off 'high' theatre from 'low'. For Tyrone, the romance of Shakespearian greatness is what matters clearly, but even this is a complicated matter in any event: it is associated with an escape from poverty and factory work into some world of higher ambition that lasted only very briefly before he tumbled into the different factory-work world of commercial theatre. In one of the several confessional episodes of Act Four, Tyrone retraces his career:

> That God-damned play I bought for a song and made such a success in – a great money success – it ruined me with its promise of an easy fortune. I didn't want to do anything else, and by the time I woke up to the fact I'd become a slave to the damned thing and did try other plays, it was too late. They had identified me with that one part, and didn't want me in anything else. They were right, too. I'd lost the great talent I once had through years of easy repetition, never learning a new part, never really working hard.

> Thirty-five to forty thousand dollars net profit a season like snapping your
> fingers! It was too great a temptation.
>
> (152–153)

This is a capsule history of commercial theatre as culture industry and
reification whereby the alienation enforced by poverty and factory drudgery becomes for Tyrone the not-so-different alienation brought about by 'a
great money success'. The actor, by definition a protean player of many
parts, becomes typecast and so thoroughly identified with one part that he
can never again be effective in another. Against this:

> Yet before I bought the damned thing I was considered one of the three or
> four young actors with the greatest artistic promise in America. I'd worked
> like hell. I'd left a good job as a machinist to take supers' parts because I loved
> the theater. I was wild with ambition. I read all the plays ever written.
> I studied Shakespeare as you'd study the Bible. I educated myself. I got rid
> of an Irish brogue you could cut with a knife. I loved Shakespeare. I would
> have acted in any of his plays for nothing, for the joy of being alive in his
> great poetry. And I acted well in him. I felt inspired by him. I could have
> been a great Shakespearean actor, if I'd kept on. I know that! In 1874 when
> Edwin Booth came to the theater in Chicago where I was leading man,
> I played Cassius to his Brutus one night, Brutus to his Cassius the next,
> Othello to his Iago, and so on. The first night I played Othello, he said to our
> manager, 'That young man is playing Othello better than I ever did!'
>
> (153)

How much of this is the overblown fantasy of the great career that might
have been is hard to tell; all the Tyrones are addicted to romancing their
pasts and purpling their lost potential. But it is clear that Tyrone's veneration for Shakespeare was always more than a matter of commitment to
high art and was motivated also by a dream of self-transcendence, self-
negation even, something that would allow him to come 'alive in his great
world of poetry' as opposed to a life-denying factory drudgery. However, to
attain this apparently nonalienated existence lived through Shakespearian
poetry, Tyrone had actually had to alienate himself anyway by working 'like
hell' and training his voice to shed his Irish brogue to sound more properly
English and to acquire some of the second-hand Yankee refinements that
the wealth he acquires in the commercial theatre buys him. Small wonder,
therefore, that the role that the 'black Irish' Tyrone played best was
Othello, Shakespeare's study of a self-alienated Venetian-assimilated
Moor who tries to pass in a white world not his own, only eventually to
be undone by the insecurities that continue to plague him.[41]

Pitted against this revered Shakespeare in *Long Day's Journey* are Jamie's
and Edmund's Decadents, those early precursors to or initiators of the

bourgeois-repudiating modernism that is, after its own fashion, as committed to the grand vocation and elevated status of art as ever 'Shakespeare' was. Or, to put it another way, the Decadents cultivate an idea of art as something so rarefied that bourgeois commerce must certainly poison it, and thus art is obliged for its own preservation to flee the reified world of the everyday into the realm of the purely artificial or into the sanctuaries of the sordid where bourgeoisie logic cannot operate. Jamie's and Edmund's tastes are not exactly the same. Edmund, the would-be poet, has read Nietzsche, whom Jamie dismisses as '[y]our pet with the unpronounceable name' (79). Jamie's own affinity for the Decadents has always been less bookish and more first-hand, lived out in person in Broadway's bars and bordellos. The difference between Shakespeare and the Decadents is that Shakespeare has always been made to stand for some sort of positive and healthy affirmation of life and literature as well as for the moment of early English Renaissance national self-assertion and emerging imperial ascendancy. The Decadents, in contrast, are more typically configured as latecomers and register the terminus of that long historical cycle and of English world and bourgeois literary dominance; they mark literature's precipitous retreat in a kind of hothouse literary self-breeding that high modernism would only intensify. If Shakespeare appears in the springtime of England's and Europe's ascent to world supremacy, the Decadents represent the autumn of that ascendancy, thus signalling a crisis rather than a rejuvenation of literature.

James and Mary Tyrone associate Edmund's consumption and spiritual despondency not just with his elder brother's malign influence, but also with his bookishness and taste for the decadent and nihilistic. Unwilling to acknowledge Edmund's illness, Mary insists that his frailty is just an act learned from the modern poètes maudits:

> Saying you're going to die! It's the books you read! Nothing but sadness and death! Your father shouldn't allow you to have them. [. . .] A boy your age with everything before him! It's just a pose you get out of books! You're not really sick at all!
>
> (93)

Later when father and son try to understand each other, James Tyrone too lashes out against his son's literary taste asking, 'Where the hell do you get your taste in authors?' (136):

> That damned library of yours! Voltaire, Rousseau, Schopenhauer, Nietzsche, Ibsen! Atheists, fools, and madmen! And your poets! This Dowson, and this Baudelaire, and Swinburne and Oscar Wilde, and Whitman and Poe!

Whoremongers and degenerates! Pah! When I've three good sets of Shakespeare there *(he nods at the large bookcase)* you could read.

(137–138, italics in the original)

For James, who sounds here like some papal index librarian or T. S. Eliot, the Pope of Russell Square, when modern post-Enlightenment literature divorced itself from God it condemned itself, Faust-like, to try to master the world on its own terms, this overreaching leading inevitably to despair and a loss of vitality. Any modern audience schooled in modern literature will assume, however, that Tyrone's belief that all this modern despair might be shed simply by turning back to God and to the three sets of Shakespeare is just a delusion, a recovery of lost innocence as impossible for the elder Tyrones, themselves lapsed Catholics, as for their atheist sons.

Though it has little of Joyce's comedy, *Long Day's Journey* binds its narrative action to the diurnal movement of the clock over a single day and thus morning hope must give way inevitably to deepest night and irrevocable disillusion. The Decadent turning away in disgust from the degraded world of the bourgeoisie and capitalism, and from bourgeois solaces in any affirmative notion of literature (or 'Literature'), would set modernism on a path of negation of progress and affirmation that it would have to follow through to its bitter post–World War II completion. *A Long Day's Journey into Night* and *Waiting for Godot* are just two of the most extreme theatrical examples of where this logic would take the theatre. The bookcases that seem at the opening of the play in Act One to be a register of the Tyrones' self-improving middle-class aspirations have come by the final Act Four to stand for something more sinister: as a compendium of modernity's fading grand hopes in art, Enlightenment, self-improvement and descent into deepest despair.

It is fitting that what comes flamboyantly to life in Act Four therefore is the voice of the Decadents, especially Baudelaire, Wilde, Swinburne and Dowson, not the theatre of Shakespeare. But, paradoxically, what comes to life on stage when Edmund and Jamie, in a splendid sequence of set pieces, deliver themselves of their recitations of these poets, most of whom died before their fiftieth year, is a poetry of departure and death. Edmund begins these performances with 'They are not long, the weeping and the laughter' from Dowson's Horatian '*Vita Summa Brevis Spem Nos Vetat Incohare Longam*' and then recites Arthur Symons's translation of Baudelaire's prose-poem 'Enivrez-vous' from *Paris Spleen*, this followed soon after by Symons's translation of Baudelaire's 'Epilogue'. From there, Edmund turns to Dowson's 'Cynara', its title taken from Horace's *Odes*, a poem Jamie likes to declaim to his fat prostitutes. Next, Edmund renders one of his own poems about trollops spattering in puddles of stale beer on honky-tonk tabletops, assuring his father that is an 'Original, not Baudelaire' (156), before commencing the long soliloquy on the fleeting 'moment of ecstatic freedom' he experienced at sea when, 'For a second there is meaning! Then the hand lets the veil fall and you are alone, lost in the fog again, and you stumble on toward nowhere, for no good reason!' (156). After these performances, an even more drunken Jamie returns home, reciting first a snatch of Kipling, then a few verses of Wilde's 'The Harlot's House', then a stanza of Kipling's doleful 'Mother o' Mine', then from Rossetti's 'A Superscription' from the long sonnet-sequence *The House of Life*. As the play nears its end and Mary, lost in morphine, finally comes downstairs to the drunken menfolk, Jamie recites a last time from Swinburne's 'A Leave-taking', the verses bidding farewell to any hope for his mother's recovery and by extension to any hope for Jamie's own reclamation from alcoholic nihilism.

What we get in Act Four, in sum, is a veritable bonfire of late Victorian or early modernist *misère* transported to America in second-hand English translation from Second Empire France or from England in the twilight hour of its empire before World War I. James Tyrone vainly tries to proffer Shakespeare as a tonic to counter all this terrific morbidity, but his own recitations, 'We are such stuff as dreams are made on, and our little life is rounded with a sleep', (134) from Act Four of *The Tempest* rebound against him by testifying to late Shakespeare's own melancholy ruminations on the brevity of life and the frothy frailty of the theatrical arts. Tyrone's snatches from Shakespeare throughout this act always seem rhetorically pale against the extravagant verbal fire of his sons' recitations of the moderns. And as the play winds to its curtain, the tragic Shakespeare of *Macbeth* or *Hamlet* infiltrates O'Neill's closing scenes when Mary, who first stalks about sleeplessly upstairs like some insomniac Lady Macbeth and then descends downstairs all dishevelled like the mad Ophelia, delivers her closing soliloquy to lost faith, lost hope. Controverting James's fond conviction that 'Shakespeare' is a wholly healthy antidote to a diseased and despairing modern literature, the English playwright here seems to testify against that idea, his darker works and more tormented creations now, as in 'Scylla and Charybdis', suggesting an anguished rather than easeful Bard.

By this concluding act, the play has indeed become a kind of Frankenstein's monster, a weave of bits and pieces made by merging the modern Decadent poets and Shakespeare's famous mad scenes. George Steiner, like many a critic of O'Neill's 'bad writing', argues that the verses taken from the Decadents are meant to highlight the 'adolescent inadequacies of those who recite them'. However, these borrowings back-fire, Steiner feels, because when performed on stage, '[t]he energy and glitter of Swinburne's language burn a hole in the surrounding fabric' of O'Neill's own pallid writing.[42] Harold Bloom, no less critical of O'Neill's stylistic shortcomings, believes that 'a singular dramatic genius is always at work in O'Neill's stage directions', and that therefore everything that lies dead on the page rises to vivid life on stage.[43] However, *Long Day's Journey* might be viewed more productively perhaps as acting out a version of what Frederic Jameson has termed 'that fierce competition for cultural preem-inence between the various media' transacted within certain works. [44] Here, that competition is most obviously conducted between the books documented in such detail in the opening stage directions and the theat-rical spoken word represented by the actors James and Jamie Tyrone especially. But to these we must add the many verse set pieces that attest to the beauty of poetry and the wordless music of Mary Tyrone, the would-be nun who can only play schoolgirl-level renditions of Chopin with an old woman's stiffened fingers. Edmund, the would-be poet in the play, as a boy learned to recite *Macbeth* to win a bet with his father, but dismisses his own adult poetry as a '[s]tammering [that] is the native eloquence of us fog people' (157).

The various artistic media may vie here, then, but in O'Neill's play the competition proves to be a contest not of the articulate but of the crippled arts. All of them – high or low, mass or elite – appear either shopworn with use or reified to death. Shakespeare is an iconic portrait; the Great Books are stage furniture. James's career-long repeat performances of *The Count of Monte Cristo* or the party piece recitations of the Decadents beloved by the drunken younger Tyrones suggest a world where everything comes alive only to be trapped in despairing performances that blur into repet-itively performed despair. Throughout the last act, James Tyrone is referred to by Jamie as 'old Gaspard, the miser', (161) a reference to Robert Planquette's comic-opera *Les cloches de Corneville* (1877). Mary's final descent from upstairs provokes from Jamie: 'The Mad Scene, Enter Ophelia!' For Mary and James, Edmund is merely acting out the part of the poète maudit or 'just a pose you get out of books!' (93) Jamie appears as a drunken second-rate Mephistopheles or Iago, full of malice yet more hapless and hopeless than sinister. 'What's happened to our game? Whose play is it?' (145) Tyrone asks Edmund as the two play cards, to which his son replies, 'Yours, I guess' (146). The question reminds the audience that in some ways this is everybody's and nobody's play because all of the Tyrones have equal claims on our interest, yet all appear to have played out their cards and are trapped in already overfamiliar, over-literary theatrical roles.

Given, then, that the last act comes to its audiences as a series of performance pieces, we are not perhaps in O'Neill's last play all that far after all from the vaudevillian theatre of James O'Neill, his father, or of the nineteenth-century American Shakespearian theatre as described earlier by Levine, where set pieces from Shakespeare and others were played for laughs. The essential difference is that in *Long Day's Journey* the boisterous crudity of the music hall has ceded to a funereal world of high cultural aspiration where the only true notes are failure and desolation, where early modernist *misère* is now becoming some sort of late modernist vaudevillian *misère* doomed to repeat itself to the point of exhausted travesty – a Decadent literature of exhaustion giving way to an exhausted literature of Decadence. Mary wishes to recover her childhood virginity and the tender solicitude of the Blessed Virgin and Mother Elizabeth, but is condemned to live as a 'hophead' Lady Macbeth. Tyrone, the would-be great Othello, has shrunk to Gaspard the Miser. Jamie is a Broadway flophouse Mephistopheles only, a second-hand reciter of the second-rate Dowson. Edmund, the would-be Conradian adventurer or naturalist slum-monger, and the O'Neill stand-in, bears the name of the dead older O'Neill sibling Eugene was conceived to replace but wears also the name of Shakespeare's most destructive villain. What we have here, in sum, is a modernism that is able to make every kind of suffering articulate but can only aestheticize that suffering or make it numbly pleasurable, not redeem it. Literature secures its dearly bought 'autonomy' only to become a kind of 'highbrow junk'. Like Mary's morphine or James's whiskey, it can sedate or sublimate suffering, but not heal it. The expression of modern suffering *in extremis*, modernism's greatest accomplishment, threatens to become just another performance, in equal measure virtuosically impotent and impotently virtuosic.

## IV

'Nobody really believes in "culture" any more, the backbone of spirit [*Geist*] has been broken, and anyone who pays no attention to this and acts as though nothing had happened, must crawl like an insect, not walk upright. The only authentic artworks produced today are those that in their inner organization measure themselves by the fullest experience of horror, and there is scarcely anyone, except Schoenberg or Picasso, who can depend on himself to have the power to do this'.[45] Thus wrote

Theodor Adorno in 'The Aging of the New Music', a lecture delivered in 1954 and published in German in 1955, the year before *Long Day's Journey* was premiered. The proposition that nobody 'really believes in "culture" anymore' coming in the mid-1950s must initially strike us as odd. This was, after all, the great age of the expansion of the American universities, the Great Books promotions and the consolidation of all those Ivy League inductions into the classics of Western Civilization and World Literature. It was the moment when an American modernism was firmly consecrated, not just in O'Neill's case, but also in so many other ways and forms: T. S. Eliot won the Nobel Prize in Literature in 1948, William Faulkner in 1949, Ernest Hemingway in 1954. In 1955, Clement Greenberg, who had joined the American Committee for Cultural Freedom in 1950, published his essay '"American-Type" Painting'. There, he argued that American Abstract Expressionism represented the latest advance in the modernist visual arts and proposed that American or American-based artists like Jackson Pollock, Willem de Kooning, Clyfford Still, Mark Rothko and others were now to the forefront of their European peers. The 'abstract expressionists', Greenberg argued, represented modernist painting's relentless drive to shed itself of all unnecessary conventions to strip art down to 'its viable essence'. 'Perhaps it is another symptom of this same state of affairs,' he surmised, 'that Paris should be losing its monopoly on the fate of painting'. Greenberg's essay concluded on a triumphant note: 'Literature – yes, we know that we have done some great things in that line; the English and French have told us so. Now they can begin to tell us the same about our painting'.[46] Contra Adorno, Americans, it might be argued, had never cared more about 'culture' than in the post-war period and had certainly never asserted their own leadership in the arts internationally with greater confidence.

Nevertheless, there is something to Adorno's claim that the greatest works of modernism attested more and more as the twentieth century proceeded to the 'fullest experience' of the 'horror' of modernity even as 'culture' in some wider sense became more wholly industrialized. They did so, he asserted, not just in terms of content but also in terms of the 'inner organization' of their forms. It is one of history's ruses, therefore, that in the very era that the United States had needed to produce a great modernist literature to attest to America's ascendancy and to demonstrate to the world its capacity to match European achievements in the arts, that this modernism, to be true to its own constitutive logic, could affirm neither modernity nor American capitalism nor even 'art' as such. American capitalism in the Cold War era endorsed modernism and made it its official art, but modernism, before Greenberg and Pollock at least, could not readily return the compliment. From its earliest stages in the Decadent movement to its later manifestations in the immediate post–World War II era, what we now call 'modernism' had turned its back on bourgeois society and had committed itself to the idea that middle-class acclaim and lucrative commercial success, at least in any immediate terms, were hallmarks of the degraded arts only. As such, any authentic art must be prepared to suffer public incomprehension and commercial failure as the price of its authenticity. This aesthetic ideology had not prevailed when Shakespeare was canonized as the great genius of English literature or Cervantes of Spanish literature. It had not yet been instituted either when Balzac became a hero of French or Goethe of German literature. The metropolitan European nations were therefore able to place their great writers in the service of an affirmative national narrative and a humanist conception of culture, something that would prove a considerably trickier task in the age of the great modernist connoisseurs of chaos from Eliot and Pound to Joyce and Stein to Faulkner and O'Neill. The Irish and Americans alike were latecomers to the canons of world literature. The modernist masterworks that won them entry to these canons disclose in their forms, morbidly and magnificently maybe, the distress of that lateness.

By the 1950s, the Americans had indeed produced a great modernist literature and had established their country's high cultural sophistication. The twist was that sophistication in the arts was by then increasingly associated with a capacity to register the disastrous turns that capitalist modernity had taken, the same capitalist modernity that the United States had made fundamental to its own national identity and world vocation:

> 'You see I think everything's terrible anyhow', she went on in a convinced way. 'Everybody thinks so – the most advanced people. And I *know*. I've been everywhere and seen everything and done everything.' Her eyes flashed around her in a defiant way, rather like Tom's, and she laughed with thrilling scorn. 'Sophisticated – God, I'm sophisticated!'
> (17, italics in the original)

So, a distraught, world-weary Daisy Fay, a high-society American version of Eliot's death-desiring Sybil of Cumae, self-mockingly confesses herself to Nick Carraway. Daisy's desperate cynicism echoes Tom's earlier remarks that 'I've gotten to be a terrible pessimist about things' because of his conviction that '[c]ivilization's going to pieces' (14). Fitzgerald's passage captures perfectly the ways in which elite cosmopolitan cultural sophistication and terrible pessimism now seemed to require each other.

That pessimism could lend itself as much to right-wing as to left-wing conclusions: it could express Tom's fears for the future of the white race as easily as Adorno's for a totally administered world. This is not to say that modernist gloom, or the American cultivation of it, was merely the latest fashionable affectation; despite their wealth and comfort, the Buchanans' misery and purposeless drift are real enough, the lives of the Wilsons far worse. However, Fitzgerald fingers well the situational irony whereby American cultural 'sophistication', of which American modernism was the most recent and highbrow expression, ran directly counter to the official optimism, exceptionalism and affirmative confidence in the future fundamental to the ideology of the 'American Dream'.

By a curious turn of events, the modern world literary system's own intrinsic logic had dictated that American literature in the twentieth century could only become 'sophisticated' or, to put it another way, could soonest qualify to become elevated to the status of 'world literature', by testifying against most of the things that twentieth-century America had taken upon itself to embody and represent. Twentieth-century America needed not just 'culture' but a world-class 'culture', and by the mid-twentieth century 'modernism' represented the most advanced form of Western cultural achievement and distinction. In the West, 'modernism' seemed to need America too. The United States produced many of its patrons, the experts to interpret it, the galleries and universities that were beginning to shelter and promote it, the young publics keen to learn how to appreciate it. There were ways in which the two could be reconciled, but what the terms 'Americanism' and 'modernism' commonly meant seemed to be fiercely antithetical to each other. Thus, many Americans would attempt to write great modernist epics, but there would be no great 'American modernist epic'. *The Great Gatsby* is a pocket epic, one of the few novels to have escaped the elephant's graveyard of American novelistic epics where works by so many of Fitzgerald's contemporaries, from Dreiser to Dos Passos, now sleep. O'Neill rescued *Long Day's Journey* from the debris of his own gargantuan but unachieved epic ambitions. If the one appears too slight and the other too dark to be the satisfactory fulfilment of America's epic ambition, they still come as close as the United States would get in the summer of its ascendancy to meeting its desire for epic grandeur. Close maybe, but no cigar.

CHAPTER 6

# 'A Wreath of Flies?': Omeros, *Epic Achievement and Impasse in 'the Program Era'*

Henceforth, any resurrection of the Greek world is a more or less conscious hypostasy of aesthetics into metaphysics – a violence done to the essence of everything that lies outside the sphere of art, and a desire to destroy it; an attempt to forget that art is only one sphere among many, and that the very disintegration and inadequacy of the world is the precondition for the existence of art and its becoming conscious. [...] A totality that can be simply accepted is no longer given to the forms of art: therefore they must either narrow down and volatise whatever has to be given form to the point where they can encompass it, or else they must show polemically the impossibility of achieving their necessary object and the inner nullity of their own means. And in this case they carry the fragmentary nature of the world's structure into the world of forms.

– Georg Lukács, *The Theory of the Novel*, 1916.[1]

Since the autumn of 1985, the St. Lucian-born poet and playwright Derek Walcott had been hearing that he was a finalist for the Nobel Prize in Literature, but each year some other writer won. After so many years of disappointment, Walcott had almost ceased hoping that the honor would ever come to him. In 1990 – the year that 'Omeros', his tenth and most ambitious book of verse, appeared in the United States – he allowed himself to suspect that the rumors would be true at last. A widely acclaimed narrative epic, 'Omeros' invests ordinary inhabitants of St. Lucia and neighboring parts of the West Indies with the Homeric spirit of characters in the Illiad and the Odyssey. One reviewer wrote, 'If certain cardinals are said to be papable or 'Popable', then Walcott surely is 'Nobelable'.

– Jervis Anderson, 'Derek Walcott's Odyssey', *The New Yorker*, 21 December 1992[2]

243

All that Greek manure under the green bananas,
under the indigo hills, the rain-rutted road,
the galvanized village, the myth of rustic manners,

glazed by the transparent page of what I had read.
What I had read and rewritten till literature
was guilty as History. When would the sails drop

from my eyes, when would I not hear the Trojan War
in two fishermen cursing in Ma Kilman's shop?
When would my head shake off its echoes like a horse

shaking off a wreath of flies?

– Derek Walcott, *Omeros*, 1990.[3]

# I

On 24 January 1936, T. S. Eliot addressed the English Literary Society of University College Dublin and, contemplating the development of modern Irish and American poetry, invited the questions: 'Are we to conceive of the situation with regard to poetry written in English to-day, as parallel to that of the Greek decadence, or that of the Roman Empire? Must we regard London as the centre, in the same way that Athens and Rome especially were centres; Rome drawing to it the gifted writers from all parts of the Empire?' Eliot cautioned against excessively neat parallels of the modern world with the past. Nevertheless, he asserted, 'the parallel with imperial Rome is true at the moment' and certainly remained so 'so far as the British Dominions are concerned' because he did not 'know of a single poet of the slightest merit in Canada, Australia and New Zealand, though I assure you a good deal of verse is being written in those countries'. 'Whether these lands will ever arrive at distinctive literatures of their own is a question which lies in too remote a future to be discussed', Eliot surmised, but for the moment 'when a writer of exceptional merit and originality appears in any dominion, he tries to get to London'. These migratory dominion poets, Eliot continued, have generally 'brought to the English tradition nothing but themselves and their individual gifts, together with the imagery and feeling of their childhood in remote lands – that is, a certain exoticism'. What they had 'not produced', though, was 'a distinct and impersonal idiom, a separate and peculiar rhythm', something that would be the definitive mark of a new literature. The only real exceptions, Eliot allowed, were America and Ireland. These had achieved new English-language literatures and 'to think of English as spoken and written in America and Ireland as *colonial* English, I think that this is an error'. 'I believe that, as far into the future as the future concerns us', Eliot concluded, 'there must be three literatures in the English language – English, Irish and American'. These literatures, he added, would reciprocally continue to influence each other, and such interaction 'might greatly fortify the vitality of the [English] language as a literary medium, by giving it added means of cross-fertilization which the French, German and Italian languages have not got'.[4]

As we noted in Chapter 1, a somewhat similar viewpoint had been expressed by Ezra Pound in 'How to Read' in the *New York Herald Tribune* in 1929 when he pronounced that 'apart from Yeats, since the death of Hardy, poetry is being written by Americans. All the developments in English verse since 1910 are due almost wholly to Americans. In fact, there is no longer any reason to call it English verse, and there is no present reason to think of England at all. We speak a language that was English'.[5] This view of matters was later taken up by Pound-admirer Hugh Kenner and amplified in his conception of the 'three provinces' of English literature in his influential trilogy, *A Homemade World: The American Modernist Writers* (1975), *A Colder Eye: The Modern Irish Writers* (1983) and *A Sinking Island: The Modern English Writers* (1987). Summing up his view in 'The Making of the Modernist Canon' in 1984, Kenner remarked: 'Since Chaucer, the domain of English literature had been a country, England. Early in the 20th century its domain commenced to be a language, English. By about 1925 it was clear that three countries, Ireland, America and England, were conducting substantial national literatures in this language'.[6] Though this, Kenner insisted, had remained hidden from English critics like F. R. Leavis, the reality was that after World War I London simply 'ingathered' talent while 'the provinces stirred', until eventually 'England had become, linguistically speaking, a province' (56).

Had they been scanning the London literary world more keenly, Pound or Eliot might have wondered by the 1930s whether in the future there would be only 'three literatures in the English language' or whether the Caribbean might be worth watching. As the Irish Free State was settling into a period of conservative consolidation in the 1930s and the United States was replacing Britain as the world's leading power, the Caribbean was becoming a hotbed of revolutionary and literary activity. In 1936, when Eliot gave his Dublin address, the young Trinidadian Trotskyist C. L. R. James published his novel *Minty Alley*, and his play, *Toussaint L'Ouverture*, opened in the West End with Paul Robeson in the leading role. Two years later, James published *The Black Jacobins: Toussaint L'Ouverture and the San Domingo Revolution*, an epic narrative of what James described as 'the only successful slave revolt in history'. James situated the Haitian overthrow of slavery from 1791 to 1804 in the context of the French Revolution and Napoleonic empire, the struggles of European imperial powers for control of the Caribbean and the emerging twentieth-century struggles for national emancipation in Africa and Asia. Set within this international frame, Toussaint's revolution appeared as no backwater sideshow to French upheavals, but as a world-historical event in its own right, the first successful slave revolt and a forecast to African and Asian emancipation struggles still to come. 'The transformation of slaves, trembling in hundreds before a single white man, into a people able to organise themselves and defeat the most powerful European nations of their day, is one of *the great epics* of revolutionary struggle and achievement', James wrote. 'Why and how this happened is the theme of this book'.[7]

James was not alone. In 1919, the Jamaican Claude McKay, a writer and activist who had already won reputation in the Harlem Renaissance, moved to London, visiting Russia in 1922, and then spent over a decade living in various parts of Europe and North Africa. In 1932, Jamaican poet Una Marson also came to London, joined the League of Coloured Peoples and the International Alliance of Women, and then moved regularly between England and Jamaica in the 1930s and early 1940s before spending an extended part of her life in the United States. In 1934, the Dominica-born Jean Rhys published *Voyage in the Dark*; she later became more famous for *Wide Sargasso Sea*, published in 1966. In 1935, George Padmore, James's Trinidadian compatriot, a communist and pan-Africanist, was compelled to relocate from Europe to London also. After World War II, other Caribbean writers followed the same path to the English capital. Louise Bennett was the first black student to study at the Royal Academy of Art in London in 1945; Sam Selvon moved to that city in 1950, V. S. Naipaul in 1954, Wilson Harris in 1956.

Crisscrossing restlessly between the Caribbean, the United States, Russia, Africa and England, these young Anglophone West Indians moved mainly in different literary circles to those of the expatriate high modernists like Eliot, Pound, Woolf, Lewis or Joyce. They moved mostly in different circuits too to their Francophone or Hispanophone contemporaries who gravitated more towards Paris. In the French capital, René Maran was the first black writer to win a Prix Goncourt in 1921. In 1928, Alejo Carpentier, later associated with the term *lo real maravilloso*, fled Cuban dictatorship for Paris and immersed himself there in avant-garde modernist circles throughout the 1930s. Aimé Césaire studied in France in the École Normale Supérieure and founded *L'Étudiant noir* there in 1935 before returning to Martinique in 1936 to write his long poem *Cahier d'un retour au pays natal*, published in 1939. In 1943, Franz Fanon escaped Vichy-controlled Martinique to go to British-controlled Dominica to join the Free French forces. Caribbean writers and activists were still migrating to the old European metropolitan centres, but their eyes were on revolutionary events and avant-garde innovations not only in Europe, but also in Africa, South America, the United States and in their own region. Like the Irish or American modernists who had settled in London and Paris earlier in the twentieth century, Caribbean writers were congregating in European capitals. Their dreams of changing the world were just as or even more ambitious, though their geographical and cultural horizons were wider and less Europe-fixated than those of their American or Irish antecedents.[8]

Contemporary literary historians stress that literary institutions, writers and readerships existed in the Caribbean region well before the 1930s, and they rightly draw attention to how the diasporic writers in twentieth-century London constructed themselves as the 'founders' of an entirely new literature.[9] It is proper to acknowledge that longer pre-twentieth-century literary history, but the rupture-making effects of the many forms of anti-colonial writing conducted in European capitals after World War I cannot be denied, and a new twentieth-century West Indian literature – like Irish and American literatures before them – was in part at least created overseas. If Eliot could assert in Dublin in 1936 that Irish and American writers in English were no longer writing colonial literatures written in '*colonial* English', the Caribbean émigré writers to London and Paris in the age of European imperial decline and American ascendancy had ambitions to establish their own autonomous nations and literatures also. The obstacles to achieving any kind of literary distinction had been considerable in the United States and Ireland; in the Caribbean, a poorer region with a brutal history of slavery and racial division, the obstacles that needed to be overcome were clearly huge. Divided into jurisdictions under British, French, Spanish and Dutch imperial control, the archipelago could boast no single great literary capital like London, Paris or New York where literary-intellectual activities might be concentrated. In addition, the metropolitan languages promoted by the region's education systems were restricted mainly to the professional classes or coastal towns; beyond these enclaves, most people spoke creole or patois, most of these dialects uncodified for educational or other official uses. Finally, given the archipelagic nature of the Caribbean and the fact that various islands were controlled by different European nations, it was difficult to channel the region's political or literary aspirations into any single emancipation struggle or cultural nationalist movement like the Irish or Harlem Renaissances.

The Caribbean response to these conditions was to turn what might easily seem like crippling destitution to advantage by making the region's eclectic mix of indigenous, African, Indian and European languages, folk-cultures and musics its greatest cultural resource. The region's geopolitical location at the 'crossroads' of Europe, Africa, India, the United States and Latin America meant that the islands could be envisaged as a kind of spaghetti-junction through which all sorts of transcontinental intellectual and political energies passed. In this manner, the periphery might be imagined as a hub in ways that resemble Franco Moretti's conception of Paris as a 'great western "X"' situated advantageously between southern and northern Europe.[10] Boasting successive waves of revolutionary or radical intellectuals, avant-garde writers, both diasporic or locally situated, as well as critics and scholars of international significance, the modern Caribbean region stands as a rebuke to those who automatically associate peripheries with literary penury or who consider their primary cultural function to be merely adoptive and adaptive.

Nevertheless, however culturally resourceful peripheral intellectuals may be, the underlying material conditions that make a region peripheral to begin with are hard to overcome. The construction of a modern 'Caribbean Literature' is a real and remarkable achievement, but, like cultural Germany in the nineteenth century before Bismarck, there was not nor still is any consolidated or unified Caribbean state to match. The short-lived Federation of the West Indies (1958–1962), founded when a community of Anglophone Caribbean polities tried to pool resources to alleviate postcolonial dependency, represented a short-lived attempt at archipelagic statehood, but its failure arguably led afterwards to more cautious forms of decolonization and to ongoing dependency on metropolitan states and corporate power. The relentless aggression directed at Cuba after its socialist revolution demonstrated how hostile the international order remained to any radical attempts to overhaul Caribbean society. As European imperial influence in the region waned after World War II, the influence of the United States increased. Indeed, the United States' rise to become a new imperial power had actually commenced in the Caribbean in 1898 when it seized Cuba and Puerto Rico from Spain in the Spanish–American War. Over the course of the twentieth century, there would be several further American invasions of the West Indies, though it is American economic power that has probably most shaped the region. The creation of a new Caribbean Anglophone literature can be celebrated as the emergence of a new 'fourth province' of English literature, then, but what exactly does it mean to be a new literary 'province' (as Eliot in 1936 claimed Irish and American literatures to be) in conditions of ongoing foreign domination, racial division and economic subordination?

When Derek Walcott won the Nobel Prize in Literature in 1992, shortly after the publication in 1990 of his epic *Omeros*, his achievement was widely regarded as a moment when Caribbean literature in English finally won the 'world' recognition for which writers in the region had long been working. Walcott's reputation has suffered since because of charges of sexual harassment, but his achievement was widely celebrated at the time as a tribute not only to the poet's own considerable literary accomplishments, but also to the vitality of Caribbean writing more generally. By the 1990s, the region could boast not only of a host of internationally feted writers of earlier generations, from Claude McKay to Jean Rhys to Aimé Césaire and Alejo Carpentier, but also of many contemporary international writers of distinction. In the 1990s, the Nobel Prize was awarded to several writers from what might be regarded as 'postcolonial' or 'peripheral' regions. Octavio Paz won the award in 1990, Nadine Gordimer in 1991, Seamus Heaney in 1995; V. S. Naipaul became a second (or third) Anglo-Caribbean winner in 2001. Such awards might be taken as a sign that the world literary system was becoming less Eurocentric and in the process of significant change. In 2000, Gao Xingjian became the first Chinese writer to be awarded a Nobel, signalling perhaps the Swedish Academy's sense that a new millennium might be opening up not just in politics but in literature too.

Still, even if changes were afoot, Walcott's award also testifies to continuity as much as to change. In the passage cited at the head of this chapter, Jervis Anderson notes that Walcott had been deemed 'Nobelable' since the mid-1980s, but that that award was not clinched until after he achieved an epic. That epic bears in its title a homage (as James Joyce's Irish epic had earlier done) to Homer, the ur-figure of European literature. Moreover, as Anderson's essay goes on to relate, Walcott had by the 1990s spent several decades working in American universities and *Omeros* was published by a New York publisher. That publisher's chairman, Roger Straus, made a trip to London in 1990, as he apparently did every autumn during the Nobel season of announcements, armed on the occasion with a tip – false as it proved – that one of two of his firm's authors, Walcott or

Gordimer, would win the coveted prize. As Anderson notes, Straus had reason to be confident 'since his firm, Farrar, Straus & Giroux, had had six Nobel Prize winners since 1980' (71). Straus may have been disappointed in 1990 when the award went to Paz, but he did not have to suffer long: as already noted, Gordimer secured the award a year later in 1991 and Walcott the following year in 1992. The awardees might be from Johannesburg or Castres, but the publishers were American, with the publishing director navigating between New York, London and Stockholm. Many things had changed since the high modernist era, and others might still be changing, but even as London had ceded to New York, the established Euro-American centres of the world literary system were still holding.

In this chapter, I read Derek Walcott's *Omeros* as an epic work that attempts both to register the conditions of its own possibility in a neoimperial and now-American-centred world literary system and as a rather desperate attempt to overcome these conditions by a kind of aesthetic fiat. My intention is not to represent *Omeros* as the *summa* of all West Indian writing, though Walcott's consecration in 1992 as the first non-white literary Nobel Prize winner from the Caribbean is a notable moment for the region's literary standing. Just as it may be argued that without the previous efforts of Wilde, Shaw, Moore, Yeats, Synge and Gregory, *Ulysses* might never have been possible, so too there might be no Walcott or *Omeros* without C. L. R. James, McKay, Marson, Rhys, Césaire, Carpentier, Fanon, Bennett, Brathwaite, Naipaul, Kincaid, Glissant, Conde and many others. This is not because Walcott is necessarily any more hospitably receptive to all of these regional authors or influences than Joyce in his time was to his Irish compatriots. In fact, Walcott's relationship to his fellow writers in the Caribbean seems often as least as prickly as those of Joyce, Yeats and other writers of the Irish Revival period to each other. However, the epic is a capacious genre that swells to its own epic-ness precisely by swallowing into itself so many of the other earlier or contemporary forms and preoccupations available to it from its region. Here, I will want to argue, while *Omeros*, like *Ulysses*, is triumphant with a sense of its own epic virtuosity, it is equally shot through with a countervailing sense of failure and limitation: the limitations of Caribbean emancipation, Walcott's personal failures as husband and father, the difficulties of creating a satisfactory epic in the modern age. In *Omeros*, as in the works of Joyce, O'Neill, Fitzgerald and others, the sense of a society and landscape submitted to processes of commodification that bite relentlessly deeper into art and life alike persists, but if these conditions are bitterly resented there seems to be no hope of any agency in sight that might be able to dispel them. This makes of *Omeros*, as in the Irish and Irish American cases earlier mentioned, an epic without a hero or any real sense of heroic possibility and one in which success and failure therefore seem finally inextricable. In worldly and aesthetic terms, *Omeros* is for Walcott a moment of remarkable mastery over self, over craft, over rivals. But that mastery proves fragile and somewhat forced because the poem's back seems to bend under the burden of its epic ambitions, and towards its conclusion its vision becomes almost apocalyptic as it acknowledges that the Caribbean region is sliding into climate catastrophe and into increasing penury for its poor even as its writers win fame. As the final line from the passage from *Omeros* cited as epigraph to this chapter allows, in this context an epic poet's garland of honour might well be only a workhorse's 'wreath of flies'.

Much scholarly debate on *Omeros* has turned on what it might mean to produce a late modernist or postcolonial epic. Walcott's critics have debated the degree to which the work is indebted to its Western borrowings or successfully differentiates itself from earlier epics, and they have pondered why Walcott's long poem, having invoked so many classical and modernist epic precedents in its earlier books, swerves in its closing sections and disavows, or appears to do so, its own conspicuous epic investments.[11] In the lines from Book Six that head this chapter, the poet-persona seems to construe all his aesthetic classicism as so much 'Greek manure under the green bananas'[12] and to repudiate his stubborn desire to see in every local fisherman's quarrel some shimmering of the Trojan War. Here, Walcott overtly interrogates the afflatus of epic and asks whether the epic impulse elevates the poor or serves only to insult their ordinary everydayness by sweeping them into its aggrandizing Homeric machinery. In later commentaries on the poem, most famously in his 1997 essay 'Reflections on *Omeros*', Walcott continues to worry this question: why epic?

Why epic indeed? The questions Walcott poses, whether in the poem itself or the later essay, are ultimately more an instigation to the reader to reflect on epic than any repudiation of the mode. Peripheral writers have always prized the epic because it is regarded as the most prestigious poetic genre, the one through which they and their regions can best hope to make a lasting mark on the literary world. Indeed, it is precisely at this pivot-moment when it most appears to interrogate epic that *Omeros* in fact most avows (rather than disavows) its commitment to the form and rehearses more particularly a sense of epic best articulated in Hegelian-Lukácsian conceptions of that genre. For Lukács, most famously in the *Theory of the*

*Novel*, all theories of epic by definition come too late. They must inevitably do so, he proposes, because the age of epic proper, for which Homer is always the exemplary instance, is one in which meaning is immanent to existence and there is thus no wounding breach between the self and the ordinary everyday world, no need for theory. As such, the age of epic, as Paul Fleming, parsing Lukács, puts it, 'has no seeking, no philosophy, no questions (only answers), and therefore no theory, not even its own'. Regarded thus, 'the *theory* of epic begins [only] when the *age* of epic has ended'[13] and the world of Greek epic is in its fullness of being, its rounded totality, by definition the radical other to our self-alienated modernity. That modernity can only guess what it has gained and what lost by measuring itself against a classical epic form that the moderns can neither return to nor yet disavow the will to recreate.

To some, Lukács's conception of epic may seem to rehash the most naïve form of German idealism with its romantic veneration of ancient Greece (the worst kind of 'Greek manure', as Walcott puts it). But Lukács's deployment of this idealized conception of Greece and Greek epic seems wholly self-conscious and self-critical. Thus, in the passage cited at the top of this chapter, the Hungarian critic clearly stipulates that: 'Henceforth, any resurrection of the Greek world is a more or less conscious hypostasy of aesthetics into metaphysics – a violence done to everything that lies outside the sphere of art, and a desire to destroy it'. In other words, because the age of the Greeks and classical epic is so radically other to our modernity, a modernity defined by questions rather than answers, by endless philosophy and theory, by alienated seeking rather than contented at-homeness with the world, modern epic can never again achieve a classical perfection of form. Or, it cannot do so at least without doing intense violence to life and to art alike. Thus, Lukács concludes, '[a] totality that can simply be accepted is no longer given to the forms of art' and the modern arts therefore must either 'narrow down and volatilise whatever has to be given form to the point where they can encompass it' – must squeeze the world to make it more amenable to form – 'or else they must show polemically the impossibility of achieving their necessary object and the inner nullity of their own means' – meaning art must confess its inability to find forms adequate to the modern condition and consciously make this failure part of its subject matter. 'And in this case', Lukács sighs, the forms of modern art are obliged to 'carry the fragmentary nature of the world's structure into the world of forms'.[14]

When, therefore, in Book Six the poet-persona or 'Walcott' figure in *Omeros* turns to the reader and asks why all this attempt to elevate the lowly Helen, Hector, Achille and the rest by rendering them in terms of classical Homeric models, the answer surely is that while the dream of a Saint Lucian or Caribbean people so at home with themselves and the world, so replete with meaning as to be without need for either Art or History, might be desirable, it is also as impossible as any recovery of the supposed perfection of ancient Greek epic would be. However, it would also be self-defeating to surrender the desire for some wholly meaningful and unalienated existence. By Walcott's logic, the contemporary need for art and history is testimony to the irrevocably alienated character of things, a sense of alienation that is – as we shall see – intensified in some of the later passages of *Omeros* to apocalyptic proportions. Given this fundamental discord that informs modernity and the arts of modernity, a successful epic, one that managed to achieve a wholly satisfying integration of form and content, would, in Lukácsian or Walcottian terms, be attainable only by doing coercive violence to its subject matter and thus represent, paradoxically, a form of failure. Even so, it is equally the case that merely to own up to the limits of modern epic, to self-reflexively highlight the fragmentariness that fractures even its most virtuosic contemporary forms, is to concede a further kind of failure, the failure of art to overcome the problems it articulates, or, to cite another Walcott line, to 'enter that light beyond metaphor' (271). If epic achievement is still recognized as a sign of literary greatness, something that can secure Nobel Prizes and lasting fame, for the modern epic success and failure have been hard to distinguish.

## II

Walcott's career-path models the kind of upwards-and-outwards curve typically associated with a successful professional progression from the status of 'local' or 'national/regional' to 'international writer'. It also reflects the wider reorientation of Caribbean letters generally as these have pivoted from an Anglophone- or Francophone-centered metropolitan European axis to a North American one. Walcott attended the University of the West Indies in Jamaica in the early 1950s, and his earliest works were mostly published in the Caribbean in this period. His work was then taken up in England, some of it appearing in the BBC's *Caribbean Voices* programme, and one of his early plays, *Henri Christophe*, was produced in London in 1952.[15] In 1962, the English-based Jonathan Cape published *In a Green Night*, Walcott's first collection of poems to appear outside the Caribbean; Cape continued to publish his work in England until 1980 when he moved to Faber and Faber. By the

1960s, however, Walcott was also finding American publishers. Robert Lowell helped him to secure the publication of his *Selected Poems* with Farrar, Straus and Giroux in 1964, the company with which Walcott would remain for the rest of his career.[16] By the 1970s, Walcott was spending extended teaching stints in the United States, and in 1981 he was appointed as Professor of Creative Writing at Boston University. After he won the Nobel Prize for Literature in 1992, he continued to teach in the United States and Canada but spent more of his later years on Saint Lucia, dying there in 2017, his passing honoured by a state funeral in recognition of his achievements.

In Walcott's case, this widening career circuit that took him from the Anglophone Caribbean to London and then to New York and Boston is interestingly complicated by the fact that Saint Lucia's popular vernacular is not English but Kwéyòl, a French-lexicon creole known locally as patois. Because Saint Lucia had been a much-contested French colony before it finally came under English control in 1814, the island shared this language – with its combination of French vocabulary and West African syntax – with the Francophone islands of the Antilles. Saint Lucia's English education system had tried to eradicate Kwéyòl, but it remained the language of the lower social classes and of the more rural parts of the island particularly, and its official status has become a matter of some controversy since independence.[17] *Omeros* acknowledges this Francophone linguistic context by using snatches of Kwéyòl, but these usages are sparing and usually accompanied by immediate translation internal to the poem so they offer no serious obstacle to *Omeros*'s English-language readers. Extended passages in *Omeros* refer to eighteenth-century British and French naval wars to secure control of the Caribbean and allude more particularly to the Battle of the Saintes, in which the British Admiral George Brydges Rodney won a decisive victory over the French fleet under the Comte de Grasse in 1782. Rodney captured the French fleet's flagship, the *Ville de Paris*, in this battle; a typhoon sank the vessel en route to England to mark the British victory.

*Omeros* repeatedly mentions the sinking of the *Ville de Paris* and the mythological Paris, associated with the famous judgement of Paris concerning the beauty of Hera, Athena and Aphrodite and Paris's winning of Helen of Troy. Because the name Helen is synonymous with Saint Lucia, 'The Helen of the West Indies', it is not fanciful to read these epic British-French naval rivalries and the English victory over the French as both a reference to the island's remote colonial past and a nod towards the contemporary predominance of English-language cultures over their

Francophone counterparts. As a onetime French colony that had retained its Catholic culture and a French patois, Saint Lucian literary effort might be directed towards France rather than England, but as a writer with English and Dutch as well African ancestry, Walcott's career always bent towards the Anglophone rather than Francophone world. Though he later remarked that he had proposed initially to have written his epic in French Creole – 'I tried to do it in "patois" [but] I ran out of vocabulary. That's ignorance of the language' – *Omeros*'s linguistic politics would suggest that Walcott accepts his work's inscription in this longer history of imperial and neo-imperial Anglicization even as he also protests elements of that history.[18]

*Omeros* is divided into seven books, these comprising sixty-four, three-section chapters, which are rendered, to use Walcott's own terms, in patterns 'roughly hexametrical with terza rima form' to offer 'a combination of a Homeric line and a Dantesque design'.[19] The Homeric line and Dantean design give the poem its high style and epic shape, but its narrative momentum relies on an intricate weave of multidirectional journeys that take readers imaginatively on transoceanic voyages to early modern Africa and across late twentieth-century Europe and America. The poem's canvas is impressively panoramic. It takes in several centuries of modern European imperial history stretching from eighteenth-century Franco-British rivalry in the West Indies to the fall of the British Empire after World War II, and an American history running from the nineteenth-century genocide of the Native American peoples to the present day when the 'Walcott' persona visits North American cities, universities and art galleries. *Omeros*'s totalizing ambitions are obvious, but so too is the episodic, even picaresque, quality of the multistranded narrative, something that accentuates the difficulty of attaining any kind of graceful wholeness of form despite the work's impressive integrative drive. At the level of story, most of the actions described in *Omeros* are too humdrum domestic to be truly epic in any conventional sense, but the broad scope of the work's historical and geographical reach and the high style of its telling convey nonetheless an epic ambition.[20]

To discover something like a 'politics' in all this, it will be necessary to consider some of the constitutive antagonisms or oppositions that structure *Omeros* and to see how these are managed and to what effect. At the most basic narrative level, the reader encounters the 'ordinary' Saint Lucian working-class figures: the fishermen, waiters and waitresses, taxi drivers, farmers, rum-shop owners and so on, who round out *Omeros*'s domestic plot. Here, the crucial antagonism is between Achille and Hector for the love of the 'real' Helen, a sensual young black woman who appears across the narrative in various guises as a sexually harassed but proud-spirited waitress, stroppy housemaid, unmarried mother and street-trader of cheap touristic goods or services. On this narrative stratum, there is a curious dissonance throughout between progressive and regressive conceptions of postcolonial temporality. This is because *Omeros* works in one direction towards an affirmative therapeutic 'healing' of Saint Lucia's inherited colonial antagonisms, yet simultaneously highlights how these lower-class Saint Lucians continue to be victimized in the present moment as service workers in the tourist industry or as poor fisherfolk on seas increasingly fished out by industrial trawlers.

At a second, more metacritical level, *Omeros* is, as Paul Jay has rightly observed, 'less a poem about the Caribbean than a poem about *writing about the Caribbean*'.[21] In this regard, the most striking antagonisms are figured in terms of an opposition between Plunkett, a retired British soldier, pig farmer and amateur historian, and 'Walcott', the poet-persona who is native to the island but who spends much of his time away from Saint Lucia on exilic odysseys across other continents. Plunkett's and 'Walcott's' ambitions are both motivated by erotic fantasies about capturing the 'real' Helen, but their opposition is conceived in terms of a struggle to master the Saint Lucian national narrative, to tell the story of the 'Helen of the West Indies'. This antagonism between Plunkett's History and 'Walcott's' Art has a geo-literary dimension, because Plunkett is the non-indigenous settler of English-Scottish ancestry who actually farms the land of Saint Lucia whereas 'Walcott', who might appear to have greater claim by race and birthright to the island, roves nomadically farther outwards and away from his island as the narrative progresses. Both figures struggle to capture the story of the 'Helen of the West Indies' in their respective mediums, then, but neither belongs to the island or the island to him in any simple sense. On a third level, these antagonisms come to crisis at the level of form itself as the final books of *Omeros* explore several possible modes of closure – Homeric, Dantean, Miltonic, Joycean – without ever really committing strongly to one specific denouement over another. Oscillating between different kinds of endings, the poem veers between affirmative and apocalyptic closure as much at the level of style or form as of content.

The early sections of *Omeros* offer the fullest treatment of the humbler classes of Saint Lucia. Here, the dramatic element converges on the unhappy triangular relationship of Achille, Helen and Hector, and on Philoctete, who has developed a foul-smelling cancerous leg wound. The crucial events on this narrative plane relate how Hector, frustrated by the low returns from fishing and wanting more money to impress Helen, abandons his fisherman's trade to purchase a transit van to taxi tourists from Castries harbour to the island's scenic sites. Though Helen leaves a frustrated Achille to live with Hector and bears their child, Hector continues to worry that she still loves Achille more. Hector also misses the seas and is frustrated by his work as taxi driver. He discharges his inner rage at his situation through reckless speeding, this eventually leading to his death when his van, the Comet, crashes, killing him. Achille, too, is a tormented figure, initially because Helen leaves him for Hector, later because the industrial trawlers that overfish the local seas render his livelihood increasingly precarious. When Hector is killed, Achille and Helen are reconciled and he will father her baby. This healing and reconciliation is prefigured by a hallucinatory voyage back to Africa, described in extended detail in Book Three, in which Achille encounters his African ancestors, relives a version of the Middle Passage and returns to his Caribbean island with a renewed sense of self and cultural heritage. This positive overcoming of a degrading history of slavery and racial victimization is seconded by the story of Philoctete, whose foul-smelling wound is finally healed by Ma Kilman, a Catholic woman who practises Obeah, and who finds the African herb on the island that restores Philoctete to health. These narratives might appear to conclude affirmatively with Philoctete's cure and Achille's and Helen's restored relationship, but the end of the poem still finds Achille desperately searching with Philoctete for better fishing waters, his livelihood insecure. Personal narratives of overcoming, then, are offset against a backdrop of environmental devastation that suggests ultimate disaster rather than reassuring denouement.

Read in Auerbachian or Hegelian-Lukácsian terms, this proletarian stratum of *Omeros* is conveyed in a curiously mixed form of Greek and biblical epic modes. Many of the characters on this level bear heroic Greek names – Hector, Achille, Helen, Philoctete, Seven Seas (also named Saint Omere) – though most are poor West Indian Catholics of African background, and as such they are as types closer to the nomadic shepherds and fishermen of Old Testament narrative, as described by Erich Auerbach, than to Homer's ruling-class kings and warriors.[22] To the degree that *Omeros* is a Homeric poem, its epic age of world-shaking or world-making military struggles belongs exclusively to the past: to the eighteenth-century British and French naval wars, to the struggles of Africans in the Middle Passage and Native American peoples on the American Plains, or to Dennis Plunkett's World War II. However, in the time-present of the poem, the conflicts are small-scale and domestic – between Helen, Hector and Achille – rather than world-consequential, and in this respect at least *Omeros* is closer to the *Odyssey* (and to Joyce's *Ulysses*) than to the *Iliad*, because its forward momentum depends on voyages and perambulations in strange lands more than on titanic conflict.

To the extent that there is real conflict at all in the present in *Omeros*, it has to do with the direction of lower-class Saint Lucian life. Where is history taking these lower-class African-descended peoples of Saint Lucia? In what direction does it point them? Are they leaving behind long centuries of slavery and vicious colonial oppression and moving into a better future, or simply exchanging one kind of colonial servitude for another, neocolonial kind? In many ways, *Omeros* displays a clear antipathy to progressive notions of time and modernizing development and admits that its aesthetic ideology is essentially romantic anti-capitalist and past-looking. When Hector sells his fishing boat to purchase his taxi, the futuristic-sounding 'The Comet', he makes more money but hates the work. His rough driving makes him a danger to himself and to his community, his speeding representing a death-wish, and his final accident is a virtual suicide. At the beginning of Book Six, Chapter XLV, 'Walcott' returns to Saint Lucia and is picked up by one of Hector's fellow taxi drivers who chatters idly about Hector's death. While driving through Castries, this driver remarks to his unconvinced passenger, 'The place changing, eh?' and 'All to the good'. 'Walcott' silently demurs, '*That* would make me a stranger', and confesses that, on hearing this statement, 'The gap between the driver / and me increased' (228, italics in the original). This little encounter is prefaced by the poet-persona's much-cited rueful reflection: 'Art is History's nostalgia, it prefers a thatched / roof to a concrete factory, and the huge church / above a bleached village' (228). Though the acknowledgement that art (or Art) prefers old things to new – thatched roofs to concrete factories – sounds penitent, *Omeros*'s preference for and dependence on journeys into the past is clear enough. Walcott's work, in other words, requires those allusions to the British-French naval wars, the sufferings of the Middle Passage and the Native American wars and the vistas of World War II and the fall of the British Empire to achieve something of the panoramic grandeur of classical epic. Moreover, its voyages into the past function therapeutically: Achille's journey back to Africa is restorative, and to cure Philoctete's wound Ma Kilman leaves the Catholic Mass she attends to travel back into the rural uplands of Saint Lucia to find an obscure African plant that will heal her friend's cancer. Each of these movements apparently backwards in time – to early modern Africa, away from the town into the mountains – is clearly life restoring, whereas Hector's association with taxi driving and reckless speed (that speed actually a reflex distress brought about by his discontent with 'progress' and 'change') is what leads to his death. It is not the case that *Omeros* expresses some unqualified desire to return to the past, but more the case, as Hector's death underlines, that it fears some catastrophic rush of relentlessly modernizing time, and looks for some alternative 'therapeutic' connection of present and past to allay its anxieties about the nature of modernization.

If we shift attention from the economic temporalities of developmentalist and anti-developmentalist time to political time, *Omeros* seems even more at odds with itself and epic form. The only moment in that work when we see the more lowly Saint Lucians engage in politics occurs in Book Two, which describes the electoral campaigns that attended the island's independence in 1979. Here, the island's two main parties, the conservative United Workers' Party (UWP) and the social democratic Saint Lucia Labour Party (SLP), are represented as largely similar to each other despite rhetorical differences, this causing Maljo, a poor worker, to start his own campaign and to recruit Hector and Philoctete as his assistants. However, Maljo's efforts to found a new movement are rendered largely in terms of comic bathos. Maljo's lack of skill on the hustings with a poor-quality microphone earns him the nickname 'Professor Statics' from the amused lower-class Saint Lucians. After a hapless electoral performance, Maljo leaves the island for Florida to become an orange picker, his migration suggesting that for lower-class Saint Lucians independence proves to be largely a non-event.

If C. L. R. James's *The Black Jacobins* represents an earlier Caribbean narrative that renders its history of slave rebellion in high heroic, romantic and epic modes, *Omeros* is a becalmed epic for which the large dramas of history already belong to the past, whereas the region's current conflicts can find expression only in the modes of pathos, satire or farce. Both works, we might say, belong to their times: James's to the revolutionary epoch of the 1930s, Walcott's to the 'end of history' moment in the 1990s when liberal capitalism appeared to have emerged victorious from its contests with fascism and communism and when strong alternatives to its dispensation seemed hard to find.[23] Nevertheless, this begs the question as to whether an 'end of history' moment can afford an epic or of what kind. Is *Omeros* more Joycean than Homeric, more comic mock epic than classical Homeric epic, its high epic scope and style all out of kilter with its lack of contemporary dramatic action and conflict of high consequence?

*Omeros*'s braided temporalities – modernizing and anti-modernizing, retrospective and futurist – remain to the end suspended in teetering balance. Walcott, it appears, can no more find a 'third way' aesthetically between a traditionalist romantic anti-capitalism, which smacks of conservatism, and a futurism that suggests an obliteration of the past, than Maljo can find a way between the UWP and SLP. For readers who incline towards a more affirmative reading in the poem's unfolding, the text offers considerable support. As mentioned already, Achille's imaginative return to Africa is a recuperative voyage that bridges his ancestral past and his present and results in an exuberant homecoming that sees him recover Helen, purge his earlier jealousy of Hector and parent Hector's child with Helen without grudge. After Hector's death, Helen too overcomes her earlier discontent and acquires new maturity and dignity. Ma Kilman cures Philoctete, and towards the poem's close we see Achille and Philoctete perform an African ceremony on Boxing Day, the two men dressed as transvestite stick-fighters complete with masks, stilts and handcrafted musical instruments. With this merging of the Boxing Day mumming and African dance, at a time of seasonal turning, *Omeros* seems to offer a final vison of syncretic cultural harmony, the androgynous warrior-women blending genders, religions and cultural heritages in a street performance of simple dignity. Here, Walcott's work comes close to a kind of multiculturalist vision that celebrates hybrid plurality as a kind of solution to the Caribbean's complex mix of racial cultures and histories.

For the reader suspicious that all this closing harmony of cancer cured and conflict reduced to ritual combat represents a version of what Adorno called 'reconciliation under duress', Walcott's epic also offers, however, a far darker, even apocalyptic vision.[24] In the opening pages of Book One, the reader finds Philoctete leading tourists into the Saint Lucian hills to watch the felling of trees from which fishermen's canoes are made. However, this tree felling is depicted as an act of violence against nature that triggers memories of the early modern deeds of tribal slaughter and slave taking that brought Philoctete's ancestors to the Caribbean: 'The bearded elders endured the decimation / of their tribe without uttering a syllable / of that language they had uttered as one nation, / the speech taught their saplings: from the towering babble / of the cedar to green vowels of *bois-campêche*' (6). By the end of *Omeros*, this introductory tree-felling and language-eradicating scene takes on a more sinister cast as the poem offers up multiple vistas of a wholly destructive aggressive war on nature. That war is now conducted by the industrial trawlers that overfish the Caribbean seas and by the tourist business and credit card finance economy that transforms all islands from the Aegean to the Caribbean to Hawaii into more or less standardized pleasure resorts. In Chapter LX of Book Seven, this interleaving of a genocidal past, ecologically ruinous present and ill-omened future finds its most explicit expression:

> He [Seven Seas] had never seen such strange weather; the surprise
> of a tempestuous January that churned
> the foreshore brown with remarkable, bursting seas
>
> convinced him that 'somewhere people interfering
> with the course of nature'; the feathery mare's tails
> were more threateningly frequent, and its sunsets
>
> the roaring ovens of the hurricane season,
> while the frigates hung closer inland and the nets
> starved on their bamboo poles. The rain lost its reason
>
> and behaved with no sense at all.
>
> (299–300)

A local analogue for Homer, Seven Seas's intimations of Holocaust-like ('roaring ovens') climate change and a deranged nature summon up a vision in which the long imperial past and a terrifying future fuse into one seamless temporality, a once apparently progressive or modernizing time now showing itself capable of producing wholly regressive outcomes:

> Seven Seas would talk
> bewilderingly that man was an endangered
>
> species now, a spectre, just like the Aruac
> or the egret, or parrots screaming in terror
> when men approached, and that once men were satisfied
>
> with destroying men they would move on to Nature.
>
> (300)

Here, the whole genre of epic, Greek or Christian, fed on human wars and the making or breaking of empires, culminates in an irreversible war on 'Nature' boding common destruction for all. If there is any intimation of oneness here, it is not a positive harmonious version leading towards androgynous syncretic cultural mixing and happy hybridity, but only the negative homogeneity of capitalist commodification and its ravaging consumption of resources anti-climaxing in the dead end of planetary destruction.[25]

   'Walcott' and Plunkett are more middle class than Achille, Hector and their companions; they speak Standard English and both are writers.

If Hector, Helen and Achille are humbler versions of epic Greek warriors or biblical herders, 'Walcott' and Plunkett, each bearing Anglo rather than Greek names, resemble Homer's gods insofar as they can fly through the skies by air travel or attain transcendental overviews of sorts by means of writing grand narratives. In Plunkett's case, this desire for transcendental vision is linked to his fascination with the once globe-spanning British Empire and to Henry H. Breen's compendious *St. Lucia: Historical, Statistical and Descriptive*, a 423-page overview of the island published in 1844, which the former Major uses as one of his research sources. Originally of lower-class English origins, though he later discovers his family ancestry is actually Scottish, Plunkett fought with Montgomery in North Africa during World War II and still suffers from the injuries acquired there. Married to Maud, an Irish Catholic who nursed him during his wartime hospitalization, and disgruntled with a post-war England still stewing in ugly class wars, Plunkett has retreated to Saint Lucia to find an Eden for his Maud and his old age. Their marriage is contented but lacks a son: this lack, his wartime traumas and his fascination with their imperious maid, Helen, provoke in him a desire to travel across the full extent of the quickly disappearing British Empire and then to go back in time to retrace his own family origins and the history of Saint Lucia. However, Plunkett's proposed post-war 'masochistic odyssey through the Empire, / to watch it go in the dusk' and his wish to visit its outposts 'from Singapore / to the Seychelles' and track its battle fortunes from 'the first musket-shot that divided Concord' to 'some hill-station of Sind' comes to nothing because Maud persuades him that 'It'll eat up your pension' (90).

Maud too longs to travel to revisit Ireland, but because Plunkett worries about the expense of such a trip, that journey is also endlessly deferred. Thus, Maud can recover her own lost island only through memory or by means of Thomas Moore's 'Bendemeer's Stream', a tune later adopted by Percy French for his famous song, 'The Mountains of Mourne'. The plangently melancholic character of these nostalgias, whether for 'the afterglow of an empire' (227) or for pastoral versions of a lost Ireland, is evident throughout. As time advances, though, these return journeys are abandoned and nostalgias for old empires or homelands are overcome. Even before Maud dies and is buried in Saint Lucia, Plunkett forsakes his historical researches and recommits himself to his farming and his wife so that eventually 'England seemed to him merely the place of his birth' (61). Shortly before Maud dies, Plunkett also has a spiky encounter with Hector, whose speeding taxi-van nearly runs him and Maud off the road.

Plunkett angrily refuses the term 'honky' (a derogatory term used for whites) and tells Hector and his companions: 'I haven't spent / damned near twenty years on this godforsaken rock / to be cursed like a tourist. Do you understand?' (256). Plunkett's army officer manner and the term 'godforsaken rock' sit uneasily with his claim to be accepted as a fellow-national with the African Saint Lucians, but his attachment to the island and its inhabitants is sincere. When Maud dies, he forsakes his sergeant major tones to his workers, and when 'Walcott' returns to the island he finds the Major standing humbly outside the bank in a line of local farmers. Now, the poet figure recognizes that 'I saw that he was / one with the farmers, transplanted to the rich dirt / of their valleys' and that he 'never wanted the privilege / that peasants, from habit, paid to his complexion' (268). 'Walcott' also acknowledges his own affective affinities with the Plunketts – 'There was Plunkett in my father, much as there was / my mother in Maud' (263) – and *Omeros* offers through this couple's narrative a compassionate account of white attitudinal decolonization. These white settlers on the island may never fully rid themselves of post-imperial melancholy or even of some residual sense of white superiority, but their desire for respite from the conflict of wars and their love of Saint Lucia are allowed due dignity. The lower-class islanders like Achille, Helen and Philoctete attend Maud's funeral Mass, and this acknowledgement matters more to Plunkett than the presence of the island's middle-class notables.

The Plunketts' travels, like those of Achille, are essentially imaginary. The poem takes the Plunketts on fantasy treks out to the empire or Ireland and Achille back to an ancestral Africa, but the voyages ultimately bring all three figures more securely home to Saint Lucia. Is this the case for the narrator 'Walcott' also? In his case, the journeys are 'real' and are career-motivated rather than urged by ancestral attachment to other continents. From the beginning, 'Walcott's' peregrinations are linked to literature and more particularly to Great Books. In Book One of *Omeros*, the narrator revisits the family's old home, now tellingly converted to a printing office, and meets there the ghost of his father, Warwick, who had imparted to his son the vocation to be a writer. These scenes are *Hamlet*-resonant, but convey little of the anguished mimetic rivalry with the Bard that is evident in Joyce's *Ulysses* or O'Neill's *Long Day's Journey*. The ghost of Warwick Walcott does complain that his 'bastard father christened me for his shire: / Warwick. The Bard's county', but confesses that nevertheless he had never 'felt part / of the foreign machinery known as Literature' (68). Warwick tells his son, 'I preferred verse to fame, but I wrote with the heart / of an amateur. It's that Will you inherit. / I died on his birthday, one April' (68).

Afterwards, this ghost father takes 'Walcott' on a walk through the colonial-era Castries in which Warwick had grown up, bringing him to the corner barbershop owned by an anarchist and Garveyite. There, Warwick remembers 'On their varnished rack, / *The World's Great Classics* read backwards in his mirrors' (71), and recalls how as a child he used to recite from these works to the barber. Later, in Book Four, Chapter XXXVI, this scenario is revisited when Warwick again appears and tells his son that they might leave the cold of Boston for 'a warmer place', meaning perhaps the purgatory where Warwick, like Old Hamlet's ghost, resides:

> But before you return, you must enter cities
> that open like *The World's Classics*, in which I dreamt
> I saw my shadow on their flagstones, histories
>
> that carried me over the bridge of self-contempt,
> though I never stared in their rivers, great abbeys
> soaring in net-webbed stone, when I felt diminished
>
> even by a postcard. Those things I wrote to please
> your mother and our friends, unrevised, unfinished,
> in drawing-room concerts died in their own applause.
>
> Way back in the days of the barber's winding sheet,
> I longed for those streets that History had made great,
> but the island became my fortress and retreat,
>
> in that circle of friends that I could dominate.
> Dominate, Dominus.

> (187)

In these visitations, 'Walcott's' profession is paternally conferred on him by an Old Hamlet–like ghost-father who had been raised in a colonial city and who had inherited a Shakespeare-inflected love of literature and a desire to see the greater world inspired by his love of *The World's Classics*. However, Warwick had felt too intimidated by the 'foreign machinery known as Literature' and by the diminishment of his own island in the light of that literature's greatness to ever dare to become more than an 'amateur'. That word conveys both the purity of one who loves literature innocently for its own sake but also the timidity of one who dares not aim higher. When he tells his son, 'It's that Will you inherit', then, and that 'before you return, you must enter cities, / that open like *The World's Classics*', the injunction stresses an imperative to world travel stimulated by literature that the stay-at-home father never had the confidence to undertake himself and that is now vicariously handed on to his son. Nevertheless, 'Walcott' is also instructed to retain as part of this 'Will you inherit' the amateur's non-professional, non-commercial reverence for Shakespeare and the literary classics, even as he exceeds the father by becoming the cosmopolitan and much-travelled worldly writer.

To remain as the stay-at-home writer is to play it safe and opt for a kind of easy domestic priority ('in the circle of friends I could dominate'), whereas to venture out into the world is to have the courage to take on the literary greats of other lands on their own domain and even to 'Dominate' them there. When father and son first meet in Book One, Warwick tells his son, 'Fame is that white liner / at the end of your street, a city to itself', one much finer 'than anything Castries could ever hope to build' (72–73), thus fundamentally linking literary distinction to travel, expatriation and whiteness. Then, the ghost-father shows his son a Hellish Dantean vision of a file of African women colliers bearing panniers of coal to steam those great cruisers of white privilege and charges him to hold to his vocation with similar stubborn determination 'and walk up that coal ladder as they do in time, / one bare foot after the next in ancestral rhyme' (75). To become a great writer, then, is to overcome the timidities of the colonial-era father and to work the drudgery of poor African women workers into the very metre of his poetics, thus remaining faithful to one's ancestral past. However, that vocation also requires the son to board 'the white liner' of 'Fame' that carries him away from Saint Lucia, the better to return to it eventually neither a cowed amateur like Warwick nor drudge like the female colliers but like a conquering, homecoming Odysseus. Though it is without the more visceral oedipal love-hate animus towards Shakespeare evident in Joyce or O'Neill, and conveys a gentler sense of filial and Shakespeare-claiming piety, the conception of the writer in *Omeros* still smoulders with *ressentiment*, fierce competitiveness, mimetic desire and anxiety, and a will to dominate before returning home victorious. To win literary distinction, 'Walcott' must surpass his father's amateurish domestic verse, forsake the small comforts of local acclaim and precedence, be prepared to travel afar and conquer a world literary system that is intrinsically white.

Despite 'Walcott's' father's associations with Shakespeare and *The World's Classics*, when 'Walcott' leaves Saint Lucia it is to go not to the Old World but the New. Book Four, the most autobiographical and confessional in *Omeros*, deals with the poet's shamed isolation and self-loathing in Boston after the break-up of his marriage. There, he develops an interest in the Trail of Tears that saw the forceful removal of several

Indian nations from the southern United States across the Mississippi in the nineteenth century, and becomes fascinated by Catherine Weldon, a white Swiss-born immigrant who had become assistant to Sitting Bull and the Sioux people of the Great Plains. Book Four also recounts 'Walcott's' visit to the Museum of Fine Arts in Boston and describes encounters there with Homer Winslow, Herman Melville and Augustus Saint-Gauden's bronze frieze *Memorial to Robert Gould Shaw and the Massachusetts Fifty-Fourth Regiment* of African American Civil War soldiers. Now, 'Walcott' is revisited by Warwick Walcott and bid again to travel the world's cities as recounted above: Book Five then takes the narrator-poet on some version of a New World grand tour of Europe of the kind that Henry James, Ezra Pound and T. S. Eliot had all undertaken in an earlier era.[26]

'Walcott's' grand tour is in some ways, though, an unconventional one, with none of the once obligatory pilgrimages to Italy, despite *Omeros's* debts to Dante, or France, despite Saint Lucia's French connections. Instead, the poet persona's travels take him from Lisbon to London and from London to Dublin and onwards from there to the coastlines of Greece, Turkey and Venice, these latter places viewed more remotely as though they were brief cruise-liner or airline stopovers. Lisbon, London, Dublin and the Aegean are all cities or regions associated with epic poets – Camões, Pound, Eliot, Joyce, Homer – but despite the literary fame of these capitals, the city-visitations in Book Five have a cameo-like quality and convey something of the short-stay, whistle-stop, 'must see' haste of modern city-only tourism. The high modernists had often spent their entire adult lives as émigrés in Europe's capitals, but Walcott's tour has the rushed-through sensation of modern travel. By contrast, his life in the United States appears more vividly in *Omeros* and has a more immersive feel to it. The point, in short, is that Europe in *Omeros* belongs to the past, not quite the remoter pasts reflected in Achille's return to Africa or Plunkett's obsession with eighteenth-century Franco-British naval wars, but to a now-faded literary era nonetheless.

Moreover, in a New World still fraught with racial resentments and deepening commodification, Europe's cultural wealth appears to the contemporary Saint Lucian traveller to have more to do with aesthetically cleansing or 'absolving' history than with engaging it. Hence, in Chapter XL, which marks the end of the European odyssey:

> What my father
>
>> spiritedly spoke of was that other Europe
>> of mausoleum museums, the barber's shelf

of *The World's Great Classics*, with a vanity whose

> spires and bells punctually pardoned itself
> in the absolution of fountains and statues,
> in writhing, astonishing tritons; their cold noise
>
> brimming the basin's rim, repeating that power
> and art were the same, from some Caesar's eaten nose
> to spires at sunset in the swift's half-hour.
>
> Tell that to a slave from the outer regions
> of their fraying empires, what power lay in the work
> of forgiving fountains with naiads and lions.
>
> (205)

What begins as a voyage of homage to the European cities and literary greats rounds off in disillusion with the apparent inextricability of empire and art. The Europe that 'Walcott' visits is not the fabled Europe of his father's colonial imagination whetted by *The World's Great Classics*, but a continent of 'mausoleum museums' where art's amnesiac function seems to be to whitewash the continent of its imperial sins.

Yet, when in the next chapter, XLI, we find 'Walcott' back in the United States, he discovers himself only in a new empire and new subordination:

> Service. Under my new empire. The Romans
> acquired Greek slaves as aesthetic instructors
> of their spoilt children, many from obscure islands
>
> of their freshly acquired archipelago. But those tutors,
> curly-haired, served a state without equestrians
> apart from statues; a republic without class,
>
> tiered only on wealth, and eaten with prejudice
> from its pillared base, the Athenian *demos*,
> its *demos* demonic and its *ocracy* crass,
>
> corrupting the blue-veined marble with its disease,
> stillborn as a corpse, for all those ideals went cold
> in the heat of its hate.
>
> (206, italics in the original)

The transition from Old to New World here is a passage from a once-imperial Europe that now wants aesthetically to whitewash its imperial past to a currently imperial America still wholly in denial of its empire – in the Caribbean and elsewhere – and that has perverted its republican ideals, compromised like Greece's and Rome's from the start by slavery, only to stew in hatreds seething beneath that denial. The trope of the colonial subject-race as intellectual tutor-servants to their crasser Roman overlords is an old one, and Irish writers from Wilde to Joyce deployed it because it reflects the bondsman's claim to spiritual, intellectual or linguistic superiority over the master. For 'Walcott', it now applies to himself, trapped in teaching service at Boston University. Some readers will feel this analogy of the well-paid and prestigious writing professor with the Greek or American slave, or with Native Americans crushed by genocide, to be misapplied. However, 'Walcott' insists on his links to the oppressed despite acknowledging also his artistic affiliations to earlier New England intellectuals like Emerson and Thoreau:

> Privileges did not separate me, instead
> they linked me closer to them by that mental chain
> whose eyes interlocked with mine, as if we all stood
>
> at a lectern or auction block. Their condition
> the same, without manacles. The chains were subtler,
> but they were still hammered out of the white-hot forge
>
> that made every captor a blacksmith.
>
> (210)

The racial wordplay on 'white-hot forge' and 'blacksmith' is clear enough, but to whom exactly do the plural pronouns 'them', 'their' and 'they' refer? Does the passage allude to the privileges that the celebrity writer enjoys and that separates him from the sufferings of America's racial minorities? Or does he claim that despite those privileges he still knows in his bones what it is to be an oppressed and rage-filled minority subject in a university environment sustained by white privilege?

'Walcott's' father-bestowed vocational mission may have required him to see the world's great cities and to become a professional writer whose metrical feet would forever record the sufferings of Saint Lucia's female colliers fuelling the great 'white liners' of 'Fame'. However, that mission's success brings him to Boston, New England repeating the imperial domin-ion of Old England, 'all colonies inherit their empire's sin' (208), and forces into awareness new modes of mental 'service'. The worlds of culture and art, education and aesthetics are as shot through as any other with race politics. As a successful cosmopolitan professional writer, 'Walcott' has certainly entered the cultural 'service'-chain at a higher level than bead-selling Helen back in Saint Lucia, but the feeling of servitude that lingers even in the uppermost tiers of this American-dominated cultural economy still smarts. To become a triumphant success, 'Walcott' must leave his Caribbean island to spend much of his life in the US university system, only then to discover when he returns to his ever-more Americanized island-home that it can never be a homecoming to the Saint Lucia he left. Achille returns to Saint Lucia more at peace with himself perhaps but still doomed to fish fished-out seas, and in a closing image we see him wrathfully protesting tourist cameras. 'Walcott', a late modernist writer fishing his own over-fished literary seas, has not only to turn to Homer, Virgil, Dante, Joyce and others to make his Saint Lucia noble and himself 'Nobelable', but he is also obliged to submit to 'service' in the new American empire to attain recognition at the top of his profession.

All of the poet's disparate selves come together in the sense that they comprise and round out the grand narrative that is *Omeros*, but there is little to suggest that they ever become one with each other in any satisfyingly integrated way. If all of the significant figures in the poem are versions of Walcott, they all stand also for facets of the modern Caribbean writer. Like Achille, that writer is a fisher in well-fished or even fished-out waters. Like Helen, the writer can be compelled to sell trinkets of local colour to European or American tourists. Like Plunkett, he or she depends on History for narratives of high drama and conflict, yet dreams of retreat from history to an Edenic Caribbean island. Like 'Walcott', Walcott is an émigré writer in an America that may be a modern-day version of ancient Greece and Rome, but it is a copy that doesn't summon to mind any ancient splendour or classical harmony, only memories of the slave systems that subtended those republics.

As *Omeros* comes to a close in Book Seven, Chapter LVIII, 'Walcott' is conducted with Homer as guide into a volcanic underworld, his grimmest invocation of Dante's *Inferno*. There, the poet and guide can smell 'the foul sulphur of hell in paradise', and he is offered a ringside view of a 'Pool of Speculation' where 'the traitors / who, in elected office, saw the land as views / for hotels and elevated into waiters / the sons of others, while their own learnt something else' (289). Soon afterwards, poet and guide come to the edge of a pit of poets:

> Selfish phantoms with eyes
> who wrote with them only, saw only surfaces
> in nature and men, and smiled at their similes,
>
> condemned in their pit to weep at their own pages.
> And that was where I had come from. Pride in my craft.
> Elevating myself. I slid, and kept falling
>
> towards the shit they stewed in.
>
> (293)

Appalled, 'Walcott' recognizes some affinity with these wretches and nearly slides into 'the shit they stewed in', but Omeros grips his hand and pulls him clear. The invective against poets and politicians who sell out the island is more vehement here than anywhere else in *Omeros*. For a moment, at least, that exasperation with the uselessness of a postcolonial comprador bourgeoisie acquires a near-Fanonian intensity. However, it is never wholly convincing. This is partly because to reduce the problems confronting the island to corrupt politicians, real estate speculators and superficial poets who lack true conviction in craft risks oversimplifying the deeper systemic issues involved, or confusing symptom with cause. And also because *Omeros* seems so much concerned otherwise to purge rage and resentment rather than to express them, to work towards an affirmative and celebratory vision rather than towards vitriolic condemnation. Moreover, as 'Walcott's' near slippage into this morass of corruption suggests, only a thin line separates those who sell out and those who don't, and that line is hard to draw with conviction. The ominous tree-felling scenario that opens *Omeros* reminds readers that forests are felled to make not just canoes but also paper, and that while paper records the spoken word, it privileges some languages over others, English over Kwéyòl, for example. One of the running jokes threaded across *Omeros* describes a waiter, Lawrence, hurrying perpetually across the beach sands with trays of drinks 'like a Lawrence of St. Lucia' (23) to serve his customers. This is an obvious parody of Lawrence of Arabia's *Seven Pillars of Wisdom*, another modern Homeric epic of would-be post-imperial emancipation. Here, Saint Lucia's postcolonial emancipation appears not as the stuff of epic vision for which T. E. Lawrence strived, but only as material for a diminished, degenerate mock epic. Rendered at once grandly dressed and obsequiously subservient by the tourist industry, the 'Waiters in bow-ties on the terraces' laugh at Achille's anger when he rages against the tourist cameras, their would-be superiority to the simple fisherman 'the laugh of a wounded race' (299).

## III

*The Antilles: Fragments of Epic Memory*, Walcott's Nobel Lecture booklet, opens with the poet visiting Felicity, a village in Trinidad, 'with friends from America'.[27] There, they witness preparations for the *Ramleela*, a nine-day reenactment of the *Ramayana*, a Sanskrit epic. The set-up here recalls that of the opening of *Omeros*, though with the Nobel-winner now in the role of Philoctete, a local guide showing foreign visitors around.

In beautifully evoked scenes, Walcott describes small Indian boys running about and aiming arrows into the air, drummers preparing their drums, actors playing the roles of princes and gods entering the field where the epic will be performed. 'I had often thought of but never seen *Ramleela*', Walcott remarks, 'and had never seen this theatre, an open field, with village children as warriors, princes, and gods. I had no idea what the epic story was, who its hero was, what enemies he fought, yet I had recently adapted the *Odyssey* for a theatre in England, presuming the audience knew the trials of Odysseus, hero of another, Asia Minor epic, while nobody in Trinidad knew any more than I did about Rama, Kali, Shiva, Vishnu, apart from the Indians, a phrase I use pervertedly because that is the kind of remark you can still hear in Trinidad: "apart from the Indians"'. However, this Indian epic, he stresses, is quite different to his London-performed Homeric counterpart. *Ramleela* requires none of the English actors' willed determination to enter into a world of make-believe because it belongs to a time when epic and epic performances were a matter of 'faith':

> Multiply that moment of self-conviction when an actor, made-up and costumed, nods to his mirror before stepping onstage in the belief that he is a reality entering an illusion and you would have what I presumed was happening to the actors of this epic. But they were not actors. They had been chosen; or they themselves had chosen their roles in this sacred story that would go for nine afternoons over a two-hour period till the sun set. They were not amateurs but believers. There was no theatrical term to define them. They did not have to psych themselves up to play their roles. [. . .] They believed in what they were playing, in the sacredness of the text, the validity of India, while I, out of the writer's habit, searched for some sense of elegy, of loss, even of degenerative mimicry in the happy faces of the boy-warriors or the heraldic profiles of the village princes. I was polluting the afternoon with doubt and with the patronage of admiration. I misread the event through a visual echo of History – the cane fields, indenture, the evocation of vanished armies, temples, and trumpeting elephants – when all around me there was quite the opposite: elation, delight in the boys' screams, in the sweet-stalls, in more and more costumed characters appearing; a delight of conviction, not loss. The name Felicity made sense.

This returns us to the conception of epic expressed in Lukács's *Theory of the Novel*. The Walcott passage invokes a notion of ur-epic, Indian not Aegean here, which retains a sense of sacred totality foreign to the modern age. This is the world of epic and epic theatre that has its origins in an epoch that has answers before questions, that performs its rituals in open fields, not darkened auditoriums, that knows happiness and not the modern plague of exilic self-doubt and self-questioning. Trained as a modern poet-ethnographer to think of the *Ramleela* as a diminished fragment of some greater original Asian version or as an elegiac diasporic reconstruction of a lost homeland, Walcott has to remind himself that the communal joy in this reenactment represents something quite different. He should not, he admonishes himself, foist the 'pollution' of doubt on this event because '[t]he sigh of History meant nothing here'.

Later in the Nobel lecture, Walcott oscillates, as he does in *Omeros*, between two conceptions of his own version of Caribbean epic. One idea of epic is modern and modernist, in which such joy in creation as belongs to the contemporary epic poet must come not from some pre-given wholeness or harmony but from lovingly re-piecing an inherited broken-ness: 'Break a vase, and the love that reassembles the fragments is stronger than that love which took its symmetry for granted when it was whole. [. . .] Antillean art is this restoration of our shattered histories, our shards of vocabulary, our archipelago becoming a synonym for pieces broken off from the original continent'. It is hard not to think here of Henry James's *The Golden Bowl* or T. S. Eliot's *The Waste Land* and of the modernist insistence on fragmentation and art as a willed effort of (impossible) restoration. Walcott's other idea of epic is anti-colonial, non-European, maybe even anti-modernist because it founds its mission on a rejection of melancholic conceptions of the Caribbean world as a diminished place, something that stems, he avers, from the archives of Victorian travel writing and finds its exemplification in Claude Lévi-Strauss's *Tristes Tropiques* (1955). Because he and his peers are native to the region and feel none of this exilic European sense of the Caribbean's inadequacy to supposedly better places, they write, Walcott asserts, with a confidence unhampered by this burden of European modernist moroseness. This is an American and Antillean Adamic benediction to which Walcott has often laid claim: namely, the good fortune supposedly bestowed on writers who belong not to the dusk of an Old Europe but to the dawn of a still-emerging New World and are therefore gifted to write without world weariness.[28] Here, we might recall the Yeats, invoked earlier in Chapter 2, who had contended that contemporary French and English literatures were in their golden sunset while reawakened Irish and other peripheral litera-tures exuded in contrast the freshness of a new epoch.

However, even as Walcott tries to find a positive version of the poet as either loving restorer of modernity's shattered world, a refurbisher of broken totalities, or as author graced to be at the beginning rather than end of his region's literary revival or arrival on the world stage, the old doubts reappear. Thus, as his lecture draws to its end, he finds himself again excoriating the 'benign blight that is tourism' that 'can infect all of those island nations, not gradually, but with imperceptible speed, until each rock is whitened by the guano of white-winged hotels, the arc and descent of progress'. 'How quickly it could all disappear!' he exclaims. 'A morning could come in which governments might ask what happened not merely to the forests and the bays but to a whole people'. As in *Omeros*, the vision of a happy Adamic Antilles relishing the sunlit mornings of its literary creation day succumbs swiftly to a vison of apocalyptic destruction.

In an acerbic yet grudgingly admiring essay on Walcott, 'The Worm in the Bud', V. S. Naipaul laconically describes the Saint Lucian as 'a kind of Robinson Crusoe, but with the pain of a modern Friday'.[29] Walcott's career started strongly, Naipaul writes, but was followed by a slump in the 1950s, this ascribed by Naipaul, predictably enough – in the manner of Henry James writing on Hawthorne – to the thinness of Caribbean life and culture. However, 'Walcott found his own way around that emptiness', Naipaul contends, when he 'began to fit his island material to older, foreign work' (23). Walcott was then lucky enough, Naipaul adds, to be 'rescued by the American universities' where his reputation was remade not as 'that of a man whose talent had been all but strangled by his colonial setting', but rather as 'the man who had stayed behind and found beauty in the emptiness from which other writers had fled' (25).

This is a caustic estimate but not an uninsightful one. Perhaps Walcott was indeed compelled, as Naipaul remarks, to leave Saint Lucia for the United States to make his career as an émigré and win his Nobel Prize. A voyage from periphery to the centre remained necessary even if over the course of the century the centre itself had changed. However, if Walcott had remade his native region to fit 'older, foreign work', so too had Joyce, Eliot, Pound, Fitzgerald and O'Neill. What distinguishes Walcott from these precursors, and of course also from the émigré Naipaul who had removed himself to England, is the 'rescue' by the American universities, something not so available to earlier high modernist generations. The high modernists had gone not to the United States but to Paris and London, the then capitals of the world literary system. In *Omeros*, as we have seen, 'Walcott' finds on his pilgrimage only an imperial Europe fading into post-history, 'that other Europe / of mausoleum museums' (205), and returns, however unhappily, to his world of "service" in the United States.

'Rescue' is also Mark McGurl's key claim in *The Program Era*: namely, that the American university system's writing programmes had salvaged post–World War II versions of late modernism by serving as a buffer between literature and marketplace. While some critics lament this contemporary merger of literary production and the university creative writing school, McGurl demurs. Hasn't the university's cultivation of a mass of talent created, he asks, a largely positive 'system-wide rise in the excellence of American literature in the postwar period?'³⁰ Far from bemoaning the fact that contemporary America lacks writers equal to the great world-bestriding mandarins of Poundian high modernism, we should, McGurl suggests, risk 'a strategic triumphalism' (129). Instead of decrying the supposed limitations of 'the program era' – the term deliberately invokes a successor era to Kenner's now outdated 'Pound era' – why not celebrate 'a surfeit of literary excellence, an embarrassment of riches'? If the post–World War II period has produced no single outstanding genius to match the achievements of Pound or Eliot, Stein or Faulkner, this is more than compensated for by a general rise and democratic levelling in accomplishment. Even if the field of contemporary literary achievement seems flatter than in the Pound era, it is also wider and more richly and variously populated. So much so indeed that 'being the dominant figure in Shakespeare's time or even Pound's time was, by comparison to today, as easy as cake' (129).

'A surfeit of literary excellence' or a 'wreath of flies'? *Omeros* was clearly a bid for old-style mandarin high modernist dominance or pre-eminence, however outmoded that ambition may seem to McGurl. And Walcott's epic offers a view of the United States and the American creative writing programme that ultimately comes closer in many respects to that of *La République mondiale des Lettres* than to that of *The Program Era* because Pascale Casanova and Walcott each see connections between the well-resourced American university and its writing programmes, American corporate publishing, capitalist commodification and US world domination – connections to which McGurl seems indifferent or he deliberately underplays. But then McGurl writes, sanguinely, as an American critic from within that American university system, Casanova, fretfully, as a freelance intellectual from a Paris fearing that city's decline in an American-dominated world of global English. Belonging to neither of these metropoles, Walcott was obliged to navigate between older European and newer American centres as he made his bid for fame and strove to create a great Caribbean epic. The mix of self-assurance and self-interrogation, distress and determination, that defines *Omeros* suggests that for Walcott, as for Joyce before him, high ambition to make a lasting mark on world literature had to live with an uneasy awareness that literary achievement might do nothing to redeem the ongoing plight of his country or to prevent the conscription of his epic to the glory of resented empires.

# Notes

## Chapter 1

1 Ezra Pound, 'How to Read', *New York Herald Tribune*, 1929, collected in *Literary Essays of Ezra Pound*, ed. T. S. Eliot (New York: New Directions, 1968), 15–40, 33–34. All further references are to this edition and page numbers are cited in the text.

2 Hugh Kenner, 'The Three Provinces', in *A Colder Eye: The Modern Irish Writers* (New York: Alfred A. Knopf, 1983), 11–18, 15.

3 Pascale Casanova, *The World Republic of Letters*, trans. M. B. DeBevoise (Cambridge, MA: Harvard University Press, 2004 [1999]). The contemporary critical literature on world literature and Casanova more specifically is too extensive to be cited here. Some key texts include David Damrosch, *What Is World Literature?* (Princeton, NJ: Princeton University Press, 2003); Christopher Prendergast, ed., *Debating World Literature* (London: Verso, 2004); Wai Chee Dimock, *Through Other Continents: American Literature across Deep Time* (Princeton, NJ: Princeton University Press, 2006); Emily Apter, *Against World Literature: On the Politics of Untranslatability* (London: Verso, 2012); Eric Hayot, *On Literary Worlds* (Oxford: Oxford University Press, 2012); Franco Moretti, *Distant Reading* (London: Verso, 2013); Alexander Beecroft, *An Ecology of World Literature: From Antiquity to the Present Day* (London: Verso, 2015); Pheng Cheah, *What Is a World?: On Postcolonial Literature as World Literature* (Durham, NC: Duke University Press, 2016); and Aamir Mufti, *Forget English! Orientalisms and World Literatures* (Cambridge, MA: Harvard University Press, 2016). For a useful overview of the history and theory of world literature, see Theo D'haen, *The Routledge Concise History of World Literature* (London: Routledge, 2012).

4 Eric Hayot, 'On Literary Worlds', *Modern Language Quarterly* 72: 2 (2011): 129–161, 129. On world systems analysis and literary worlds, see Hayot, *On Literary Worlds*, and David Palumbio-Liu, Bruce Robbins and Nirvana Tanoukhi, eds., *Immanuel Wallerstein and the Problem of the World: System, Scale, Culture* (Durham, NC: Duke University Press, 2011).

5 On world literary systems, see also Franco Moretti, *Atlas of the European Novel* (London: Verso, 1998), *Graphs, Maps, Trees: Abstract Models for a Literary*

*History* (London: Verso, 2005) and *Distant Reading*, as well as Moretti's essays 'Conjectures on World Literature', *New Left Review* 1 (January/February 2000): 54–68, and 'More Conjectures', *New Left Review* 20 (March/April 2003): 73–81.

6 E. R. Curtius, 'Remarks on the French Novel', in *Essays on European Literature*, trans. Michael Kowal (Princeton, NJ: Princeton University Press, 1973), 437–445, 437.

7 Casanova, *The World Republic of Letters*, 45–73. Direct quotations are referenced in the text.

8 Casanova, *The World Republic of Letters*, 73–75.

9 On Herder's work, see John K. Noyes, *Herder: Aesthetics against Imperialism* (Toronto: University of Toronto Press, 2015), and Vicki A. Spencer, *Herder's Political Thought: A Study of Language, Culture, and Community* (Toronto: University of Toronto Press, 2011).

10 See also Pascale Casanova, 'Combative Literatures', *New Left Review* 72 (November/December 2011): 123–134, 127–128.

11 Casanova, *The World Republic of Letters*, 115–125.

12 See also my 'The World Literary System: Atlas and Epitaph', *Field Day Review* 2 (2006): 196–219.

13 On contemporary debates on the Eurocentrism of comparative literary studies and attempts to move beyond this, see Haun Saussy, ed., *Comparative Literature in an Age of Globalization* (Baltimore: Johns Hopkins University Press, 2006).

14 George Bernard Shaw, *The Apple Cart: A Political Extravaganza* (New York: Brentano's, 1931), 96. Further references to this edition are cited in the text.

15 Franco Moretti, *Signs Taken for Wonders: Essays in the Sociology of Literary Forms*, trans. Susan Fischer, David Forgacs and David Miller (London: Verso, 1983), 209, italics in original. It would be more accurate, in my view, to suggest that by appropriating 'modernism' the United States constructed itself as heir and guarantor of 'Western culture', extending that term's reach to include Europe and the Americas with the United States itself as its highest stage of achievement.

16 On American critical appropriations of modernism, see David A. Hollinger, 'The Canon and Its Keepers: Modernism and Mid-Twentieth-Century American Intellectuals', in *In the American Province: Studies in the History and Historiography of Ideas* (Bloomington: Indiana University Press, 1985), 74–91.

17 Giovanni Arrighi, *The Long Twentieth Century: Money, Power and the Origins of Our Times* (London: Verso, 1994). Direct quotations are referenced in the text.

18 Arrighi, *The Long Twentieth Century*, 27–84.

19 Arrighi, *The Long Twentieth Century*, 46–58.

20 Arrighi, *The Long Twentieth Century*, 47–74 and 269–300.

21 Arrighi, *The Long Twentieth Century*, 64–66.

22 Arrighi, *The Long Twentieth Century*, 269–300.

23 On the English insistence that their academies were less 'theoretical' and more liberal than their European counterparts, see Colin Trodd, 'Academic Cultures: The Royal Academy and the Commerce of Discourse in Victorian London', in *Art and the Academy in the Nineteenth Century*, ed. Rafael Cardoso Denis and Colin Trodd (Manchester: Manchester University Press, 2000), 179–193.

24 On the modernist avant-gardes, see Renato Poggioli, *The Theory of the Avant-Garde*, trans. Gerald Fitzgerald (Cambridge, MA: Harvard University Press, 1968 [1962]); Matei Calinescu, *Five Faces of Modernity: Modernism, Avant-Garde, Decadence, Kitsch, Postmodernism* (Durham, NC: Duke University Press, 1987 [1977]); and Peter Bürger, *Theory of the Avant-Garde*, trans. Michael Shaw (Minneapolis: University of Minnesota Press, 1984). See also Perry Anderson, 'Modernity and Revolution', in *Marxism and the Interpretation of Culture*, ed. Cary Nelson and Lawrence Grossberg (Urbana: University of Illinois Press, 1988), 317–338.

25 On this topic, see Priscilla Meyer, *How the Russians Read the French: Lermontov, Dostoevsky, Tolstoy* (Madison: University of Wisconsin Press, 2008), and Leonid Livak, *How It Was Done in Paris: Russian Émigré Literature and French Modernism* (Madison: University of Wisconsin Press, 2003).

26 See Katerina Clark, *Moscow, The Fourth Rome: Stalinism, Cosmopolitanism, and the Evolution of Soviet Culture, 1931–1941* (Cambridge, MA: Harvard University Press, 2011), 172, and chapter 5 more generally.

27 The works of Georg Lukács represent the most widely read example of this conception of literary history. See in particular *The Historical Novel*, trans. Hannah and Stanley Mitchell (Lincoln: University of Nebraska Press, 1962 [1938]) and *Studies in European Realism*, trans. Edith Bone (London: The Merlin Press, 1972 [1950]).

28 For an analysis of the ways in which Soviet intellectuals remained fascinated with Paris and Western culture, see Eleonary Gilburd, *To See Paris and Die: The Soviet Lives of Western Culture* (Cambridge, MA: Harvard University Press, 2018).

29 For useful overviews, see James McFarlane, 'Berlin and the Rise of Modernism, 1886–96', in *Modernism: 1890–1930*, ed. Malcolm Bradbury and James McFarlane (Harmondsworth: Penguin Books, 1976), 105–119, and Charles W. Haxthausen and Heidrun Suhr, eds., *Berlin: Culture and Metropolis* (Minneapolis: University of Minnesota Press, 1990).

30 See Franz Kuna, 'Vienna and Prague, 1890–1928', in *Modernism: 1890–1930*, ed. Malcolm Bradbury and James McFarlane, 120–133, and Marjorie Perloff, *Edge of Irony: Modernism in the Shadow of the Habsburg Empire* (Chicago: University of Chicago Press, 2016). The classic overview of Viennese modernism remains Carl E. Schorske, *Fin-De-Siécle Vienna: Politics and Culture* (New York: Vintage Books, 1981 [1961]).

31 See Eric Cahm, 'Revolt, Conservatism and Reaction in Paris, 1905–25', in *Modernism: 1890–1930*, ed. Malcolm Bradbury and James McFarlane, 162–171, 167.

32 See 'The Situation of the Writer in 1947', in *'What Is Literature?' and Other Essays* (Cambridge, MA: Harvard University Press, 1988), 141–238, 189. All other references are to this edition and page numbers are cited in the text. For Casanova, Sartre's great fame and refusal of the Nobel Prize in 1964 are evidence of Paris's continuing post–World War II global prestige. In a limited sense, she is right, but Sartre's more sober analysis attests that a situation can continue to look the same for a while even after circumstances have in fact fundamentally altered. Casanova's work ignores Moscow and the Soviet world and downplays the rise of New York and the United States. Sartre, writing in 1947, makes no such errors.

33 Ewan Horowitz, 'London: Capital of the Nineteenth Century', *New Literary History* 41: 1 (Winter 2010): 111–128, 114. Further references are included in the text. See also Malcolm Bradbury, 'London, 1890–1920', in *Modernism: 1890–1930*, ed. Bradbury and McFarlane, 172–190. On the artistic bohemias in Paris and London, see Jerrold E. Seigel, *Bohemian Paris: Culture, Politics, and the Boundaries of Bourgeois Life, 1830–1930* (New York: Penguin, 1987), and Peter Brooker, *Bohemia in London: The Social Scene of Early Modernism* (Basingstoke: Palgrave Macmillan, 2004).

34 Walter Benjamin, *The Arcades Project*, trans. Howard Eiland and Kevin McLaughlin (Cambridge, MA: Belknap Press of Harvard University Press, 1999), 26. On Paris more generally, see also Walter Benjamin, 'Paris, the Capital of the Nineteenth Century' and 'The Paris of the Second Empire in Baudelaire', in *The Writer of Modern Life: Essays on Charles Baudelaire*, trans. Howard Eiland (Cambridge, MA: Belknap Press of Harvard University Press, 2006).

35 On the role of émigré writers in English modernism, see Terry Eagleton, *Exiles and Émigrés: Studies in Modern Literature* (London: Chatto and Windus, 1970).

36 On Irish emigration and diaspora, see Timothy W. Guinnane, *The Vanishing Irish: Household, Migration, and the Rural Economy in Ireland, 1850–1914* (Princeton, NJ: Princeton University Press, 1997).

37 William Dean Howells, *Literature and Life: Studies* (New York: Harper and Brothers, 1902), 174. Further references are included in the text.

38 Van Wyck Brooks, *Letters and Leadership* (New York: B. W. Huebsch, 1918), xi–xii. All further references are to this edition and page numbers are cited in the text.

39 Major contemporary studies of the Irish Literary Revival include Declan Kiberd, *Inventing Ireland* (London: Jonathan Cape, 1995) and P. J. Mathews, *Revival: The Abbey Theatre, Sinn Féin, the Gaelic League and the Co-operative Movement* (Cork: Cork University Press, 2003). For a summary overview, see Emer Nolan, 'Modernism and the Irish Revival', in *The Cambridge Companion to Modern Irish Culture*, ed. Joe Cleary and Claire Connolly (Cambridge: Cambridge University Press, 2005), 157–172.

40 See Ann Douglas, *Terrible Honesty: Mongrel Manhattan in the 1920s* (New York: Farrar, Straus and Giroux, 1995), 4.

41  Douglas, *Terrible Honesty*, 14.
42  On the Harlem Renaissance, see David Levering Lewis, *When Harlem Was in Vogue* (Oxford: Oxford University Press, 1981); Jervis Anderson, *This Was Harlem: A Cultural Project 1900–1950* (New York: Farrar, Straus and Giroux, 1982); and Houston A. Baker, Jr., *Modernism and the Harlem Renaissance* (Chicago: University of Chicago Press, 1987). See also Douglas, *Terrible Honesty*, chapters 2, 8 and 10.
43  On Greenwich Village, see Douglas, *Terrible Honesty*, 18–21. And on London, see Brooker, *Bohemia in London* and Michael K. Walsh, ed., *London, Modernism, and 1914* (Cambridge: Cambridge University Press, 2010).
44  On American and African American literary expatriation in Paris in this era, see J. Gerald Kennedy, *Imagining Paris: Exile, Writing and American Identity* (New Haven: Yale University Press, 1993); Michel Fabre, *From Harlem to Paris: Black American Writers in France, 1840–1980* (Urbana: University of Illinois Press, 1991); and Brent Hayes Edwards, *The Practice of Diaspora: Literature, Translation, and the Rise of Black Internationalism* (Cambridge, MA: Harvard University Press, 2003).
45  On the American exiles in London, see Alan Holder, *Three Voyagers in Search of Europe: A Study of Henry James, Ezra Pound, and T.S. Eliot* (Philadelphia: University of Pennsylvania Press, 1966); Stanley Weintraub, *The London Yankees: Portraits of American Writers and Artists in England, 1894–1914* (New York: Harcourt Brace Jovanovich, 1979); and Alex Zwerdling, *Improvised Europeans: American Literary Expatriates and the Siege of London* (New York: Basic Books, 1998).
46  On English resistances to modernism, see Perry Anderson, *English Questions* (London: Verso, 1992), chapter 2, and Gabriel Josipovici, *What Ever Happened to Modernism?* (New Haven: Yale University Press, 2010).
47  T. S. Eliot, 'The Three Provincialities', *The Tyro* 2 (1922): 11–12.
48  Geoffrey Elton, *Notebook in Wartime* (London: Collins, 1941), cited in Leonard Diepeveen, *The Difficulties of Modernism* (London: Routledge, 2003), 104.
49  Jed Esty, *A Shrinking Island: Modernism and National Culture in England* (Princeton, NJ: Princeton University Press, 2004), 3.
50  Howells, cited in Alex Zwerdling, 'The European Capitals of American Culture', *The Wilson Quarterly* 17: 1 (Winter 1993): 126–136, 133.
51  James, cited in Zwerdling, 'The European Capitals of American Culture', 133.
52  See, for example, Ehrhard Bahr, *Weimar on the Pacific: German Exile Culture in Los Angeles and the Crisis of Modernism* (Berkeley: University of California Press, 2007).
53  On American Cold War cultural politics and modernism, see variously Serge Guibault, *How New York Stole the Idea of Modern Art: Abstract Expressionism, Freedom, and the Cold War*, trans. Arthur Goldhammer (Chicago: University of Chicago Press, 1983); Frances Stoner Saunders, *Who Paid the Piper?: The CIA and the Cultural Cold War* (London: Granta Books, 1999); Robert

Genter, *Late Modernism: Art, Culture, and Politics in Cold War America* (Philadelphia: University of Pennsylvania Press, 2010); Andrew N. Rubin, *Archives of Authority: Empire, Culture, and the Cold War* (Princeton, NJ: Princeton University Press, 2012); and Greg Barnhisel, *Cold War Modernists: Art, Literature, and American Cultural Diplomacy* (New York: Columbia University Press, 2015).

54 Lewis Mumford, *The Golden Day: A Study in American Literature and Culture* (Boston: Beacon Press, 1957 [1926]), 107–108.

55 F. Scott Fitzgerald, 'Echoes of the Jazz Age' (1931), in *The Crack-Up: With Other Uncollected Pieces, Note-books and Unpublished Letters*, ed. Edmund Wilson (New York: J. Laughlin, 1945), 14.

56 Edmund Wilson, *Axel's Castle: A Study of the Imaginative Literature of 1870–1930* (New York: Farrar, Straus and Giroux, 2014 [1931]).

57 Edmund Wilson, *Letters on Literature and Politics, 1912–1972*, ed. Elena Wilson (New York: Farrar, Straus and Giroux, 1977), 149–151, 151. All further references are to this edition and page numbers are cited in the text.

58 Zwerdling, 'The European Capitals of American Culture', 133.

59 John Peale Bishop, 'The Arts in America', in *The Collected Essays of John Peale Bishop*, ed. Edmund Wilson (New York: Charles Scribner's Sons, 1948), 166–174, 166. All further references are to this edition and page numbers are cited in the text.

60 For more on this matter, see Joe Cleary, 'Realism after Modernism and the Literary World-System', *Modern Language Quarterly* 73: 3 (2012): 255–268.

61 For Casanova's account of the assimilated writer, see *The World Republic of Letters*, chapter 7.

62 See Andrew Gibson, *Joyce's Revenge: History, Politics, and Aesthetics in* Ulysses (Oxford: Oxford University Press, 2002).

63 James Joyce, *Ulysses: The Corrected Text*, ed. Hans Walter Gabler (New York: Vintage Books, 1986 [1922]), 28.

64 See, however, my 'Irish American Modernisms', in *The Cambridge Companion to Irish Modernism*, ed. Joe Cleary (Cambridge: Cambridge University Press, 2014), 174–192, and Tara Stubbs, *American Literature and Irish Culture, 1910–1955: The Politics of Enchantment* (Manchester: Manchester University Press, 2013).

65 The classic accounts of Victorian conceptions of the Irish are L. Perry Curtis's *Anglo-Saxons and Celts: A Study of Anti-Irish Prejudice in Victorian England* (Bridgeport, CT: University of Bridgeport, 1968), and *Apes and Angels: The Irishman in Victorian Caricature*, rev. ed. (Washington, DC: Smithsonian Institution Press, 1997). On how the Irish became 'white', see David R. Roediger, *The Wages of Whiteness: Race and the Making of the American Working Class* (London: Verso, 1991); Noel Ignatiev, *How the Irish Became White* (New York: Routledge, 1995); and Matthew Pratt Guterl, *The Color of Race in America, 1900–1940* (Cambridge, MA: Harvard University Press, 2001).

66 See Mark McGurl, *The Program Era: Postwar Fiction and the Rise of Creative Writing* (Cambridge, MA: Harvard University Press, 2009).

## Chapter 2

1 Cited in James Pethica, ed., *Yeats's Poetry, Drama, and Prose* (New York: W. W. Norton, 2000), 261–262.

2 Ezra Pound, *Patria Mia* (Chicago: Ralph Fletcher Seymour, 1950), 32–33. All further references are to this edition and are cited in the text.

3 For useful general overviews on these events and movements, see Bernard Bailyn, *The Ideological Origins of the American Revolution* (Cambridge, MA: Belknap Press of Harvard University Press, 1967); David Dickson, Dáire Keogh and Kevin Whelan, eds., *United Irishmen: Republicanism, Radicalism and Rebellion* (Dublin: Lilliput Press, 1993); Thomas Bartlett et al., eds., *1798: A Bicentenary Perspective* (Dublin: Four Courts Press, 2003). On North American Fenians, see Patrick Steward and Bryan McGovern, *The Fenians: Irish Rebellion in the North Atlantic World, 1858–1876* (Knoxville: University of Tennessee Press, 2013).

4 On the nativist versions of American modernism, see Walter Benn Michaels, *Our America: Nativism, Modernism, and Pluralism* (Durham: Duke University Press, 1995), and for an Ascendancy-focused overview of the Irish Revival and modernism, see W. J. McCormack, *Ascendancy and Tradition in Anglo-Irish Literary History from 1789 to 1939* (Oxford: Clarendon Press, 1985).

5 See Perry Anderson, 'Modernity and Revolution', *New Left Review* I: 144 (March/April 1984): 96–113. For a cogent summary of the critical literature on these topics, see Janice Ho, 'The Crisis of Liberalism and the Politics of Modernism', *Literature Compass* 8: 1 (2011): 47–65.

6 The choice of Tocqueville and Arnold as key intellectual sources for the prehistory of American and Irish modernisms is to some extent selective because the multiple crosscutting intellectual discourses that contributed to these respective literary 'renaissances' are obviously more intricate than any single chapter can chart. Tocqueville and Arnold both owe debts to Edmund Burke, for example, and to various other European liberal and conservative traditions that cannot be considered here. Nevertheless, Tocqueville's and Arnold's centrality to late nineteenth-century developments in Irish and American cultural nationalisms, and to the modernisms that responded critically to those nationalisms, is not to be underestimated and the topic is still under-researched. Gustave de Beaumont and Tocqueville are best known for their work on the United States, but both were also fascinated by Ireland and Irish experiments in liberal democratic politics within the United Kingdom, and Arnold wrote on both Ireland and America. For some key works, see Alexis de Tocqueville, *Alexis de Tocqueville's Journey in Ireland, July–August, 1835*, trans. and ed. Emmet Larkin (Washington, DC: Catholic University of America Press, 1990); Gustave de Beaumont, *Ireland: Social, Political and Religious*, trans. W. C. Taylor (Cambridge, MA: Belknap Press of Harvard University Press, 2006); Matthew Arnold, *The Study of Celtic Literature* (London: Smith, Elder, & Co., 1900 [1867]); Arnold, *Irish Essays and Others* (London: Smith, Elder, & Co., 1882); and Arnold, *Discourses in*

*America* (London: Macmillan, 1984 [1885]); and 'Civilization in the United States', *Nineteenth Century* 23 (April 1888): 481–496. For accounts of Arnold's impact on Irish cultural nationalism, see Seamus Deane, *Celtic Revivals: Essays in Modern Irish Literature, 1880–1980* (London: Faber and Faber, 1985), and *Strange Country: Modernity and Nationhood in Irish Writing Since 1790* (Oxford: Clarendon Press, 1997). For Tocqueville and American culture, I have drawn most heavily on Sheldon Wolin, *Tocqueville between Two Worlds: The Making of a Political and Theoretical Life* (Princeton, NJ: Princeton University Press, 2001), and Lucien Jaume, *Tocqueville and the Aristocratic Sources of Liberty*, trans. Arthur Goldhammer (Princeton, NJ: Princeton University Press, 2013).

7 See Alexis de Tocqueville, *Democracy in America and Two Essays on America*, trans. Gerald E. Bevan (London: Penguin Books, 2003), 508. All further references are to this edition and are cited in the text.

8 The relationship between the novel and journalism touched on by Tocqueville has a long history in British and American literatures, and the importance of later journalists such as Mark Twain, Stephen Crane or Ernest Hemingway to the development of a more distinctively American national literary idiom might seem to bear out Tocqueville's remarks. On related topics, see John C. Harstock, *A History of American Literary Journalism: The Emergence of a Modern Narrative Form* (Amherst: University of Massachusetts Press, 2000), and Richard Keeble and Sharon Wheeler, eds., *The Journalistic Imagination: Literary Journalism from Defoe to Capote and Carter* (London: Routledge, 2007).

9 For a useful summary of Tocqueville's American reception, see Matthew J. Mancini, *Alexis de Tocqueville and American Intellectuals: From His Times to Ours* (New York: Rowman & Littlefield, 2006), and on his European intellectual sources, see Lucien Jaume, *Tocqueville and the Aristocratic Sources of Liberty*.

10 Thoughtful general studies of the complexities of nineteenth- and early twentieth-century Anglo-American literary relations include Robert Weisbuch, *Atlantic Double-Cross: American Literature and British Influence in the Age of Emerson* (Chicago: University of Chicago Press, 1986); Leonard Tennenhouse, *The Importance of Feeling English: American Literature and the British Diaspora, 1750–1850* (Princeton, NJ: Princeton University Press, 2007); Laura Doyle, *Freedom's Empire: Race and the Rise of the Novel in Atlantic Modernity, 1640–1940* (Durham, NC: Duke University Press, 2008); and Brook Miller, *America and the British Imaginary in Turn-of-the-Twentieth-Century Literature* (New York: Palgrave Macmillan, 2010).

11 Wolin, *Tocqueville Between Two Worlds*, 316. All further references are cited in the text.

12 On Tocqueville and later conceptions of American society, see Claus Offe, *Reflections on America: Tocqueville, Weber and Adorno in the United States*, trans. Patrick Camiller (Cambridge: Polity Press, 2005).

13 Matthew Arnold, *The Study of Celtic Literature* (London: Smith, Elder & Co, 1900 [1867]), 5. All further references are to this edition and are cited in the text. For wider studies of Arnold, see Lionel Trilling, *Matthew Arnold* (New

York: Columbia University Press, 1949), and Stefan Collini, *Arnold* (Oxford: Oxford University Press, 1988). On Arnold and Celtic literature, see Rachel Bromwich, *Matthew Arnold and Celtic Literature: A Retrospect 1865–1965* (Oxford: Clarendon Press, 1965), and Deane, *Celtic Revivals*.

14 The complex family romance underlying Arnold's attitude to things Celtic is worth noting. In the early pages of his lecture he refers to his father, Thomas Arnold, a militant Saxonist, and recalls: '[W]hen I was young, I was taught to think of Celt as separated by an impassable gulf from Teuton; my father in particular, was never weary of contrasting them; he insisted much oftener on the separation between us and them than on the separation between us and any other race in the world; in the same way Lord Lyndhurst, in words long famous, called the Irish "aliens in speech, in religion, in blood"' (14-15). However, Arnold's mother, Mary Penrose, was of Cornish extraction and one of her son's biographers notes that Arnold wrote in 1859 to his sister Lucy on their family roots remarking, 'I have long felt that we owed far more, spiritually and artistically, to the Celtic races than to the somewhat coarse Germanic intelligence readily perceived, and become increasingly satisfied at our own semi-Celtic origin, which, as I fancy, gives us the power, if we will use it, of comprehending the nature of both races'. The unmarked 'we' here, as Joep Leerssen notes, can refer to the Arnold family specifically or to the English generally, but Arnold's conception of his own hybridity is clear. See Clinton Machann, *Matthew Arnold: A Literary Life* (Basingstoke: Macmillan, 1998), 65–66, and Joep Leerssen, 'Englishness, Ethnicity and Matthew Arnold', *European Journal of English Studies* 10: 1 (2006): 63–79, 71–72.

15 Matthew Arnold, *The Popular Education of France* (London: Longman, Green, Longman and Roberts, 1861), 169. All further references are to this edition and pages numbers are cited in the text.

16 Arnold's *Discourses in America* is an unoriginal, sub-Tocquevillian work that reiterates long-standing English truisms about American cultural dependence and lack of sophistication. Franklin and Emerson are cited as promising exceptions to the low literary attainment of the United States but neither is regarded as comparable to the best European writers. Arnold's admiration for Emerson, the only writer he considers extensively, comes with a reiterated insistence that he is not 'a great poet, a great writer, a great philosophy-maker'. However, Emerson's *Essays* are preferred for their optimism to Carlyle's distempered disdain for happiness, and Emerson's value 'for both the branches of our race' is stressed. Arnold, *Discourses in America*, 29, 32.

17 For more detailed studies of Arnold's deployment of nineteenth-century race, ethnic and religious discourses, see Fredric E. Faverty, *Matthew Arnold, the Ethnologist* (Evanston: Northwestern University Press, 1951); Robert J. C. Young, *Colonial Desire: Hybridity in Theory, Culture and Race* (London: Routledge, 1995); Miriam Leonard, *Socrates and the Jews: Hellenism and Hebraism from Moses Mendelssohn to Sigmund Freud* (Chicago: University of Chicago Press, 2012); and Edward Alexander, *Classical Liberalism & the Jewish Tradition* (New Brunswick: Transaction Publishers, 2003).

18 On Celticism in the United States and its impact on several American 'renaissances', see Michael Soto, *The Modernist Nation: Generation, Renaissance, and Twentieth-Century American Literature* (Tuscaloosa: University of Alabama Press, 2004), chapter 2.

19 Henry James, *Hawthorne* (New York: AMS Press, 1969 [1887]), 43–44.

20 Critics have disagreed on how to interpret this work's significance. Most have viewed it in terms of a Bloomian 'anxiety of influence' psychodrama whereby James has to purge himself of a significant paternal but provincial predecessor to establish his more cosmopolitan credentials. Gordon Fraser partially disputes this reading and asserts that James writes, rather, with a canny eye to the English literary establishment, promoting Hawthorne's accomplishments while acknowledging his defects, but nevertheless insisting on the growing merits of American literature and thus positioning himself to take up a prominent place as Hawthorne's successor in a transatlantic marketplace. Michael Anesko adds a fascinating twist by arguing that James's *Hawthorne* plagiarizes from French critic Émile Montégut's *Nathaniel Hawthorne* (Paris: J Laisné, 1866). In this account, Montégut displayed a Tocquevillian interest in 'the problematic nature of democratic individualism' (38) and had written many essays on American literature. For Anesko, James and, later, T. S. Eliot were both keen to camouflage Montégut's influence on their respective versions of Hawthorne. Anesko's reading evidences Tocqueville's ongoing influence on European and American conceptions of American letters. However, it also supports Pascale Casanova's stress on the importance of French critical approval to the establishment of non-French writers in the nineteenth and twentieth centuries. See Gordon Fraser, 'The Anxiety of Audience: Economies of Readership in James's *Hawthorne*', *The Henry James Review* 34: 1 (Winter 2013): 1–15, and Michael Anesko, 'Is James's Hawthorne Really *James's* Hawthorne?', *The Henry James Review* 29: 1 (Winter 2008): 36–53.

21 John Dos Passos, 'Against American Literature', *The New Republic*, 14 October 1916, 269–271, 270.

22 T. S. Eliot, cited in Tony Tanner, 'American Canon', *boundary 2* 37: 2 (2010): 71–87, 73.

23 Amy Lowell, *Tendencies in Modern American Poetry* (New York: Macmillan, 1917), 5.

24 James Joyce, 'The Day of the Rabblement', in *Occasional, Critical, and Political Writing*, ed. Kevin Barry (Oxford: Oxford University Press, 2000), 50–52, 50.

25 W. B. Yeats, 'Hopes and Fears for Irish Literature', in *Uncollected Prose by W. B. Yeats: First Reviews and Articles 1886–1896*, vol. 1, ed. John P. Frayne (New York: Columbia University Press, 1970), 247–250, 248. All further page references to this reported account of Yeats's lecture appear in the text.

26 W. B. Yeats, 'Nationality and Literature', in *Uncollected Prose by W. B. Yeats*, ed. Frayne, 266–275, 268.

27 W. B. Yeats, 'The Celtic Element in Literature', in *W. B. Yeats: Early Essays*, ed. George Bornstein and Richard J. Finneran (New York: Scribner, 2007), 128–138, 129. All further page references appear in the text.

28 Ezra Pound, *Patria Mia*, 21. All further page references are to this edition and appear in the text. Pound sent this work to Chicago in 1913 but it was lost when the firm was dissolved and was not published until thirty-seven years later. However, in 1915, *Poetry* magazine published three articles with the titles 'The Renaissance: I – the Palette' (*Poetry* 5: 5 (Feb 1915): 227–234), 'The Renaissance II' (*Poetry* 5: 6 (Mar 1915): 283–287), and 'The Renaissance: III' (*Poetry* 6: 2 (May 1915): 84–91), and these cover similar ground.

29 For wider discussions of Pound's reflections on American art, education and criticism, see Stephen G. Yao and Michael Coyle, eds., *Ezra Pound and Education* (Orono: National Poetry Foundation, 2012); Cary Wolfe, *The Limits of American Literary Ideology in Pound and Emerson* (Cambridge: Cambridge University Press, 1993); and K. K. Ruthven, *Ezra Pound as Literary Critic* (London: Routledge, 1990).

30 As is well known, Pound and Yeats were intimates in this period and wintered together in Stone Cottage, Sussex, from 1913 to 1916. How they mutually influenced each other is debated, but see especially James Longenbach, *Stone Cottage: Pound, Yeats and Modernism* (New York: Oxford University Press, 1988).

31 Pound writes, 'At any rate, it does not lie within the scope of this essay to deal with the possible status of the arts under socialism, or to consider the possibilities of any new form of government, or to consider absolute justice and the rights of active and passive property. I write barefacedly. You may call me an opportunist if it gives you the least taint of pleasure or of satisfaction', *Patria Mia*, 69.

32 'As for "The Humanities", the courses in these branches would seem to draw a preponderance of the dullest or weakest of the students, to wit, men who at worst want to become schoolmasters, and, at best, professors. And even then they are subjected to a system which aims at mediocrity, which is set to crush out all impulse and personality; which aims to make not men but automata', *Patria Mia*, 80.

33 See Mark McGurl, *The Program Era: Postwar Fiction and the Rise of Creative Writing* (Cambridge, MA: Harvard University Press, 2009).

34 For a recent study on modernism and decadence, see Vincent Sherry, *Modernism and the Reinvention of Decadence* (Cambridge: Cambridge University Press, 2015).

35 See Michael Soto, *The Modernist Nation*, 58 and 188, note 7. Soto notes that before F. O. Matthiessen's *American Renaissance: Art and Expression in the Age of Emerson and Whitman* (London: Oxford University Press, 1941), the '"American Renaissance" of the nineteenth century was universally called the "New England Renaissance"' (188). Soto contends that the Irish Revival had a major impact on American criticism and literature and suggests that Irish influence 'can be traced along a direct line from Dublin and London to

Boston, New York and Philadelphia' (65). Irish writing found important receptions in the works of Van Wyck Brooks and Cornelius Weygandt as well as in the more nationalist American literary journals generally. On links between the Irish and Harlem Renaissances, see Tracy Mishkin, *The Harlem and Irish Renaissances: Language, Identity, and Representation* (Gainesville: University Press of Florida, 1998).

36 Valery Larbaud, 'The Rebirth of American Poetry', *The Living Age* 311 (1921): 589–594. Cited in Soto, *Modernist Nation*, 73.

37 For a sense of 1922 as watershed, see Michael North, *Reading 1922: A Return to the Scene of the Modern* (New York: Oxford University Press, 1999), 3–30.

38 On liberalism and empire, see Uday Singh Mehta, *Liberalism and Empire: A Study in Nineteenth-Century British Liberal Thought* (Chicago: University of Chicago Press, 1999); Jennifer Pitts, *A Turn to Empire: The Rise of Imperial Liberalism in Britain and France* (Princeton, NJ: Princeton University Press, 2005); and Duncan Bell, *Reordering the World: Essays on Liberalism and Empire* (Princeton, NJ: Princeton University Press, 2016).

## Chapter 3

1 William Dean Howells, 'American Literature in Exile', *Literature and Life* (New York and London: Harper & Brothers Publishers, 1902), 202–205, 203.

2 Frank Norris, 'The Frontier Gone at Last', *The World's Work*, February 1902, cited in Frank Norris, *Novels and Essays* (New York: Literary Classics of the United States, 1986), 1183–1190, 1187. All further references are to this edition and page references are cited in the text.

3 Ezra Pound, 'Date Line', in *Literary Essays of Ezra Pound*, ed. T. S. Eliot (New York: New Directions, 1996), 74–90, 82. For key texts on this topic see: Daniel Katz, *American Modernism's Expatriate Scene: The Labour of Translation* (Edinburgh: Edinburgh University Press, 2007); Alex Zwerdling, *Improvised Europeans: American Literary Expatriates in London* (New York: Basic Books, 1998); Stanley Weintraub, *London Yankees: Portraits of American Writers and Artists in England, 1894–1914* (New York: Harcourt Brace Jovanovich, 1979); and Alan Holder, *Three Voyagers in Search of Europe: A Study of Henry James, Ezra Pound, and T. S. Eliot* (Philadelphia: University of Pennsylvania Press, 1966).

4 George Moore, *Confessions of a Young Man* (1888), 254–255. Cited in James E. Miller Jr., *T. S. Eliot: The Making of an American Poet, 1888–1922* (University Park: Pennsylvania State University Press, 2005), 224.

5 Pascale Casanova, *The World Republic of Letters*, trans. M. B. DeBevoise (Cambridge, MA: Harvard University Press, 2004 [1999]), 205–219, 207. Page references are cited in the text.

6 Cited in Lyndall Gordon, *Eliot's Early Years* (Oxford: Oxford University Press, 1977), 83–84.

7  Henry Adams, *The Education of Henry Adams* (New York: The Heritage Press, 1918 [1907]), 298.

8  On the ways in which James, Pound and Eliot adapted or failed to adapt to English society, see Zwerdling and Holder, cited in note 3.

9  See Franklin Henry Giddings, *Democracy and Empire* (New York: Macmillan, 1901); Brooks Adams, *The New Empire* (New York: Macmillan, 1902); John R. Dos Passos, *The Anglo-Saxon Century and the Unification of the English-Speaking People* (New York: G. P. Putnam's Sons, 1903); Theodore Roosevelt, *National Strength and International Duty* (Princeton, NJ: Princeton University Press, 1917); and James Truslow Adams, *The Epic of America* (Boston: Little, Brown, 1931). More generally, see Stuart Anderson, *Race and Rapprochement: Anglo-Saxonism and Anglo-American Relations, 1895–1904* (London: Associated University Presses, 1981).

10  Giovanni Arrighi, *The Long Twentieth Century: Money, Power and the Origins of Our Times* (London: Verso, 1994), chapter 1 and pp. 28–37 especially.

11  Joseph Conrad, *Nostromo: A Tale of the Seaboard* (London: Penguin Classics, 2007 [1904]), 62–63.

12  For useful studies of finance, reification and commodification in these works, see Stephen Ross, *Conrad and Empire* (Columbia: University of Missouri Press, 2004); Jonathan Freedman, 'The Decadent Henry James: British Aestheticism and the Major Phase', in *Professions of Taste: Henry James, British Aestheticism, and Commodity Culture* (Stanford: Stanford University Press, 1990), 202–260; and Miranda El-Rayess, *Henry James and the Culture of Consumption* (New York: Cambridge University Press, 2014).

13  Henry James, *The Golden Bowl* (New York: Alfred A. Knopf, 1992 [1904]), 5. All further references are to this edition and page references are cited in the text.

14  See Margery Sabin, 'Competition of Intelligence in *The Golden Bowl*', in *The Dialect of the Tribe: Speech and Community in Modern Fiction* (Oxford: Oxford University Press, 1987), 65–105.

15  As well as Sabin just cited, my reading of *The Golden Bowl* is informed by Margery Sabin, 'Henry James's American Dream in *The Golden Bowl*', in *The Cambridge Companion to Henry James,* ed., Jonathan Freedman (Cambridge: Cambridge University Press, 1998), 204–223; Thomas Peyser, 'The Imperial Museum', in *Utopia & Cosmopolis: Globalization in the Era of American Literary Realism* (Durham, NC: Duke University Press, 1998), 135–168; Mark Seltzer, '"The Vigilance of Care"', in *Henry James and the Art of Power* (Ithaca: Cornell University Press, 1984), 59–95; Jonathan Freedman, 'The Decadent Henry James: British Aestheticism and the Major Phase', in *Professions of Taste*; and Ruth Bernard Yeazell, *Language and Knowledge in the Late Novels of Henry James* (Chicago: University of Chicago Press, 1976).

16  Arno J. Mayer, *The Persistence of the Old Regime: Europe to the Great War* (New York: Pantheon Books, 1981).

17  On Bob Assingham as a symptom of British imperial decline, see Stephen D. Arata, 'Object Lessons: Reading the Museum in *The Golden Bowl*', in *Famous Last Words: Changes in Gender and Narrative Closure,* ed. Alison Booth

(Charlottesville: University of Virginia Press, 1993), 199–229, 205–206 especially.

18 On James's attitude to Adam Verver, see Sabin, 'Henry James's American Dream in *The Golden Bowl*', 210, and on the United States as generalized space, see William Righter, 'Amerigo in an American Nowhere', in *American Memory in Henry James: Void and Value*, ed. Rosemary Righter (London: Routledge, 2004), 99–124.

19 On Chinese references in *The Golden Bowl*, see Kendall Johnson, 'James and the China Trade', *Modern Fiction Studies* 60: 4 (Winter 2014): 677–710.

20 In his Foucauldian reading of James, Seltzer remarks: 'The well-policed character of the "world" of *The Golden Bowl* is at once readily apparent and difficult to assess, apparent in that the novel displays the nexus of seeing, knowing and exercising power that, I have argued, defines the politics of the Jamesian text, problematic in that police work and supervision in the novel are so thoroughly inscribed in gestures of compassion, care, and love' (62–63). For Seltzer, surveillance is critical to both *The Princess Casamassima* and to *The Golden Bowl*, but policing and penal institutes are fundamental to the earlier novel, an internalized policing of self and others to the later one. This is persuasive but in focusing on power/knowledge and control/love, Seltzer devotes only passing attention to the roles of wealth or to the international dynamics of *The Golden Bowl*. Seltzer, '"The Vigilance of Care"', 59–95.

21 Arrighi, *The Long Twentieth Century*, 59–84, especially 66–67. Arrighi's distinction between conservative, reformist and reactionary tendencies in the period builds on Arno Mayer, *Dynamics of Counterrevolution in Europe, 1870–1956: An Analytic Framework* (New York: Harper and Row, 1971).

22 Giuseppe Tomasi di Lampedusa, *The Leopard*, trans. Archibald Colquhoun (London: William Collins and Random House, 1988 [1958]), 28.

23 See, for example, Christof Wegelin, 'The Sublime Consensus', in *The Image of Europe in Henry James* (Dallas: South Methodist University Press, 1958), 122–140. Wegelin believes that the final triumph in the novel is a shared one for Maggie and Amerigo: 'It is at any rate not the triumph of America over Europe. Rather it is the triumphant complementing of one by the other' (135). Gore Vidal, in 'Return to *The Golden Bowl*', *The New York Review of Books*, 19 January 1984, 1–9, feels that victory clearly goes to Maggie and Adam. Of the end of the novel, he writes: 'They are again as one, this superbly monstrous couple' and 'it is enough that two splendid monsters have triumphed again over everyone else and, best of all, over mere human nature' (8). For Vidal, *The Golden Bowl* is a coldly imperial allegory of US domination whose 'spirit' nevertheless 'is not imperial so much as it is ambitiously divine' (9). 'At the end of Henry James's life', he writes, 'in a final delirium, he thought that he was the Emperor Napoleon; and as the Emperor, he gave detailed instructions for the redoing of the Tuileries and the Louvre: and died, head aswarm with golden and imperial visions' (9). In 'Henry James's American Dream in *The Golden Bowl*', Margery Sabin argues that: 'At the very end, James seems to back Maggie's way of pressing the spring of an

Amerigo now converted into a perfect doll of a husband'. However, Sabin asserts that 'James's more haunted total vision [. . .] shows how Maggie's triumph over abjection not only requires brutal domination of others, but also remains dominated by specters of what she has sought to banish and control' (221). Charlotte's dispatch to America confirms, for Sabin, 'the book's insuperable anxiety that America could not naturally come into a marriage with civilization. The very idea of civilization would have to be "sifted to sanctity" by more mysterious and horrifying translations, suppressions, and conversions before America could safely possess or even handle it' (221). These readings all appear plausible, but, however different they are, there seems consensus enough that American power – whether deemed complementary to Europe, domineering or domineering but troubled – is ascendant at the end of James's novel. My own sense is that *The Golden Bowl* offers a minor, comic and 'banal' version of the transatlantic union of Britain and the United States in the marriage of Fanny and Bob Assingham; a troubled one in the marriage of Adam Verver and Charlotte Stant, both somewhat mercenary Europeanized Americans; and a higher instance in the marriage of Maggie and Amerigo, European aristocrat firmly subordinate to his superior-minded wife. These different couplings allow for a variety of imagined outcomes, allowing James his usual twists and refusal to show a final hand.

24 On the history of American museums in this era, see Jeffrey Trask, *Things American: Art Museums and Civic Culture in the Progressive Era* (Philadelphia: University of Pennsylvania Press, 2012). Sergio Perosa tracks James's ambivalent reactions to American art collecting across his novelistic career in 'Henry James and Unholy Art Acquisitions', *The Cambridge Quarterly* 37: 1 (2008): 150–163.

25 See T. S. Eliot, *The Complete Poems and Plays, 1909–1950* (New York: Harcourt Brace and Company, 1967 [1950]), 50. I have used this edition throughout and all further page references will be cited in the text.

26 For postcolonial readings of the *The Waste Land*, see variously: Vincent Sherry, 'T. S. Eliot: 1910–1922', in *Modernism and the Reinvention of Decadence* (Cambridge: Cambridge University Press, 2015), 234–279; Jed Esty, 'Insular Time: T. S. Eliot and Modernism's English End', in *A Shrinking Island: Modernism and National Culture in England* (Princeton, NJ: Princeton University Press, 2004), 108–162; Joseph McLaughlin, '"What Are the Roots That Clutch": Money, Migration, and *The Waste Land*', in *Writing The Urban Jungle: Reading Empire in London from Doyle to Eliot* (Charlottesville: University of Virginia Press, 2000), 168–194; David Trotter, 'Modernism and Empire: Reading *The Waste Land*', in *Futures for English*, ed. Colin McCabe (Manchester: Manchester University Press, 1988), 143–153; and Eleanor Cook, 'T. S. Eliot and the Carthaginian Peace', *English Literary History* 46: 2 (Summer 1979): 341–355.

27 T. S. Eliot, 'Ezra Pound', in *An Examination of Ezra Pound*, ed. Peter Russell (New York: New Directions, 1950), 326–338, cited in James E. Miller Jr., *T. S. Eliot: The Making of an American Poet, 1888–1922*, 387.

28 T. S. Eliot, 'Letter to his Mother, 29 December 1918', in *The Letters of T. S. Eliot, 1898–1922*, vol. 1, ed. Valerie Eliot (New York: Harcourt Brace Jovanovich, 1988), 263–264, 264. All further letters in this period are taken from this volume and page numbers are cited in the text. On Eliot's involvements through Lloyd's with the post-war settlements in France, see Alexander Smith, 'The Literary Consequences of the Peace: T. S. Eliot, Ezra Pound, and the Treaty of Versailles' (doctoral dissertation, Columbia University, 2006), especially chapter 2, 'T. S. Eliot in the Hall of Mirrors', 81–144.

29 T. S. Eliot, 'Turgenev', *The Egoist* 4 (December 1917): 167. Cited in Louis Menand, *Discovering Modernism: T. S. Eliot And His Context* (Oxford: Oxford University Press, 1987), 123–124.

30 See 'Letter to Eleanor Hinkley, 1 April 1918': 'I am very glad you like James. [. . .] He is a wonderful conscientious artist, one of the very few, and more European than most English or Americans. [. . .] As a critic of America he is certainly unique' (226–228, 227). Further, in a 'Letter to his Mother, 2 June 1918', he writes, 'James was a fine writer – his book of impressions on America [*The American Scene*], written about 1907 I think, is wonderfully well written. There are so few people who will take the trouble to write well. It is full of acute criticism too' (232–233, 233).

31 T. S. Eliot, 'On Henry James', *The Little Review* (August 1918), collected in *The Question of Henry James: A Collection of Critical Essays*, ed. F. W. Dupee (New York: Henry Holt, 1945), 108–119, 108–109. Further citations are referenced in the text.

32 On this topic, see Jason Harding, The Criterion: *Cultural Politics and Periodical Networks in Inter-War Britain* (Oxford: Oxford University Press, 2002), and Jeroen Vanheste, *Guardians of the Humanist Legacy: The Classicism of T. S. Eliot's* Criterion *Network and Its Relevance to our Postmodern World* (Leiden: Brill, 2007).

33 T. S. Eliot, 'The Unity of European Culture', in *Notes Towards the Definition of Culture* (New York: Harcourt, Brace, 1949), 113–128, 121 and 122. All further references are cited in the text.

34 Eric Sigg, *The American T. S. Eliot: A Study of the Early Writings* (Cambridge: Cambridge University Press, 1989), 121. All further references are cited in the text.

35 T. S. Eliot, 'Burbank with a Baedeker, Bleistein with a Cigar', in *The Complete Poems and Plays, 1905–1950*, 23–24, 24.

36 On these and other distancing effects in *The Waste Land*, see Michael H. Levenson, *A Genealogy of Modernism: A Study of English Literary Doctrine, 1908–1922* (Cambridge: Cambridge University Press, 1984), 203.

37 Edmund Wilson, 'T. S. Eliot', in *Axel's Castle: A Study of the Imaginative Literature of 1870–1930* (New York: Farrar, Straus and Giroux, 2004 [1931]), 75–105, 82–83.

38 F. W. Bateson, 'T. S. Eliot and the Poetry of Pseudo-Learning', *The Journal of General Education* 20: 1 (April 1968): 13–27, 24.

39 T. S. Eliot, 'The Metaphysical Poets', in *Selected Prose of T. S. Eliot*, ed. Frank Kermode (London: Faber and Faber, 1975), 59–67, 65. All further references are to this edition and page numbers are cited in the text.

40 T. S. Eliot, 'Tradition and the Individual Talent', in *Selected Prose of T. S. Eliot*, ed. Kermode, 37–44, 38–39. Italics in the original. All further references are to this edition and page numbers are cited in the text.

41 Cited in Paul Douglass, 'T. S. Eliot's European Tradition: The Roles of Dante Alighieri and Matthew Arnold', in *T. S. Eliot, Dante, and the Idea of Europe*, ed. Paul Douglass (Newcastle upon Tyne: Cambridge Scholars Press, 2011), 133–145, 143.

42 Cook, 'T. S. Eliot and the Carthaginian Peace', 341–343.

43 Ezra Pound, 'Henry James', in *Literary Essays of Ezra Pound*, 295–398, 300.

44 On Eliot's erudition, see the contrasting views of F. W. Bateson, 'T. S. Eliot and the Poetry of Pseudo-Learning', cited in note 38, and William Arrowsmith, 'Eliot's Learning', *Literary Imagination: The Review of the Association of Literary Scholars and Critics* 2: 2 (2000): 153–170.

45 W. H. Auden, 'American Poetry', in *The Dyer's Hand and Other Essays* (New York: Vintage Books, 1978), 354–368, 366.

46 Franco Moretti's *Modern Epic: The World System from Goethe to García Marquez* (London and New York: Verso, 1995) lists *The Waste Land* on its opening page with an array of other 'epics' including '*Faust, Moby-Dick, The Nibelung's Ring, Ulysses, The Cantos,* [. . .] *The Man Without Qualities, One Hundred Years of Solitude*' as 'sacred texts' of the modern West and reads them as 'world texts' that map the modern supranational world system. For Moretti, a crucial feature of a 'world text' is that 'it's very long, and very boring' and thus it is typically 'an almost super-canonical form, yet one that is virtually unread'. Hence, too, 'world texts depend so closely upon scholastic institutions' for their propagation because 'they are not self-sufficient' and 'do not really work all that well' and are 'semi-failures' (1–5). Moretti doesn't mention that *The Waste Land* is so much slimmer than the other bulky works cited in his list and says little about Eliot's poem in *Modern Epic*. Nor does he deal further with the question of the university and that institution's training of specific kinds of readers despite drawing attention to it at the outset of his work. Part of my larger argument here is that *The Waste Land* invites and instructs a particular kind of diligent reader and that the work's compact brevity is part of its success, something that makes it much more likely to be read than, say, *Faust, Ulysses* or *The Cantos*. Its condensed size certainly makes *The Waste Land* better suited to the graduate seminar format.

47 See Harding, *The Criterion*, 207.

48 On Eliot's deposition of Arnold and remaking of himself as a new Arnold in higher key in *The Sacred Wood* and beyond, see Paul Douglass, 'T. S. Eliot's European Tradition', cited in note 41, and Perry Meisel, *The Myth of the Modern: A Study of British Literature and Criticism after 1850* (New Haven: Yale University Press, 1987), 71–120.

49 My sense of Eliot's later career owes debts to John Xiros Cooper, *T. S. Eliot and the Ideology of* Four Quartets (Cambridge: Cambridge University Press, 1995), though Xiros Cooper tends to downplay somewhat the American dimensions of that later career phase.

50 T. S. Eliot, 'The Man of Letters and the Future of Europe', *The Sewanee Review* 53: 3 (Summer 1945): 333–342, 336–337. Italics in the original. All further references are to this printing and page numbers are cited in the text.

51 Here, I differ to Jed Esty's reading of Eliot's career in *A Shrinking Island*, 108–162. For Esty, Eliot moves from a cosmopolitan internationalist high modernism in the 1920s towards a later insular retrenchment that seeks the organic wholeness never discoverable in the British Empire in a more self-contained domestic national culture. Eliot's ongoing concerns with both the United States and Europe sit awkwardly with this reading. On European intellectuals and the European idea in this era, see Mark Hewitson and Matthew D'Auria, eds., *Europe in Crisis: Intellectuals and the European Idea, 1917–1957* (New York: Berghahn Books, 2012).

52 See Max Horkheimer and Theodor W. Adorno, *Dialectic of Enlightenment*, trans. John Cumming (New York: Continuum, 2000 [1944]), and Erich Auerbach, 'The Philology of World Literature (1952)', in *Time, History and Literature: Selected Essays by Erich Auerbach*, ed. James I. Porter, trans. Jane O. Newman (Princeton, NJ: Princeton University Press, 2014), 253–265. Contemplating the spread of Anglo-American English globalization, Auerbach remarks: 'It may even happen that, within a comparatively short period of time, only a limited number of literary languages will continue to exist, soon perhaps only one. If this were to come to pass, the idea of world literature would simultaneously be realized and destroyed' (254).

53 See Donal Harris, 'Our Eliot: Mass Modernism and the American Century', in *On Company Time: Modernism in the Big Magazines* (New York: Columbia University Press, 2017), 141–172.

54 'Mr. Eliot', *Time* 55:10, 6 March 1950, 22–26.

55 Geoffrey Galt Harpham, *The Humanities and the Dream of America* (Chicago: University of Chicago Press, 2011), 154, and more widely 154–161. Further references are cited in the text.

56 Alex Beam, *A Great Idea at the Time: The Rise, Fall, and Curious Afterlife of the Great Books* (New York: Public Affairs, 2008), 1–5 and passim.

57 See Daniel Bell, *The Reforming of General Education: The Columbia College Experience in Its National Setting* (New York: Columbia University Press, 1966), 39. 'Just as the divisive experiences of World War I provided the impulse for the Contemporary Civilization course at Columbia College, similar troublesome problems confronting American schools during World War II prompted the establishment of the General Education Committee at Harvard. Such problems as "why we fight", the principles of a free society, the need to provide a consistent image of the American experience, the definition of democracy in a world of totalitarianism, the effort to fortify the heritage of Western civilization, and the need to provide a "common learning" for all

Americans as a foundation of national unity, were the factors that shaped the thinking of the Redbook' (39).

58 For the larger episode, see Travis Elborough, *London Bridge in America: The Tall Story of a Transatlantic Crossing* (London: Jonathan Cape, 2013).

## Chapter 4

1 'Shakespeare in Dublin', *Irish Times*, 24 March 2016, 4.

2 John Eglinton, 'The Beginnings of Joyce', in *Irish Literary Portraits* (London: Macmillan, 1935), 131–150, 145–146.

3 Cited in *Aristotle: Poetics*, ed. and trans. Stephen Halliwell, *Longinus, On the Sublime*, ed. and trans. W. H. Fyfe, revised by Donald Russell, *Demetrius: On Style*, ed. and trans. Doreen C. Innes, based on W. Rhys Roberts (Cambridge, MA: Harvard University Press, 1995), 213.

4 Larbaud's lecture was published as 'James Joyce' in *La Nouvelle Revue Française* 18 (April 1922): 385-409, 389. An English version appeared in Eliot's *The Criterion* in October 1922; see Valery Larbaud, 'The "Ulysses" of James Joyce', *The Criterion* 1: 1 (October 1922): 93–103. Ernest Boyd disputed Larbaud and fellow 'provincial cosmopolitans' for their ignorance of Irish local politics, which led Larbaud wrongly, he asserted, to associate Joyce with Sinn Féin radicalism. Larbaud's claim for Ireland's 're-entrance' into the front ranks of European literature, Boyd believed, connected Joyce to medieval Irish Catholic culture and severed him from Anglo-Irish writers of the Irish Renaissance including Moore, Yeats, Æ, Synge and James Stephens. See Ernest Boyd, 'Concerning James Joyce', *The World (New York)*, 25 January 1925, n. p., and 'Joyce and the New Irish Writers', *Current History* 39: 6 (March 1934): 699–704.

5 William Butler Yeats, 'Nobel Prize Acceptance', in *Later Articles and Reviews: Uncollected Articles, Reviews, and Radio Broadcasts Written after 1900*, ed. Colton Johnson, vol. X of *The Collected Works of W. B. Yeats* (New York: Scribner, 2000), 164.

6 Hugh Kenner, *A Colder Eye: The Modern Irish Writers* (New York: Alfred A. Knopf, 1983), 13–18, 15.

7 Pascale Casanova, *The World Republic of Letters*, trans. M. B. DeBevoise (Cambridge, MA: Harvard University Press, 2004 [1999]), especially chapters 1–3.

8 On the modularity of national literatures, see Sarah M. Corse, *Nationalism and Literature: The Politics of Culture in Canada and the United States* (Cambridge: Cambridge University Press, 1997).

9 See Harold Bloom, *The Anxiety of Influence: A Theory of Poetry* (Oxford: Oxford University Press, 1973), and René Girard, *Deceit, Desire, and the Novel: Self and Other in Literary Structure*, trans. Yvonne Freccero (Baltimore: Johns Hopkins University Press, (1965 [1961]). Bloom's theory of influence was later developed in numerous studies, including *A Map of Misreading* (Oxford: Oxford University Press, 1975), *Poetry and Repression: Revisionism*

*from Blake to Stevens* (New Haven: Yale University Press, 1976), *Agon: Towards a Theory of Revisionism* (New York: Oxford University Press, 1982), *The Western Canon: The Books and Schools of the Ages* (New York: Harcourt, Brace, 1994), and *The Anatomy of Influence: Literature as a Way of Life* (New Haven: Yale University Press, 2011). Girard's mimetic theories were also developed across his career, notably in *Violence and the Sacred*, trans. Patrick Gregory (Baltimore: Johns Hopkins University Press, 1977 [1972]), and *A Theater of Envy: William Shakespeare* (New York: Oxford University Press, 1991).

10 On Girard's differences with Freud, see René Girard, *Oedipus Unbound: Selected Writings on Rivalry and Desire*, ed. Mark R. Anspach (Stanford: Stanford University Press, 2004).

11 On this topic, see Vern Neufeld Redekop and Thomas Ryba, eds., *René Girard and Creative Mimesis* (Lanham: Lexington Books, 2014).

12 See George Moore, *Hail and Farewell!: Vale*, vol. XIII of *The Collected Works of George Moore* (New York: Boni and Liveright, 1923), 139.

13 Cited in Christopher St. John, ed., *Ellen Terry and Bernard Shaw: A Correspondence* (New York: G. P. Putnam's Sons, 1931), 110. For Shaw on Ibsen and Shakespeare, see Edwin Wilson, 'Shakespeare and Ibsen', in *Shaw on Shakespeare: An Anthology of Bernard Shaw's Writings on the Plays and Production of Shakespeare* (New York: Books for Libraries Press, 1961), 227–229, 228.

14 Ernest Boyd, *Literary Blasphemies* (New York: Harper & Brothers, 1927), 10, 72, 73.

15 Boyd, 'William Shakespeare', in *Literary Blasphemies*, 39.

16 Boyd, 'William Shakespeare', in *Literary Blasphemies*, 40.

17 Adrian Poole, *Shakespeare and the Victorians* (London: Arden Shakespeare, 2004), 231.

18 See Hippolyte Taine, *History of English Literature*, trans. H. Van Laun (London: Chatto & Windus, 1883 [1866]).

19 Edward Dowden, *Shakespere: A Critical Study of His Mind and Art* (New York: Harper & Brothers, 1901), 27, 34.

20 Wilde's comments on Shakespeare and the British Empire appeared in the *Stratford Upon Avon Herald*, 12 October 1888. For fuller discussion, see John Stokes, '"Shopping in Byzantium": Oscar Wilde as Shakespeare Critic', in *Victorian Shakespeare*, ed. Gail Marshall and Adrian Poole, vol. 1 (Basingstoke: Palgrave Macmillan, 2003), 178–191, 178.

21 See Wilson, ed., *Shaw on Shakespeare*, 5.

22 W. B. Yeats, 'At Stratford-on-Avon', in *Ideas of Good and Evil* (New York: Russell and Russell 1967 [1903]), 142–167, 159. On Yeats's complex relationship with Dowden, see Ronnie Mulryne, 'Yeats and Edward Dowden: Critical Clinamen', *Gaeliana* 6 (1984): 137–153, and Charles I. Armstrong, 'The "intimate enemies": Edward Dowden, W. B. Yeats and the Formation of Character', *Nordic Journal of English Studies* 13: 2 (2014): 23–42.

23 Yeats, 'At Stratford-on-Avon', 166. More widely, see also Oliver Hennessey, *Yeats, Shakespeare, and Irish Cultural Nationalism* (Madison: Fairleigh Dickinson University Press, 2014).

24 See Frank Harris, *The Man Shakespeare and His Tragic Life-Story* (New York: Mitchell Kennerley, 1909).

25 James Joyce, *Ulysses: The Corrected Text*, ed. Hans Walter Gabler (New York, Vintage Books 1986 [1922]), 163, 161. All further references are to this edition and page and line numbers are referenced in the text.

26 On the British Empire Shakespeare Society, see Coppelia Kahn, 'Remembering Shakespeare Imperially: The 1916 Tercentenary', *Shakespeare Quarterly* 52: 4 (Winter 2001): 456–478. More generally, see also Leah S. Marcus, *How Shakespeare Became Colonial: Editorial Traditions and the British Empire* (New York: Routledge, 2017), and Clara Calvo and Coppelia Kahn, eds., *Celebrating Shakespeare: Commemoration and Cultural Memory* (Cambridge: Cambridge University Press, 2015).

27 On Dowden and unionism, see Kathryn R. Ludwigson, *Edward Dowden* (New York: Twayne Publishers, 1973), 45. On Swinburne and unionism, see Matthew Campbell, *Irish Poetry under the Union, 1801–1924* (New York: Cambridge University Press, 2014), 168–170, 169.

28 On this topic, see Clara Calvo, 'Fighting over Shakespeare: Commemorating the 1916 Tercentenary in Wartime', *Critical Survey* 24: 3 (2012): 48–72. The Brandl lecture was published as Alois Brandl, *Shakespeare and Germany* (New York: Oxford University Press, 1913). On German Shakespeare more widely, see Andreas Höfele, *No Hamlets: German Shakespeare from Nietzsche to Carl Schmitt* (Oxford: Oxford University Press, 2016).

29 For the full text, see 'Shakespeare in Dublin', *Irish Times*, 24 March 1916, 4. My account of the Irish response to the tercentenary draws on Andrew Murphy, 'Shakespeare's Rising: Ireland and the 1916 Tercentenary', in *Celebrating Shakespeare*, ed. Calvo and Kahn, 161–181.

30 Stephen Gwynn, *Irish Literature and Drama in the English Language: A Short History* (London: T. Butterworth, 1926), 65. For detailed information on the various figures that feature in 'Scylla and Charybdis', see William M. Schutte, *Joyce and Shakespeare: A Study in the Meaning of* Ulysses (New Haven: Yale University Press, 1957), especially 30–51, and Clare Hutton, 'Joyce and the Institutions of Revivalism', *Irish University Review* 33: 1 (Spring–Summer 2003): 117–132.

31 Eglinton and Ernest Boyd wrote appreciative but critical appraisals of Dowden, each acknowledging his literary abilities but noting the latter's resolute refusal to commit to the idea of an Irish national literature. Boyd's assessment appears as 'A Lonely Irishman: Edward Dowden', in *Appreciations and Depreciations: Irish Literary Studies* (Dublin: Talbot Press, 1917), 141–162, and Eglinton's as 'Edward Dowden's Letters', in *Irish Literary Portraits* (London: Macmillan, 1935), 65–82. Boyd's essay notes that '[t]he subtle essayist "John Eglinton", whose *Two Essays on the Remnant* appeared in 1895, at once attracted [Dowden], and he is the only writer of the Revival of

whom Dowden regretted not having written a study' (149). Eglinton's portrait offers a bookish, standoffish Dowden who, as Ireland became more nationalist, campaigned for the union and then retreated into his library: 'It was easy to make little of Dowden in his later phase, when he found himself on platforms from which Rome and all its works were denounced, to the satisfaction chiefly of Protestant old ladies. [. . .] Well, the Ireland contemplated by Dowden was a Protestant Ireland: that is to say, an Ireland in which Protestant ideals were paramount. [. . .] The ideal Ireland, as conceived of by Dowden, was the rounding forth of the English connection, a luminous filling in of a hitherto blank space, a country in a word for which the glorious part remained of realising in these islands the perfect entelechy of an ideal for which he was ready to accept the name "English." However, Eglinton concluded: 'The real joke was that Calvin or even Hooker would have held up his hands in horror at the notion of calling Dowden's hesitating agnosticism by the name of Protestantism' (81–82).

32 Matthew Creasy notes that: 'Even before *Ulysses* was complete, Ezra Pound was comparing it to *Bouvard et Pécuchet*, Flaubert's last, unfinished novel about the mishaps of two clerks from Paris who retire to the countryside to pursue a sequence of failed projects, from agriculture to archaeology and literary study. Joyce, Pound announced in May 1918, "has done what Flaubert set out to do in *Bouvard et Pécuchet*, done it better, more succinct, an epitome". He would amplify this claim in two subsequent articles, his "Paris Letter" for *The Dial* and "James Joyce et Pécuchet" (written in French) for the *Mercure de France*'. See Matthew Creasy, 'Inverted Volumes and Fantastic Libraries: *Ulysses* and *Bouvard et Pécuchet*', *European Joyce Studies* 19 (2011): 112–127, 112.

33 John Eglinton, *Anglo-Irish Essays* (Dublin: Talbot Press, 1917), 79–89, 87–88. Eglinton's critique of the Revival for its lack of literary distinction here echoes, though in gentler and more reproving tones, Dowden's more dismissive critique of nineteenth-century Irish literature and the possibility that the country would ever produce a great European writer: 'I can't, however, believe Ireland will produce such a thing [as a great author], or at least anything but more long-eared asses (or at most a Duns Scotus or two); the idiotic noises the true Irishman makes from generation to generation are certainly not human, but are part of the irony on humanity of the aristophanic spirit who presides over World Drama – a chorus of asses'. Cited in Mulryne, 'Yeats and Edward Dowden: Critical Clinamen', 144.

34 Eglinton, *Anglo-Irish Essays*, 89.

35 Harris's Shakespeare, unlike William Rowe's or Edward Dowden's, finds no solace in old age and retirement: 'What had Stratford to offer Shakespeare – village Stratford with a midden in the chief street and the charms of the village usurer's companionship tempered by the ministrations of a wandering tub-thumper? [. . .] The truth is, that the passions of lust and jealousy and rage had at length worn out Shakespeare's strength, and after trying in vain to win to serenity in "The Tempest", he crept home to Stratford to die' (*The Man*

*Shakespeare and His Tragic Life-Story*, 403–404). Stephen's Shakespeare in *Ulysses* owes much to this rage-animated and eventually rage-worn Shakespeare.

36 On Swinburne and the Boer War, see Don Gifford and Robert J. Seidman, *Notes for Joyce: An Annotation of James Joyce's* Ulysses (New York: E. P. Dutton, 1974), 163–164.

37 Whitman considered Shakespeare, like Spenser and Dante, one of the great writers of European feudalism and his literary spirit as such at odds with the modern and democratic poetry needed for America and the future.

38 For a strong postcolonial reading in this manner, see Andrew Gibson, *Joyce's Revenge: History, Politics, and Aesthetics in* Ulysses (Oxford: Oxford University Press, 2002), especially chapter 3.

39 On the parallels between Stephen's envious and cuckolded Shakespeare and Joyce himself, see Girard, *A Theater of Envy*, 263–265. On Nora Barnacle's taunting of Joyce with 'Dear Cuckold', see Brenda Maddox, *Nora: The Real Life of Molly Bloom* (Boston: Houghton Mifflin, 1988), 148–149.

40 Girard, *A Theater of Envy*, 264. All further references are cited in the text.

41 Harold Bloom, *The Western Canon*, 385.

42 Bloom, 'Joyce...Dante...Shakespeare...Milton', in *The Anatomy of Influence*, 109–125, 114. All further references are to this edition and are cited in the text.

43 Bloom, *The Western Canon*, 395. All further references are cited in the text.

44 For a critique of Girard's take on motherhood, see Toril Moi, 'The Missing Mother: The Oedipal Rivalries of René Girard', *Diacritics* 12: 2 (Summer 1982): 21–31. Sandra Gilbert and Susan Gubar's *The Madwoman in the Attic: The Woman Writer and the Nineteenth-Century Literary Imagination* (New Haven: Yale University Press, 1979) offers a revisionary feminist interpretation of Bloom's *The Anxiety of Influence*.

45 For a useful summary analysis of divergent feminist accounts of 'Penelope', see Emer Nolan, *James Joyce and Nationalism* (London: Routledge, 1995), chapter 6.

46 For their respective comments on Joyce's negations of Western literature, see Erich Auerbach, *Mimesis: The Representation of Reality in Western Literature*, trans. Willard R. Trask (Princeton, NJ: Princeton University Press, 2003 [1946]), 551, and Georg Lukács, *The Historical Novel*, trans. Hannah Mitchell and Stanley Mitchell (London: Merlin, 1978 [1962]), 284, 305 and 'The Ideology of Modernism', in *The Meaning of Contemporary Realism*, trans. John Mander and Necke Mander (London: Merlin, 1972, [1963]), 18–19.

47 John Eglinton, 'The Beginnings of Joyce', 145–146.

48 Hauptmann and Fulda are cited in Wilhelm Hortmann, *Shakespeare on the German Stage: The Twentieth Century* (Cambridge: Cambridge University Press, 1998), 3-4.

49 Henry Arthur Jones, *Shakespeare and Germany* (London: Chiswick Press, 1916), 4.

50 Clare Hutton, 'Joyce and the Institutions of Revivalism', 127. As Hutton points out, Stephen's Catholic and Lyster's Quaker identities are the forms of denominational affiliation that are most highlighted in the episode. 'Lyster', Hutton observes, 'figures as the peace-maker in the chapter: unfailingly courteous and helpful [. . .], he is also endlessly deferential and polite to Stephen, "blushing" with embarrassment when the conversation about revivalism threatens to overpower the planned discussion of Shakespeare' (127). All true, but Joyce's mockery in the episode nevertheless does not spare Lyster.

51 On Joyce's rivalries with Yeats and Yeats's presence in *Ulysses*, see particularly John McCourt, '"I have met you, bird, too late, or if not, too worm and early": The Eternal Circling of Yeats and Joyce', *Journal of English Language & Literature* 62: 3 (2016): 341–359; Damian Love, 'Sailing to Ithaca: Remaking Yeats in *Ulysses*', *The Cambridge Quarterly* 36: 1 (2007): 1–10; and Russell McDonald, 'Who Speaks for Fergus? Silence, Homophobia, and the Anxiety of Yeatsian Influence in Joyce', *Twentieth Century Literature* 51: 4 (Winter 2005): 391–413. Particularly useful here is Russell McDonald's comment that Joyce deals with Yeats in *Ulysses* not directly, but always at a distance through Stephen's silent ruminations and the publicly performed parodies ascribed to Mulligan (not Stephen). The Yeats–Joyce rivalry might also be seen as one between poetry and the novel, each writer allowing the other precedence in the genre to which he did not lay special claim.

52 Barbara Fuchs, 'Golden Ages and Golden Hinds: or, Periodizing Spain and England', *PMLA* 127: 2 (March 2012): 321–327, 324. All further references are cited in the text. See also Fuchs, *The Poetics of Piracy: Emulating Spain in English Literature* (Philadelphia: University of Pennsylvania Press, 2013).

53 On the erasure of English debts to Spanish literature in the early modern period, see Fuch's *The Poetics of Piracy*; on English reworkings of Cervantes, see Ronald Paulson, *Don Quixote in England: The Aesthetics of Laughter* (Baltimore: Johns Hopkins University Press, 1998).

54 Cited in Fuchs, 'Golden Ages and Golden Hinds', 321.

55 See James Joyce, 'Ireland: Island of Saints and Sages', in *Occasional, Critical, and Political Writing*, ed. Kevin Barry (Oxford: Oxford University Press, 2000), 108–126, 109.

56 See Don Gifford and Robert J. Seidman, Ulysses *Annotated: Notes for James Joyce's* Ulysses, 2nd ed. (Berkeley: University of California Press, 1988), 147: 7:785.

57 On the many types of support that went into the final publication of *Ulysses*, see Sylvia Beach, *Shakespeare and Company* (Lincoln: University of Nebraska Press, 1991 [1956]), especially 45–62.

58 Cited in Nolan, *James Joyce and Nationalism*, 1.

59 For Ellmann's irenic reading of 'Scylla and Charybdis', see Richard Ellmann, *Ulysses on the Liffey* (New York: Oxford University Press, 1972), 81–89, especially 88–89. Ellmann writes: 'The calm [that ends this episode] is post-coital. [. . .] God the creator has fused with man the creator, both androgynous, ostlers and butchers, Iagos and Othellos, both producing, by intercourse

of contraries, life from death, generation from corruption, art from dialectic. The son without a body, as Joyce described Stephen in the first three episodes, has at the end of nine himself become capable of fatherhood. Stephen has solved the riddle of Scylla and Charybdis as Oedipus solved the riddle propounded by another double-natured creature. The answer to the sphinx's riddle was man, the answer to Scylla-Charybdis's is the act of love' (88–89). In his summary of *Ulysses and Us: The Art of Everyday Life in Joyce's Masterpiece* (New York: W. W. Norton, 2009), Kiberd argues that: 'In the scene in the National Library, after Stephen Dedalus has disowned his own theory of Shakespeare, the figure of Bloom appears before him, as if offering the beginnings of an answer: "cease to strive". He turns his back consequently on literary Dublin and follows Bloom out, finding the idea of everyday life more interesting'. Declan Kiberd, 'Ulysses and Us', *The Irish Times*, 13 June 2015. Downloaded on 8 August 2019 at: www.irishtimes.com/culture/books/ulysses-and-us-by-declan-kiberd-1.2247446.

60 For more on this topic, see James Gordon Finlayson, 'The Artwork and the *Promesse du Bonheur* in Adorno', *European Journal of Philosophy* 23: 3 (2012): 392–419, 397, 402–403.

## Chapter 5

1 F. Scott Fitzgerald, Letter to Edmund Wilson, May 1921, in *The Letters of F. Scott Fitzgerald*, ed. Andrew Turnbull (New York: Charles Scribner's Sons, 1963), 326–327, 326.

2 Eugene O'Neill, Letter to George Jean Nathan, 12 November 1929, in *'As Ever, Gene': The Letters of Eugene O'Neill to George Jean Nathan*, ed. Nancy L. Roberts and Arthur W. Roberts (London: Associated University Presses, 1987), 101–103, 102.

3 F. Scott Fitzgerald, Letter to Marya Mannes, October 1925, in *The Culture of the Twenties*, ed. Loren Baritz (Indianapolis: Bobbs-Merrill, 1970), 307–308, 308.

4 Baritz, *Culture*, 308.

5 Roberts and Roberts, eds., *'As Ever, Gene'*, 102. All further references are to this edition and pages numbers are cited in the text.

6 On American cinematic epic, see Vivian Sobchack, '"Surge and Splendor": A Phenomenology of the Hollywood Historical Epic', in *Film Genre Reader II*, ed. Barry Keith Grant (Austin: University of Texas Press, 1995), 280–307, and Melani McAlister, '"Benevolent Supremacy": The Biblical Epic at the Dawn of the American Century, 1947–1960', in *Epic Encounters: Culture, Media, and U.S. Interests in the Middle East since 1945* (Berkeley: University of California Press, 2005), 43–83.

7 On the fate of John Dos Passos's *U.S.A.* trilogy as a once-great American novel, see Michael Denning, 'The Decline and Fall of the Lincoln Republic: Dos Passos's *U.S.A.*', in *The Cultural Front: The Laboring of American Culture in the Twentieth Century* (London: Verso, 1998), 163–199. In an essay published in 1938, 'John Dos Passos and *1919*', Jean-Paul Sartre could still

declare, 'I regard Dos Passos as the greatest writer of our time'. See Jean-Paul Sartre, *Literary and Philosophical Essays*, trans. Annette Michelson (New York: Collier Books, 1962 [1955]), 94–103, 103.

8 On the rise of New York as financial and cultural capital in this era, see the chapters collected in Martin Shefter, ed., *Capital of the American Century: The National and International Influence of New York City* (New York: Russell Sage Foundation, 1993), and Ann Douglas, *Terrible Honesty: Mongrel Manhattan in the 1920s* (New York: Farrar, Straus and Giroux, 1995). On the post–World War II period, see Leonard Wallock, ed., *New York: Cultural Capital of the World, 1940–1965* (New York: Rizzoli, 1988).

9 On the rise of the American university, see Jonathan R. Cole, *The Great American University: Its Rise to Preeminence, Its Indispensable National Role, and Why It Must Be Protected* (New York: Public Affairs, 2009). On modernism and the American university, see Gail McDonald, *Learning to Be Modern: Pound, Eliot, and the American University* (Oxford: Clarendon Press, 1993), and Evan Kindley, *Poet-Critics and the Administration of Culture* (Cambridge, MA: Harvard University Press, 2017).

10 On America's complex relationship to national and international modernism, see variously Serge Guilbaut, *How New York Stole the Idea of Modern Art: Abstract Expressionism, Freedom, and the Cold War,* trans. Arthur Goldhammer (Chicago: University of Chicago Press, 1983); Frances Stonor Saunders, *Who Paid the Piper?: The CIA and the Cultural Cold War* (London: Granta Books, 1999); Andrew N. Rubin, *Archives of Authority: Empire, Culture, and the Cold War* (Princeton, NJ: Princeton University Press, 2012); and Greg Barnhisel, *Cold War Modernists: Art, Literature, and American Cultural Diplomacy* (New York: Columbia University Press, 2015).

11 On the Irish dimensions of F. Scott Fitzgerald and Eugene O'Neill, see my 'Irish American Modernisms', in *The Cambridge Companion to Irish Modernism*, ed. Joe Cleary (Cambridge: Cambridge University Press, 2014), 174–192.

12 The term is taken from Doris Sommer, *Foundational Fictions: The National Romances of Latin America* (Berkeley: University of California Press, 1991) and refers to the exceptional status that some Latin American romance novels occupied in the educational systems or national imaginations of their societies.

13 On *The Great Gatsby*'s place in the larger canons of the 'Great American Novel', see Lawrence Buell, *The Dream of the Great American Novel* (Cambridge, MA: Belknap Press of Harvard University Press, 2014), 139–174. On Fitzgerald and epic, see Marcella Taylor, 'The Unfinished American Epic: Fitzgerald's *The Great Gatsby* and the Twenties', in *The Twenties,* ed. Barbara Smith Lemeunier (Aix-en-Provence: University of Provence, 1982), 65–78.

14 On *The Great Gastby*'s relationship to Hollywood, see Jordan Brower, '"Written with the Movies in Mind": Twentieth-Century American Literature and Transmedial Possibility', *Modern Language Quarterly* 78: 2 (2017): 243–273.

15 For Eliot's letter, see Valerie Eliot and Hugh Haughton, eds., *The Letters of T. S. Eliot, 1923–1925*, vol. 2 (New Haven: Yale University Press, 2011), 813. For the general reception *of The Great Gatsby*, see Nicolas Tredell, *Fitzgerald's* The Great Gatsby: *A Reader's Guide* (London: Continuum: 2007), 77–91, and G. Thomas Tanselle and Jackson R. Bryer, '*The Great Gatsby*: A Study in Literary Reputation', *New Mexico Quarterly* 33: 4 (1963): 409–425.

16 These reviews are cited in Tanselle and Bryer, '*The Great Gatsby*: A Study in Literary Reputation', 412–413.

17 Cocteau cited in Tredell, *Fitzgerald's* The Great Gatsby: *A Reader's Guide*, 80. On the wider French reception of *The Great Gatsby*, see Michael Nowlin, 'Fitzgerald's Survival of French Neglect', *The F. Scott Fitzgerald Review* 10 (2012): 27–47.

18 See Tanselle and Bryer, '*The Great Gatsby*: A Study in Literary Reputation', 410.

19 Dos Passos, Troy and Berryman cited in Tanselle and Bryer, '*The Great Gatsby*: A Study in Literary Reputation', 418, 419, 420. For Trilling's essay, see Lionel Trilling, 'F. Scott Fitzgerald', in *The Liberal Imagination* (New York: New York Review of Books, 2008), 243–254, 251. The essay was originally published in *The Nation*, 25 April 1945, and extended to serve as introduction to *The Great Gatsby* for a New Directions printing in the same year.

20 On *Gatsby*'s Cold War reception, see also Laura Goldblatt, '"Can't Repeat the Past?": *Gatsby* and the American Dream at Mid-Century', *Journal of American Studies* 50: 1 (2016): 105–124.

21 See John Pizer, *The Idea of World Literature: History and Pedagogical Practice* (Baton Rouge: Louisiana State University Press, 2006), and Sarah Lawall, ed., *Reading World Literature: Theory, History, Practice* (Austin: University of Texas Press, 1994).

22 See Sarah Lawall, 'The Alternate Worlds of World Literature,' *ADE Bulletin* 90 (1988): 53–58. Cited in Pizer, *The Idea of World Literature*, 85.

23 F. Scott Fitzgerald, *The Great Gatsby*, ed. Matthew J. Bruccoli (Cambridge: Cambridge University Press, 1996 [1925]), 57. All further references are to this edition and page numbers are cited in the text.

24 Joss Lutz Marsh associates Gatsby with Hollywood film directors and stars and with Fitzgerald's ambiguous fascination with the cinema industry in 'Fitzgerald, *Gatsby*, and *The Last Tycoon*: The "American Dream" and the Hollywood Dream Factory', *Literature/Film Quarterly* 20: 1 (1992): 3–13. Jordan Brower, in 'Written with the Movies in Mind', suggests that *Gatsby* was, so to speak, 'born-filmic, struck in the mold of contemporary American cinema' (261).

25 See Sobchack, '"Surge and Splendor": A Phenomenology of the Hollywood Historical Epic', 280–307, 280–281.

26 On Fitzgerald's relationship to modernist distinction and commercial success, see Michael Nowlin, *F. Scott Fitzgerald's Racial Angles and the Business of*

*Literary Greatness* (New York: Palgrave Macmillan, 2007), 59–84. Nowlin contends that despite his professed reverence for high modernist writers, Fitzgerald remained sceptical of their advanced avant-garde ambitions and more fascinated with commercial success, this despite his commitment to 'serious literature'.

27 Turnbull, ed., *The Letters of F. Scott Fitzgerald*, 288. Italics in the original.

28 Brooks Atkinson, 'Theatre: Tragic Journey', *New York Times*, 8 November 1956. Downloaded on 10 May 2018 at www.nytimes.com/interactive/2012/06/17/theater/20120617-longdays.html.

29 Cited in Donald Gallup, 'A Tale of Possessors Self-Dispossessed', in *The Cambridge Companion to Eugene O'Neill*, ed. Michael Manheim (Cambridge: Cambridge University Press, 1998), 178–191, 178. On the analogy between O'Neill's history cycle and Shakespeare's, see Travis Bogard, *Contour in Time: The Plays of Eugene O'Neill* (Oxford: Oxford University Press, 1988), 369.

30 Cited in Gallup, 'A Tale of Possessors Self-Dispossessed', 178. All further references cited in the text.

31 David Savran, 'The Canonization of Eugene O'Neill', *Modern Drama* 50: 4 (Winter 2007): 565–581, 568.

32 Savran, 568. Benjamin De Casseres's phrase, which originally appeared in 'Eugene O'Neill: From Cardiff to Xanadu', *Theatre* 10 (August 1927), is cited in Savran, 568.

33 On the Federal Theatre Project, see Loren Kruger, *The National Stage: Theatre and Cultural Legitimation in England, France and America* (Chicago: University of Chicago Press, 1992), 133–184. On left-wing theatre, see Michael Denning, 'Labor on Revue: The Popular Front Musical Theater' and 'Cabaret Blues', in *The Cultural Front*, 283–322 and 323–361.

34 Eugene O'Neill, *Long Day's Journey into Night*, 2nd ed. (New Haven: Yale University Press, 2002), 167. All further references are to this edition and page numbers are cited in the text.

35 Mary Shelley, *Frankenstein, or, The Modern Prometheus* (Oxford: Oxford University Press, 1985), 217.

36 On books and allusions in O'Neill, see Robert Combs, 'Bohemians on the Bookcase: Quotations in *Long Day's Journey into Night* and *Ah, Wilderness!*', *The Eugene O'Neill Review* 33: 1 (2012): 1–13; Laurin Porter, 'Musical and Literary Allusions in O'Neill's Final Plays', *The Eugene O'Neill Review* 28 (2006): 131–146; and Laurin Porter, '"Why do I feel so lonely?": Literary Allusions and Gendered Space in *Long Day's Journey into Night*', *The Eugene O'Neill Review* 30 (2008): 37–47. On the role of Shakespeare in O'Neill's work, see Normand Berlin, *O'Neill's Shakespeare* (Ann Arbor: University of Michigan Press, 1993).

37 On language in O'Neill, see George Steiner, *Language and Silence: Essays on Language, Literature, and the Inhuman* (New York: Atheneum, 1967), 31; Harold Bloom, foreword to Eugene O'Neill, *Long Day's Journey into Night*, v–xii; and Matthew H. Wikander, 'O'Neill and the Cult of Sincerity', in *The Cambridge Companion to Eugene O'Neill*, ed. Manheim, 217–235.

38 On the anxiety of language and the tendency in Western culture to privilege speech over textuality, see Jacques Derrida, *Writing and Difference*, trans. Alan Bass (Chicago: Chicago University Press, 1978) and *Of Grammatology*, trans. Gayatri Chakravorty Spivak (Baltimore: Johns Hopkins University Press, 2016 [1974]).

39 On eloquence and blarney in constructs of Irishness, see Seamus Deane, 'Dumbness and Eloquence: A Note on English as We Write It in Ireland', in *Ireland and Postcolonial Theory*, ed. Clare Carroll and Patricia King (Cork: Cork University Press, 2003), 109–128.

40 Lawrence W. Levine, 'William Shakespeare and the American People: A Study in Cultural Transformation', in *The Unpredictable Past: Explorations in American Cultural History* (Oxford: Oxford University Press, 1993), 139–171, 140. All further references are cited in the text.

41 The term 'Black Irishman' often occurs in relation to O'Neill, as, for example, in Croswell Bowen's article 'The Black Irishman', published in *PM* in 1946 and collected in Mark W. Estrin, ed., *Conversations with Eugene O'Neill* (Jackson: University Press of Mississippi, 1990), 203–223. There, the term is used to refer to 'an Irishman who has lost his Faith and who spends his life searching for the meaning of life, for a philosophy in which he can believe again as he fervently once believed in the simple answers of the Catholic Catechism. A Black Irishman is a brooding, solitary man – and often a drinking man too' (203–204). But the term is also shadowed by associations with Blackness that the Irish had to repudiate to become 'White'.

42 See Steiner, *Language and Silence*, 31.

43 Harold Bloom, foreword to Eugene O'Neill, *Long Day's Journey into Night*, xii.

44 Fredric Jameson, 'Altman and the National-Popular, or, Misery and Totality?', trans. Robert Hullot-Kentor and Frederic Will, in *The Ancients and the Postmoderns* (London: Verso, 2015), 205–220, 206.

45 Theodor W. Adorno, 'The Aging of the New Music', in *Essays on Music*, selected, with introduction, commentary and notes by Richard Leppert (Berkeley: University of California Press, 2002), 181–202, 200.

46 Clement Greenberg, '"America-Type" Painting', in *Art and Culture: Critical Essays* (Boston: Beacon Press, 1989 [1961]), 208–229, 209, 229.

## Chapter 6

1 Georg Lukács, *The Theory of the Novel*, trans. Anna Bostock (Cambridge, MA: MIT Press, 1989 [1920]), 38–39.

2 Jervis Anderson, 'Derek Walcott's Odyssey', *The New Yorker*, 21 December 1992, 71–79, 71. All further references are cited in the text.

3 Derek Walcott, *Omeros* (New York: Farrar, Straus and Giroux, 1990), 271. All further references are to this edition and page references are cited in the text.

4 T. S. Eliot, 'Tradition and the Practice of Poetry', in *T. S. Eliot: Essays from the Southern Review*, ed. James Olney (Oxford: Clarendon Press, 1988), 10–20, 15–16. Italics in the original.

5 Ezra Pound, 'How to Read', *New York Herald Tribune*, 1929, in *Literary Essays of Ezra Pound*, ed. T. S. Eliot (New York: New Directions, 1968), 33–34.

6 Hugh Kenner, 'The Making of the Modernist Canon', *Chicago Review* 34: 2 (Spring 1984): 49–61, 52. Further page references are cited in the text.

7 C. L. R. James, *The Black Jacobins: Toussaint L'Ouverture and the San Domingo Revolution* (New York: Vintage Books, 1963), 'Preface to the First Edition', ix. My italics.

8 For critical overviews of Anglophone Caribbean literature, see Allison Donnell, *Twentieth-Century Caribbean Literature: Critical Moments in Anglophone Literary History* (London: Routledge, 2006), and Allison Donnell and Sarah Lawson Welsh, eds., *The Routledge Reader in Caribbean Literature* (London: Routledge, 1996). On the wider region, see Kristian Van Haesendonck and Theo D'haen, *Caribbeing: Comparing Caribbean Literatures and Cultures* (Amsterdam: Rodopi, 2014).

9 See Donnell, *Twentieth-Century Caribbean Literature*, and Raphael Dalleo, *Caribbean Literature and the Public Sphere: From the Plantation to the Postcolonial* (Charlottesville: University of Virginia Press, 2011). On the masculinist character of the 'foundational fathers' of exilic Caribbean writing, see Belinda Edmondson, *Making Men: Gender, Literary Authority, and Women's Writing in Caribbean Narrative* (Durham, NC: Duke University Press, 1999), and Michelle Ann Stephens, *Black Empire: The Masculine Global Imaginary of Caribbean Intellectuals in the United States, 1914–1962* (Durham, NC: Duke University Press, 2005).

10 See Franco Moretti, *Distant Reading* (London: Verso 2013), 17.

11 The literature on *Omeros* and epic is extensive. Works that inform this chapter include: Robert D. Hamner, *Epic of the Dispossessed: Derek Walcott's* Omeros (Columbia: University of Missouri Press, 1997); Line Henriksen, *Ambition and Anxiety: Ezra Pound's* Cantos *and Derek Walcott's* Omeros *as Twentieth-Century Epics* (Amsterdam: Rodopi, 2006); Sneharika Roy, *The Postcolonial Epic: From Melville to Walcott and Ghosh* (London: Routledge, 2018); Isabella Maria Zoppi, '*Omeros*, Derek Walcott, and the Contemporary Epic Poem', *Callaloo* 22: 2 (Spring 1999): 509–528; Gregson Davis, '"With No Homeric Shadow": The Disavowal of Epic in Derek Walcott's *Omeros*', *The South Atlantic Quarterly* 96: 2 (Spring 1997): 321–333; and Natalie Melas, 'Ruined Metaphor: Epic Similitude and the Pedagogy of Poetic Space in Derek Walcott's *Omeros*', in *All the Difference in the World: Postcoloniality and the Ends of Comparison* (Stanford: Stanford University Press, 2007), 113–169.

12 Derek Walcott, *Omeros*, 271.

13 Paul Fleming, 'Belatedness: A Theory of the Epic', *Modern Language Notes* 129: 3 (2014): 525–534, 525. Italics in the original.

14 Georg Lukács, *The Theory of the Novel*, 38–39.

15 For wider background works on metropolitan English-Caribbean relations, see Peter J. Kalliney, *Commonwealth of Letters: British Literary Culture and the Emergence of Postcolonial Aesthetics* (Oxford: Oxford University Press, 2013),

and Glyne A. Griffith, *The BBC and the Development of Anglophone Caribbean Literature, 1943–1958* (London: Palgrave Macmillan, 2016). See also Jahan Ramazani, *The Hybrid Muse: Postcolonial Poetry in English* (Chicago: University of Chicago Press, 2001), chapter 3.

16 On these stages of Walcott's career, see Edward Baugh, 'Introduction', Derek Walcott, *Selected Poems* (New York: Farrar, Straus and Giroux, 2007), xi–xvii, xiii. For career overviews, see also John Thieme, *Derek Walcott* (Manchester: Manchester University Press, 1999), and Paul Breslin, *Nobody's Nation: Reading Derek Walcott* (Chicago: University of Chicago Press, 2001).

17 For a general account, see Aonghas St. Hilaire, 'Postcolonial Identity Politics, Language and the Schools in St. Lucia', *International Journal of Bilingual Education and Bilingualism* 12: 1 (2009): 31–46.

18 Walcott, speaking at the University of Milan, 22 May 1996, cited in Paula Burnett, *Derek Walcott: Politics and Poetics* (Gainesville: University Press of Florida, 2000), 136 and 342, note 56.

19 Robert Brown and Cheryl Johnson, 'An Interview with Derek Walcott', *Cream City Review* 14: 2 (Winter 1990), 209–223. Cited in Hamner, *Epic of the Dispossessed*, 4–5.

20 On epic content and telling, see Luke Arnott, 'Epic and Genre: Beyond the Boundaries of Media', *Comparative Literature* 68: 4 (2016): 351–369.

21 Paul Jay, 'Fated to Unoriginality: The Politics of Mimicry in Derek Walcott's *Omeros*', *Callaloo* 29: 2 (Spring 2006): 545–559, 546. Italics in the original.

22 On the differences between Greek and biblical epic, see Erich Auerbach, 'Odysseus' Scar', in *Mimesis: The Representation of Reality in Western Literature*, trans. Willard R. Trask (Princeton, NJ: Princeton University Press, 2003 [1953]), 3–23.

23 On Saint Lucian economics and politics, see Tennyson S. D. Joseph, *Decolonization in St. Lucia: Politics and Global Neoliberalism, 1945–2010* (Jackson: University Press of Mississippi, 2011).

24 Theodor Adorno, 'Reconciliation under Duress', in *Aesthetics and Politics*, trans. Ronald Taylor (London: Verso, 1988 [1977]), 151–176.

25 On climate change in the Caribbean, see Clinton L. Beckford and Kevon Rhiney, eds., *Globalization, Agriculture and Food in the Caribbean: Climate Change, Gender and Geography* (London: Palgrave Macmillan, 2016).

26 Some critics argue that Book Five is the least integral to *Omeros*'s design. See, for example, Hamner, *Epic of the Dispossessed*, who remarks that '[i]n keeping with those critics who question the inclusion of Euro-American scenes in what is ostensibly a West Indian epic, I must agree that these scenes disrupt the general texture of the narrative' (106).

27 Derek Walcott, *The Antilles: Fragments of Epic Memory: The Nobel Lecture* (New York: Farrar, Straus and Giroux, 1992). The volume is unpaginated. All further citations are from this edition of the text.

28 On Walcott's conception of New World Adamic vision, see Breslin, *Nobody's Nation*, chapter 4.

29 V. S. Naipaul, 'The Worm in the Bud', in *A Writer's People: Ways of Looking and Feeling* (London: Picador, 2007), 3–33, 21. All further page references to this edition are cited in the text.

30 Mark McGurl, 'The Program Era: Pluralisms of Postwar American Fiction', *Critical Inquiry* 32: 1 (Autumn 2005), 102–129, 129. Further references are cited in the text.

# Index